ABSOLUTE **EROTIC,** ABSOLUTE **GROTESQUE**

Mark Driscoll

ABSOLUTE **EROTIC,** ABSOLUTE **GROTESQUE**

THE LIVING, DEAD, AND UNDEAD IN JAPAN'S IMPERIALISM, 1895–1945

Duke University Press   Durham and London   2010

© 2010 Duke University Press

All rights reserved

Printed in the United States of America
on acid-free paper ∞

Designed by Heather Hensley

Typeset in Charis by Tseng Information
Systems, Inc.

Library of Congress Cataloging-in-
Publication Data appear on the last
printed page of this book.

From DIANE

CONTENTS

This book describes how Japan rose to be a world power in a few short decades. The dominant way of narrating that rise tends to focus on centers of power, whether the center is the supposed Euro-American birthplace of modern technoscience and Enlightenment reason or is understood to be Japan's westernized metropole, Tokyo. Against this hegemonic assumption that advanced conceptual and technical forms of Euro-American and metropolitan origin are the sole causes of modern development, subalternist postcolonial studies and Marxism—the two theoretical approaches privileged here—recommend that critical attention be redirected to human life and labor, especially that inhabiting the margins and peripheries far away from centers of power. Therein the ontological energy of life and the surpluses stolen from labor (by capital) can be clearly glimpsed as the engines driving imperial expansion. In this book marginal life and peripheral labor spawned in Japan's peripheries in Korea and China will move out of the historiographical shadows to become starring dramatis personae. As the fleshly container of life and labor is the body, working bodies, desiring bodies, addicted bodies, and dying bodies are offered up as evidence for what I call the peripheral a priori: the spatiotemporal prioritizing of peripheral marginalia as the primary agents of culturo-economic change, what D. K. Fieldhouse depicted as the "metropolitan dog wagged by the tail" of the colonial periphery (cited in Uchida J. 2005, 38). In this study of Japan's imperialism, the peripheral tails wagging the dog of the imperial center are Chinese coolies, Japanese pimps working in China's treaty ports, trafficked Japanese women, and poor Korean tenant farmers—the bodies supplying the vital energy and laboring surplus that mattered (to) Japan's imperialism.

The importance of the colonial periphery for empire was a given for

Japan's political elites in the late nineteenth century, as the consolidation of nation-state institutions occurred simultaneously with imperial expansion, similar to the case of modern Germany. Yamagata Aritomo, the oligarch and two-time prime minister during the Meiji period (1868–1912), was one of the first to conceptualize the mutually constitutive nature of the colonial periphery and the imperial center in 1890. In order for Japan to defend itself against the continuing encroachments of the Euro-American powers in East Asia (intensifying with the first [1839–42] and second [1856–60] Opium Wars), Yamagata envisioned two concentric circles, with an inner circle corresponding to the coalescing Japanese state (also rendered as "cordon of sovereignty") and an outer circle to a security periphery against European encroachment ("cordon of interest"). Japanese imperialists tried with varying degrees of success to convince the Chinese and Korean inhabitants of its outer circle that Japan was sincerely concerned with protecting them as well against white imperialists. Nevertheless, paternalistic protection more often than not ceded to baser impulses to pillage resources and profit from underpaid, exploited labor. The colonies in Taiwan (from 1895), southern Manchuria (1905), and Korea (1910) quickly earned revenue at a time when Japan still relied on the London money markets for capital. More than a mere geopolitical buffer zone, the outer circle directed profits to the Japanese inner circle generated from trafficking drugs and women and jacked from Chinese coolies and Korean tenant farmers. Although the ideological code of Pan-Asianism was sometimes accessible to soften the extremes of profiteering and pillaging in the outer peripheries, even committed anti-Western Asianists like the East Asian Brotherhood ideologue Sugita Teiichi conceded the eat-or-be-eaten Realpolitik of the age when he concluded a trip to China in 1884 saying, "I wonder whether Japan will be served up as the main dish to Westerners in the coming feast, or whether we should join the guests. Surely, it would be better to sit at the table than be part of the menu" (quoted in Iriye 1980, 331). Sugita was not alone in rearticulating an early modern Japanese militarist's desire to replace China as the hegemon in the East Asian tribute-trade economic system (which led to Japan's starting the only major war in the region for centuries, the Imjin War of 1592–98) to contemporary ideologies of Pan-Asianism and Realpolitik in the 1880s (Kawakatsu 1994).

Dis-Oriented for decades by the geopolitics of cold war knowledge production, modern Japan studies have tended not to focus on the all-you-can-eat Chinese and Korean produce that Japanese capitalists gorged themselves on while dining at the imperialist table. Cheered on by the Princeton historian Marius Jansen's recommendation to fixate on the "brighter side" of Japan's history (1962, 11), scholars have either ignored Japan's Asian outer circle entirely or, when choosing to focus on it, have tended to limit their discussions to colonial institutions and practices discretely isolated from larger assemblages of force. Through the methodological optic of the peripheral a priori, my account of Japan's imperialism—which necessarily enfolds an analysis of Japan's modernity—will begin and end with the outer circle, often referred to in the early twentieth century as Japan's "darker side" (*ankokumen*). Therein, along with protecting, pillaging, and profiting from the subaltern and colonized, Japanese hustlers and petty capitalists were engaged in a battle for market hegemony with the representatives of the regional and civilizational hegemon, Qing China. The Japanese most eager to compete with and confront powerful Chinese merchants were human traffickers and thug salesmen (*tekiya*) selling cheap Japanese goods, and their successes determined the modus operandi of the outer circle for decades. Although violent, martial forms of capital accumulation were taking place inside Japan as well at this time, postcolonial studies adduces that the "state of exception" characteristic of imperialist tactics in the outer circle allowed accumulation to advance more quickly, benefiting from novel (and often criminal) techniques that were adopted later in the inner. Therefore, in stark contrast to the modernizationist assumptions of a centrifugal, diffusionist force trajectory emanating from power centers, when Japanese merchants resorted to judo and karate to physically force Koreans to buy shoddy goods, when Japanese pimps wrenched market share from Chinese increasingly unwilling to traffic women, and when armed Japanese settlers swindled and stole land in Korea, these pioneering martial arts centripetally flowed back into and impacted Japan's inner circle metropoles, where they became normal means of capital accumulation after they emerged in the outer.

My title refers to the erotic-grotesque, which was the dominant form of mass culture modernism in Japan from 1925 to 1934 and included sexology, detective fiction, graphic art, soft-core pornography, and urban anthropology. I follow the lead of Japanese Marxists of this same period in recasting the erotic-grotesque as a code for the ways the erotic—what

Deleuze and Guattari configured in the 1970s as "desiring production"—
was captured or grotesqued by capitalism in distinct political ways. In
the book's three parts I periodize the central modes of desiring production and political grotesque as biopolitics (1895–1914, with the colonization of Taiwan, Korea, and the Guandong Lease in southern Manchuria,
concurrent with an expansion of Japanese merchants and consulates
into China and Southeast Asia); neuropolitics (1920–36, characterized by the economic takeoff of Japan after the First World War and
the establishment of consumer capitalism in metropolitan areas); and
necropolitics (1932–45, dominated by a total war economy and fascist
mobilizations).

I will show that from the beginning of its imperial rule Japan's power
rode on the constituent energy unleashed by desiring, deterritorializing bodies. In part I, "Biopolitics," I introduce the four embodied subjectivities: Chinese coolie, pimp and human trafficker, Korean tenant
farmer, and Japanese sex worker. The subject of chapter 1 is immigrant
North Chinese workers, or "coolies," who single-handedly constructed
Japan's infrastructure in its Guandong Lease Manchurian colony after
the victory in the Russo-Japanese War in 1905. Approximately twenty
million coolies moved or were moved permanently to Northeast China
from 1905 until 1945, many of them to slave away in Japanese capitalist enterprises. This forced and free transfer of a subaltern population
that the sociologist Mushakōji Kinhide (2006) likens to the Middle Passage of African slaves across the Atlantic (what North Chinese laborers
themselves called the "desperation forcing us into Manchuria" [*chuang
guandong*], a phenomenon we might call the "Manchurian Passage") led
to Chinese workers outnumbering Japanese management in the same
company by as many as 300 to 1. As capital was scarce and expensive,
it was the basically free labor of Chinese coolies that made colonialism
profitable for Japanese capital in Manchuria.

In chapter 2, I turn my attention to Japanese pimps (*zegen*) and human
traffickers. These lower-class men succeeded in wrenching market control from Chinese with the only commodity they had access to: kidnapped Japanese women. By trafficking these women, several hundred
pimps became the first generation of powerful Japanese businessmen in
Asia, setting up both their own brothels and the secondary businesses
necessary to support them: kimono makers, Japanese restaurants, and
purveyors of luxury goods. The pimps would not have existed without

their prized commodity, an estimated one hundred thousand Japanese women coerced and cajoled into sex work. These women, many of whom were able to fulfill their contracts and set up their own businesses, are featured in chapter 3. Together with their young middle-class Japanese sisters who fled the confines of patriarchal Japan for the relative freedom offered by the outer circle colonies and concessions, Japanese sex workers were the pioneering businesswomen whose activities were as crucial for imperial expansion on the Asian continent as those of the pimps.

Dispossessed Korean farmers, the topic of chapter 4, were an early force in resisting Japanese settler colonialism. Their militancy impelled colonial policy in Korea to shift from encouraging settlement to subsidizing corrupt Japanese landlords, who made huge profits from oppressive rents and introduced widespread indebtedness into Korean life. Here we have arguably the clearest example of subaltern, biopolitical subjectivities forcing imperial capitalism to take on a different, more complex form.

Keeping in mind that surplus labor and life stolen from the margins and peripheries drove imperial capital accumulation, part II, "Neuropolitics," returns to the developed inner circle to uncover a new mode of capturing and grotesqueing desiring production. Japan's metropoles enjoyed a vibrant expansion of mass culture modernism after the economic takeoff following the First World War, to the extent that metropolitan readership of magazines and newspapers was the highest in the world. Focusing more explicitly on the erotic-grotesque media, I demonstrate how it both critiqued and contributed to the extension of capitalist power directly into the human nervous system: neuropolitics. Specifically, I look at the two central streams of erotic-grotesque modernism to identify the key neuropolitical subjectivities they spawned: sexologist, detective novelist, revolutionary pornographer, and the street subjectivities of the modern girl (*moga*) and modern boy (*mobo*).

In chapter 5, "All That's Solid Melts into Modern Girls and Boys," I work against the standard Eurocentric interpretation of Japanese sexology by focusing on Tanaka Kōgai and Nakamura Kokyo. Along with other Japanese sexologists, they constructed an imperialist scholarly endeavor that opposed and provincialized Europe, consolidating a technology of sex that produced an intensely libidinized Japanese masculinity. I argue that this form of heterosexual masculinity, which Tanaka and Nakamura naturalized as savage, rapacious, and insatiable and condensed as the "modern primitive," was technologized in the 1920s and returned to the outer circle to commit crimes against humanity in such places as Nanjing in December 1937 and Singapore in February 1942.

Chapter 6, "Revolutionary Pornography and the Declining Rate of Pleasure," is the first full treatment of the pioneers of erotic-grotesque modernism, Umehara Hokumei and Sakai Kiyoshi. Working across several different media, Umehara managed to gain control of two journals in 1925 through his best-selling translation of Boccaccio's *Decameron*. When his publication house came under intense police surveillance in 1927, he and Sakai moved to Shanghai, vowing to bring the erotic-grotesque "sexual revolution" to China. This chapter also introduces the important sociologist Akagami Yoshitsuge, who identified the erotic-grotesque as the capitalist media designed to penetrate directly into the human sensorium. In his important text, *The Face of Erotic-Grotesque Society*, published in 1931, Akagami exposed a neuropolitical capitalism that relied on fascinating image commodities to infiltrate the body and weaken the nerves. He theorized that a commodified *ero*, or "erotic," by soliciting consumer curiosity and colonizing human attention, substitutes for more authentic modes of desire. Part II ends with an intertext that analyzes the boom in vampire culture in metropolitan Japan in the late 1920s. By examining the work of the most famous Japanese detective novelist, Edogawa Rampo, I point to some of the ways that erotic-grotesque commodities inculcated a fascination with murder and suicide.

In part III, "Necropolitics," I show what happened to some of the subaltern biopolitical subjectivities under a new regime of rule in Japan's fascist colony of Manchukuo beginning in March 1932: kidnapped women sex workers turned into "comfort women"; pimps became state-sanctioned advisers; and coolies morphed into approximately ten to twelve million unremunerated forced laborers. Chapter 7, "The Opiate of the (Chinese) People," demonstrates the extent of imperialists' dependence on drug revenues in their occupation of China. As the central commodity in necropolitical capitalism, drugs were designed to make a killing profit from the death and incapacitation of Chinese. Some 50 to 55 percent of Manchukuo revenues came from drug sales, and by 1944, 20 percent of Manchukuo's Chinese population of forty million was seriously addicted.

Chapter 8, "Japanese Lessons," focuses on two of the main civilian leaders in Manchukuo: the fascist bureaucrat Kishi Nobusuke and the war profiteer and industrial capitalist Ayukawa Yoshisuke, the founder of Nissan. Kishi was sent to Manchukuo in 1936 from Japan's Ministry of Finance to set up the Five-Year Plan for Industrial Development, designed to prepare Japan's military for "total war" with the Soviet Union and "final war" with the United States. As he did so, he pioneered techniques in laundering the money earned from Manchukuo's extensive trafficking in drugs and humans. Moreover, in August 1937 Kishi wrote the first forced labor policy in Japan's imperialism, which authorized one of the most brutal transfers of subject peoples (Korean and Chinese) in the world. Ayukawa brought Nissan Holdings to Manchukuo from Tokyo in December 1937 and proceeded to make large profits directly through land appropriations and the use of forced labor and indirectly through the guaranteed revenue he received from the Manchukuo state. Producing the vehicles and machines that allowed Japan's army to conquer China and Southeast Asia, Ayukawa promoted a form of fascism he called *zentaishugi*, or "totalitarianism."

I conclude the book by analyzing the system of sexual slavery that characterized the necropolitics of Japan's imperialism. Drawing on new resources, I show how the 150,000 to 400,000 comfort women and forced sex workers were victims, first of the neuropolitical capitalist imperative to treat humans as disposable commodities, and then of the necropolitical command to "kill and leave undead." As further evidence of the hegemony of necropolitical sovereignty, I finish the book with a short reading of representative texts from two of the most popular Chinese writers in Manchukuo, Mei Niang and Li Zheyi.

ACKNOWLEDGMENTS

This project began back when I was a PhD student at the University of California, Santa Cruz, where I was asked to think systematically about power, pleasure, and disempowerment by my teachers Harry Berger, Chris Connery, Roberto Crespi, David Halperin, Donna Haraway, James O'Connor, Kristin Ross, Dan Selden, and Hayden White. Meeting Harry Harootunian there was life transforming, as my interests were moving in the direction of East Asia and he facilitated a move to Cornell after four great years at Santa Cruz.

Poor Brett de Bary, Victor Koschman, and Naoki Sakai. They offered a nice PhD fellowship to a student with too much theory and poor language skills, and could not have expected that thanks would take the form of covert and overt resistance to disciplinary formation. In many ways despite myself and thanks to the efforts of my teachers, Cornell was a great place for exploring ideas about Japan, East Asia, and the world. The graduate students in Japanese who contributed to my explorations included Rich Calichman, Katsuhiko Endo, Yukiko Hanawa, Lewis Harrington, Joanne Izbicki, Ayako Kano, Beng Choo Lim, Ben Nakamachi, Setsu Shigematsu, and Josh Young. My awesome Cornell *senpai* include Mark Anderson, Mike Bourdaghs, and Joe Murphy. Meeting the smart, young professors Nina Cornyetz, Bill Haver, Hosea Hirata, Tom Lamarre, and Livia Monet during my first year at Cornell gave me hope that an adult paycheck just might be in my future. Tim Murray was the best kind of mentor: intellectually rigorous, witty, and politically engaged.

I spent four years in Tokyo as a PhD student, from 1994 to 2001, and Tatsumi Takayuki and Kotani Mari were welcoming and warm during my various intellectual and political incarnations. My main *sensei* during this time were the improbable couple of Karatani Kojin and Nakahara Michiko, recently retired from Waseda University. Karatani invited me into his graduate student seminar at Hōsei for two years and was extremely generous with his time. Professor Nakahara is the epitome of the politically engaged academic; over the course of the past twenty years, working with a small collective of feminist activists, she has brought to light issues of sexual violence and gender oppression in twentieth-century East Asia. Tokyo University of Foreign Studies has been my intellectual home in Japan since 1995, and Professors Iwasaki Minoru, Nakano Toshio, Narita Ryūichi, and Yonetani Masafumi have welcomed me into their intellectual world since I first went to Tokyo and have patiently tolerated my linguistic butchery for over a decade now. Ken Kawashima and Anne McKnight were great friends and interlocutors during these years. More recently the late Miriam Silverberg and Tak Fujitani offered both friendly criticism and invested encouragement in this project, as has the wise and witty Jim Hevia.

Underpaid and underprivileged women have taught me Japanese and Chinese, and among those too numerous to mention I want to thank Hamano Shōko, Ishibashi Kyōko, and Zhou Yi. I spent one year at the Inter-University Center for Japanese Language in Yokohama and learned to speak Japanese there under the patient tutelage of fine teachers who were also fantastic human beings.

Since beginning my job here at the University of North Carolina, Chapel Hill, I've benefited from the camaraderie of arguably the best group of Japan scholars in Anglophone academe: David Ambaras, Dani Botsman, Leo Ching, Chris Nelson, Gennifer Weisenfeld, and Tomiko Yoda. My friends in cultural studies and postcolonial studies, Karen Booth, Elyse Crystal, Arturo Escobar, Larry Grossberg, John Pickles, and Eunice Sahle, keep the non–East Asian part of my intellectual life juiced on a daily basis. The UNC Chinese librarian, Hsi-chu Bollock, was immensely helpful.

This book wouldn't have been possible without a thirteen-month Japan Society for the Promotion of Science postdoctoral fellowship in Tokyo from December 2006 until January 2008. I'm not sure who was on the Social Science Research Council Japan Committee for 2006, but many thanks go to those who supported my application. Itō Mamiko, Kasahara Hikaru, Johnny and the dudes at Las Meninas, and Yabu Shiro and his leftist crowd at Jacobin in Golden Gai made my life much less lonely during that year. My activist comrades Umi Hagitani and Sabu

Kōso make my annual Tokyo stay fun and focused. My comrade Narita Kei of Irregular Rhythm Asylum helped me out on several occasions checking facts from the colonial newspapers at the Diet Library.

Since my return from Japan permanently in 2001, my work has benefited from a great group of friends and theory blabbermouths, including Srinivas Aravamudan, Jon Beller, Karyn Ball, Andrew Haas, Ranji Khanna, Wahneema Lubiano, Randy Martin, Walter Mignolo, Jackie Orr, Stephen Pfohl, and more recently Beth Povinelli and Patricia Clough.

Closer to publication time, Ken Wissoker's rare combination of humanity and professionalism shepherded the review process with a sure hand. Courtney Berger was the same capable and comedic presence she had been for my earlier project, and Leigh Barnwell took over beautifully from Courtney after she got her much-deserved promotion. Mark Mastromarino efficiently guided the manuscript through the production process. This book was also improved by the reports of three anonymous reviewers. Erika Nelson proofread the entire book, a product unimaginable without the love, life, and laughter of her older sister, my lover Diane.

ABBREVIATIONS

CK	*Chōsen Kōron* (Korea Review)
COM	*Chōsen oyobi Manshū* (Korea and Manchuria)
FMA	(Japanese) Foreign Ministry Archive
KN	*Keijō Nippō* (Seoul Daily Report)
MKS	*Manshūkokushi*. Edited by Manshūkokushi hensan kankōkai. 2 vols. Manmō Dōhō Engokai, 1971.
MSSK	*Manshū sangyōkai yori mitaru Shina no ku-ri-*. Edited by ManMon sangyō kenkyūkai. Dalian: Manshū Keizai Jihōsha, 1920.
MNNS	*Manshū Nichi Nichi Shinbun* (Manchuria Daily Newspaper)
RDQDZX	*Riben diguo zhuyi qinhua dangan ziliao xuanbian*. Edited by Jilinsheng shehui kexueyuan hebian. 14 vols. Beijing: Zhonghua Shuju Chuban, 1991.
ZDLSG	*Zhongguo dongbei lunxian shisinianshi gangyao*. Edited by Wang Chengli. Beijing: Zhongguo Dabaike Quanshu Chubanshe, 1991.

INTRODUCTION   Modern society is perverse, not in spite of its puritan-
ism or as if from a backlash provoked by its hypocrisy;
it is in actual fact, and directly perverse.

FOUCAULT, *THE HISTORY OF SEXUALITY*, VOL. 1

On 19 March 1911 the founder of modern Japanese nativism, Yanagita
Kunio (1875–1962), wrote to the prominent natural historian and bota-
nist Minakata Kumagusu (1867–1941) asking for folklore samples from
his home in Wakayama in western Japan, where Minakata had settled
after returning from fifteen years abroad. Yanagita was especially interested in examples documenting the existence of strange mountain
people (*yamabito*), goblins (*tengu*), and humanoid giants. He thought
these were all living descendants of a non-Ainu aboriginal race of Japanese who were long ago forced into the mountains by the arrival of
plains-inhabiting settlers from Northeast Asia—Asians widely recognized as the biological ancestors of nearly all Japanese. Yanagita promised to include any of Minakata's samples supporting his hypothesis in
his new journal, *Researching Native Place*. With this journal Yanagita was
attempting to build on the popularity of his collection of Japanese folklore *The Legends of Tōno*, published in 1910, to jump-start a discipline he
called *minzokugaku*, the study of native customs. Addressing Minakata
honorifically as *sensei*, Yanagita somewhat pompously proclaimed, "At
long last, a complete change in Japanese popular understanding [*koku-
ron*] regarding our customs is upon us. We here at the journal are committed to fundamentally transforming the conventional view of Japanese customs from something defensive, into something positive and
future-oriented" (quoted in Minakata 1985, 6).

The year 1911 was also the last full year of the Meiji emperor's reign
(1868–1912) and only six years after Japan's victory in a bloody campaign against Russia that made Japan an irrevocable imperial presence

in Korea and Northeast China. In his brief return letter of 21 March Minakata, a critical follower of Darwinian evolution, refuses to document the timeless existence of make-believe Japanese aboriginals. Instead, he submits that such folklore myths aren't specific to Japan at all but can be found in places as different as Ireland and South Asia. Furthermore, Minakata complains that the paucity of *any* surviving myths in his area has much to do with the way the centralizing Japanese state and prefectural development policies have been destroying human and natural life in Wakayama, from the "reckless deforestation" (*ranbatsu*) to the oppressive "shrine consolidation" which was imposing Japan's state religion, Shinto, onto local, non-Shinto sites of worship: "Whether one's concern is scholarly or nationalistic [*kokutai*], we should all be worried about these policies" (1951–52, vol. 10, 2).

Five days later Minakata posted his full response to Yanagita, beginning again with complaints about Tokyo's ongoing privatization and centralization. He updates Yanagita on the protest activities he and the Diet representative from Wakayama, Nakamura Keijirō, have been organizing and announces that he will appeal to his British colleagues for help in stopping the modernizing bulldozers unleashed by the "Japanese emperor's country" (*kōkoku*). The body of the letter responds to Yanagita's request for myths of giants and goblins. With this second letter, it's evident how different Minakata's scientific understanding of human life, evolution, and transformation is from Yanagita's mythological, static, and creationist understanding. In drawing Yanagita's attention to this difference, Minakata opens his response by discussing some data he came across in the religious section of the Museum of Natural History in London, including ancient Greek myths about genitalia. He explains that stories of superhuman body parts, such as the enormous nose of the *tengu* goblin or the long legs of giants, are normally understood as symbols for genitalia. He wonders if Yanagita's giants and goblins might not be better understood as sacred and erotic objects, the sort people invest with socioreligious meaning. In other words, Minakata lectures, they don't refer to actual entities but function as substitutes, "what scholars refer to as fetishes" (1951–52, vol. 10, 12–13).

Yanagita was not convinced. He claims in his return post on 30 April that he has "proof" of his actually existing Japanese aboriginals in the form of similar myths collected from different areas of Japan; they all depict the Ur-Japanese communicating with the locution "Ho! Ho!

Ho!" Minakata's response was sent in two installments, the first on 18 May and the second a week later. Although he didn't realize it at first, Minakata quickly figured out that Yanagita didn't consider the contents of folk myths to be fictional. In what couldn't have been an auspicious opening for the hopeful Yanagita, Minakata begins by denying the presence of similar myths in Wakayama. After dismissing Yanagita's claim, Minakata tries to prod him into a consideration of modern, Darwinian theories of evolution. Wouldn't it make more sense to assume, he reasons, that when these folk myths refer to supernatural creatures the referents are the monkeys and baboons that were the ancestors of all humans? Going over the various sources, he deduces, "All these narratives are evidently talking about big monkeys" (1951–52, vol. 10, 24–25).

Finally, Minakata directly addresses the Ho! Ho! Ho! phonemes that Yanagita has been averring are the linguistic signature of indigenous Japanese giants: "People who aren't well-educated lack correct information. Let me just note one more thing about the issue of human giants. Here where I live there's a shrine where a bird makes the Ho! Ho! Ho! sound. A friend went to investigate for himself and it turned out to be a horned owl [mimizuku]. The stuff that's been left there is unmistakably horned owl shit" (1951–52, vol. 10, 32–33). He seems hopeful that the brute facticity of the owl shit will brake Yanagita's desire to ground Japaneseness in the mountain folk and giants of an ethnoracially pure Japan, severed from the Asian mainland. But the thin-skinned Yanagita senses Minakata's condescension and responds defensively by questioning his patriotism. On 13 October Yanagita denounces him: "Although you've shown us a proper patriotic attitude with your work on the shrine issue, with everything else you're much too cosmopolitan. Elitists like you turn your back on all Japanese scholarship" (quoted in Minakata 1985, 130–31).

Because Minakata relished the exposure that he got from publishing in Yanagita's journal, he learned to soften his critiques. However, after five years of their marriage of convenience it became clear to him that Yanagita would yield no ground on his antiscientific creationist take, and so Minakata took to ridiculing him. A well-known instance of this (Tsurumi K. 1978; Figal 1999) appears in their final correspondence. At his wit's end with Yanagita, he attempts one last dismissal of the absurd giant and goblin theory of a pure Japanese ethnogenesis, and with it Japan-centered nativism. In his last known letter to Yanagita, dated midnight, 23 December 1916, Minakata recalls a specimen-collecting outing with a colleague in the summer of 1908. Half naked, the two botanists found themselves screeching out while hurtling down a steep mountain slope waving their mosquito nets, unable to stop themselves from the momentum. Here's Minakata telling the story: "There was a group of twenty or so village wives tending the fields at the bottom of the mountain. They shrieked out 'Strange entities have come down from the Heavens!' when they saw us and took off. Only when we reached the bottom did we realize why they were terrified: they thought we were superhuman demons" (1951–52, vol. 11, 290–91). In his parting slap down to Yanagita he declares, "*I* am your mountain giant and goblin."

I've set up Yanagita's and Minakata's disputes carried out on the cusp of Japan's colonial empire because they represent continuing attempts to configure subjectivity and system creation. This book breaks from a model of scholarship still present in East Asian studies that emphasizes a more or less homogeneous Japanese cultural nationalism severed from Asia. Marginalizing the canonical Yanagita and the paranoid cultural particularism for which he has served as privileged synecdoche, I follow Minakata's itinerant cosmopolitan along with Japanese postcolonial scholarship by Yonetani Masafumi (2006) and others that track the historicopolitical relation between Japan and its East Asian ethnoracial and symbolic donors. Although there's no doubt that many Japanese elites in the mid-nineteenth century recognized the need to adopt select elements of European technoscience, they acknowledged this not out of admiration for an assumed European superiority. Rather, Japanese leaders understood that defending themselves in the inner circle and East Asian others in the outer circle against the Euro-American agents of advanced technology threatening their sovereignty—gunboat imperialists, drug runners, and rampaging free traders intent on forcefully "opening up" the region that had been the center of world trade for a millennium—meant that they had to inject themselves with certain immunities. The reform leader Fukuzawa Yukichi explicitly recommended in the 1880s that Japan needed to "catch measles" from Euro-America (1960, 231). Given the historical encounter produced by the First Opium War (a confrontation more properly referred to, in critical response to Samuel Huntington's Eurocentric global mapping of the "West and the Rest," as the "East and the Beast"),[1] Japanese elites understood that the best means of protecting themselves from the Euro-American beasts and realizing their centuries-long dream of replacing China as the center of the East Asian tribute trade system (Hamashita 1988) would be through controlled exposure to its toxicity. This strategy of immunological self-exposure was popularized in the late nineteenth century as *wakon yōsai*, "Japanese spirituality, Western technology."

In the sixteenth and seventeenth centuries, eager to reverse nagging trade deficits with China (source of the textiles and china that European consumers coveted), Spain and Britain forcefully established peripheries in the New World where they could readily expropriate surpluses. Building on these economic martial art tactics Marx called the "primitive accumulation" of capital, by the 1830s Britain was finally ready to invade China's empire from its Indian colony. In their successful campaign to terrorize East Asians into submission to unequal trade, events that James Hevia (2003) brilliantly ironizes as "English lessons," British imperialists imposed a system of treaty ports and colonial cities on the China coast—"Every one of them," the enraged Rosa Luxemburg wrote in 1913, "[was] paid for with streams of blood, with massacre and ruin" (1968, 394). In response, Japan's elites rushed ahead with a program to detain and contain Beastification. Their ultimate goal was to send the white predators home and dethrone the weak Qing rulers of China as the imperial hegemon in East Asia and the Asia-Pacific. Immunologically, this required a commitment to injecting themselves with pathogens from the Euro-American Beasts, what the mainstream historiography on Japan has preferred to call "modernization."

In this book I offer a new (and in some ways *old*) analysis of how beastialization took place under Japan's imperialism in Asia. Here, I share a hermeneutic with recent anticapitalist scholarship on East Asia by Hyun Ok Park (2005) and Ken C. Kawashima (2009) that builds on materialist work emphasizing the construction of a capitalist periphery and colonial plunder. I'm writing this introduction in November 2008 in the midst of a severe global economic downturn caused primarily by greedy First World finance capitalists throwing away the hard-earned money of the middle and working classes. If now isn't the time to refuse the naturalization of capitalism and the ideological insistence on its benevolent and civilizing character, then there never will be a time. Although it wouldn't be right to overlook the impact of certain conservative tendencies in Anglophone postcolonial studies, it's clear that until quite recently the influence of U.S.-based modernization scholarship has been the strongest in censoring anticolonial and anticapitalist critiques of Japan's imperialism. For example, in the introduction to the canonical volume on the subject, *The Japanese Colonial Empire, 1895–1945*, Mark Peattie mystified readers with the following remark: "[Although] a just apportionment of good or evil in the results achieved defies the most objective observer of Japanese colonialism . . . it is possible to enumerate broad categories of change which could be termed 'modernizing'" (1984, 44–45). In foreclosing on the question of profit and power (in other words, by not asking *Cui bono?* Who benefits?) modernization historians unwittingly echo Monty Python's *Life of Brian* (1979). In this film the revolutionaries plotting to overthrow the Roman imperialists and install a Judea People's Republic try to incite a group of fellow locals by asking, "What have the Romans ever done for us?" When confronted with the litany of modernizing successes installed by Roman imperialism—roads, sanitation, good booze—the leader can only admit what is ideological common sense to modernizers everywhere: imperialism always delivers the goods to its colonies. Anti-imperialists and leftist cultural studies scholars who deny this are duped and deluded.

Against the modernizationist Peattie and the Pythons both, in this book I foreground the ways human and nonhuman resources stolen from colonial and domestic peripheries, together with excessive profits jacked from colonized renters and subaltern wage laborers, built Japan's imperial behemoth. Rosa Luxemburg's de-naturalizing insistence that "capital employs force as a permanent weapon" (1968, 371) is seconded by Marx, who warns in *Capital Volume 1*, "Accumulation of wealth on one pole is . . . at the same time accumulation of misery, the torment of labor, slavery, brutalization and moral degradation at the opposite pole" (1977, 799). Against modernization theory's disregard for the pain and power differences cleaving gender, class, and colonizer-colonized relations in Japan's imperialism ("All benefited," Peattie scolds leftist scholars [1984, 37]), Marx's fundamental point is well taken, that capitalist systems exist only because a large part of workers' lives is stolen: "The present wealth . . . is based on the theft of alien labor time" (1973, 705). Reframing Marx's language and transcoding it into the mass culture discourse of Tokyo in the 1920s, capitalists depend on the mugging grotesque of the living, erotic labor of subaltern and proletarian others for their very existence. Although some of the secondary and tertiary effects of Japan's imperialism could arguably be construed as "modernizing" for those who still accept that idiom, the suffering of colonized subaltern laborers enduring existential states Mbembe (2003) defines as "being-in-pain" was its primary cause. In this sense, Japan's imperialism was irrefutably modern; there was nothing late or lacking about it. But it was modern in many other ways as well. So in this book I link dialectically the *necro*-logic of expropriation—colonial pillage and capitalist profiteering, what I call, following the Japanese sociologist Akagami Yoshitsuge (1931), the *grotesque*—with the *bio*-logic of creative, desiring life, what I call, after Minakata and his followers, the *erotic*.

Kokutai versus Hentai

Minakata's biologics intuited that the dynamism inhering in productive life is what is most crucial for power to capture and contain, and his writings on the shrine consolidations reflect this. In a famous opinion piece written in 1912 he called the Japanese state's theft of collective labor and common lands in Wakayama "domestic imperialism" (1951–52, vol. 8, 193–98). Of the 3,700 local shrines 3,100 had been shut down and their land sold off by November 1911; for the first time common property had been privatized, with the profits going to corrupt Shinto priests Minakata thought were in the pockets of land-grabbing capitalists (Figal 1999, 203). These shrine consolidations and the accompanying deforestation are best construed as examples of the primitive accumulation of capital, what David Harvey (2003), updating Marx, calls "accumulation by dispossession." On 22 August 1910 Minakata was arrested and imprisoned for his militant protests against the shrine policy. For several years he'd been doing all he could to prevent privatization, including extensive fieldwork documenting Wakayama's pillaging by Tokyo politicians and profiteers.

Minakata's direct action protests against accumulation by dispossession in Wakayama were the culmination of two decades of research and writing on the dialectic between production and reproduction, energy and system, and chaos and containment. Beginning with his research on the erotic energy absorbed by the Tibetan mandala, and continuing with his analysis of the ways totem communities direct potentially antisystemic desire toward pacifying and unifying individuals around one shared symbol, he saw how the Japanese state was similarly stealing the labor of humans and other species that had created life-worlds in Wakayama. The state relied for its very existence on expropriating the creativity of life. Although nation-state institutions concocted what he called "systems" (*seidō*), these systems were but a posteriori phenomena, parasitic entities that relied on the world-making capacity of lively others for their derived existence (1951–52, vol. 11, 201). Similar to the dialectic of "living labor" and "vampire capital" that Marx established in *Capital*, Minakata's emphasis on life and its ontological primacy over and against the secondarily ontic mandala, totem, and generalized "system" was yet another source of disagreement with Yanagita.

One of the ways this disagreement played out was through Minakata's anger at Yanagita's policy of rejecting erotica for *Researching Native Place*. Several scholars have noted Yanagita's statement assuming his "responsibility as editor not to publish obscenity" (Matsui 1993, 515). Minakata fumed to his friends, such as Mutu Go: What kind of system of the Japanese folk would insist on censoring such crucial aspects of everyday life? (1951–52, vol. 12, 410–29). He linked Yanagita's erotophobia to the way local authorities, following the lead of metropolitan elites, wanted to discipline older erotic practices in the countryside. As Alan Christy points out, Minakata complained that in a neighboring village, the police had just issued regulations outlawing the old custom of "hooking up" (*yobai*), or recreational sex: "Tokyoites might chuckle when they hear of this, but still today there's hardly a village in Japan where cruising doesn't occur every evening" (quoted in Christy 2010, 318–19). Minakata connected Yanagita's erotophobia with this kind of infiltration of the repressive "family-state" (*kazoku kokka*) ideology into peripheral areas. He understood Yanagita's nativism project as translating into modern terms the older discourse of essential Japaneseness, what he referred to as *kokutai* (国体). Minakata implicitly opposed *kokutai*, rendered as the static "Japanese essence," with the standard biological concept of *hentai* (変体), or "mutating organic matter." His most important scientific work involved tracing the hybrid genealogies of slime molds and other forms of *hentai*. In the early twentieth century he started using the *hentai* homonym 変態 (the "modality of human transformation") to speak about a similar process in humans (Nakazawa 1993). For Minakata this transcoding of mutable plant and bacteria *hentai* onto the human species underscored their transformative, structure-producing energy.

By the time of his correspondence with Yanagita, Minakata had grasped the transformations of all forms of life in terms of what he called in English "emanation," which he privileged over the narrower, Darwinian "evolution" (1951–52, vol. 9, 154). Frustrated with scientific attempts to reduce species evolution to processes that fit neatly into classificatory systems, his emanation as "nonlogical change" (*henka*) was chaotic, excessive, and disorderly—fundamentally resistant to systemic capture. Rather than seeing the relation between biological classification and creative life, observer and observed, or totem and erotic energy as neutral and natural, he identified an irresolvable and agonistic tension between them. When applied to the realm of individuals in political societies, this entailed a high-stakes cat-and-mouse game of capture and resistant escape.

Perhaps nothing expresses their differences more than the disagreement over the issue of violence and human sacrifice. One of Minakata's critical refrains held that, as Yanagita lacked even a basic understanding of anthropological concepts like gift giving and exogamy, his system of native customs was destined to be inert and static. A fortiori, as Minakata explained in a letter to Nishimura Shinji in 1927 (1951–52, vol. 12, 87–96), Yanagita's refusal to accept the fact of human sacrifice and the abjection of alterity in the boundary-establishing rituals of societies meant that his nativism ignored the problem of violence (*bōryoku*). For his part, Minakata chose to emphasize the ways totemic and other kinds of societies attempt to siphon off productive life and secure permeable boundaries through rituals such as sacrifice and the exogamous exchange of women.

Following from this understanding, the historical fact of human sacrifice was a given for Minakata (Matsui 1993, 597–601). During the debates about it in Japan in the mid-1920s, he went so far as to argue that it was still practiced: "Using human sacrifices as supports for buildings and other structures occurs even now" (Minakata 1992, vol. 2, 225). His long essay on sacrifice, written in 1927, is a tour de force of global knowledge that begins with examples from Japan's *Heikei Monogatari* and classical Chinese sources. He relates that in the Spring and Autumn Annals era (722–481 B.C.), Chinese officials, "trying to secure castle walls . . . pushed a a terrified queen into the wall's foundation and sacrificed her" (227); likewise in fourteenth-century Bombay and ninth-century Japan, a queen's living daughter was built into castle walls as a sacrifice. Minakata considered human sacrifice a testament to both political structures' vampirism of human labor and the attempt to cover up this vampirism, as in totemic sacrifice. He polemicized that through the erasure of the world-making energy in human eroticism and life on one side, and the refusal to consider the ways systems and societies need to "grotesque" or capture this energy on the other, Yanagita's methodology foreclosed on sociopolitical change. In other words, what is implicit in Minakata's philosophy is that between the vital productivity of desire (the erotic), called "living labor" in Marx and "desiring production" in Deleuze's and Guattari's *Anti-Oedipus* (1983), and the violent usurpation of this desire by hegemonic power (the grotesque), called "anti-production" by Deleuze and Guattari and simply "capital" by Marx, lies an unresolvable war.

Minakata's theories of emanation, life, and totemism were controversial during his lifetime. In one of his pieces on totemism showing how plant and animal totems are used to categorize humans, he pointed out that the name Kumagusu itself is a combination of bear (*kuma*) and wisteria (*kusu*). The polemicist Miyatake Gaikotsu suggested that the second character in the Kumakusu compound actually derived from *kuso*, which means "shit." This was Miyatake's way of dismissing Minakata's theories as so much *kumakuso*, or "bear shit."

Totem Philosophy

While Miyatake was putting up a stink, Minakata's metaphysics of life and desire was anticipating the central philosophical anthropologies of Japan's imperialism. The philosopher and policy intellectual Miki Kiyoshi (1897–1945) recommended in the 1930s that political leaders should ground Japan's empire on the world-making vitality of its human subjects, arguing that "the truth of the state relies on the human body" (1967, vol. 8, 15). In 1937 he accepted the invitation to head the cultural section of Prime Minister Konoe Fuminaro's Shōwa Research Association and became one of the philosophical architects of Japan's late imperialism. In that important position he combined Heidegger's intensity of thrown *Dasein* with Marx's focus on human labor's productivity. Widening the sources of productivity in Marx to natural life—"Nature is technological and produces like humans"—Miki conceived a "new humanism" designed to transcend the dualism separating living affect (pathos) and truth (logos) by fusing all vital production monologically to what he called the "myths of the state," a process he homologized to totemic operations in primitive societies (10, 22).

Miki's invocation of the totem in 1938, simultaneous with the construction of the imperialistic East Asian Co-Prosperity Sphere, was inspired by Tanabe Hajime (1885–1962), his teacher in philosophy at Kyoto University and the most important philosopher in Japan during the 1930s and 1940s. In his magnum opus, *Shu no Ronri* (The Logic of Species), Tanabe deployed totemism to open his theory of "absolute dialectics" (*zettai benshōhō*). Building on the Aristotelian and Hegelian tripartite schema of individuum (*ko*), particular species (*shu*), and universal genus (*rui*), he installed a vertically antagonistic relation between individuals and their species, a negativity that is mediated by universality. Along with this oppositional relationality between species and genus, he also established a horizontal antagonism between different ethnoracial species, with the universal mediating this as well. Similar to the ways an overarching tribal totem sutures together different clans into one shared community, the universal dialectically absorbs antagonism from different species and transforms it into positive identity.

Writing against both theories of organic society and the ideology of secular liberalism that emphasized consensus, Tanabe posited, "Social totality isn't a harmonious gathering of parts, but rather is a complex system of mediation where the individual [*ko*] maintains a productive antagonism towards the species [*shu*], and the species [*shu*] maintains a productive antagonism towards the whole [*rui*], whereby each part is also part of some other part" (1963, vol. 6, 62). The standard classificatory separation of the three elements gives way in his system to a mediated immunological identity, where each is a "hybrid [*kongōmono*] that exists only through antagonistic relation with something other" (62). Immunologically, each part of the trivium both shares and repels aspects of the other parts. On the side of the individual subject, Tanabe was insistent that for self-consciousness grounded in freedom, it was essential that the subject experience a negating discontinuity from its ethnoracial species. For there to be a sense of subjective difference from species (and therefore self-consciousness), the individual's *immediacy* with respect to its species must be broken. At this point, species is seen antagonistically by the subject as something intent on restricting its freedom and grotesqueing its vitality. As species itself had earlier become sovereign through the "violent usurping [*sandatsu*] of the mother's womb" for its own control (70), the subject immunologically retains certain aspects of its species, before opposing the rest with its newfound "will to power" (196).

After the two-stage negation of the mother-object by the patriarchal species and of the speciesized group by the individual subject, the subject enters a third stage. While the second negation contradictorily confirms the relation with the ethnocultural group (a confirmation that is also an immunological guarding against), it impels a leap beyond this particular into the universal genus (*rui*), embodied for Tanabe in Japan's multiethnic empire. Like the individual, the particularistic group achieves its contradictory identity only by its negative belonging to the universal empire. As Japan's empire was extending rapidly from Korea to Manchukuo and then into northern and central China, imperialists were terrified of decolonial nationalisms in the outer circle, and Tanabe attempted a philosophical recommendation of why Korean, Taiwanese, and Manchukuoan Chinese should reject their particularized species for self-conscious membership in the universality of Japan's empire (Sakai N. 1995). Although it was natural that colonized species would maintain a relation of negativity to the imperial state, the most modern, self-conscious of colonized subjects would recognize the transcendent superiority of Japan, as evolved imperial life meant for Tanabe the overcoming of brute biological species life (*sei*) and the seeking of universal belonging through the mediations of absolute dialectics. As the conclusion shows, "modern life" for Tanabe becomes absolutized only by self-consciously dying for Japan's empire. The philosophical project of absolute dialectics culminates in the imperial state's possessing the power to invert death and life, by calling death in imperial war the highest form of life.

Even before this explicitly necropolitical turn in the in early 1940s, Tanabe's imperial state possessed awesome grotesqueing capacities through its directorship of the "infinite hybridization of the world" (1963, vol. 6, 196). Although for Tanabe production and desire were on the side of individual subjects, the imperial state functioned as final guarantor of identity and the receptor of each subject's will to power. While subjective life for Tanabe was more complex than the creative power of vital entities in Minakata, they both situated political power as derived from natural life. To be sure, Tanabe downplayed the rationality of both subjective desire and biocultural group existence; his system featured a trade-off: living biopower provides systemic dynamism, while universality grants identity and logothetic rationality to dynamic life. Nevertheless, these aspects share a great deal with Minakata's emphasis on ecological life as the productive energy grounding all sociopolitical systems.

The notion of the immunologically mutual contamination of hegemonic power with subjective freedom that I find in Tanabe's dialectical philosophy and Minakata's biophilosophy finds a contemporary correlate in Michel Foucault's theory of power. Intending to delineate a modern form of power following on the heels of the breakdown of early modern disciplinary power (which solicited docility and demanded confinement), Foucault's understanding of biopolitics is, in my view, consistent with the philosophical architecture of Minakata and Tanabe. Although he later deployed his theory of power in multiple ways, the central impetus behind the shift from disciplinary power to what he called a "nondisciplinary" form of political rule was to underline the generating productivity of life. Biopolitical modernity, defined as the entrance of "life into history," represents for Foucault the new awareness by hegemonic rule that power can most effectively extend its domain not through the coercive "exercise of sovereignty over the fine grain of individual behaviors" (2007, 66), but by retreating from its scrutinizing surveillance and employing a more neutral optic that focuses on the population: "Unlike discipline, which is addressed to bodies, the new nondisciplinary power is applied not to man-as-body but to the living man; ultimately, if you like, to man-as-species" (2003, 243).

After these first attempts to theorize biopolitics in his lectures in 1975–76, Foucault returned from a sabbatical year to give the College de France lecture series in 1977–78, published as *Security, Territory, Population*. When he resumed his exploration of biopolitics, nondisciplinary power assumed a character that has been downplayed in the secondary literature. Appearing after discipline's withdrawal from coercion and incarceration, emergent nondisciplinary power begins to allow the naturalness of *bio*-life and vitalist desire more free rein. As Foucault explained, although the problem for disciplinary power was "how to say and legitimize 'no,'" the problem for nondisciplinary power was "how . . . [to] say yes to desire" (2007, 66, 73). During these lectures on nondisciplinary power he often linked biopolitics to the economic theory of laissez faire. Drawing attention to the Physiocrats' causal linkage of desire and exchange and the wealth and health of the population, Foucault claimed that the new challenge for hegemonic political power would be to understand that when it says "yes to desire," this releases individual subjects to do all the hard work for it. For Foucault, hegemonic power begins to grasp the fact that in modernity "life" is stronger than it is; as with Minakata and Tanabe, the vitalism of desire is the motor force for power. Consequently, power needs injections of immunities from vital desire for it to survive; rejecting its sovereign separation from lowly life, it recognizes the need to become *hentai* with and immunologically hybridized to it.[2]

Donna Haraway proposed a related reading of biopolitics as immunology two decades ago: "The immune system . . . constructs the boundaries for what may count as self and other in Western biopolitics" (1991, 204). But this is not the standard interpretation. The scholarship on biopolitics has been primarily concerned with tracking the institutional implementation of modern science in the forms of hygiene campaigns, maternity clinics, and disease prevention. In this sense, biopolitics takes life as its object so as to improve, prolong, and control it. However, when we pause to analyze Foucault's famous sound byte of biopolitics—*faire vivir, laisser mourir*—the common understanding of biopolitics as the embrace of living populations by medical science and demographic statistics is encoded only in the first clause, improving life (*faire vivir*). The second clause, letting die off (*laisser mourir*), doesn't simply mean killing, but something like "allowing something to die off if that is its inherent tendency." Jasbir K. Puar astutely reads this second clause thus: "Death becomes a form of collateral damage in the pursuit of life" (2007, 32). Although at times improving life necessitates murderous killing, what is accented in *laisser mourir* is the nonchalant indifference of biopolitics, a neutrality that fully opposes disciplinary power's obsession with proper postures and docile demeanors. However, as Foucault explicitly invokes the liberal economic doctrine of *laissez faire* (let them fare for themselves) in his later lectures on biopolitics, it's clear that the aim of biopolitics is to improve (some) lives while laissez-faire-ing others. In other words, certain populations within a body politic will be selected for health maintenance and disease control, while other populations will be *left to fare for themselves*. Select population groups will enrich themselves and society as a result of this nonchalant freeing, while others are released into what Judith Butler (2004) calls the "precarity" of probable death. What's important is that even the populations selected for life up-grades receive a Get out of Jail Free card, courtesy of biopolitics' indif-ference.

In my reading, biopolitics vectors in two directions in its concern with life: one leads to health and the other to wealth. This is to say that life as species-population needs to be improved on in terms of health, while life as desiring production needs to be released from its carceral confines to work for capital accumulation, something made explicit in Foucault's lectures of 1978, *The Birth of Biopolitics*. To add a Marxist sup-plement to biopolitics' vector of wealth, life is liberated so surplus can more readily be expropriated from living labor. Although its nondisci-plinary nature precludes it from commanding, biopolitics can "direct the flows of population to this or that region or activity." When biopolitical power liberates to more effectively expropriate, Foucault writes, "popu-lation is aware of what it wants, yet unaware of what is being done to it" (2007, 105).

In part I of this book, "Biopolitics," I argue that the two distinct vec-tors of "enhancing life" and "letting people fare for themselves" aptly depict the period following the collapse of what scholars have iden-tified as the confining Neo-Confucianism of Japan's Tokugawa world ([1603–1867]; Ikegami 1995). Few would dispute the fact that modern medicine and sanitation systems followed the "enhancing life" vector of biopolitics during the consolidation of Japan's nation-state in the 1890s and early twentieth century. As far as the second vector is concerned, the historian Irokawa Daikichi (1985) broke scholarly ground in show-ing how previously confined subjects were released from disciplinary domination in Japan during the interregnum spanning the close of the Tokugawa era and the period when the new Japanese constitution was promulgated in 1890. As one of the tactics of biopolitics is to "direct population flows," I focus on groups of the one million Japanese "liber-ated" to emigrate abroad, the twenty million Chinese immigrant laborers ("coolies") working permanently or seasonally in Japan's Manchurian colony beginning in 1905, and the masses of Korean farmers "liberated" from their land to become tenants to Japanese capitalist landowners. Largely neglected in the scholarship, these "biopolitical subjectivities" were the ontological motors and constituent energy of Japan's imperial-ism. Japanese ideological discourse of the Meiji era (1868–1912) intuited this new sense of biopolitical laissez-faire-ing, whereby subjects were now seen as personally responsible for "making a better life for themselves" (*risshin shusse*) or for "making a quick buck and instant success" (*ikkaku senkin*) in the outer circle peripheries. Contemporary pundits such as Fukuzawa Yukichi (1835–1901) recognized the importance of deconfined Japanese émigrés making something of their lives while working abroad, as the remittances they sent back to Japan provided crucial revenue for local governments in addition to desperately needed foreign currency for the Japanese state. Furthermore, colonial officials such as Gotō Shinpei understood that North Chinese coolies were the driving force for Japan's colonial lease in Manchuria, where they physically installed its entire infrastructure.

Articulating biopolitics to an uneven chaotic capitalism brings Foucault and Marx into a productive tension. As Foucault understood biopolitics as a form of rule wherein capitalist discipline was not yet immanent to it, Marx referred to a similar kind of sociohistorical condition as the "formal subsumption" of labor to capital. Designed to explain a shift away from a feudal and early modern disciplinary stasis, formal subsumption is the superimposition of commodity production and wage labor onto older social formations. Capital uses the preexisting arrangement of labor and technology and transforms them slightly; production now becomes commodity production solely for the market, and working hours are dictated by surplus value extraction: "The process of production has become the process of capital itself," geared toward "the sole purpose of using money to make more money" (Marx 1977, 1020). This subtle though significant shift leaves the specific content of early modern work denied and "living labor" killed and reified by the violent abstraction of the wage regime, placing the capitalist in the new position of the "direct exploitation of the labour of others" (1019).

Following Foucault's recommendation to see political power hunting in the margins for life to grotesque and South Asian subaltern studies' insistence on looking at the flexible yet violent extractions of the colonial state, I start this work with an analysis of how biopolitics worked in Japan's colonial periphery in the first twenty years of empire on the Asian continent, 1895–1915. Although we'll witness only a formal subsumption of living labor to capitalism, the biopolitics of Japan's colonial-peripheral capitalism will be shown to produce both enhanced populations of people and new subjectivities. I argue in part I that these biopolitical subjectivities are crucial for an analysis foregrounding the antagonism between ontological desiring production (erotic) and ontic political capture (grotesque). While mainstream scholarship on Japan largely refuses to see the painful expropriation of the surplus produced by embodied, living labor as productive of imperialism, my focus in part I is to show how the ongoing operations of vampirizing and grotesqueing biopolitical subjectivities quite literally *produced* Japan's imperialism and pushed capitalism to take on a more complex regime of grotesqueing.

In part II, I call this more complex regime *neuropolitics*. Although in biopolitics living labor alone possessed the animating capacity to, as Marx put it, "awaken things from the dead," when formal subsumption gives way to real subsumption in neuropolitics, living labor itself is transformed into "dead, objectified labor" encrypted in mass-produced commodities and industrial machinery alike (Marx 1977, 289). Different from formal subsumption, capitalist real subsumption as Marx identified it is that which controls more aspects of social relations—an intensified immunology which bolsters capital's power of parasitism and guards against threats. Although Marx's privileged example for real subsumption is the industrial factory, real subsumption's tendency is to work on society itself (Negri 1991). Marx theorizes that on the foundation established by formal subsumption "there now arises a technologically specific mode of production—*capitalist production*—which transforms the nature of the labor process and its actual condition. Only when that happens do we witness the *real subsumption of labour under capital.*" Locating a shift from absolute to relative surplus value expropriated by capital from labor, he writes, "With the real subsumption . . . a complete (and constantly repeated) revolution takes place" (Marx 1977, 1034–35).

Marx revealed a set of displacements in the shift from formal to real subsumption. The most important is that which evolves from the mystification of isolated workers ostensibly owing their very existence to capitalists, to the mystification that modern society itself is a gift from capitalism (Read 2003). In part II, I follow a similar line of displacement. The fundamental dialectic of living labor against the capitalist grotesque in part I is displaced in neuropolitics onto the commodification of all human sensations. The material effects of this displacement are both intensified and reflected on in erotic-grotesque modernism. One of my main concerns here is to analyze the process of commodity fetishism saturating Japan's metropoles under real subsumption. As individuals and society are ideologically misconstrued to be conceived by capitalism, metropolitan societies fall victim to an inhuman inversion in which "the *increasing value* of the world of things proceeds in direct proportion to the *devaluation* of the world of humans" (Marx 1988, 71; emphasis in original). Intensifying a process begun in biopolitics, "the worker puts his life into the object; but now his life no longer belongs to him but to the object" (72). Therefore, the instrumentalized worker is left with no other choice but to try to buy back his or her life in the form of commodity substitutes, what erotic-grotesque social scientists in the 1920s called a "second life." This process of buying back as a consumer one's life stolen by capital as a producer will reveal neuropolitics' central command. While the command of biopolitics is to enliven, and leave (the rest) to fare for themselves, the fascinating commodities on display in metropolitan capitalism conspire with neuropolitical domination to "stupefy and modify." A constantly stimulated stupefaction is the generalized condition of humans living in what Walter Benjamin called the "dreamworld" of metropolitan capitalism. Working to shock and awe metropolitan subjects into a state of stupefaction, neuropolitical capitalism then allows stunned subjects to purchase a substitute "second life" back from capitalism in the form of consumable commodities.

So we'll track a shift from the emphasis on the formal subsumption of labor and the production of biopolitical subjectivities in part I to the production of an entire commodified (second) life-world in neuropolitics under real subsumption in part II. As we do so, we will track a shift from the centrality of living labor to that of commodified, dead labor as it is grotesqued into mass-produced consumer goods and fixed-capital machinery. The production of subjectivities will also shift to those of popular sexologist, erotic-grotesque cultural producer, and modernologist market researcher—the subjectivities responsible for opening new pathways for capitalist real subsumption extending directly into the human nervous system and facilitating the stimulation and stupefaction of metropolitan consumer-subjects.

In part III, "Necropolitics," I track the ways the neuropolitical production of affect elicited an even more intensive subsumption of laboring bodies under capitalism in Japan's Manchukuo colony. Continuing my heuristic focus on the antagonism between the erotic as desiring production and the grotesque as political-economic capture, I extend this fundamental antagonism from one that featured living labor formally subsumed to biopolitical capitalism to one that centered on dead, commodified labor in neuropolitics to, finally, "living-dead" or undead labor subsumed by necropolitical capitalism through its constituent subjectivities of drug dealer, war profiteer, and fascist new bureaucrat. This displacement of the fundamental Marxist antagonism between labor and capital (living labor ➔ commodified, dead labor ➔ undead labor) has its corollary in the hegemonic shift from bio- to neuro- and then necropolitics in the directional that moves from life ➔ second life ➔ undead death.

Consequently, real subsumption in Japan's Manchukuo colony (1932–45) doesn't lead to the expansion of use-values and the production of new collective subjects, as it normally does. Rather, it takes advantage of the absolute surplus extraction latent in formal subsumption (where there is often no concern to reproduce workers in a way that they show up ready and rested for work the next day) with the relative surplus extracted from technomachinic inputs. I call this rare combination of extensive, absolute surplus extraction up to and including the death of the worker, with intensive inputs into the production process, *deformal subsumption*. Although Marx had uncovered in *Capital* the "tendency to force the cost of labor towards absolute zero" (1977, 748), the unremunerated, forced labor of between ten and twelve million Chinese in Manchukuo as the quintessence of deformal subsumption was only one aspect of necropolitical rule. Another aspect was the flooding of Manchukuo with opium and Japanese-produced heroin and morphine. Therefore, in addition to production, aspects of consumption in necropolitics also worked against systemic reproduction.

In addition to these deathly circuits of production, consumption, and extortion, colonizer sovereignty in Manchukuo can be qualified as a huge state of exception, wherein the suspension of the law characterized the regime's sovereignty from the beginning. In an influential essay, Achille Mbembe depicts the qualities of hegemonic power ruling in the state of exception as that which generates "death that lives a human life" (2003, 12). Rendering necropolitical sovereignty as the "subjugation of life to the power of death," Mbembe identifies necropolitics as invested in "the creation of *death-worlds*, new and unique forms of social existence in which vast populations are subjected to conditions of life conferring upon them the status of *living dead*" (15, 40). Frantz Fanon earlier identified something close to Mbembe's depiction of necropolitical death-worlds in *A Dying Colonialism*, where he insisted that "the colonized person . . . perceives life not as a flowering or a development of an essential productiveness, but as a permanent struggle against an omnipresent death" (1965, 128). In part III, I show how necropolitics worked together with deformal subsumption to not only murder many Chinese in Manchukuo, but to wreak vengeance on the biopolitical subjects mainly responsible for Japan's capitalist imperialism in the first place. Through deformal subsumption in colonial fascism, the subjectivities left to fare for themselves by biopolitical capitalism (coolies, sex workers, colonized renters) were de-ontologized and killed off by a necropolitical regime that succeeded in inverting and absolutizing living labor's centrality for imperial capitalism.

Finally, I show that imperial necropolitics rejects all hybrid pathogens and purges itself of immunological modernity tout court. In this sense, it is "overcome," as H. D. Harootunian (2000) has argued. But it's important to also emphasize the continuous present of overcoming; in Tanabe's dialectics, the pathogenic quality of immunities is constantly absolutized into that which can only receive identity papers from Japan's universal empire. As Japan's mastermind of total war, Ishihara Kanji, outlined, after passing through the stages of immunization (receiving injections from European technology, incorporating the vast resources of East Asia, etc.), Japan would be ready to take the place of the United States as the site of global universality. As Ishihara imagined, the blessings of *kokutai* (Japan's de-immunized organic body) could be offered to everyone. However, I show how biopolitics is purged by necropolitics when bioimmunities *within* become necroimmunities guarding Japanese *from* all others. The horizontal immunological relation with Euro-America and East Asia and the vertical immunology between capital and labor are foreclosed on. With the emergence of necropolitics in Japan's imperialism, the erotic as living labor is absolutized by power as the grotesque itself become *absolute*, in the sense of "cut off" and without mediations. The *hentai* and "perverse" admixtures of immunological modernity become purified into the dream of Japan as the unmediated and nonhybrid occupier of universality. As I show in the conclusion, this process culminated in a kind of suicidal *autoimmunity*, whereby Japan started eating itself.

But before we get all dizzy up here in clouds of speculative theorizing, it's best to descend to firm materialist ground and introduce the single most important subjectivity in Japan's imperialism: the Chinese coolie.

PART I **BIOPOLITICS**

1

COOL(IE) JAPAN   [The coolies'] one passion seemed to be patient, eternal toil. Nothing stopped them in their work. And in that manner they laid the foundation of economic and financial power. . . . The history of the development of Manchuria is the story of the Shantung Coolie, nothing more.

ADACHI KINNOSUKE, *MANCHURIA: A SURVEY*

We must find new lands from which we can easily obtain raw materials and at the same time exploit the cheap slave labor that is available from the natives of the colonies.

CECIL RHODES

Desire, combined with what North Chinese themselves called the "desperation pushing us into Manchuria" (*chuang guandong*), drove one of the largest movements of people in modern history. What Thomas Gottschang and Diana Lary (2000) call the "great migration" to northeastern China saw roughly twenty-five million people move there from the densely populated North China provinces of Shandong and Hebei from 1890 to 1940. Only the century-long emigration of fifty-two million people from Europe between 1840 and the 1930s was larger. To talk about migration initially in terms of desire is not to downplay the various forces that induce the desperately poor to sever themselves from home and enter a labor diaspora. In the case of the Shandong "coolies," even considering the relatively short several-hundred-mile move into neighboring northeastern China, it would be hard to underestimate the miserable conditions in which poor farmers, skilled workers, and itinerant laborers found themselves in the 1890s and early twentieth century.

After the Second Opium War, Euro-American powers imposed the

"Open Door" policy of free trade with China, designed to provide easier access for their capitalists, hungry for market share of what had been, until the 1840s, the world's largest economy. This regime of unequal treaties laid the groundwork for the initial accumulation by dispossession of North China by England, the United States, Germany, and others. Northeast China was likewise forcefully inserted into the global economy, first by Russia and Britain and then by Japan.

The areas in China being buffeted by these political and economic pressures had, during the Qing Dynasty (1644–1911), suffered droughts in 233 of those years and floods in 245 of them. Environmental and geopolitical catastrophes like these impelled some Japanese elites to foreground what Wendy Brown calls, in a somewhat different context, the "states of injury" of hapless Chinese (Brown 1995). However, as Brown warns, hegemonic power is working whenever states of injury are enumerated. The injurious state of Chinese coolies at the hands of brutal Euro-American colonizers and gunboat imperialists was played up by Japanese imperialists intent on showing how, as Asians, their own treatment of Chinese labor was necessarily brotherly and humane. The civilizing missionary positions taken by Japanese colonizers were proclaimed with the confidence that a racial unity with Chinese and shared cultural history with China would mystify the fact that coolie labor—waged much lower than it was sold—single-handedly produced value in Japanese-controlled and colonized Northeast China.

Japanese colonialists also justified the move to continental Asia as a selfless desire to civilize. They pointed to their tentacle-like railroad system—first laid down on top of an incipient Russian base in 1905 and continually expanded until the end of the Second World War—and the discounted fourth-class passage that seasonal Chinese workers occasionally received to usher them to multiple labor sites as Japanese imperialism's emblem of a modernizing system. This emblem, of course, was also a symptom of capital's need for cheap labor. For the new railroads were Japan's imperial response to the problem identified by Foucault as specific to both capitalism's formal subsumption and to biopolitics: the problem of population. Railroads answered the question of the population with the fixed capital to "attach workers firmly to the production apparatus, to settle them or move them where it needs them to be—in short, to constitute them as a labor force" (Foucault 1997, 34).

To extend only slightly the epigraph from the journalist Adachi, the history of the de- and repossession of Northeast China by Japan's imperialism is the story of the Chinese coolie, nothing more. Japanese dreams of empire in Asia built on the backs of cheap coolie labor surfaced even before the consolidation of its modern nation-state in 1868. In London in 1862 the Satsuma diplomat Godai Tomoatsu was reported to have "asked about the possibility of using Chinese and Indian laborers under Japanese direction to establish an East Asian center of industrial economic power" (Jansen 1965, 59–60). This wish was fulfilled immediately after the treaty ending the Russo-Japanese War was signed in New Hampshire on 5 September 1905. Thereafter, Tokutomi Sohō, Natsume Sōseki, and other imperialists saw Japan's imperial future in the Manchurian present embodied in the reserve army of coolie labor. Sōseki was initially disconcerted by the sheer number of "filthy" coolies he saw when he first landed at Dalian Harbor in September 1909, describing them as "a surging multitude . . . buzzing and swarming like angry wasps" (2002, 39). The famous novelist was invited to visit Japan's new colony by his school friend Nakamura Zekō, the second president of the South Manchurian Railway Company. However, by the end of his trip through Manchuria he came away with a glowing report of the capacity for coolies to slave tirelessly for Japanese capitalist concerns, never complaining even among themselves, "as silent as people who had lost their tongues" (65). Their willingness to work robotically "from morning to evening without pause" led Sōseki to conclude his travelogue to East Asia, written for the bourgeois readers of the *Asahi* newspaper, "Chinese coolies are superb workers . . . moreover, they are utterly compliant" (66; translation modified).

Sent on a fact-finding mission in 1923 to document the extent of Japan's colonial provenance on mainland China, the journalist Adachi Kinnosuke twice marvels in his chronicle at the surging multitude — what he racially others as the "black tide" — of coolies laboring tirelessly for capitalist enterprises in Manchuria. He first narrates how Northeast China was "conquered" by illegal coolie migrants from neighboring Shandong province in the nineteenth century. Although the Qing first tried to ban and then to restrict migration into their home region of the Northeast until 1878 to protect cultural homogeneity, rich landlords secretly encouraged destitute coolies to work their land. Adachi explains, "Native Manchurians who owned the land liked the Chinese workmen to come into Manchuria. Why? For just one all-sufficient reason: they could turn over the farm lands to the Chinese and enjoy their simple life by the sweat of somebody else's brow" (1925, 42).

The "pull" elements of the labor market needs of the capitalist and landlord class were matched with "push" factors enumerated by Adachi in terms borrowed from Japanese colonial discourse of the early twentieth century. Although an ensemble of environmental, geopolitical, and economic causes were often invoked to explain the social chaos impacting North China as the Qing dynasty imploded, the overriding cause identified by Japanese colonizers for poor Chinese migrants coming to Manchuria was raciological: Chinese are genetically programmed for slave-like work. Reassuring his readers that there was nothing mysterious about the historical fact of Manchuria's being "conquered" and "colonized" initially by coolies, Adachi hypothesizes coolly, "No race known to history has ever beaten the Chinese in patience and persistence of striving for the thing their hearts desired" (1925, 42). This essentialist explanation of the coolie's *desire* for the kinds of labor that no other race of people would do was self-evident, "as simple as it is apparent" (44).

> It was the ability of the Chinese coolie to live on cheap, coarse food—such food as is given to cattle in other lands. . . . Not only that but thriving on it. Even to this very day the physique, the power of physical endurance, of the Chinese coolie is the eternal wonder of the Japanese. Beside the Chinese coolie the Japanese workmen are pale and puny. With the sensational rise in living expenses in the Far East in recent years, I found, last year, the coolies in Manchuria were living on seven cents a day. (44)

Adachi strips coolie labor of all demands and nearly all human needs. The only thing that remains is "their one passion—patient, eternal toil. Nothing stopped them in their work" (44). With the Chinese willing to dine on cattle fodder and dog food, there was no reason for Japanese capitalists to pay them any more than the going rate for animal shelter and feed; they needed just enough to socially reproduce their labor so as to guarantee another long day of expropriating surplus. By 1860 Marx was using the term "Chinese wages" (1977, 749) as a code for the miserable remuneration tossed at the most oppressed class of workers in the world. Many Japanese capitalists thought to themselves, Why pay Chinese more, when there are no coolie *demands* for higher wages and no manifest coolie *needs* other than that of living for work? Given this population racism toward Chinese coolies, the proper response for Japanese colonizers appeared to be a fortunate convergence of capital and biopolitics: provide conditions that would expand Chinese life by guaranteeing arduous work. So Japan's colonial territory in the Guandong Lease and South Manchuria was turned into a massive composite of job fair, debtor's prison, and labor camp.

Japan's Manchuria

The signifiers "Manchuria" in English and "Manshū" in Japanese are part of a colonial discourse designating these terms as unrelated to China's territorial sovereignty. Until the communist victory in 1949, the area was called in Chinese Dongsansheng, the Three Eastern Provinces. It is referenced in contemporary Mandarin simply as Dongbei, or the Northeast. The region was in the midst of political and economic reform when Japan defeated Russia and obtained the latter's lease on the southern part of the Liaodong Peninsula in 1905. Along with the Guandong Leased Territories, totaling 3,462 square kilometers, Japan claimed a narrow strip of land containing the Russian-built South Manchurian Railway and the profitable Fushun coal mine. The area that came to be called the South Manchurian Railway Zone was only 260 square kilometers, while the line itself had a total length of 1,105 kilometers. In addition, Japan obtained rights from the Qing government to establish Japanese settlements in four major Manchurian cities. In 1906 the Qing allowed a Japanese consulate general to be established in Manchuria's capital city, Fengtian (Mukden), and smaller ones in Changchun, Kirin, Andong, Yingkou, and Xinmintun (Sakatani 1980). Although deterritorializing energy in the form of Japanese traffickers and sex workers had come to the area beginning in the 1870s, followed the next decade by small groups of *sōshi* solders of fortune, the victory over China in 1895 allowed many Japanese imperialists a chance to develop a taste for this part of China, and their devouring began in earnest in 1905. The agency that came to direct these hungry incorporations was the South Manchurian Railway Company (SMR).

The SMR was created in November 1906 by the Emperor Meiji's decree for the purpose of managing the coal mines and railroads won from Russia. Its corporate offices were in the new warm water port of Dalian, then under construction. Two months earlier Japan's Guandong government general (*Kantō totokufu*) was set up to exercise juridical and civilian control over the colonial territories and railway zones, working in tandem with Japan's Guandong army, which was responsible for security in the leased territories, railway zones, and consular areas. The SMR was also a vital source of colonial power. Despite the fact that it was established as a commercial enterprise with shareholders, the SMR immediately began to operate as a de facto ministry of colonial affairs in the Guandong Lease. While its official directive focused on the need to bring the universal, and purportedly neutral, gifts of capitalist development and modern civilization to the region, its real mission, as Matsusaka Y. T. argues, "was nothing less than the colonization of Northeast China" (2001, 4). Indeed, the SMR's founders, including its first president, Gotō Shinpei, explicitly invoked Britain's East India Company as their model (Andō 1965, 33–35). Such colonial enterprises operated "not as mere businesses," Gotō argued when the SMR charter was being drawn up, but as entities that "represented the state and accordingly exercised a measure of the sovereign power of the state" (Matsusaka 2001, 91). Gotō was effectively saying that the SMR should follow the precedent he established when he led Japan's colonizing enterprise in Taiwan.

Biopoliticians on Drugs

Gotō was a polyglot and a doctor who studied hygiene and immunology in Germany for eighteen months in 1890 and 1891, receiving his medical degree in Munich. As the result of his published article on the importance of quarantining soldiers returning from war (together with incessant letter writing to officials offering scientific answers for the health and immunological problems of the day), he was given an appointment in the army's Health Bureau. There, Japan's first modern immunologist directed a quarantine system for soldiers returning from the war with China in May and June 1895 (Tsurumi Y. 1937, vol. 1, 694–96; Mikuriya 2004, 104). The success of Gotō's program led to his appointment at the Home Ministry, where one of his major proposals urged the Foreign Ministry not to outlaw opium in Taiwan—despite a majority in favor of doing just that—but to regulate its use and profit from the monopoly Japanese would enjoy as the only wholesale dealers. Furthermore, they could extract money by requiring Chinese retailers and opium den proprietors to pay taxes and fees to the Japanese. Prime Minister Itō Hirobumi was convinced, and in February 1896 he ordered the Taiwan governor general to implement Gotō's policy (Gotō S. 1911, 58–59; Liu 1983, 74–75).

In 1897 Gotō set up the Bureau of Opium in Taiwan to monopolize importation, production, and sales of the drug. His plan was to fix the price so high that, together with the custom duty on British opium, it would generate 2.4 million yen annually—the same amount as the total tax revenue obtained by Japanese colonizers for 1897 (Matsushita 1926, 38). In 1898 and 1899 government opium revenues constituted a whopping 46 percent and 42 percent of all revenues of the Taiwan colonial government (Liu 1983, 185). During the first few years, when colonial administrators were under immense pressure to release Japanese domestic taxpayers from the burden of colonization, opium was the commodity that answered this demand. Some Japanese elites, frustrated by the unexpectedly high costs of colonization in the first years, had even called for selling Taiwan to France. I don't think it's stretching the point to suggest that there might not have been any Japanese colonization without this commitment to drug dealing. Although it fell gradually as a percentage of total revenue, the opium revenues increased every year until 1918, when they peaked at over eight million yen. During the First World War opium still made up 16 percent of total revenue. After 1905 some of the huge profits came from the export of opium to Manchuria, where Japanese wholesalers began to compete legally (after two decades of black market dealing) with Chinese for the profitable opium market there. Coolie laborers would be among their loyal customers. Gotō confessed to the sensitivity surrounding Japan's drug dealing in 1914, when, referring to the opium profits, he conceded, "[The] measures used to attain rapid financial independence were expedients that could have caused us acute embarrassment if discovered by foreigners" (1921, 50).

After three chaotic years of colonization in Taiwan Prime Minister Itō appointed Kodama Gentarō governor general in January 1898. Three months later, Gotō Shinpei was named to the powerful position of chief of civil affairs; the two would henceforth rule together in what is known as the Kodama-Gotō regime, which turned colonial capitalist rule upside down in Japan's first colony. Together they viciously undercut the Chinese merchants in the urban areas and market towns, reoriented family farm production vertically to guarantee Japanese industrial profit and food exports to Japan, and occasionally resorted to illegal land grabs and other "accumulation by dispossession" prerogatives of the colonial state. By 1905 Taiwan was economically self-sustaining and, until the end of the Second World War, handed over revenues directly to Japan's Finance Ministry (Tsurumi E. P. 1967). The profits generated from the railroad and opium monopolies played a central role.

With assistance from Tsurumi Yūsuke (1937), Patricia Tsurumi (1967), a recent monograph on Gotō by Daba Hiroshi (2007), and some of Gotō's early writings, I've identified four axioms of Gotō's colonial rule in Taiwan. The first is his often invoked but rarely explained "life principle" (*seibutsu no gensoku*). This crucial notion is deployed initially in his first book, *The Principles of National Hygiene* (*Kokka eisei genri*) of 1889. This text introduces the basic issue concerning the physiology of human adaptation: human infants can't exist alone and therefore need social structures to support them. Because humans are eternally "unsatisfied animals" (41), to achieve "physiological integrity" they require a "sovereign" to intervene and instruct them to adapt properly to their surroundings. Through this process of sovereign imposition, the state's role is to insert modern subjects into an "organic body" (Gotō S. 1978, 91).

Gotō often invoked his notion of life principle in preparing for a new task. He used it when he was appointed chief civilian administrator in Taiwan (Tsurumi Y. 1937, vol. 2, 38), when he became the president of the SMR in 1906, and again in a famous speech in 1916 outlining his imperialistic "theory of Japanese expansion" (*Nihon bōchōron*). He was appointed to Taiwan nearly a decade after *The Principles of National Hygiene* was written, and by that time his previous prescription for the top-down imposition of science onto docile subjects was complicated by both his critique of the "tyranny" of European colonialism and his official respect for traditional Chinese customs. What he called the "science of life," found most readily in "systems of industrial production, hygiene, education, transportation, and policing," would have to meet halfway with the accumulated history of Taiwanese culture and Chinese customs—their own life principle. When he was asked by his new boss Kodama exactly what he meant, he responded, "It's respecting [*omonzuru*] Taiwanese custom, if you want me to put it in a nutshell. Besides, it's impossible to suddenly turn a mediocre flounder [*hirame*] into an excellent sea bream [*tai*]. Life principle follows from the imperative to respect customs" (quoted in Tsurumi Y. 1937, vol. 2, 38–39).

Gotō reasoned that the problems that hampered Japanese rule during the first three years of the Taiwan colony were a direct result of military solutions being applied to what were demonstrably administrative problems. The previous military governors general tried to force the flounder-like Taiwanese into becoming superior Japanese sea bream— the same kind of cultural tyranny characteristic of European colonizers. However, Gotō's life principle impelled him to look for other fish to fry.

His second axiom, then, is knowledge about and respect for the local, the most important aspect of which was Chinese customary law. Many elite males of Gotō's generation (1857–1929) were taught the Chinese classics, inculcating a bias toward Chinese cultural forms. This willingness to incorporate aspects of the culture of the colonized was derived from his critique of European colonizers' disposition to "impose their own culture" onto local conditions. "Cultural tyranny," Gotō argued in 1914 in a famous speech provincializing Europe, was the predictable result of such nonscientific colonialism based on mere "lies about civilization [*kyogi no bunmei*]." For Japan to be recognized as the preeminent Asian leader, it had to continue with the "humanistic, enlightened colonial policy" that Gotō established in Taiwan (1944, 64–70, 62). It's important to point out that this injection of local customs into the operating system of the colonizers is constitutive of what I'm calling *immunological modernity*. Arguably the most important institutionalization of this modernity in the form of immunities of local, Taiwanese customs was the Research Center for Taiwanese Customs and Tradition, which opened in 1901. The center published reports on Taiwanese ethics, religion, and custom (Mikuriya 2004, 140–45). After the first decade of colonial rule the Research Center morphed into the central institution of colonial biopolitics by adding research on demographics and health.

Before identifying the third axiom, I want to introduce Gotō's mature understanding of life principle. In a lecture he gave in 1916 outlining his "theory of Japanese expansion," life shows up not as the physiological vulnerability we saw in his text of 1889, but as biopolitically liberated and defiantly desiring. In his earlier take on life he assumed a dialectic between the individual and human group structure, what he called simply "the state." Beginning around 1910 his thoughts about desire, sociality, and imperialism found their crystallization in the slogan *seimeiyoku*, or "desiring life." Here, life was not the tentative subject threatened by the various health predicaments of the 1880s (cholera, malnutrition, etc.) but was excessive, always desiring more than what it already had. In 1916 Gotō explained this ec-static quality as "the superhuman power [*shinpiryoku*] to constantly push out and create the new, assimilating and conquering one's surroundings without stopping. Far beyond mere survival or static existence, desiring life [*seimeiyoku*] is the unbounded power of expansion that continues to labor without any rest" (2004, 558).

In 1889 the constant absence of human satisfaction was seen as a lack or deficiency that had to be supplemented. Conversely, in 1916 individual subjects are always desirous of more than what they already have, and society's role is to mediate the tensions that inevitably arise between them. Moreover, as Gotō assumes an isomorphy of individual, society, and empire, societies also possess this quality of desiring life that necessarily puts any society into conflict with its neighbors. While the "imperial state" mediates the tensions displaced from individuals onto society, Gotō doesn't specify any mediating agency for the inevitable conflict between empires. Nevertheless, he suggests that this conflict will culminate in a struggle between the humanistic imperialism of Japan and the tyrannical rule of what he often called "white imperialism."

The third axiom is the assumed beneficence of capitalist markets. The economic modernization of Taiwan was largely directed by Gotō, who managed to make the colony profitable in seven years. He accomplished this initially by "rationalizing" the land tax system, which followed from his insistence that owners have legally recognized contracts for private property. His second step was to instruct Japanese and Taiwanese police to guarantee the regular functioning of local markets during times of instability. The third measure was his regulation of customs and duties, following from his consolidation of a port shipping system and railway overhaul. The last move in grounding capitalism indelibly on the island was to increase revenue flows from the opium and railroad monopolies (Daba 2007). The profits from the colonial monopolies ballooned, growing from around 500,000 yen in 1896 to over ten million in 1905, to seventeen million in 1907, right after Gotō left for Japan's new colony, the Guandong Lease in Manchuria (Ka 1995).

These policies, lumped together by colonial elites as the "business management of Taiwan" (*Taiwan keiei*), were soon adopted in Northeast China after the Qing government and international pressure forced a reluctant Japanese military to demobilize there after the victory against Russia in 1905. Although Gotō had an excellent working situation with General Kodama, his relationship with the rest of the army was fraught throughout his tenure as chief civilian administrator in Taiwan. It would be wrong, though, to see the demobilization as a desire on Gotō's part to marginalize Japan's military. Rather, as one of Japan's most thoughtful imperialists, Gotō argued in 1906 for a widening of the concept of military power from how it was then understood in Japan. He rendered this new enlarged concept, one that quickly became the main slogan in Japan's Northeast China policy, as *bunsōteki bubi*, literally, "military arms" (*bubi*) in "culturo-civilian disguises" (*bunsōteki*). Almost a decade later he defined this as a colonial policy that sought to use "civil affairs" (*bunji*) to prevent other countries from invading Japan's territory, thereby supporting the military in "any potential crisis" (1944, 78).

Bunsōteki bubi is often rendered into English as "civil management." However, given Gotō's emphasis on economic transformation through capitalist rationalization in Taiwan, together with the fact that he had just agreed to be the first president of the colonial capitalist enterprise the SMR, the most important civilian aspect of this colonial policy was the business of merchant and industrial capitalism. Gotō had to devise tactics to advance two different and conflicting strategies in Japan's newest colony; one was geared toward keeping what Japan won on the battlefield in 1904–5 (military control), and the other toward the smooth expropriation of surplus by Japanese in Manchuria (business). He conceived the "military arms with culturo-civilian disguise" phrase as a way to wage what he and others called a "peaceful war" (*heiwa no sensō*) through capitalist business. The French military strategist Clausewitz's famous aphorism, "War is the continuation of politics by other means"—which Foucault reversed to describe biopolitics—might be troped here in considering Gotō Shinpei's designs for colonial capitalist rule in Manchuria. Therefore, my updated translation for *bunsōteki bubi* is *business as the continuation of war by other means.* Imperial elites such as Itō Hirobumi and Kodama early on saw the corporate capitalist offices of the SMR as a dressing room full of disguises for military hegemony. Right before the signing of the Treaty of Portsmouth in September 1905 Kodama argued that Japan's most "urgent post-war strategic policy in Manchuria" was to establish "multiple covert projects under the pretext of running a railroad company": "The SMR must pretend that it has nothing to do with politics or military affairs" (quoted in Tsurumi Y. 1937, vol. 2, 651).

Which brings us to Gotō's fourth axiom, his notion of competition:

tōsō. In the first decades of the twentieth century *tōsō* as competition or struggle was often deployed with "coexistence" (*kyōzon*). When read together these signifiers form one of the Japanese translations of social Darwinism's "survival of the fittest," and Gotō's principal readers have taken this phrase as evidence of his social Darwinism. However, it seems clear that the previous axioms complicate, if not disprove this altogether. Like other social scientists in Japan (and elsewhere) in the early twentieth century, Gotō was much more of a Lamarckian. Lamarck's insistence on acquired or learned characteristics as inheritable (to say nothing of life principle) is what Gotō would be referencing in his insistence on the benefits of colonial tutoring. Gradually turning tasteless Taiwanese flounders into scrumptious Japanese sea bream is a Lamarckian conceit par excellence.

Although I refuse to link Gotō with social Darwinism, his rendering of competition makes perfect sense when it is networked to biopolitical capitalism. Coexistence (*kyōzon*) always implies competitive struggle (*tōsō*) when Japanese businessmen are competing with Chinese merchants in Taiwan, when Japanese merchants are competing with Chinese for control of the soybean trade in Northeast China, and when Japanese capitalists struggle with colonized Chinese and Korean labor to keep wages down. In his only full-length study of biopolitics, Foucault argues that competition is always central to capitalist regimes. Over and against the ideological mystification that insists that the capitalist marketplace tends toward a just "equal exchange of goods," Foucault reminds us that neoclassical economic theory emphasizes "competition and inequality" (2008, 119–20). Competition and inequality were therefore close to natural laws that Gotō assumed when applying life principles to capitalist markets in Japan's colonies.

Business as a Continuation of War by Other Means

Gotō had in effect laid down a challenge to Japan's imperialists: Figure out a way to harness the transformative power of "desiring life" to scientific colonialism and capitalism in Japan's new colony and produce subjectivities grounded on his life principle policy. When he agreed to be the first president of the SMR in July 1906 he wrote a memorandum to all the top Japanese political leaders explaining his acceptance. He claimed that he and Kodama foresaw a second major war with Russia, and to prepare for this and to support capitalist expansion, they recommended flooding the region with Japanese immigrants. Gotō was openly critical of Japanese elites who refused to construe colonization as the difficult process it had to be to achieve success: "Today, some people attribute our suzerain position in Korea to our having been victorious in war. In reality, this outcome wasn't achieved in so straightforward a fashion. The truth of the matter is: our acquisition of Korea owes everything to the recent history of the immigration of our people to the region" (Minami Manshū Tetsudō Kabushiki Gaisha 1919, 110–11).

Gotō argued forcefully during his two-year tenure as SMR president that a more welcoming "Open Door" trade environment would lure Japanese farmers and merchants into Japan's new colonial territory. An attractive business climate, fertile farmland, and colonial biopolitics (hospitals, schools) would persuade poor and adventurous Japanese to come and settle. But Gotō's dream of populating Manchuria with Japanese settlers wouldn't be realized until the 1930s, with the establishment of Manchukuo. It fell afoul of the obsession with "quick money and easy success" (*ikkaku senkin*) that characterized the attitudes of most Japanese when they looked to and journeyed to Manchuria.

Laissez-Faired

Profiteering required low wage floors in Northeast China, and Japanese capitalists eyed covetously the reserve armies of North Chinese migrants rushing into the region to escape environmental and political crises. The SMR was one of the early culprits here. Although Gotō often imagined his company to be the engine pulling Japanese settlers into Manchuria, from the beginning the SMR was ordered by the emperor, via its imperial charter, to operate in the black. Although most elites assumed the SMR would offer preferential treatment to Japanese employees, after eighteen months, and while Gotō was still president, in 1908 it undertook a major cost-cutting initiative. That year the SMR fired two thousand Japanese and replaced them with part-time Chinese workers (Hirano 1983, 476). Excepting managerial staff, from that point on, and in flagrant violation of the SMR's ideal staffing scenario of an equal split between Chinese and Japanese (Matsusaka 2001, 143), the ratio of Chinese to Japanese workers grew exponentially. By early 1913, the Guandong governor general stated that the policy of encouraging Japanese labor flows was a "complete failure" owing to the surplus of Chinese coolies "willing to accept ridiculously cheap wages" (*MNNS*, 14 February 1913). By 1915, Chinese outnumbered Japanese in all unskilled labor positions in the SMR.

Charting a wage pattern that would hold until the mid-1920s, the main colonial newspaper in Northeast China, the *Manchuria Daily Newspaper* (*Manshū Nichi Nichi Shinbun*) reported that the average daily wage for skilled dockworkers employed by the SMR's Dalian wharves in March 1909 was 91 cents for Japanese and 44 cents for Chinese. For unskilled coolies it was 29 cents (*MNNS*, 21 April 1909). However, in what must have had a severe dampening effect on emigration, when Japanese ventured into the interior of Manchuria they often found themselves competing with Chinese at a similar skill level for the same wage. A *Manchuria Daily Newspaper* report of 1 July 1909 told of a sharp drop in daily wages for Japanese in the interior, owing to an "imbalance of supply and demand." Even more ominous for those hoping for a Japanese influx, daily wages for unskilled labor in Dalian unwittingly supported Gotō's Pan-Asian rhetoric by not discriminating between Chinese and Japanese. In April and May 1915 average wages for Japanese *jinrikisha* cab drivers were the same as for Chinese drivers, 35 cents a day (*MNNS*, 20 June 1915). Unfortunately for unskilled Japanese labor thinking of relocating to Manchuria, Kodama's and Gotō's ideal baseline calling for increasing Japanese immigration vectored in one direction, while the bottom line for the SMR and private capital veered off in an opposing direction.

As I mentioned earlier, Foucault argued that biopolitical regimes assume an excess of life: "Biopower is in excess of sovereign right. This excess of biopower [makes it] possible for man not only to manage life, but to make it proliferate" (2003, 254). The political problem to be solved in Manchuria was how to establish the groundwork for rapid capital accumulation. The debate between Japanese colonization understood as a physical occupation by Japanese settlers (Gotō's vision) and the business management of the region geared toward the quick expropriation of surplus (Japanese merchant and industrial capitalists' vision) really lasted only two years. "Chinese wages" were too low to resist, and heretofore undreamed-of profit margins beckoned hungry capitalists. After Gotō returned to Japan to become more involved in domestic politics, in 1915 the president of the SMR, Nakamura Yūjirō, was openly discouraging Japanese farmers from coming to Manchuria. But he offered this advice to Japanese capitalists interested in the same real estate: "[The capitalist] will be all the more blessed economically if he can make skill-ful use of Chinese workers, whose strong points lie in their willingness to accept the lowest standards of living and to tolerate the extremes of the climate" (quoted in Matsusaka 2001, 191).

This decision not to support Japanese immigration to Manchuria meant that two biopolitical subjectivities were consolidated right at the beginning of Japan's colonization: Chinese laborers and Japanese capitalists. A quintessentially Marxist divide between Chinese sellers of commodified labor on the one hand, and Japanese purchasers of these commodities on the other defined the parameters for the formal sub-sumption. Hirano Kenichirō argues that in the second year of the Guan-dong Lease, Japanese capitalist enterprises large and small realized it was best for them to "simply exploit unskilled Chinese laborers" (1983, 155). The most exploitable was coolie labor from Shandong.

In a study of the migration patterns of these workers conducted in 1927, C. Walter Young (1929) discovered that the SMR had maintained between ten and twenty job recruitment centers in Shandong and Hebei provinces. Until the mid-1920s the SMR was directly recruiting contin-gent workers for their two coal mines, in addition to their wharf facili-ties. The SMR wasn't the only company luring coolies to Manchuria; Mitsui and Yalu Lumber preceded the SMR to Shandong, with Yalu Lum-ber generating spectacular profits for their efforts. In an interview with a reporter from the *Manchuria Daily Newspaper*, Yalu's director general, Hashiguchi Minato, sang the praises of cheap Chinese labor. He related that while there were 45 corporate staff members, 23 Japanese and 22 Chinese, the remaining 30,000 workers in his company were North Chi-nese migrants, a number he hoped to increase to 50,000 in the next few years (*MNNS*, 10 January 1909).

In the introduction I briefly invoked what Marx called the formal subsumption of labor to capital. Something less than the complete en-closure of labor to a capital logic infecting all aspects of life, formal sub-sumption exhibits "an economic relationship" whereby labor is never-theless forced to become "far more continuous and intensive" than it had been previously (1977, 1026). The labor force producing value for the Japanese company Yalu Lumber consisted of seasonal migrant workers leaving their villages in Shandong sometime in March and returning in October or November. The harsh winters in northern Manchuria made logging nearly impossible for four months, so a great number of the Chinese workers returned regularly to the milder Shandong to pass the winter. In other words, a majority of these workers split their lives between a temporality determined by commodity capital and one determined by older, agricultural rhythms.[1] Occasionally market logics pervaded even this temporality in the form of cash-cropping and merchant loans, but a portion of it remained autonomous (Kong 1986, 43–57).

Most of the hiring practices of coolies employed seasonally and on yearly contracts were also embedded in formal subsumption. Despite the presence of Japanese companies' recruitment stations in Shandong, the great majority of Chinese workers in Manchuria were recruited through the established system of *laoxiang batou* (hometown boss). Although it became dominant in Manchuria after the relaxation of immigration restrictions for Han Chinese in 1878, this system was first consolidated in southern China, where it predated the establishment of the treaty port system by European powers in the 1840s. The "predicament of coolie labor" had already undergone a major shift before Chinese migrant labor emerged as the driving force of capital accumulation in Japan's colony in Northeast China after 1905.

The period of the global coolie trade ran from the third decade of the nineteenth century to 1874, when the Qing government outlawed the practice. This period is usually characterized by the system of indentured labor, whereby Chinese and South Asians were contracted to a Euro-American owner for anywhere from one to seven years. Again, this indentured system combining free and forced labor of Chinese for white Euro-American capital was preceded by a more informal system of coolie trade centered around Hong Kong, Xiamen (Amoy), and Guangzhou, conducted exclusively by Chinese merchants. This trade mainly sent indigent Chinese men from the coastal cities to sites of earlier Chinese overseas settlement: Malaysia, the Dutch East Indies, and the Philippines. This Chinese trading of poor workers would set the precedent for the system used by Chinese and Japanese companies in Manchuria after 1878.

What is often called the *laoxiang guanxi* (local connections) system of bringing workers to Manchuria was centered on either the *batou* or *gongtou* (work head) leader. These men recruited poor men who were fellow *laoxiang*, either from the same village or from neighboring villages. The number of men in any one group ranged from five to one hundred or more, although twelve to fifteen was the ideal number from the perspective of both welfare and control. The most important aspect of the *batou*-recruit relationship was shared locale; recruiters were trusted because of the accountability *batou* were expected to assume because of their shared community. The *batou* invariably accompanied his recruits on the journey to Manchuria and normally acted as their foreman once they arrived (Lu 1987; Minami Manshū Tetsudō Kabushiki Gaisha 1934). Recent interviews with surviving recruits from the 1930s and 1940s underline the fact that the relationship between boss and recruits normally entailed something beyond a mere commodity transaction (Gottschang and Lary 2000). Of course this "beyond" differed in each case, but it is clear that many of the Chinese wouldn't have gone to Manchuria at all if it hadn't been for the relative security they felt within the *batou*-recruit system (Manzhou yiminshi yanjiu hui 1991).

Once in Manchuria the *batou* would delegate the daily work routines to either the *gongtou* or the *batou*'s own underling, the *xiao batou*. The *batou* stayed busy managing the more skilled workers in his group, such as the cook (*zuofande ren*) and accountant (*xiansheng*). Normally the *batou* paid the unskilled coolies daily with funds received from the company. According to the most detailed study of this system, published in Japanese in 1944, the *batou* passed the wage down first to the accountant and then to his assistant, the *xiao batou*. The researcher Nakamura Takatoshi (1944) claimed that with each of the three handlings—company to *batou*, *batou* to accountant, accountant to *xiao batou*—so much of the wage was skimmed off the top that the coolie was often forced to borrow money from the *batou* just to survive.[2]

Accounts from the Second World War like Nakamura's overlook the very different relations of production that determined the distinct ways labor was subsumed under capital. Earlier Japanese depictions of the *batou* system were less stigmatizing than the wartime versions, like Nakamura's, which were designed to justify complete control of Chinese labor by Japanese imperialists, who, when they weren't imposing a brutal regime of forced labor, assumed a totalized, real subsumption of labor under capital. For example, the important colonial monthly *Korea and Manchuria* (*Chōsen oyobi Manshū*) carried a feature on coolies in Dalian in January 1913 called "Coolies and Coolie Camps." It describes a much less oppressive situation between a *batou* and his recruits. Reporting on two coolie groups, the author claimed that it was standard for coolies to receive 85 percent of their wages directly from the *batou*, who took 10 to 15 percent from each coolie. Coolie wages were 40 cents a day, and each worker got 4 or 5 cents removed by the *batou*; 22 cents each day went to the accountant to pay for room and board. The remaining 13 cents were "usually saved." However, these coolies were no slouches when it came to partying: "Because of their passionate interest, coolies also engage in hobbies like bird-feeding and gambling; there are ten different gambling events. Although very little money is waged at gambling, the lucky winners always celebrate either by getting all dressed up and heading downtown to flirt with [*jareru*] women, or visiting one of the opium dens in the city. For 5 or 6 cents they can spend hours smoking in the dens, stoned all day" (117).

When the SMR first started recruiting unskilled Chinese labor in the early twentieth century Japanese managers disliked the *batou* and *laoxiang guanxi* system. After attempting to install "scientific" labor management schemes at large facilities, such as the Fushun coal mine—rewarding particularly obedient and hardworking coolies with promotion to *xiao batou* positions, offering skills training—the SMR quickly resigned itself to using the Chinese practice (Andō 1965, 116–17; Eda et al. 2002, 497–98). It proved to be more profitable in the long run. Except for the SMR, Mitsui, and Yalu Lumber, who all recruited skilled workers directly from Shandong, the major Japanese employers took advantage of the older Chinese practice and outsourced recruitment of skilled and unskilled labor starting in 1906. The main history of the huge Japanese construction industry in Manchuria, *A Survey of Construction in Manchuria* (*Manshū Kenchiku Gaisetsu*), relates that the construction industry realized that there were "zero construction workers" available for hire when the large coal mine and railway projects started up in 1906 (Kenchiku Gakkai 1940, 437). They simply had no alternative but to plead their case to the Chinese *batou*. Consequently, a significant amount of leeway was granted to them, and *batou* quickly adapted to the new demand environment. The *batou*-recruit system provided workers to companies for short-term contracts, offering, in David Tucker's understanding, "the advantages of a temporary employment agency to an industry that undertook many seasonal and temporary projects" (quoted in Kratoska 2005, 30). In addition to the transfer of risks (sickness and insubordination) and costs (food and lodging) to the *batou*, it was clear to Japanese that the migrants overwhelmingly preferred contact and contracts with their own *laoxiang* acquaintances. *A Survey of Construction in Manchuria* concluded that taking full advantage of the *batou* system was a no-brainer: "Good *batou* are like money in the bank" (Kratoska 2005, 31).

For the approximately 35 percent of migrants who chose to venture to Manchuria outside of the *batou* or the Japanese recruitment systems, either with families or alone, life was much more difficult. Many of them ended up associating with *batou* anyway. The implicitly ethical codes embedded in the *laoxiang guanxi* system impelled many *batou* to advance money to workers, to cover emergency expenses, and even to remit savings back to their families in North China. Most Chinese migrants were reluctant to use banks for these services, especially Japanese banks. Because of the importance of the *batou* in this colonial labor system, some decent *batou*, such as the Cui brothers, attained a saint-like stature in North China (Eda et al. 2002, 218). Less scrupulous *batou* rip-off artists were executed by communist cadres after they established power in 1949. Unlike *batou* who accompanied their recruits to Manchuria, full-time recruiters who worked directly with Japanese companies or the military were universally despised as *zhuzai*, or "flesh merchants" (Gottschang and Lary 2000, 107).

Dalian, Biotopia

Right after the Russo-Japanese War the Japanese military in Northeast China commissioned a major study of the economic prospects for the region. Until then, elites thought that Manchuria held out very little in the way of opportunities for surplus extraction for Japanese capital. Kodama Gentarō requested that an assistant of Gotō's in Taiwan named Ishizuka Eizō (1866–1942) lead the study. Ishizuka was one of Gotō's staff of civilian administrators credited with making an "underdeveloped" Taiwan both economically self-sufficient and profitable for Japanese business within the first decade of colonization. The army gathered together a team of seventy-five people for Ishizuka, including businessmen, translators, and experts from Japan's Ministry of Agriculture and Commerce (Matsusaka 2001, 50). After conducting his research mainly in October and November 1905, Ishizuka began releasing classified memoranda from the findings in December 1905; the full results were made public in eight volumes in 1906, dealing with agriculture, business, industry, and natural resources (Kantō totokufu, 1906). Ishizuka's "Survey of Manchuria's Development" surprised political and business elites by suggesting a strong potential for Japanese capitalism in the region, based on the untapped agricultural and industrial potential supported by cheap resources and basically free Chinese labor.

Business as a continuation of war by other means meant completing the major port facilities of Dalian first. When the Russians halted construction of the port in 1903 owing to the impending military conflict, only about one-third of the infrastructure was in place. The SMR quickly went about finishing Pier 1 and constructing Piers 2 and 3 from scratch. All told, the reconstruction of Dalian Harbor ordered by Gotō included three huge breakwaters, four piers, and large-scale embankments. Dalian became, in the matter of a few years, the most commercially vibrant port in Northeast Asia. The "Dalian strategy" of Japanese imperialism entailed rerouting the soybean trade through SMR's modern customhouses in Dalian on its railroads, undercutting the Chinese merchant hegemony centered on the older port of Yingkou.[3]

In a short five years the SMR moved quickly to double-track and update its main 239-mile line from Dalian at the bottom of the Liaodong Peninsula straight into the heart of soybean distribution in central Manchuria. It also widened Japan's light military rail to the standard commercial gauge of four feet, nine inches for the 170-mile expanse running from the Korean border at Andong to Manchuria's capital city of Fengtian. This last job was finished in October 1911 and cost the equivalent of U.S.$12 million. Adachi Kinnosuke quotes SMR sources estimating that if an operation of similar scale had been undertaken in the United States it would have cost ten times what it did in Manchuria (1925, 121). Given labor costs in 1910, it would have been three times as expensive inside Japan. Thanks to coolie laborers who did all the physical work necessary, by 1911 all the centerpieces of Japan's imperialism in Manchuria were complete: the railways, modern port and customs facilities, and the city of Dalian made over as the most modern Asian metropolis, replete with boulevards 178 feet in width, twice as wide as those in Paris (Tsurumi Y., vol. 1, 1937, 878–79). There were also two modern coal mines and smaller urban environments with hospitals and schools all along the Railway Zone of the Guandong Lease. Repeating the economic growth pattern from Taiwan, the volume of trade from Dalian doubled from 1905 to 1906, doubled again in 1908, and then managed to double one last time in 1909. Based in the city, the *Manchuria Daily Newspaper* proudly tracked Dalian's meteoric rise, from the seventeenth busiest port in China in 1908 to the seventh in 1909 (*MNNS*, 24 November 1909). Earlier that same year, in a spasm of pride, the newspaper claimed that Dalian was gradually "replacing Shanghai and Hong Kong as the most important port on China's coast" (*MNNS*, 31 July 1909).[4] The Japanese newspaper of record was honest enough to concede that the rise of Dalian would have been "impossible without cheap Chinese workers" (*MNNS*, 16 December 1908).

When Gotō Shinpei moved to Dalian in December 1906 to begin his tenure as the first president of the SMR, he installed the operating system for Asian colonization that he had debugged in Taiwan. The first element of this would be the insistence that colonization pay for itself (Gotō S. 1944, 114), and his first appointments for the corporate leadership of the SMR reflected this. Gotō's handpicked assistant was the former director of financial affairs for the Taiwan governor general's office, Nakamura Kimitake. Two of the first directors hired were businessmen, Inukai Shintarō and Tanaka Seijirō, both from the Mitsui Company with experience in Manchuria (Tsurumi Y., vol. 1, 1937, 699). However, Gotō also knew how to take advantage of scholarly knowledge to advance the project of empire. As he had done in Taiwan, he established biopolitical institutions in the form of a research center for Manchurian culture and demography and appointed Professor Okamatsu Santarō of Kyoto University as director (Mikuriya 2004, 146–47). Okamatsu was ordered by Gotō to hire only Japanese proficient in Chinese, because this center in the SMR's large Research Division (Chōsabu) would be conducting extensive fieldwork in southern and northern Manchuria (Kobayashi 2005b).

Coolie Customizing

One of the people hired by Okamatsu to lead a study was also a member of a group that formed in the wake of Ishizuka's "Survey of Manchurian Development" project. Aioi Yutarō was a founding member of the Manchuria-Mongolia Industry Research Group, where he began studying the productive capacity of coolie labor in 1910. In 1908 Okamatsu put Aioi together with some SMR translators and fieldworkers to conduct the first comprehensive study of Chinese coolies in Manchuria. Although sections of the study were released earlier to the twin sponsors of the project, the work wasn't published in full until May 1920. As Aioi explained in the preface, the publication of the research was interrupted by the "events" of the First World War.

Aioi's book, *The Manchurian Industrialist's World Looks to the Chinese Coolie* (*Manshū Sangyōkai yori mitaru shina no ku-ri-*) provides all the information that Japanese investors need to take full advantage of what Aioi refers to repeatedly as the still untapped "power source" (*gendōryoku*) for Japanese capitalism in China: cheap coolie labor. After stating on the first page "Chinese workers = coolies," he gets his readers' attention by stating that, according to information from the Dalian wharves, there were 1,148,916 coolies involved in nonfarm work in southern Manchuria in 1912, working on the wharf, as taxi drivers, and loading and unloading freight, coal mining, and packaging. The number of nonfarmer coolie laborers disembarking in Dalian Harbor doubled to 2,219,890 in just five years (MSSK, iii). Because of this unprecedented profit environment, Japanese capitalists needed a special approach. Referring indirectly to the widespread abuses of Chinese workers by Japanese capitalists that were only alluded to in the Japanese press, Aioi advises that because of the "huge amount of profit" that each coolie body represents, and given "the massive number of coolies, there's no point in cheating any individual coolie." Even though the potential for profit to be made from them grows every year, there will be "an eventual price to pay . . . if Japanese capitalists aren't honest with the coolies" (4).

But rest assured, investors aren't in for a sermon here. Aioi tells capitalists that he has been researching the "coolie issue" (*ku-ri- mondai*) since 1908 with an SMR group, and then with his own Manchurian Industrialists World since 1911. Thus he bases his findings on over a decade of research and fieldwork to recommend a double focus in approaching the coolie problem. Using his ace card of capitalism = civilizing mission straight off, Aioi doesn't see any contradiction in conflating the profit motive with "the best methods to save coolies" (MSSK, 4). But more than that, in a deft download of Gotō's biopolitical life principles, Aioi proffers that the challenge facing Japanese colonial capitalists in relation to the coolies will be to simultaneously "attend respectfully to their beliefs" and everyday customs while guaranteeing that they are the "beneficiaries of hygiene, education, and medical care" (5–6). Aioi concludes his preface with this advice: "We have to both provide them with the best of what we have, and respect their ethnoracial identity [*minzoku-sei*]. By respecting them we can expropriate the most out of them" (6).

The body of Aioi's book is divided into two long sections. The first takes up the theme of the "conditions of coolie life," and the second offers recommendations for coolie treatment. The section on conditions is prefaced by a short bit on the "real activities of coolies." Aioi fills in some gaps in the knowledge about coolies by giving Japanese readers the following colonial definition: "The English definition of a coolie is a Chinese local who has been employed by a foreigner, normally as a *shafu* cabbie or tenant farmer. Coolies go to places like Mongolia, Man-churia, Indo-China and South America and some of them get rich in those places. But not all coolies are poor workers for foreigners. They also include Qing youth who long for exciting adventures" (MSSK, 3). Aioi concedes that despite the presence of thrill-seekers in their num-bers, for the most part coolie laborers are unwittingly in the "driver's seat of international commerce," where, despite the fact that they per-form all the physical labor for capitalist enterprises in many parts of the world, "[they] are robbed of one half of their earned money to balance the account ledgers of international trade" (4). The main reason coolies get ripped off is that they are forced to deal with "foreigners" and travel long distances by sea to unfamiliar places. Aioi's main argument in this book is that because of the almost unlimited productivity latent in coolie bodies, there's no need for Japanese capitalists to continue cheat-ing and exploiting them after the fashion of white Europeans; the legal expropriation of surplus by capitalists purchasing coolie labor will be enough to make all Japanese rich. To prod Japanese into their "natu-rally" respectful deportment toward coolies, he identifies their modus vivendi and cultural attitudes.

As far as everyday necessities, coolies hardly have any at all: "Any-thing will do as far as clothing is concerned," and they prefer "simple food" (MSSK, 21, 23). The most important single fact about coolie be-havior is that, unlike Japanese, who "work to make a better life," coolie lives consist of almost nothing "but hard work" (25). They rarely go to bars or brothels, and except for the occasional visit to the local opium den their lives "revolve completely around work." Even their frequently noted weakness for "betting small amounts of money on card games and dice" only happens in their rooms late at night after a hard workday (25).

Anticipating the reluctance to hire coolies because of unbridgeable cultural differences, Aioi reassures Japanese employers that as a discreet population Chinese coolies barely have any culture at all. Lacking cultural and even material needs, coolies are quite content slaving the days away in a near infrahuman state, interrupted only by their nightly card games and weekly visits to the nearest opium den. These last are merely what Marx called the "means of subsistence" that coolies use to prepare themselves for the next twelve- or fourteen-hour day of grueling physical labor. (No doubt opium also worked to ease the pain of what Anne Anlin Cheng [2001] calls the "racial melancholia" of the subaltern.) Therefore, the key strong point of coolies is their sheer willingness to endure almost any kind of physical hardship without complaint. This is broken down into three positive points: they never get sick; their passive and obedient (*jūjun*) nature is just right to guarantee smooth capital-labor relations; and they are physically taller and stronger than Japanese and therefore have more stamina (MSSK, 31–32). At least at first glance, they would appear to be the ideal colonial labor force. However, there are identifiable weak points and, Aioi concedes, some minor drawbacks to utilizing coolie labor.

The first is that they are for the most part unskilled and "stupid" (*kibin de nai koto*). Generally speaking, owing to their low educational level coolies are able to perform "only very simple tasks" (MSSK, 33). Handling complex machines and following written directions are too complicated for them. The second significant weak point is connected to their lack of culture and religion. Because they have "no sense of responsibility" and can't distinguish right from wrong, their bosses and managers need to keep a "close watch over them." Although this surveillance is normally handled by the Chinese *batou* and *xiao batou*, Japanese capitalists should be aware of the possibility that coolies will steal things at work sites. The final weak point is the minor issue that, "when compared to Koreans, Chinese coolies don't like strict term conditions for loans" (33–34). But Aioi mollifies this weakness by contending that they rarely borrow money anyway: "Chinese are known throughout the world as passionate about saving money" (34).

Resorting to a ubiquitous colonial ideology that justified Japan's imperialism as based on a shared, and immunological, ethnoracial identity, Aioi next contrasts the use of immigrant labor in Manchuria to the conditions of immigrant labor in other places: "In Western Europe there's open hostility to immigrant labor; in Manchuria that's not at all the case. Without the problem of racism, people here understand that immigrant workers are only trying to make money. In fact, there are many regions in Manchuria where coolies are thanked warmly for coming to work" (MSSK, 45). Not only do white Europeans universally discriminate against immigrants, but in their own involvement in the global coolie trade British merchants ship coolies everywhere under horrible conditions. Here, Aioi is referencing the distinction established in Japan's imperial discourse around 1910 between "sea coolies" (coolies transported overseas to work) and "land coolies" (*riku no ku-ri-*). In a *Manchuria Daily Newspaper* feature titled "Sea Coolies vs. Land Coolies," Uchida Tomiyoshi clarified the distinction in a self-serving way:

> The Chinese junks that are carrying coolies at sea are terrible compared to the Japanese facilities here in Dalian. Here, everything is different; we have a modern, civilized port city. Through the various jobs that coolies do, like loading and unloading, economic growth has taken off. We should respectfully call them "coolie sama" as thanks for all they've done. . . . In Dalian you often see coolies taking the bus and paying their fare like anyone else. These land coolies [*riku no ku-ri-*] have much better lives than the sea coolies [*umi no ku-ri-*] and my sincere hope is that there be no further increase in the number of sea coolies. (*MNNS*, 1 January 1913)

The abuses of the Euro-American sea coolie trade were well documented by 1906, when Japanese capitalists began using exclusively coolie labor in Manchuria. Although Uchida's article isn't explicit about the abuses attributable to the "long-distance coolie trade," the signifier "sea coolies" would have clearly referenced this for Japanese readers. Aioi mentions the Euro-American abuses twice in his book, once stopping to recommend the shorter immigration into Manchuria as infinitely preferable.

The first transpacific shipment of Chinese coolies was sent to the French West Indies from Singapore in 1845, and within two years a complex system of intercontinental coolie trade was set up at Xiamen by two British firms. Each enjoyed close ties to British consular officials and

American shipping companies. Syme, Muir and Company went so far as to set up what the local Chinese called a "pigsty" (*chu-tsai kuan*) right in front of their firm; it was an exact replica of the barracoon used to cage African slaves. In this pigsty enslaved Chinese were stripped naked, examined for diseases, and, if approved, forced to put their name on a labor contract. After signing for their indenture, they were branded or painted with a letter signifying their destination: *c* for Cuba, *p* for Peru, *s* for the Sandwich Islands, and so forth (Irick 1982, 26–27). From 1847 to 1853 tens of thousands of coolies were exported to the Americas from Xiamen; from the mid-1850s until the suppression of the trade in 1874 many more were sent from Macau and Hong Kong.

The treatment of the coolies was so bad that the Qing government eventually sent an expedition to investigate abuses in 1874. The results of that investigation were published in Chinese and English under the title *Chinese Emigration: Report of the Cuba Commission, 1874*. From testimonies given to the Cuba Commission by coolies, it seems that after landing in Havana the exhausted coolies were led to barracoon cages by guards on horseback brandishing whips. The coolies were routinely treated like cattle, their meals and movements carefully watched (17). From the barracoons they were brought to quarantine stations, where their long hair queues were cut off. Next they were sent to the market to be sold. Once they were on display the humiliation continued, as they were classified by first, second, or third grades, according to their physical prowess and apparent strength. When the buyers made their selection, the coolies were forced to remove all their clothes for inspection in front of the consuming public. After being sold, they were dragged to farms, plantations, factories, and mines, "to face," in Yen Ching-Hwang's words, "their real masters" (1985, 64).

Aioi, Uchida, and other Japanese imperialists never failed to assume that because of their ethnoracial closeness to Chinese, the ravages inflicted on transpacific sea coolies would never be replicated against the land coolies in Manchuria. Those kinds of abuses were unimaginable in an enlightened land where colonizers like Uchida felt compelled to address the lowliest of Chinese workers as *ku-ri- sama*, "most honorable coolie." For Aioi, this kind of respect was appropriate given China's "long and distinguished history" and the fact that coolies were the sine qua non for Japanese capital accumulation in Manchuria. Indeed, he begins his section on policies toward coolies by stating, "All aspects of Manchurian business hinge on coolies" (MSSK, 76).

The second half of *The Manchurian Industrialists' World Looks to the Chinese Coolie* details Aioi's policy recommendations. He reminds Japanese that very little would have been accomplished to date (1918) in Manchuria without coolie labor. But all of that—the trains, the wharves, the coal mines, almost the entirety of the great city of Dalian—pales in comparison to the still untapped potential for growth. Extolling this potential, he unfolds a utopia of capital accumulation: "A more extensive utilization of coolies will mean expanded production, which will increase the import trade, which will also contribute to an increase in the number of special trains for immigrant coolies, which will help with regulating our railway market, which necessarily means the expansion of Manchurian trade and the increase of exports to Japan" (MSSK, 77). For this projective causality to materialize, however, there are several aspects of Manchuria's infrastructure that must be upgraded. The most important of these is improved accommodations for coolies: "Up until now, their wandering lifestyle [*furō ikikata*] of the coolies takes them anywhere, but Japanese industrialists haven't provided adequate infrastructure that might encourage them to settle down; the infrastructure for coolie accommodations in Manchuria right now is terrible" (78, 82). Public restrooms need to be made available closer to urban work sites, and Chinese-speaking social workers need to be made accessible (79–80).

Aioi concludes his recommendations by wondering why Japanese businessmen have largely ignored the purchasing power of coolies. "Coolies are consumers too," he reminds his readers, "and we can profit from this" (MSSK, 84). Recognizing this will lead to a win-win situation, where it will be "easier for capitalists to benefit from coolies," and Japanese will be successful in luring "even more than the several hundred thousand coolies flooding into Manchuria at the present annual rate" (85–86). In urging capitalists to embed coolies deeper into both Japanese colonial production and consumption, Aioi is in effect calling for a shift from the formal subsumption of labor under capital to real subsumption. Regrettably, Japanese capitalists have been content with the formal subsumption of labor to capital. However, Aioi invites capitalists to reflect deeper on coolies' innate "power source," power that could potentially drive the whole mode of capitalist production in Manchuria toward a new and more profitable complexity. Astute businessmen can "already witness the ways in which coolies have transformed capitalism" (86). Now it's up to Japanese capitalists themselves to respond positively to the challenge provided by coolie labor.

Aioi failed to mention some of the infrastructure then available to coolies. The Japanese labor management company Fuchang Gongsi started building a complex of coolie dormitories in Dalian called Heikanzō in 1911. By 1923 eighty-nine modern brick dormitories were available to house up to thirteen thousand coolies (Hirano 1983, 164–65). The facilities were impressive, especially the public bath and the heating and sewage systems. Moreover, shop owners rented stores at the compound to sell goods to the coolies. The facilities at Heikanzō would appear to answer Aioi's challenge to move toward the real subsumption of labor under capitalism. However, given the fact that there were at the very least two million coolies in the Guandong Lease by 1917—compared to roughly 100,000 Japanese—and proper facilities for only fifteen thousand or so, we can assume that many coolies lived "like primitive people or beggars in Japan, drifting around from job to job and sleeping outside in the fields": "Those living in the cities will squat anywhere that protects them from the rough elements" (*COM*, January 1913, 116).

So despite the rhetoric of Pan-Asianism impelling Japanese to nurture coolies in a civilized fashion, it seems that most of the unskilled Chinese immigrants to Manchuria lived a life of extreme hardship, some sense of which we get in Aioi's study and in the interviews conducted by Diana Lary. Furthermore, despite the fact that migrant laborers were able to remit about 40 yuan each year to their families in North China (when average annual income for rural households was about 100 yuan),[5] average wages in the first and second decade of the Guandong Lease weren't great. Earlier, I cited the 1913 wage of 40 Japanese cents a day for coolies working on the wharves and residing at the Heikanzō in north Dalian. It's clear from the coolie wage rates reported in the *Manchuria Daily Newspaper* that the wharf coolies were the aristocrats of unskilled labor in Japanese-controlled Manchuria. Coolies who did not work on the wharf consistently made one-third to one-half less in the 1907–18 period. For example, a newspaper feature printed in summer 1909 reports the regularization of coolie wages (except wharf coolies) in southern Manchuria as between 23 and 25 cents per day (*MNNS*, 16 June 1909). Coolies doing seasonal agriculture work made even less.

In the spring of that year the SMR's Wharves Office gave the average daily wages of dockworkers for 1908 as 91 Japanese cents for Japanese stevedores, 44 cents for Chinese coolie stevedores, and 29 cents for nonstevedore coolies (*MNNS*, 21 April 1909). But these coolies averaging 29 cents a day were still technically wharf coolies, and coolies working in coal mines and in the Japanese timber industry made 6 to 9 cents less per day (*MNNS*, 16 January 1911). Although comparative wage studies of unskilled workers in Northeast and North China show that wages were consistently two or three times higher in the Northeast,[6] ethnographic studies done by SMR researchers after Aioi's book was published show that coolies in Dalian often spent half of their wages on basic food needs, which was twice as much as the percentage they had to spend back home in North China (Yamamoto K. 1927). Praising the thrifty coolies in Manchuria for living on 7 cents a day in 1923 in the face of a "sensational rise in living expenses," Adachi Kinnosuke was oblivious to the fact that coolies who did not work on the wharves were averaging only 20 to 22 cents a day at that time (1925, 44).

With dormitory rates at Heikanzō running at 18 to 20 cents per day without food, most Chinese migrant workers in urban areas simply could not afford decent shelter. Except for the main coolie housing at Heikanzō and smaller coolie dormitories at the Japanese coal mines and at charities (all these together had the capacity of housing only 5 percent of nonfarm coolies in 1917), accommodations were prohibitively expensive. Most coolies in a *batou* group resigned themselves to sleeping outside in the ubiquitous "coolie tents" or in makeshift shacks arranged by their *batou* at "work camps" (*hamba*). We can assume that the one-third of migrants coming to Manchuria on their own were squatting anywhere there was shelter from the elements. When not sleeping outside, exposed "like beggars in Japan," many of the Chinese migrants depicted by Japanese journalists slept in the structures bombed out during the previous two wars Japan had waged in and around the region. Littered throughout Northeast China, these structures were rarely enclosed and never sound. Business as the continuation of war by other means attained a wretched literalness here, as these war-ravaged ruins became the dormitories for the workers driving the shift from military competition to capitalist competition. In these monuments to the new business model of colonialism, coolies were often easy prey to thieves working alone or for warlord groups.

It's important to remember that although the wage rate in Manchuria was not enough for most coolies to rent rooms at 20 cents per day and have any money left over to remit, it did allow them to subsist on the animal feed mentioned by Adachi and the leftovers referred to by Aioi. Destitute Chinese migrant workers could save a little money and still have some left over to purchase the basic means of subsistence that enabled them to endure another long workday. And that included opium, sold by Japanese and Korean dealers often working for Japanese colonial officials. As was the case in Taiwan, the profits from the opium market were essential for the extension of Japanese imperialism in mainland China. Here again, we come across business as a continuation of war by other means.

Japan's Imperial World Is Flat

Almost all Japanese accounts of Chinese migrant workers during the first and second decade of the twentieth century provide a glimpse into the everyday brutality of what Marx called the imposition of an "alien regime," the formal subsumption of labor under capital. This subtle though significant shift from previous modes of production put colonizer capitalists in the novel position of the "direct exploitation of the labour of others" (Marx 1977, 1019). Marx identified the shift to formal subsumption as characterized primarily by an "economic relationship of supremacy and subordination" (1026). Even in the self-congratulatory discourse of *The Manchurian Industrialists' World Looks to the Chinese Coolie* there are references to how this colonial version played out between Chinese migrant workers and Japanese managers working for the SMR (MSSK, 78–79). Andō Hikotarō cites the commonplace exploitation of Chinese migrant workers at the two SMR coal mines of Fushun and Yentai, where beginning in 1911 there were annually over a thousand deaths or serious injuries; in both 1926 and 1927 there were over ten thousand *reported* deaths or serious injuries at the two sites (1965, 115).

The population racism and production of biopolitical subjectivity inherent in formal subsumption made coolies into superhumanly strong workers, subhumanly stupid individuals, and doglike in their willingness to obey Japanese colonizers and their Chinese bosses alike. Unlike hotheaded Koreans and proud Japanese workers, coolies never caused their superiors any trouble (MSSK, 38). This production of coolieness as sometimes stoned on opium and otherwise helpless and "comfortably numb" in the face of Japanese subjugation naturalized a treatment of them determined by both the exploitation of formal subsumption and the colonizer-colonized relation. Japanese could feel good about themselves for providing coolies with jobs. In the words of a contemporary cheerleader for neoliberal capitalism, Thomas Friedman, they slept well at night (better than "their" coolies sleeping outside in tents, at least) knowing they had leveled their imperial world flat enough to excite labor and commodity markets. However, the abjection that revealed the lies of Japanese imperialists was visible even in the prose of the *Manchuria Daily Newspaper*, which reported on a steamer carrying three thousand Chinese coolies bound for a Japanese work site in northern Manchuria that capsized, killing all but eight coolies (*MNNS*, 21 March 1913); coolies frequently driven to suicide by overwork (1 August 1913); coolies brutally murdered by rogue Japanese (24 February 1913; 16 June 1911), or found dead from a drug overdose (15 January 1915; 5 April 1915).

The treatment of Chinese migrant workers at the hands of Japanese capital is epitomized in the way they were registered in the same freight category as inanimate commodities arriving by ship into Dalian by the SMR's Wharf Office. A short *Manchuria Daily Newspaper* article related that although human (read: Japanese or Euro-American) passengers were categorized separately, Chinese migrant workers were classified "together with soybeans and light machinery" (*MNNS*, 16 June 1909). Already dehumanized by Japanese imperialists' depictions of them as a "black tide" and as biopolitical subjectivities who "live only to work," drifting and cultureless, now coolies were left for dead (*laisser mourir*) on the outskirts of Dalian or inside collapsed SMR coal mines. The discursive production of Chinese migrant workers as "living only to work" had its biopolitical correlate in their being gratefully "worked into life." As we saw briefly above, and as is demonstrated in part III, the mobilization for total war necessary for the "liberation of Asia" transformed this state of being "worked into life" ever so slightly as "dying to work," which tragically morphed into the full necropolitics of being "worked to death."

2

PERIPHERAL PIMPS Each new colonial expansion is accompanied, as a matter of course, by a relentless battle of capital. . . . Any hope to restrict the accumulation of capital exclusively to "peaceful competition" rests on the pious belief that capital can rely upon the slow internal process of a disintegrating natural economy. Force is the only solution open to capital; the accumulation of capital, seen as a historical process, employs force as a permanent weapon.

ROSA LUXEMBURG, *THE ACCUMULATION OF CAPITAL*

If money comes into the world with a congenital bloodstain on one cheek, capital comes dripping from head to toe, from every pore, with blood and dirt.

KARL MARX, *CAPITAL*, VOLUME 1

On 18 September 1918 the Japanese consulate in the Manchurian capital of Fengtian sent an internal report to the Japanese foreign minister in Tokyo, our old friend Gotō Shinpei. The report updated the Foreign Ministry on a situation concerning five Japanese human traffickers (*shūgyō-sha*, "those engaged in ugly business"), who had been under investigation by the consular police since 24 January. On that day they were brought into the consulate and "warned" about the extent and nature of their operations after several complaints had been filed at Japanese consulates in Northeast China (FMA, "Collections of Improper Business," vol. 2).[1] Even though the Japanese police proffered "concrete advice on how to clean up their business" during the January interviews, the communiqué of 18 September relates that these traffickers had evidently ignored the recommendations. Despite the fact that their activities had been monitored by the consular police for seven months, the report states they had refused to alter the "nature of their business." All five were thereby "forbidden to conduct business in Manchuria."

The report is the fourth of five correspondences sent from Fengtian to the Foreign Ministry in Tokyo dealing with the five human traffickers. While updating Gotō and his staff on their situation, in this report and a final one the Fengtian consulate provides some background on the men and warns the Foreign Ministry that the closure of this one case does not mean the problem has been solved: "At any one time our consular police force keeps an eye on several hundred of these traffickers. . . . We are doing everything within our means to keep track of their activities."

The final correspondence in the case was addressed to the new foreign minister, Uchida Yasuya, and dated 12 November 1918. It informs Tokyo that owing to the dispatch of some of the Manchuria-based soldiers to Siberia and the related thinning of the security forces attached to the Fengtian consulate, Japanese pimps and traffickers had been operating with renewed impunity. After relating this unfortunate backtracking following the banning of the five traffickers on 18 September, the Fengtian Japanese consulate appears intent on lowering any of the expectations the Foreign Ministry might have had about restricting the operations of Japanese human traffickers, something that was not only tarnishing Japan's image in Europe and North America, but severely undercutting Japanese imperialists' claim of "civilizing Asia." The Foreign Ministry was particularly sensitive to the growing chorus of Chinese leaders calling for an outright ban on the practice, as Japanese had recently taken to kidnapping and pimping Chinese women. As the report sent on 12 November indicates, the demand for trafficked women originated primarily from Russian civilians and Japanese soldiers. This had been the case since the Russo-Japanese War, when "human traffickers accompanied the Japanese Army and provided women for them": "For the last fourteen years, loyal Japanese soldiers have continued to come to these men's establishments. . . . [Unfortunately] many soldiers have caught syphilis from these women. Therefore, we should require regular medical examinations of them; only when the women have received a clean bill of health can we allow our soldiers to frequent these brothels."

I haven't been able to find any reaction from Gotō to the reports of trafficking. Although he was juggling many issues at this time, including reframing Japan's entire diplomatic relationship with the new Soviet Union, the lack of a response suggests that he didn't consider the matter important. Knowing the situation on the ground in Northeast China as well as he did, it is unlikely that he would have been surprised. In fact, in late 1905 he and others were desperately looking for ways to get Japanese soldiers demobilized and off the streets. Consolidating a tighter circuit between army barracks and the brothels recently set up by the same pimps who procured women for soldiers during the war would doubtless have been seen as a step in the right direction. When Gotō and other officials moved to set up a licensed prostitution system in their new capital, Dalian, in late 1906 (the year all Japanese-run brothels in Manchuria came under the jurisdiction of the nearest consulate), they relied on these very men. In other words, the traffickers expanding their business from one directly connected to the Japanese army in Manchuria to one responding to military and civilian demands for prostitutes and concubines was exactly what Gotō was advocating in his colonial policy of capitalist business as a continuation of war by other means, *bunsōteki bubi*. Although Japanese consular officials in China referred to human trafficking as "ugly business" in their internal correspondence with the Foreign Ministry beginning in 1895, and therefore different in some aspects from the "pretty" fixed-capital projects of the SMR, it *was* business. As such, it would compete with Chinese merchants dominating this and all other commercial activities in Northeast and Southeast China and therefore could contribute to Japan's imperial expansion. Furthermore, because the market-oriented activities of the pimps grew primarily out of their connection to the army in Manchuria, they could easily be reoriented back to the military when policy so demanded. This is exactly what happened in the 1930s. The "comfort system" of forced sex work would have been difficult to consolidate without the enthusiastic cooperation of pimps and traffickers working closely again with Japan's military.

Nevertheless, there are some hints that Gotō may have ordered one of his assistants to advise the Fengtian consulate to apply the protocol established for licensed Japanese prostitutes—set up earlier in Dalian—to Chinese sex workers in Manchuria. If this was not the case, then Gotō's program of life principles and scientific colonialism was already becoming ingrained in colonial ideology, as the final recommendations from the Fengtian consulate parroted the program established first in Taiwan and then used in the Guandong Lease, which required regular medical examinations for women sex workers. Such routine exams for women within the framework of a licensed system was a direct application of Gotō's biopolitical axiom of "life principles" and was isomorphic with his opium policy in Taiwan. In other words, no matter how unseemly a particular practice (human trafficking, drug dealing), Japanese colonizers should do everything in their power to biopolitically enhance its hygienic environment and encourage Japanese to profit from the production and consumption circuits connected to it.

Much had changed between 1895 and 1918. Japan emerged after the First World War as a major imperial power with a vibrant industrial capitalism. Intensifying global antipathy against prostitution resulted in international treaties outlawing trafficking and sex with minors.[2] Increasing competition between Japanese and Chinese merchants in Northeast China was due to the gradual return of the dispersed Chinese merchants now lured back by the SMR-led economic boom in the region after the Russo-Japanese War and by the Manchurian warlords' growing autonomy and prosperity. In 1918, although the Japanese consulates still felt pressured to limit the activities of the pimps, their quick resignation to restrictions on Japanese and Chinese *women*, rather than continuing surveillance of the Japanese male traffickers, must have been a relief of sorts for the overstretched consuls. This important matrix of Japanese business activity in China would henceforth carry on more or less as before.

Historically adjudicating this "more or less as before," and the subjectivities so produced, is the goal of this chapter. Using the internal correspondence of the Foreign Ministry, Japanese press accounts from China and western Japan, diaries of Japanese ship captains, oral testimonies of kidnapped women, and the diary of Muraoka Iheiji, the most famous Japanese human trafficker of the late nineteenth century and early twentieth, I'll try to provide some account of how and why Japan's imperialism produced the subjectivity of the pimp and procurer. Whether referred to as pimps (*zegen*), human traffickers (*shūgyōsha*), or flesh merchants (*jinshinbaibaiya*), without these Japanese men there would have been much less extensive kidnapping and deployment of the so-called comfort women later on.[3] However, my aim is to demonstrate the centrality of the pimps for Japanese capitalist successes and market penetration in Asia in the thirty to forty years before they assisted the Japanese army in setting up the infrastructure for forced sex work. In 1937 Muraoka Iheiji said that two-thirds of the bosses of large Japanese enterprises in the Asia-Pacific began their business careers as low-level human traffickers (Muraoka 1960, 57).[4] Even if his autobiography carries only the 75 percent credibility granted it by most scholars, an investigation of how this worked historically is called for.

The revisionist economic history of Hamashita Takeshi (1989, 2003) and Sugihara Kaoru (1996, 2002) has shown how important the Chinese merchant networks were in relinking Japanese trade with East and Southeast Asia after the forced opening of Japan's treaty ports in the 1850s and 1860s to Euro-American trade. Whether acting on their own or using their centuries-long expertise as middlemen for *arriviste* European market animals and gunboat imperialists, the Chinese merchants managed trading networks between the treaty ports on the China coast and Nagasaki (where they and Dutch merchants were granted exclusive trading rights during the 230 years of Japan's partial closure), Kobe, Osaka, and Yokohama. It would be impossible to fully apprehend the centrality of the Japanese pimps to Japanese imperialism without first foregrounding the importance of Chinese merchants in reestablishing Japanese trading links with Asia.

The historical work done on the trafficking of Japanese women and girls by Morisaki Kazue (1976), James Warren (1993), Yamazaki Tomoko (1995), and Hirakawa Hitoshi and Shimizu Hiroshi (1999) has focused primarily on Japanese male traffickers in Southeast Asia. However, it's clear that beginning in the late 1850s, in addition to the silk and silver that Chinese merchants were sending to Asian markets from Japan, they were also supervising the movement of another precious commodity: young Japanese women. From the cases in the Foreign Ministry archives and the writings of the Japanese pimps themselves, it's obvious that Chinese merchants preceded Japanese in trafficking Japanese women to Asia. First, for Japanese women to end up in the places they did in considerable numbers by the mid-1880s (Harbin, Fengtian, Shanghai, Hong Kong, Xiamen, Hanoi, Singapore) would have required the direction of Chinese merchants who dominated commerce in all these places. Without some assistance by Japanese-speaking Chinese merchants and their male and female underlings, individual Japanese women could not have found their way to brothels in continental Asia where they were sold outright to white Europeans or Chinese. Internal correspondence between Japanese consulates in Asia and the Tokyo Foreign Ministry in the 1880s and 1890s has detailed Chinese involvement in trafficking

Japanese women (FMA, "Matters of Improper Business," vol. 1, cases 2, 5, and 13). There is evidence of Chinese traffickers of Japanese women to Northeast China as late as 1908 in the *Manchuria Daily Newspaper* (*MNNS*, 25 March 1908). After that, the market was gradually dominated by the three hundred to four hundred Japanese pimps estimated to be working in Northeast China by 1918. But it took several decades of battle over this lucrative market for Japanese men to finally gain the upper hand over their Chinese competitors.

It is difficult to find anyone connected to Japanese merchant circles in Asia during this period who didn't consider the sex workers' contribution crucial to Japanese capitalist expansion. The pioneering presence of Japanese prostitutes was recognized as indispensable for the spread of related Japanese consumer products: beer, sake, Japanese food, makeup, and Japanese clothes. In a survey of Japanese business development in Southeast Asia written in 1919, Tsukuda Kōji and Katō Michinori state frankly:

> Small business [*go shaku*] men originally followed the Japanese prostitutes before spreading through Southeast Asia. The prostitutes needed Japanese food, beverages, clothes and many other Japanese products. Their demand was met by the strange Japanese variety-goods store, which peddled a wide range of products. As the Japanese store also sold to non-Japanese in these areas, Japanese commodities became widely popular. The strength of Japan's Southeast Asian trade today is not thanks to the large merchant houses like Mitsui; the trade was first developed by the Japanese variety-goods dealers. Behind these merchants is the shadow cast by the Japanese prostitutes. (Quoted in Hirakawa and Shimizu 1999, 20)

Katō Hisakatsu, a ship's captain who plied the trade routes from Nagasaki to China and Southeast Asia for three decades beginning in the 1890s, wrote that throughout the Asia-Pacific region until the First World War Japan's most well-known exports were coal, raw silk, and women: "Almost every place that my ships went, Japanese traffickers had established flesh-markets [*jinniku no ichi*] selling what they called 'packs of whores' [*rōshi no mure*]" (1931, 61).

Katō's memoirs differ from more recent accounts in that Japanese women sex workers and pimps and procurers are always understood as a couple; one is impossible without the other. In his text *From the*

Diaries of a Ship's Hand (*Sendō no nikki kara*, 1924), Katō refers casually
to the trafficker–sex worker couple as the "truth of human trafficking
[*shūgyōfuron*]." Only later do we get an image of the lonely, brave Japanese sex worker sacrificing her body to send money back to her family
and establish markets for her country's products in Asia. This image of
the tragic pioneer for Japan's imperial capitalism really gets solidified in
the first two decades of the twentieth century and essentializes Japanese
sex workers. Before their essentialization, several of the most important
Japanese intellectuals recognized the male trafficker–sex worker couple
and recommended more of them. The most influential intellectual figure
in Japan during the 1880s and 1890s, Fukuzawa Yukichi, publicly encouraged the emigration of poor Japanese women to work as prostitutes in the treaty ports in Asia, becoming what Neferti Tadiar calls "bio-
territories" for Japan (2009, 105). Fukuzawa insisted that modernizing
Japan had no use for the women except for their potential foreign currency earnings, and that sex work in the booming cities of Hong Kong,
Shanghai, and Singapore would benefit the women, their families, and
their nation. In 1882 he wrote, "People should not criticize these women
for traveling abroad for prostitution. Since the government's policy is to
increase emigration, these women should be granted the freedom to do
so" (quoted in Terami-Wada 1986, 307).

Futabatei Shimei, the scholar of Russian literature and author of
Floating Clouds (*Ukigumo*), which is considered the first modern Japanese novel, lived off and on in Northeast China and Siberia for years and
witnessed firsthand the influence of Japanese sex workers on Russians
and Chinese. According to his friend, the translator Uchida Roan (1859–
1922), when Futabatei was living in Harbin, Manchuria, during the 1890s
he seriously considered running his own brothel, which would include a
network of Japanese male pimps and older Japanese women to run the
establishment. In his biography of Futabatei published in 1914, Uchida
reveals that everyone in Futabatei's circle was familiar with his "theory
of trafficking Japanese women [*shūgyōron*]." According to Uchida, Futabatei considered Japanese sex workers essential for Japan's imperialism
in Asia, because the erotic power they held over Russians and Chinese
meant that these male customers would quickly become "Japanized and
start buying exclusively Japanese products": "They first start out paying for sex with lower-class Japanese prostitutes. Next, they move on
to more expensive Japanese women, and before long they're obsessed

with all Japanese products" (2001, 372–73). Uchida relates that Futabatei considered it his "patriotic duty" (*aikoku gimu*) to support this process of Japanization by getting personally involved in the business of
trafficking women.

Although neither of these writers directly refers to pimps and procurers, they both knew from their frequent travel outside Japan that it
was impossible for poor, illiterate Japanese women to make their way to
brothels in places like Harbin, Manchuria, or Singapore by themselves.
Whether explicitly in the case of Futabatei, or implicitly in the case of
Fukuzawa, their respective "theories of trafficking Japanese women"
recognized the role of male traffickers. Mori Katsumi and other scholars casually state that all of the thirty to fifty thousand Japanese women
doing sex work abroad in the first decade of the twentieth century were
assisted to some degree by pimps (1959, 111). It is important to remember
that in the first fifteen years of Japanese women doing sex work in Asia,
the activities of the pimps and procurers would have been controlled by
Chinese men in Japan. When Muraoka Iheiji was hired by the Japanese
consulate in Shanghai in 1887 to conduct a six-month investigation of
the market environment in Northeast and North China, his awareness
and growing anger that Chinese men were trafficking Japanese women
and girls gradually overwhelmed his other observations.

Because of his previous work experience in Northeast China, Muraoka was hired by the Japanese consulate in Shanghai to accompany
one of their staff and the army lieutenant Uehara Yasuku on a secret mission. Spending five months, from June to November 1887, scouting out
Japanese opportunities in Manchuria (nearly two decades before the
Ishizuka survey), he contributed to the first major investigation of business prospects in Northeast China. Muraoka and the staff officer note
several things. The first is that, in Muraoka's own words, "We rarely run
into any Japanese men." The second, and deeper, impression is their
discovery of the large number of Japanese sex workers in the cities and
towns they visit. Muraoka is taken aback by the diverse backgrounds of
the women, with "samurai daughters" (1960, 17) as numerous as women
from poor farming villages. What doesn't seem to surprise him is the
fact that almost all the Japanese women they interview plead for help
in returning. Although we get little in the way of their own words, one
woman describes being "brought" (*tsurerareta*) against her will by Chinese merchants in Nagasaki to Manchuria, where the Chinese sold her

for the equivalent of four hundred dollars, a considerable sum of money. Two women describe being pimped and brought to Manchuria by a Chinese merchant who had set up a business in Kobe that lasted for four years (19).

The almost complete absence of Japanese men leads Muraoka to assume that almost all of these Japanese women have been "brought by Chinese" to China (1960, 18–19). Excepting a handful of Japanese men working for Chinese warlords and five or six more exporting soybeans from a Mitsui shop in Beijing, there are no other conclusions to draw. Muraoka deduces that the Chinese have brought the Japanese women to Northeast China, at which point they were either sold directly to Russian criminals and Chinese warlords or sent to brothels run by Chinese merchants. The Japanese group from Shanghai takes note of the other commodities plentiful in Manchuria: the abundance of opium grown in the area and sold by Chinese merchants and the huge soybean production and trade. At the end of the investigation Muraoka ponders the opportunities that Japanese women, opium, and soybeans hold for male Japanese businessmen in Manchuria (19–20); all they need is some initial support to begin battling with Chinese merchants for market control.

Although he was contracted by the Japanese consulate to investigate business opportunities in Manchuria, at each stop Muraoka makes in his later business survey trips in the 1890s and later (Shanghai, Singapore, Kuala Lumpur, Manila) he undertakes a similar scan of the commercial environment, never failing to note the strength of the local Chinese merchants. If Japan is going to be the most powerful country in Asia, he opines, Japanese must understand that Chinese merchants are their main competition. For Muraoka, Europeans are mere consumers of the commodities peddled by the Chinese and Japanese, not serious competitors for commercial hegemony. Offering himself as the poster boy for a new breed of aggressively competitive Japanese merchant—one of the main characteristics Foucault insisted was solicited in the biopolitics of liberal capitalism—Muraoka brags about his varied tactics of competing directly against Chinese merchant capitalists, where on two occasions he resorted to using Japanese martial arts in street fights against them (1960, 8, 23).

When the first Japanese women were trafficked to Asia for sex work, they came from places where Chinese merchants had established either long-term (Nagasaki) or short-term (Yokohama, Kobe) market control of trade routes with Asia. In his *Autobiography* Muraoka inserts several surveys of the hometowns, ages, and buyers of the Japanese women and girls sold to places in Asia; almost all of them hail from these places in the beginning. It's only after the Japanese pimps and procurers begin to control the trafficking racket and establish the countrywide practice of kidnapping that we see Japanese women and girls coming to Asia from many different parts of Japan. The Chinese traffickers used a variety of techniques for procuring, while the Chinese bosses handled the payoffs to shipping company officials and port and consular officials in Japan and Asia, occasionally hiring European men to act as husbands and "protectors" of the Japanese on the overseas trip (FMA, "Verification Record for Passports").[5] The hiring of Europeans to traffic Japanese was rare; on the other hand, the hiring of Japanese *chinpira* (young gangster) underlings by Chinese merchants and warlords was widespread throughout Northeast and Southeast Asia.

This is the first instance in his *Autobiography* where Muraoka's sense of Japanese nationalism is palpable. He returns to Shanghai in December 1887 from his trip to Manchuria determined to change the intolerable situation in which Chinese men have control over the profits expropriated from Japanese sex workers. He nowhere states what the Japanese consular official and military officers thought about the situation, but from the Japanese consulate's subsequent support of Japanese traffickers in Shanghai and Hong Kong (where they managed to wrestle most of the market for Japanese girls and women from the Chinese), it's highly unlikely that the imperial officials didn't share Muraoka's feeling in this regard.

Muraoka accidentally finds himself in a position to directly challenge Chinese merchants seven months later, in Xiamen. In the meantime, inspired both by the selfish pursuit of the huge profits he realizes can be made in Northeast China from pimping and procuring Japanese women and by a proprietary paternalism that allows him to construe this same pimping and procuring as "rescuing" and "saving" Japanese females from predatory Chinese, he uses the savings from his investigative work for the army to establish a prostitution ring in Shanghai with thirteen Japanese females, several of whom he has kidnapped himself.[6] During the time he's consolidating a small trafficking business in Shanghai in April and May 1889, he hears rumors circulating among the small Japanese business community about kidnapped Japanese females being "imprisoned" (*kankin*) as sex slaves by Chinese merchants and sailors in Xiamen (1960, 28). Based on information from several different sources, including Japanese consular officials, sailors, and Japanese brothel owners in Shanghai, Muraoka decides to transfer his business south to Xiamen in an attempt to "rescue" (*kyūshutsu*) the helpless Japanese from the clutches of these Chinese.

So in late June 1889 he moves his entire brothel operation down the China coast to Xiamen, where he intends to save the estimated five hundred enslaved Japanese (1960, 28). When he arrives there he quickly realizes that all the Japanese women working for Chinese brothel owners in Xiamen have been kidnapped from Japan, and each "lost their virginity" to Chinese men. Feeling a growing humiliation at the extent of the Chinese merchants' trafficking business, he requests help from the British consular police, and, embellishing the lurid narrative of the situation of the enslaved Japanese females with each new visit to the British police, he's finally invited to participate in a raid on one Chinese house in August. The operation "frees" six Japanese females, all of whom had been imprisoned by Chinese for at least one year. Astonishingly, Muraoka is given official custody of the six women,[7] and he immediately sells five of them to Hong Kong and keeps one as his "wife"; as such she's forced to do sex work in Muraoka's own Xiamen brothel, the sole Japanese brothel in the port city at this time (30). Another "rescue" operation requested by the Japanese consulate several months later, and carried out by Muraoka's men with the assistance of the Chinese metropolitan police, succeeds in extracting fifty-five Japanese women from their Chinese merchant masters (30). Once again Muraoka is given custody of all the Japanese women.

At this point the local Chinese traffickers decide they have had enough and start threatening him. After one more raid even some of the European customers of the Chinese traffickers are getting angry at all the complications, and Muraoka decides the heat is too much for him. So after successfully selling off all fifty-five of the Japanese women rescued during the second raid to brothels in Hong Kong and Singapore (and generating huge profits, as he paid absolutely nothing for the women), in December 1889 he decides to leave town and set up shop in Singapore, where he hears the business environment constructed by the British authorities is more welcoming for Japanese traffickers. With several men he has hired in Xiamen and a few of his "wives" from Shanghai (the others were sold off to individual Europeans or Chinese brothels *again*), he lands in Singapore with lots of capital to begin one of the most extensive trafficking businesses of the era. In four years' time Muraoka claims to have kidnapped and stowed away 3,122 Japanese women—largely from areas in western Japan—to Singapore to be either sold there or shipped off to even more remote destinations, such as Bombay and Australia, to work in brothels.

The scholar Mori Katsumi corroborates much of Muraoka's account based on his interviews with Japanese women who claim to have been bought as virgins by Chinese and then imprisoned for anywhere from one to three years in and around Xiamen (1959, 102). Several of the women claim to have been sold by kidnappers at markets in Xiamen to rich Chinese, who then moved them from the coastal city to the Chinese mainland and kept them as concubines in their residences there. Several of these women could have been among those "saved" by Muraoka and his underlings. In any case, it's important to make absolutely clear that over a period of three years some of these women would have been kidnapped or transported against their will three or four times. First they were bought or kidnapped in Japan by Chinese, or by Japanese men working for Chinese. Next they were sold in Hong Kong or Xiamen to their Chinese masters. The sixty-one women "rescued" or kidnapped again by Muraoka were, with the exception of a few who were forced to work in his brothel, sold again by him to Singapore or Hong Kong, where they would most likely have ended up in Japanese brothels. Some would surely have been bought out of their brothels again by individual men, Chinese or European. As a male writer, it's difficult to even begin to imagine how this process impacted the Japanese women and girls subjected to it. At the very least, in pondering this series of staggeringly violent market transactions we might begin to free ourselves from culturalist profiling (Japanese culture solicits meekness and subservience from its women) and begin to think as materialists about how Japanese sex workers in Asia earned the reputation of being submissive, obedient, and willing to have sex with anyone with the money to pay. The word *trauma* seems deficient when asked to explain the aftereffects of being produced as infrahuman, commodity bodies by the explosive confrontation of Euro-American gunboat imperialism with this regional struggle over markets that defined Muraoka Iheiji's battle for profits with Chinese traffickers. Nevertheless, a kind of trauma caused by the serial dispossession of the kidnapped women contributed to the process of turning Japanese sex workers into the kind of dehumanized objects that Diane Sommerville (2006) argues black female slaves were for their male captors. A technology of sovereign and severe Japanese masculinity was produced for the pimps and traffickers—the first important male Japanese imperialists in Asia—through the violent trafficking and commodification of enslaved Japanese women and girls. Moreover, the subjectivization of sex workers as animalistic, corporeal things to be manipulated by male capitalists established a precedent for how colonial labor would be similarly devalued by Japanese imperial capitalists later on.

Pimp Personae

Most pimps and procurers were second or third sons of poor farming families who, losing out to elder brothers in inheritance, had little hope of a decent life if they stayed with their family during the tough times of mid-nineteenth-century Japan. Muraoka Iheiji was an exception in that he was the eldest son of a poor Nagasaki family, born in 1867. His father died in Tokyo in 1877. Rather than burdening his mother with one more mouth to feed, Muraoka did odd jobs for a while, and at seventeen decided to take a job as a ship's hand working the Nagasaki–Hong Kong trade route in 1885. Using the windfall profits he made selling the rescued Japanese women, he eventually set up a major trafficking operation in Singapore, based in a large compound and employing twenty-four men. All these employees had criminal records in Japan or had left the country just ahead of the police. The stories of the other big-time continental Asia–based Japanese pimps are similar to Muraoka's. Matsuo Kashirō was born a year after Muraoka, also in Nagasaki, as the second son in a poor farming family. He was arrested in Nagasaki for the murder of a younger Japanese rival moving in on his territory in Indo-China. The police report stated that Matsuo began his career as a pimp trafficking Japanese women from Nagasaki to Korea and China in the late 1880s. As soon as Taiwan was colonized by Japan in 1895 he set up a large operation in Taipei, with fifty-six women and a dozen ex-con employees. As there were very few Japanese businesses this large in colonial Taipei at the time, it's unlikely that Gotō Shinpei wasn't aware of what Matsuo was doing. From his corporate headquarters in Taipei, Matsuo built his own market that trafficked Japanese women in the South China Sea area, the famous Nagasaki-Korea-Shanghai-Taiwan–Hong Kong route. To take advantage of the high demand for Japanese sex workers in the Chinese treaty ports at this time (Japanese were known to agree to monthly medical checkups, and lavish kimono and cosmetics accentuated their exotic novelty for Chinese and European consumers) Matsuo transferred his operations to Hong Kong in 1900, which allowed him to extend his business into Southeast Asia (Warren 1993, 219).

Muraoka provides the background of some of his employees when he describes how he set up his huge business in Singapore. One of his men, Ueda Tomosaburō, was orphaned at fourteen, and soon afterward he realized that the neighborhood kids were stealing grain from his family's shed. So he built an intricate booby trap with a powerful explosive that ripped the leg off one of the boys and hurt a second. He was placed in a juvenile prison until he was twenty (1960, 58). After working for Muraoka for several years he set up his own trafficking business in Australia before returning home to Shimane, Japan, where he refashioned himself as a wealthy landowner and respected citizen. A second underling, Sakata Junzaburō, seduced his boss's daughter and then left Nagasaki with another woman, deciding to return a year later with the hope that the boss's daughter had given birth to his son in the interim, in which case he intended to become heir to the company. Instead, his former boss had him put in prison, but he managed to escape to Singapore (54–55). Matsuda Hitoshi had been in and out of jail in Japan for armed robbery, murder, and kidnapping. The serial rapist Takamine Kunijirō had contracted such a bad case of gonorrhea that he had to sleep in an awkward position on his side (*yokone*) for over a year (55). Minakata Fujiyoshi stole all his grandmother's savings, and after she ratted on him he was forced to flee Amakusa for Hong Kong.

With this merry band of murderers, rapists, and rip-off artists Muraoka set up a small trafficking empire in Southeast Asia. I use *empire* deliberately here because he regarded his business operations as indispensable both for Japanese capital accumulation domestically and for Japanese commercial hegemony over Chinese merchants throughout Asia. Many contemporary Japanese observers expressed the same sentiment, however euphemistically. Muraoka was well aware that people knew how central Japanese sex workers were in the first two decades of Japanese imperialism in Asia, yet he thought they hypocritically refused to give credit to the male traffickers who did the hard work of getting the women from rural Japan to the thriving port cities on the China coast and Manchuria. As a way of explaining his own behavior in the face of this hypocrisy, after he completed his first "rescue" operation in Xiamen and proceeded to sell off the women, he jotted down exactly what he was doing and for whom. Some of his comments are addressed directly to Japanese hypocrites who condemn what he does as "immoral."

> First, in making money, I can send some back to my family in Japan. This is my way of providing extra cash to Japan as well, as the folks back home all have to pay taxes. Second, through my trafficking activities I've been able to buy my friends land and houses in Nagasaki. Third, I always remember the lessons I learned from my first boss and try to stimulate Japanese business interests wherever I go. Fourth, my business satisfies basic human needs for affection and community; it just worked out well for me that I was able to make lots of money at the same time. Finally, to sum all this up, I guess my greatest immorality is "when you work hard at business, you profit from it" [*jigyō jitoku*]. (24–25)

More than a confession of any wrongdoing, this is a testament to the modernizing effects of human trafficking. It is also biopolitical bragging, as Muraoka insists he is improving the lives (*faire vivir*) of populations of Japanese. Furthermore, his litany of immoralities is nothing but the ideological common sense of Japanese capitalism of this era. The resort to irony is an attempt to work out his frustration over the fact that elites were largely unwilling to openly praise human trafficking as they praised other business practices in Japan at this time. So it's left to this indignant trafficker to reveal some fundamental truths of capitalist business as a continuation of war by other means. We saw in the first chapter how this war was fought with and against Chinese immigrant labor to Manchuria. Here, on the China coast, business was driven by battles against Japanese girls and women, forcefully kidnapped in Japan and stowed away for several weeks to distant lands, where they were sold like animals or Chinese coolies to men with capital. Muraoka also comes close to delineating how his business as war is necessarily fought *with* Japanese women against Chinese merchants and British imperialists and by Japanese male pimps *against* Japanese women. He identifies this constitutive contradiction often using colloquialisms from his native Nagasaki. In so doing he is able to rhetorically conflate criminal businessmen like himself with the male elites of Japan, from whose fraternity he feels he has been unfairly excluded.

Muraoka scribbled the following phrases on the ship leaving Xiamen for Singapore, having gotten into trouble for "rescuing" two Japanese women who'd been sold by Chinese traffickers. He cites liberally from the ideological program code of the self-made man that was popular in Japan at this time (Kinmonth 1981): "Women are the downfall of men; women are the machines that generate business [*jigyō*] for men. Women are the forces that lead men into hell; women are the instruments that guide men on the road to success [*shusse*] in the world. Women are the contraptions that pull men into doing evil business; women are men's fate. Women are the main sacrificial foundations [*hashira*] of the state; relying on women is certain ruin" (Muraoka 1960, 40).

Muraoka explains in his autobiography that as his business expanded, he intuited even more of the contradictory logic driving Japanese imperialism's expansion in Asia. When he's setting up his first major business operation in Singapore in January 1890 he pens a smirky confession of all his "sins."

> Okay, I'll admit that my Japanese trafficker brothers in Shanghai and Tianjin are basically shit-stew [*kusomiso*], just like me. But think about it this way: by doing evil, you'll get the death penalty; by doing good, you'll get into heaven. But doing some good and some evil will land you right in the middle of this here world—hahahaha. . . .
>
> But let's think about what this combination of good and evil really means. Of course, kidnapping and human trafficking are two of the greatest evils, but I was already a villain to start with. I usually think that villains like me just do things out of self-interest, with no concern at all for Japan. Then I think again and realize that making the kind of money I can by selling women will turn me into a major businessman and take some of the financial pressure off Japan. I'm not the only one who thinks that villains who get their hands on lots of money suddenly turn good [*maningen*]; the petty thieving stops immediately and serious business starts. Evil changes quickly into good. With this in mind I decided to build the "convicts dormitory" in Singapore as a place where all my men could reform themselves by making patriotic sacrifices for Japan. My men would reform themselves by developing

each area in the Pacific through extending our prostitution business. I thought this would contribute to a far-sighted, 100-year plan of development for Japan. (1960, 47, 49–50)

This prescient projection of Japanese capitalist expansion is translated for the petty criminals when CEO Muraoka gathers them all together to launch his new Singapore operation. Here, Muraoka explains to his employees that he is giving them one last chance to redeem the sins of their recent past, and in so doing become respectable Japanese. The opportunity that will allow them to turn their lives around, provide penitence for their criminal acts against the mother country, and contribute positively to Japan is basically the chance for them to compete successfully against the Chinese merchants. If his henchmen are willing to follow his example and work tirelessly to succeed, their acts will not only benefit themselves and their trafficking operation, but will allow other Japanese to profit in their footsteps. Muraoka thinks to himself before his pep talk, "I formed this group of cons with the expectation that they would develop the Asia-Pacific. Although people refer to them as killers, thieves and crooks, I firmly believed that if they were provided with the right opportunities they could all become honest businessmen. I was confident that I was the one who could lead them down the path towards reform" (1960, 55). Then he addresses his men:

You're probably thinking that you pretty much figured out what we'll be doing, but I bet you don't get the real reason. Regular people say that you're all a bunch of killers and thieves. Even more extreme than that, it's said that you freely chose to get involved in these criminal affairs. In other words, even though you were all raised as Japanese citizens, you willfully made yourselves into enemies of the Japanese nation [*kokka o ada ni shi*]. You've destroyed what it is that made you Japanese, and this has led you down a path of ruin. . . . However, I'm about to let you have a chance to redeem yourselves and play an important role in the business future of Japan. You are all going to make lots of money and along the way relieve some of the financial burdens on Japan. You will be able to redeem yourselves in the eyes of our country and become respectable citizens again. But for this to happen, you must be willing to work with me. I'm asking you to stay committed and don't ignore any business opportunity that comes your way. Within just a few years, you will be dressing up our country in expensive brocade and doing honest work, feeling a new confidence to expand business that will increase Japanese exports into Asia. . . . However, keeping with our larger goal of helping Japan by becoming successful businessmen, it will be necessary to commit one final crime. (56)

Capitalism, the Martial Art

Reading Muraoka's address to his traffickers through the Rosa Luxemburg epigraph on the extra-economic violence necessary for capital accumulation aptly depicts the impulse behind his efforts. There is absolutely nothing natural or inevitable about the sacrificial process of accumulation. She writes, "Capitalism employs force as a permanent weapon," and Muraoka explains that this "final crime" is the forceful kidnapping of Japanese girls from western Japan. He then describes how the women will be brought to his corporate headquarters in Asia, where they will be "broken in"—raped and terrorized into submissive obedience—before being sold off. Luxemburg's martial "force," one of Marx's "methods of force" necessary for capitalism (1977, 928), is casually ordered here by Muraoka as the necessary evil that will lead to all the subsequent good: erstwhile rapists and human traffickers redeemed as model Japanese citizens, lucrative markets in Asia wrenched away from Chinese merchants, and Japan properly established as a wealthy imperial country. None of the good of capital accumulation can happen without the necessary evil of kidnapping and sexually terrorizing Japanese women. Even if Muraoka hadn't included judo in the training exercises for his young traffickers, everything else here is enough to show how capitalism is the ultimate martial art.

In several places in his *Autobiography* Muraoka states explicitly what has recently become common knowledge for scholars paying attention to the role of sex workers in Japan's imperialism: they were the sine qua non for Japanese commodity capitalism in Asia (Brooks 2005; Fujime 1995). However, we also need to see prostitution as, in Marx's problematic gender code, "only a *specific* expression of the *general* prostitution of the laborer" (1988, 133).[8] Bourgeois economists would erase the generality of all labor as prostitution pimped by capital and describe the role sex workers played in capital accumulation in continental Asia as a "multiplier" for the various Japanese products and services: textiles, makeup, and the beer and sake sold at Japanese brothels and restaurants. Muraoka is refreshingly demystifying as his welcoming speech gets more detailed:

> Because of the constant demand for Japanese girls, even in the most remote villages in the South Pacific we'll be able to set up brothels. This will enable the sundries stores and then the small merchants to come over from Japan right behind us. When the shackles are removed from the Japanese merchants and they're given the chance to operate freely, they'll be successful. All the different parts of society will then be mobilized towards business [*shakaiha shuttyōsho o dasu*]. In this society consisting of nothing but business, it will no longer be considered appropriate to refer to brothel owners and traffickers as "pimps," they will be businessmen pure and simple. And thanks to their single-minded dedication to business, in no time at all other Japanese developers will rush into their area; ships filled with products from Japan will be the next to arrive. Gradually, the entire area surrounding them will become prosperous as well. (1960, 57–58)

But for all this to happen, Muraoka's businessmen have to commit their "final sin" of kidnapping women. If we can accept 75 percent of what Muraoka claims is true, his men forced approximately twenty-five hundred Japanese women and girls to go to various parts of Asia during the decade of the 1890s for the dual ends of accumulating capital and magically redeeming his motley crew of rapists and thieves. It's important to state that these were but a fraction of what Sonoe Sachiko estimates to be over one hundred thousand Japanese women sex workers sold throughout the Asia-Pacific region from the 1870s to the 1930s (2000, 104). But out of all the Japanese pimps, Muraoka claimed to be the most experienced in the martial art of kidnapping and quickly selling women, and was anxious to pass his wisdom on to his men.

Muraoka's concrete instructions are fairly basic. The men were to "kidnap women exclusively in the countryside," with a focus on poor and illiterate women. He warned them, "Take precautions that all your movements are hidden, never write anything down, and never use my name in any of your dealings" (1960, 57). Because the act of physically getting women onto a ship to be stowed away always entailed resistance from the women and could be observed by port security officials, his men should be "especially discreet when doing so." "When you get the girls ready to sneak on the ship, make sure you have bribed the police, consular officials, and the ship's bosses and captains beforehand. If you're unable to do that, try to distract the police with stories about home and show them pictures, while you arrange to have the women hidden in the bottom of the ship" (57).

The operation of stowing women away for three- and four-week trips to Hong Kong and Singapore normally entailed the cooperation of Japanese port officials and ships' captains on the Japanese side, and British and Chinese authorities in Shanghai, Hong Kong, and Singapore. It has been well documented that, when not openly assisting traffickers, British officials tacitly supported Japanese sex workers being kidnapped and sold in their colonial cities of Hong Kong and Singapore (Miyaoka 1968; Warren 1993; Hirakawa and Shimizu 1998).[9] Their traumatization was construed in popular discourse as Japanese sex workers being subservient, demure, and obedient (stereotyped in *Madam Butterfly*), leading to British consumers overwhelmingly preferring them over Chinese and Southeast Asian sex workers. Considering Japanese sex workers' obedience and the fact that they usually cooperated with the biopolitical requirements for regular medical examinations,[10] British authorities were in no hurry to restrict the supply of kidnapped Japanese women.

Muraoka does not explain the mechanics of stowing away (*mikkō*) in his *Autobiography*, but with an estimated thirty to forty thousand Japanese women kidnapped and transported between 1885 and 1915 (Mori K. 1959) it's fairly easy to form a narrative. Although on occasion sex workers traveled from Japan to other parts of Asia legally, the great majority were stowaways, as it was quicker and cheaper for traffickers to simply bribe officials and boat captains. But first procurers had to get them to a ship.

Different stratagems were used to get women to consider leaving their hometowns. Procurers often returned to towns and villages near where they themselves were raised; there it was easy to gather information about families who were particularly bad off and to arrange meetings either with parents or, more often, with the girls by themselves. Taking advantage of the familiar, they would then weave fantastic tales about the exotically foreign and the riches to be had working as housekeepers in the new Eurasian cities of Singapore and Hong Kong. An elderly Amakusa woman related how in 1890 a pimp in the guise of an itinerant salesman deceived poor farm girls with images of a "dreamland" opposed in every way to their poverty-stricken lives in Kyūshū:

"One day a smooth-talking man appeared on my island; he was selling sea-products made in Nagasaki. In the stores in town he was telling everyone interesting stories about foreign lands. Salmon was plentiful in Vladivostok; as kids played in boats, the salmon jumped into them. Gold nuggets were waiting to be picked up. I got close to him at my grandmother's house" (quoted in Ichioka 1977, 6–7). In 1904 Minami Haru was approached by a procurer who promised this seventeen-year-old Amakusa girl that she could earn nearly seven yen a month working as a barmaid abroad. In her own words, Minami explains why she decided to take a chance on the unknown. "It was very difficult for a woman to earn even one yen a month at that time. My father was a day laborer, and there were five other children in our family. I decided to take the offer. I was taken to Kuchinotsu port that night by small boat and then transferred to a foreign ship. In the hold of the vessel I encountered about twenty other girls. We were only given a crust of bread each day for twenty-nine days—the length of the passage to Singapore" (Warren 1993, 216).

The pimps and procurers often worked in teams, dividing up the tasks between them: the initial contact with the girls and women, transporting them from their town or village to a port, and the final work of forcefully loading them onto coal barges or merchant ships. The sheer volume of women kidnapped and stowed away at any one time (with as many as fifty women being put onto one vessel en masse) required traffickers to physically accompany the women in the holds and furnace rooms of ships to prevent them from trying to escape or alert deckhands. This appears to have been an innovation introduced by Japanese traffickers (Miyaoka 1968). The methods used by the Japanese chaperones to keep the women compliant under extreme conditions (often the only place in the ship's hold to hide women was the area surrounding the coal burner, and these spaces sometimes became literal infernos) ranged from some semblance of human kindness to rape and murder.

The trafficker Tada Kamekichi raped and strangled a women he was bringing from Nagasaki to Singapore, finally tossing her lifeless body into the sea. Apparently, this was to set an example to the other seven women who had defied his orders to make extra money by having sex with some of the crew during the passage (Warren 1993, 219; Hane 1982, 221). The women survivors sent a letter of grievance to the Foreign Ministry in Tokyo signed in their own blood.[11] These women were perhaps lucky to survive, as there are many examples of women dying horrible deaths, buried beneath shifting cargo or incinerated by fires set by coal furnaces. One incident that received international attention and forced the Japanese authorities to pay more attention to stowaways involved the postal ship *Fushiki Maru*. When the ship reached Hong Kong on 26 March 1890 twelve stowaways were found in a locked, blood-spattered coal bunker. Being locked in for at least two days, eight had apparently died of asphyxiation, while four were barely alive. One of the dead was a male trafficker named Aburaya. The four survivors filed a report with the port authorities in Nagasaki, which is now in the Foreign Ministry archives. They claimed that the trafficker Aburaya lured them on board with promises of riches in Hong Kong. He forced the women to dress as coal coolies (*sekitan ku-ri-*), and when they descended into the bowels of the ship they were shut deep into a coal bunker. The day after they entered the bunker the steel door was locked tight, and the entire compartment became an oven, being adjacent to the firebox and group of furnaces. As the temperature climbed steadily, seven women and Aburaya went into convulsions and bled from the nose as they suffocated (FMA, "Collections of Improper Business," vol. 1).

There are several cases documented by ships' captains and now in the Foreign Ministry archives of women taking matters into their own hands. Katō Hisakatsu reported one incident that took place en route from Nagasaki to Hong Kong: "When my engineer went to investigate the loss of pressure in a water pipe, he discovered a group of girls, who, in the last stage of dehydration, had chewed a hole in the pipe to get water. Buried under the coal beside them were the brutally hacked bodies of their kidnappers, on whom the girls had taken a horrible revenge as what they thought were their last hours approached" (1924, 33). In a second incident four Japanese women appeared at the police headquarters in Singapore on 25 September 1892 to report the death of a Japanese male who fell overboard en route from Hong Kong. The women, all recent arrivals from Nagasaki, claimed that they hadn't known the man before boarding the ship in Hong Kong (FMA, "Matters of Improper Business," vol. 1, case 37).

These and other examples go some way toward depicting the ontological ferocity of the kidnapped women. However, scholars don't agree on the degree of complicity and agency of the women in the kidnapping.

Among the several Japanese scholars who have addressed this, the feminist Morisaki Kazue (1976) stands out by refusing to downplay the desire of the women to escape poor home situations and therefore contribute later on with frequent remittances made from sex work. Although I respect Morisaki's position, I believe it makes more sense to follow Mori Katsumi's and Yamazaki Tomoko's (1999) estimate that approximately 90 percent of the women were kidnapped and stowed away largely against their will. In each case the traffickers preyed on and grotesqued the women's desire for something different, distorting the desire for a "something else" as a desire for "everything else" the women ever wanted: freedom, excitement, and pride at remitting money to their indigent families. Moreover, the family was sometimes given some kind of payment by the procurers, both as an inducement to their daughter's obedience and as a form of hush money so they wouldn't inform the police.

The subjectivity of the male trafficker needs to be seen as the production of a form of freed, laissez-faired life, a biopolitical production originating from the urgent needs for capital accumulation on the part of the Japanese state, combined with the new desires of poor Japanese men elicited by imperial opportunities in continental Asia. Japanese traffickers like Muraoka and Matsuo illustrate perfectly Rosa Luxemburg's hidden truth of the process of capital accumulation: that it can occur only through violent force, a necessarily grotesque and grotesqueing production. In the case of poor women in western Japan, a preexisting structure of seasonal and permanent migration existing from the fifteenth century (occasionally including migration for sex work in the biggest port city in Japan at that time, Nagasaki) was grotesqued almost beyond recognition by the formal subsumption of desiring immigrant labor under capitalism.

Marx argued that the new exploitation characteristic of formal subsumption, whereby capital directly confronts labor, could be seen most clearly in the colonies and peripheries of imperial powers. There the older structure of reliance on cultural supports and customary networks in the old country was severed. Although the worker was just as dependent on the capitalist, in the peripheries this "dependence must be created by artificial means" (1977, 937). In other words, a whole new (gendered) structure of domination and exploitation had to be constructed in Japan's imperial periphery. The subjectivity of the pimp and procurer arises from this need of capital to concoct new modes of subordination to it.

Thanks to the efforts of Muraoka Iheiji and other Japanese traffickers, the situation that Muraoka observed in Manchuria in 1887 was gradually reversed after the Russo-Japanese War of 1905. Slowly, Chinese men and women began working for *Japanese* human trafficking operations. A report in the *Manchuria Daily Newspaper* reveals that Chinese male and female couples were working for Japanese trafficking operations to bring women from Nagasaki to Manchuria, something that would have been impossible before Japan's colonial Guandong Lease (*MNNS*, 12 January 1915). These Japanese-controlled human trafficking enterprises also relied on Chinese men and women to procure *Chinese* women for their extensive operations in Northeast Asia, completely inverting the earlier pattern of Chinese merchants employing Japanese men to kidnap Japanese women (*MNNS*, 17 February 1908). Capitalist business as a continuation of war materialized by the new generation of Manchuria-based Japanese traffickers like Utsumi Iwao—many of whom had learned the ugly business from working with Muraoka (*MNNS*, 31 May 1910)—was expanding quickly thanks to the desiring production of this central biopolitical subjectivity, the peripheral pimp.

3

**EMPIRE IN
HYSTERICS**

Hysteria is often used to describe women's psychic character. Like the word "emotional" it is not at all insulting, rather it is a way of showing respect for the special characteristics of women.

KOREA REVIEW, JUNE 1916

These Japanese prostitutes travel all over the Asian continent, lose any sense of their home country [*bōkokuteki*], and fall tragically into hysteria.

SEOUL DAILY NEWS 16 MARCH 1923

In November and December 1919 the Seoul-based monthly *Korea Review* (*Chōsen Kōron*) began to actively promote a sister journal it had been planning for several years. Meant to address the needs and concerns of its women readers of Japanese, *Women's Continental World* promised features on the "new colonial woman" and the new governor general's psychiatric hospital in Seoul, and "tales of romance between Japanese and Koreans." In December 1919 the *Korea Review* previewed the last piece, promising an exposé on the shiny, modern facility filled with female sacrifices to Japan's colonial presence in Asia. One Japanese patient was said to be afflicted with "severe hysteria" (*mōretsu na histeri-*), with symptoms running to insomnia and acute delusion, including thinking that she was really Korean.[1]

Colonizer men oscillated between praising Japanese women for their crucial contributions to empire and condemning them for being too independent, and masculine ambivalence was reflected in the metaphors used to describe colonizer women. They often coded women as wandering birds who had "left the nest of Japan." Depending on whether their hatching process had been successful, the women were destined to be either imperial success stories or fall into a life of drugs, lesbianism, and sex work. Whether or not they succeeded in becoming heroines of Japan's empire, they were ultimately characterized as ornithic wanderers (*rurō*), drifters (*nagaremono*), and *rōnin*, lordless women warriors who had escaped the nest (*sudachi*). Both the *Manchuria Daily Newspaper* and the *Korea Review* regularly published articles that, to a great extent, praised these women. For example, a six-part series in the former called simply "Leaving the Nest" describes Arata Suhako as a young, beautiful, unmarried hair salon owner who was a "model for Japanese capitalism in North China" (*MNNS*, 27 March 1924). Motohashi Shizuko, a professional pianist who performed regularly in Dalian concerts and bars, was also "beautiful, unmarried and carefree": "This prominent member of Manchuria's music world *left the nest* as soon as possible" (*MNNS*, 6 April 1924, emphasis added). However, the same series included a narrative about an unnamed, attractive college graduate who didn't want to settle down to a boring life as a mother in Japan, so she went off to northeast Asia with high hopes, only to end up in Dalian's red-light district. The article concludes with the warning "There is no way to predict whether a young woman is ready to leave the nest or not." But one thing is clear: the colonies hold out both opportunity and danger (*MNNS*, 10 April 1924). The opening of the governor general's psychiatric hospital in Seoul in 1919 is the terminus of sorts to twenty-five years of imperial ambivalence about how to adjudicate the slippage between opportunity and danger, because after 1920 the women who were unable to take proper advantage of the opportunities afforded them were routinely profiled as "hysterics."

The subjectivization of colonizer women as "hysterics"—the more modern and sexological coding for ornithic wanderer—mattered women's bodies. Unlike the biopolitical subjectivization of coolies and pimps, this profiling as hysteric often condemned and confined women inside Japan while biopolitically freeing them in the colonial periphery. This peripheral liberation, however, lasted only until 1920. The recurrent exposés in the *Korea Review* on the hysterics incarcerated at the new psychiatric hospital suggest that by the early 1920s imperial sexology consistently stigmatized single, colonizer women as insufficiently Japanese owing to an excess of intimacy with colonized Koreans, Chinese, and Russians. The cure for these women in Korea became in-patient confinement, as it was inside Japan. During the preceding three decades the cure for these same symptoms of assertive independence and proximity to non-Japanese alterity was adamantly out-patient. Although "hysteria" wasn't common parlance in Japanese before 1920, these same essentialized female traits were affirmed during the first decades of Japan's empire in Asia. Whether as sex workers, small businesswomen, or wanderlusting "Asian drifters" (*tairiku rōnin*), they were praised as indispensable agents in extending Japan's imperialism. (This is why pimping them, despite being "ugly business," was countenanced and even supported.) "In a very real sense," Barbara Brooks writes, "Japanese sex workers and women in the 'entertainment' business were the pioneers of this frontier" (2005, 300).

Like Minakata Kumagusu's privileging of *hentai* over *kokutai*, Michel Foucault distinguishes the imperialistic "deployment of sexuality" from the conservative inner circle "regime of family alliance." The deployment of sexuality inducing Japan's imperialism featured a vast system of commercial sex as its axis, building on the patriotic profiteering of pimps and human traffickers. Japan's colonial periphery was allegorized as a permissively utopian Garden of Eden, where Japanese males could transact for sex with "Chinese, Korean, Japanese, and Russian Eves" free from sin or responsibility of any kind (*CK*, "Four Segments on Colonial Women," March 1916, 84–92). The colonial monthlies *Korea Review* and *Korea and Manchuria* functioned as free advertising for the commercial sex industry by publishing feature stories on brothels, replete with pictures of sex workers. The *Manchuria Daily Newspaper* ran a monthly column called "Using the Red-Light District" that featured advice on Dalian's restaurants and brothels where Russian, Chinese, and Japanese sex workers could be purchased on the cheap. The male colonizer could heed the recommendation of the advertisements in this paper for more "rewarding sex with medically examined prostitutes" (*MNNS*, 19 March 1924) without suffering the social stigma against commercial sex that was intensifying inside Japan.

Anecdotal evidence of the size and scope of Japan's sex industry outside of the newspapers and colonial monthlies has been available for some time in the diaries of male Japanese colonizers. The private diaries of a Japanese schoolteacher in Korea, composed from 1922 to 1930, provide confirmation of the extent of sexual consumerism. Even with Christian and socialist influences in his family, Jōkō Beijirō admits to monthly and occasionally weekly trips to brothels to buy the bodies of Korean and Japanese women, with the visits continuing sporadically after his marriage to a fellow Japanese schoolteacher (*Jōkō Beijirō nikki*, vols. 22, 34).[2]

The central element in Japanese imperialism's deployment of sexuality in Asia was an extensive system of licensing Japanese women and girls as prostitutes to work in the new treaty ports in East Asia. This system was energetically supported by both Japan and the Euro-American powers. Gotō Shinpei's "enlightened" colonial apparatus in the Guandong Lease immediately moved to establish a licensed prostitution system similar to the much smaller one installed in Taiwan in 1897, collecting much needed taxes on the brothels, and fees for each sex worker registered (Song 1998). Biopolitical "life principles" clearly meant letting the good times roll for men of means in Asia. Gotō the hygienist, and colonial sexologists in general, excited these consumer desires (by naturalizing them as "biological elements") and then garnered crucial revenue by profiting from them.

The feminist historian Fujime Yuki has shown how the modern Japanese state was sustained by the expansion in sex work beginning in the 1870s. She points to the fact that the system of licensed prostitution established inside Japan after the opening of the treaty ports in the 1860s was a continuation of the system used in the seventeenth and eighteenth century in Japan's cities. Fujime claims that this early modern system was interrupted and reconfigured by new global demand led by British and Russian soldiers and Chinese merchants. When combined with the Japanese state's desire to extract surplus from these sources, brothel owners were forced to interface directly with state power in ways they hadn't before. The newly linked prostitution system provided tax revenues directly to national and local governments, monies that often spelled the difference between red and black budgets for administrations newly expected to finance hospitals, police forces, and armies. After the Russian and British navies demanded medical examinations of Japanese women sex workers in Nagasaki and Yokohama in the 1860s, examinations became compulsory for Japanese sex workers globally, providing their pimps and brothel owners with a substantial competitive advantage (Fujime 1995, 1999).

Fujime has also exposed the deceit of the early Meiji state, which showed a more wholesome face to erotophobic Christian imperialists and a more biopolitically hygienic face to erotophilic European sailors and merchants demanding physician-inspected Japanese women for

purchase. The government passed several pieces of legislation ostensibly designed to regulate sex workers: the Order to Free Prostitutes in
1872, legislation passed later in 1872 called the Regulations Concerning
Brothels and Prostitutes, and the Criminal Code for Prostitutes in 1876.
As a response to criticism from Christian missionaries who accompanied
rowdy sailors and merchants into the new Japanese treaty ports, these
regulations allowed the Japanese government to deny that human trafficking continued to occur in Japan. However, appropriating some of
the Christian rhetoric, the new laws permitted prostitution (now legally
codified as "the shameful occupation") as a mode of poverty relief,
based on the "free will" of the sex worker. Fujime concludes:

> The 1872 Order to Free Prostitutes ostensibly abolished human traf-
> ficking. Nevertheless, the subsequent legislation of the 1872 Regula-
> tions Concerning Brothels and Prostitutes created a loophole through
> which such trafficking was permitted if it was based on the free will
> of the prostitute. In 1902, the Japanese Supreme Court recognized
> prostitutes' right to leave brothels. At the same time however, it also
> legislated prostitutes' obligations to repay all outstanding debts, vali-
> dating the pretext of free will. Legally, even though women were free
> to leave brothels, those with no other livelihood could only continue
> working as prostitutes. The illusion which held that, since prostitu-
> tion was based on free will all prostitutes thereby chose to be prosti-
> tutes, became the foundation for the modern Japanese state's under-
> standing of prostitution. (quoted in Fujime 1997, 140; translation
> modified)

The civil codes of modern Japan insisted that wills, like markets, remain free. And as free will was the ground for modern subjects, the
freely chosen occupation expressed the essence of the person. In other
words, the state was legislating essentialism as part of the production of
biopolitical subjectivity. This allowed the Japanese state to hide the material reasons for women becoming sex workers, reasons that have everything to do with capitalism and military imperialism. Heavy tax burdens
on farmers led directly to young daughters being sent off to brothels,
which in turn led to higher tax revenues for the state and higher profits
for brothel owners. Furthermore, the demand for brothels increased as
Japan's military grew exponentially beginning in the 1880s.[3] In other
words, it's only half correct to privilege Japanese women as the pio-

neers of imperialism in Asia, as this ignores the systemic elements of biopolitical capitalism and militarism that made such pioneering much more than a choice freely made by young women. Sex workers were constituted and grotesqued by the imperial state almost as much as they were constituent, productive forces of it. In both sex workers and Chinese coolies the minimum requirements for the formal subsumption of labor under capital are present and accounted for: labor is "freed" from the means of its self-reproduction and wealth is "liberated" to become capital and search for the highest returns.

As in the case of Chinese labor, capitalism produced the subjectivities of coolie laborer and colonizer employer on the model of Marx's two fundamental subjectivities of free laborer and capitalist. The abstract similarity between poor Japanese women and Chinese immigrant labor nevertheless conceals a differently formed subjectivity. The regime of biopolitical production took the freeing of poor women's living labor and turned it into an essentialized psychological profile and subjectivity. We saw in the case of destitute Chinese labor how biopolitics took some of these same predicates of hysteria—drifting, homelessness, lack of culture—and subjectivized the coolie as subdued, subjugated, and manipulable. The profiling of Japanese sex workers in Asia as liberated, exuberant, and desiring-productive led to a quite different subjectivization. In their case, subjectivizing them as wandering, severed from home and haven, and willing to engage in sex for money—*on the loose* in every sense—was both cause and effect of their being coded as hysterics.

The subjectivization of hysteria by colonial doctors and sexologists (Tanaka Kōgai, Mori Tsūyoshi), colonial gossip columnists (Ishimori Sei'ichi), and later on in the colonial novels of Yuasa Katsuei and other writers, was caused by the presence of Japanese sex workers (*karayuki-san, geisha, shōgi, joshigun*) as the crucial first wave in Japan's imperial expansion into the Asian continent. However, these male writers frequently conflated sex workers with the equally unprecedented presence of economically independent and unmarried Japanese women in the colonial cities.[4] In so doing they codified deployable misogynist descriptions such as the "poisoned woman in Asia" (*tairiku dokufu*), the "Seoul hussy" (*Keijō bakuren*), and the "Dalian wormy snob" (*Dairen mushi*). By 1920 *hysteric* could be utilized to depict any unmarried Japanese woman living semi-permanently in continental Asia.

Imperialism as Women's Business

Unlike in any other colonial encounter, there were equal numbers of Japanese colonizer men and women in the cities of Korea and Northeast China. This historical uniqueness led to the popular understanding that Japan's empire was "women's business." Compared to men in the colonial periphery, Japanese women were found to be "better at languages, business, and the management of empire" (*MNNS*, 16 October 1921).[5] Their myriad contributions included working as judges, lawyers, bankers, police officers, and detectives.

Although Euro-Americans visiting Japan's colonial territories were shocked to witness the large numbers of women in positions of authority (*KN*, 14 March 1923) and even in more familiar occupations, Japanese colonizer women were considered by male imperialists to be unusually independent and erotically sovereign. So much so that in Dalian and Seoul they were said to be capable of managing multiple husbands and lovers (*MNNS*, 18 November 1920) or of refusing relations with men altogether (*CK*, April 1914).[6] Until the late 1920s colonizer women were assisted in their goal of being independent from men by the establishment of women-only credit unions in the cities of Fengtian and Dalian founded by nouveau riche (*narikin*) hairdressers, nurses, and sex workers (*MNNS*, 1 and 4 February 1920). The economic and political clout of women colonizers led some at the time to suggest that modern Japanese feminism received its major stimulus not from Euro-American first-wave feminism, but from the example of independent Japanese women living in the periphery of empire (*MNNS*, 17 May 1918; *KN*, 6 June 1923).

It should go without saying that the celebratory male discourse of Japanese women being the pioneers of imperialism contained a conflicted ambivalence, and a consequential double bind overdetermined Japanese women's lives on the Asian continent. On the one hand, they were expected to carry out all of the affective and reproductive labor of empire in conversation groups and language exchanges with colonized women and men, as schoolteachers and nurses, through women-operated and -owned small businesses catering to Korean and Chinese women, doing sex work, and more.[7] On the other hand, by performing this labor they ran the risk of being profiled as a hysteric for becoming "too Korean" or "too Chinese." So while the onus of carrying out the colonial policy of assimilation (*dōka*) was placed on Japanese women's shoulders, there was a constant danger that these same women would be accused of losing their Japaneseness when they became too much like, and too intimate with, the Asian colonized. Gotō Shinpei's immunological modernity required a proper balance of Asian pathogens in the Japanese body; too much and the imperial immune system crashes.

Binarized against a detached and discriminating male agency of colonial elites and businessmen, Japanese women living in continental Asia were said to be susceptible and suggestible, a contagious sponge for things non-Japanese. When women were identified with hysterical traits, their absent moral agency was considered the cause: they "caught" or "contracted" their desires and identities indiscriminately from the place of the Asian other (Fuss 1995, 107–40). Therefore, in the colonies, what Judith Butler calls the "girling of the girl" induced proto-hysterical Japanese women to interact more intimately with the colonized, positively fulfilling the everyday requirements of colonial assimilation (1993, 7). But at the same time, this impossible double bind exposed Japanese women to the hysteria profile written by male officials that included the negative quality of being anti-Japanese, a judgment that often contained the power to confine them in psychiatric institutions or, what was sometimes worse, married and in lockdown inside patriarchal homes in Japan.

The etiology of hysteria in modern Japanese sexology consolidated the coding of women who had been robbed of their will and who were morally and psychologically defenseless when faced with alterity. The editor of the important sexology journal *Abnormal Psychology*, Nakamura Kokyo, recorded cases of hysterics who became adept in Korean, French, and Chinese, without any prior exposure to those languages, while they were patients in his clinic for hysterics at Chiba University (1930, 17–19, 31). Nakamura quickly became the most respected expert on hysteria in Japan and published often on the phenomenon in the mass-culture women's magazines. His series of articles on hysteria appeared in *House Wife's Friend* from 1929 to 1931 and were collected as a book in 1932. As the most influential work done on hysteria before the Second World War, they warrant a closer look.

Nakamura begins by claiming that hysteria is not innate (*sententeki*) and that it is only in rare cases that hysteria is caused by the psychosomatic particularity of women (1932, 1–2). Yet nowhere does he discuss concretely any cases of male hysteria. He asserts (as he does through-out his writings) that the cause of hysteria is for the most part capital-ist modernity itself, chiefly "the frequent contact with unknown people and the speed with which this occurs" (3). From this analysis of the modern world he recapitulates sexological gynophobia: "Hysterics mix up their own desires with the desire of the other. . . . This confusion of desires is said to be close to the liberal feelings of sympathy, empathy, and gratitude. But actually, these liberal feelings are internally narcis-sistic, while the hysteric is characterized by an external narcissism or affirmative narcissism [*sekkyokuteki jikochūshinshugi*]" (4).

The second section of *The Treatment of Hysteria* (*Hisuteri- no ryōhō*) outlines the symptoms of hysteria, beginning with "sudden shifts in at-tention from self to other, and from excessive love to profound hate" (Nakamura K. 1932, 7). Although it was first seen as a cause, Nakamura also ascribes the second symptom to narcissism: "Hysterics are always trying to attract other people's attention, and this need explains their rapid transition phase where they adopt the desire of others, internal-ize that, and then imagine it to be their own" (7). The fact that hysterics quickly sense when their immediate surroundings do not affirmatively mirror them means that they will search for ways to be loved in new en-vironments. Thus "they are prone to fall in love too easily and become erotically indulgent" (8). Nakamura ends this introduction by claiming that this fundamental form of hysteria is characterized by "1. curiosity; 2. vanity; and 3. mimesis [*mohōsei*]," leading hysterics to inevitably mix up "fantasy and reality" (8–9).

Although this is the most measured in tone of the accounts of hys-teria by Japanese male authors of the period,[8] the central thematics of drifting, susceptibility to alterity, ability to mime other languages and customs, and hypersexualization are consistent with other work on hys-teria done inside Japan in the 1920s. That body of work almost always connected its denigration of female sexuality to the emerging urban subjectivities of the "new woman" (*atarashii onna*) and the "modern girl" (*moga*). This kind of stigmatization was consistent inside Japan and by 1930 was articulated to a defense of traditional "Japanese culture." These same signifieds of hysteria—wandering, contagious susceptibility to the other's language and culture, being oversexed and hyperindepen-dent yet lacking in moral and subjective agency—were articulated to a different regime of power in the colonial periphery, with dramatically different effects. Although I've pointed to some gender-specific tension surrounding the designation of hysteria in the colonial periphery, there is a surprising absence of overt gynophobia when compared to the texts published inside Japan. It is to those differently inflected colonial texts that we'll now turn.

Contact and Contagion

Hysteria was *the* description of single Japanese colonizer women. Its widespread use to describe Japanese women living in continental Asia suggests the need to reframe the standard understanding of the representations of women in Japanese sexology and psychiatry within a larger context of colonial empire. Again, the cure for bourgeois hysterics inside Japan was rest and relaxation through confinement to the home or hospital (Nakamura K. 1932, 134–42); in the colonies this was reversed. This is because working-class and peasant women were both encouraged and forced to leave their hometowns to brave biopolitical capitalism and colonialism in the outer circle.

Mori Tsūyoshi, the head psychiatrist at the Governor-General's Hospital in Seoul from 1914 to 1918, and later in charge of all patients at the new Seoul psychiatric hospital, wrote frequently for the *Korea Review* on hysteria as an effect of colonizer women's displacement from Japan. In a two-part series published in September and October 1916 he identified hysteria as the "disease of modern civilization" (*CK*, September 1916, 148–50) and the primary effect of the increasing demands, both psychic and physical, caused by modern development. First he criticizes European sexology's essentialism (in part because more recent advances suggested that hysteria strikes men as easily as women [148]), which he dismisses as focusing ludicrously on wandering wombs and oversexed women. Here, we are presented with a confident tone dismissive of European sexology, and one that refuses a biological reading of hysteria. The first installment gives a history of previous interpretations and claims that in the Japanese colonies hysteria is actually something quite different from European pseudo-scientific conceptions.

In part 2 of the essay "The Symptoms and Treatment of Hysteria," he implies that standard hysterical symptoms define the psychic and material situation of Japanese colonial *women*, who suddenly become the privileged object of his colonial psychiatric power-knowledge (*CK*, October 1916, 132–36). In this essay Mori presents the classic description of hysteria as a double bind, whereby women are represented as alternately being in *excess of* and *lacking in* male normative psychosomatic qualities (cognitive reason, sexual restraint, emotional distance, physical strength, etc.). The causes of this are given as the "modern conditions of psychic shock, displacement, restlessness, and drifting"— in other words, "the social conditions of most women" in the colonies (132). Mori opines that to a nonspecialist these women probably seem like the "fiercely independent and socially rebellious type . . . who don't like to take orders from anyone" (133). He reports that these Japanese women are, in fact, everywhere in colonized Korea, but instead of seeing them as "strong, difficult and independent women," as most male imperialists do, they are actually quite vulnerable and require medical attention.

Mori's analysis situates hysteria in part as specific to working women in colonial capitalism. As most of the Japanese women who went to Asia were peasants and from the lower class, they were constantly struggling to make ends meet. Taking advantage of the easier access to capital and business opportunities available to colonizers, a great number of these women opened small businesses or did social and sex work. This, of course, required a proximity to Koreans, Chinese, and Southeast Asians that few men experienced and resulted in friendships, relationships, and marriages.

Again, colonizer men were markedly conflicted about women's proximity to the Asian other. For example, in a *Korea Review* feature of March 1916 a group of male doctors and pundits discuss their views on "colonial women" (*CK*, March 1916, 85–92). All the men agree that there are lots of beautiful and powerful Japanese women living in Korea and Manchuria, and they echo each other (hysterically) in contrasting these dynamic and productive colonial women against the passive women living inside Japan (87). One of the writers cites the colonial common sense that Japanese imperial expansion on the Asian continent would frankly be impossible without them (88). But the effects of the separation from the homeland have produced both an erotic "looseness" (*hōshō*) and a general moral laxity. Furthermore, these women tend to "treat men as playthings" (89). Yet while the women seem solely interested in their own pleasure and profit, they also seem to pick up their own "personal" desires from wherever they are. Moreover, the hunt for pleasure and profit necessitates close commercial contacts, friendships, and erotic relations with Chinese and Koreans. Because of their nature as simultaneously "selfish," "susceptible" (*dōka sareru*), and "sympathetic," they are "perfect to carry out our colonial policy of assimilation."[9] But the male panelists fear that as these Japanese women advance Japan's mission in Asia, they could get lost and "assimilated" to the "colonial feeling" (87) that so easily seduces women cut off from the homeland. One man wonders out loud, "Although there have been many success stories . . . isn't it easy to see that the colonies are leading these women down a path of tragic ruin [*chinrin*]?" and "Shouldn't something be done to cure this hysteria?" (91, 90).

Here's the double bind in clear ideological terms: the colonial condition reproduces hysteria, and at the same time hysteria supports, augments, and intensifies Japan's colonial imperialism. Hysterics sympathize with and are susceptible to the colonized other, creating crucial links and mediations between male colonizers and colonized. But because of the contagiousness of hysteria, Japanese hysterics quickly become indistinguishable from the colonized other, something colonizer males perceive as dangerous. The "sympathy, suggestibility, and selfishness" of colonizer hysterics is perceived as creating a parallel structure of colonial power, one much more effectively "assimilationist" than the differently gendered top-down structure of colonial subordination. However, because it exists separate from paternal authority, the unpredictability of the parallel structure of horizontal power eliciting the contagiousness of hysteria can get out of control and become threatening to male colonizer hierarchies.[10]

The *Korea Review*'s popular exposé of colonial life, "Strange, Uncanny Illusions That Appear and Disappear" (*CK*, "Kiki kaikai hengen shutsubotsusen," September 1913), often featured investigative articles about hysterics by its author, Ishimori Sei'ichi. Following the older genre of the tabloid-like *tsuzukimono* (sensationalized serial narrative), the long three-part feature published in summer 1914 profiles several femmes fatales (*kidai dokufu*) who evidently "left the nest" too early.[11] The feature expresses a psychosexual ambivalence typical of Japanese colonizer men. On the one hand, Ishimori seems fascinated and seduced by these women, but on the other, he derides them as pathetic victims of colonialism, similar to the psychoanalytic analysis of the projection of male castration anxiety onto the iconic figure of the independent woman (Doane 1989). Ishimori writes that he is both "scared out of his wits [*dogimo o nuita*]" and sexually aroused (*kōkotsu*) at the prospect of investigating these "sexy, mysterious women . . . parking themselves wherever they wish all over Korea and Manchuria" (*CK*, June 1914, 115).

He investigates one woman referred to only as the "gold-toothed turtle" (*kinba no okame*), who had come to the colonial periphery ten years before and quickly won "business contacts in Korea and China" (*CK*, June 1914, 116). She was apparently involved in various moneymaking schemes, such as counterfeiting (*gizō*), blackmailing, and swindling activities connected to money laundering. Her sex appeal—seducing Russians, Chinese, Koreans, and Japanese alike—was said to be inseparable from her ability to work effectively with bankers and commercial capitalists (116). She had worked these connections into her own small empire, allowing her such unspeakable luxuries as automobiles, a cache of firearms (118), and paying pretty, young male gigolos (Japanese and Korean) for attention when and where she wanted it (117). She is rumored to have shot people in bars, and Ishimori claims to have personally witnessed her target practice with pistols (118). This combination of violence and seductiveness makes her a feared competitor in the gambling parlors of Seoul and Pusan.

While Ishimori makes his way around Seoul (Keijō), and later Dalian, he provides readers with a detailed ethnography of Japan's prized colonial cities. In Seoul his investigation introduces readers to the black market underworld of colonial corruption, with Chinese warlords and Japanese swindlers involved in all-night gambling and drinking parties. These players are ushered around Seoul by women cab drivers and exhibit an open disdain toward both the Korean municipal police and the Japanese colonial gendarmes. In Dalian Japanese are in a fierce turf battle with local Chinese and Russian underworld criminals. Ishimori depicts structures of identification and desire that evoke an astonishing degree of fluidity between colonizer and colonized. The investigation narrates instances of Japanese women paying for sex with colonized men; Japanese women who prefer "darker men" (*CK*, July 1914, 112); and, obsessed by these women, Japanese men who phantasmatically project a world of female omnipotence in the imperial periphery. Here, the overpowering presence of the woman Ishimori calls the "hysterical gold-toothed turtle" reshuffles ethnoracial hierarchies. Her darker boyfriends include Chinese, Korean, and Japanese,[12] and they are similarly binarized against her white makeup and pale skin. She's caught teasing her boyfriends by making them put dirty mud on their faces to high-light their lack of refinement, although Ishimori quips that they weren't exactly "sentimental types [*kanshōteki*]" who "liked poetry and things like that to begin with" (111). Her blackface minstrel suitors weren't sentimental types, for sure, but they were still helplessly in thrall to her.

A June 1916 essay from *Korea Review* titled "What Are Men Looking For in Women?" asserts that, unlike inside Japan (*naichi*), in the colonies women who are "independent, unpredictable, and deeply involved with the colonized" are considered very attractive: "If this is called 'hysteria' then that should be something that is respected, not despised" (78). The male writer continues by claiming that "so-called hysteria appears to be an essential ingredient [*jūyō na yōso*] of colonial development" (79). A May 1913 article from the same journal depicts a "hysterical" woman who had come to the colonies and wound up becoming involved in illegal financial schemes. Describing her as a "hussy" (*haku-ren*) and a "new woman"—narcissistic, with short hair, and as masculine as any man—the writer invokes a stream of sexological adjectives to code her as "wandering" and "drifting." He concludes that when this kind of hysterical woman comes to the colonies from Japan, she will either get rich in business or end up in a brothel (112).

The double bind of fallen brothel girl or elevated businesswoman intensifies the related double bind of being compelled to associate intimately with Koreans and Chinese and, because of this interactivity, running the constant risk of being abjected for it. What's important is that in both the first and second double bind, the either/or effects follow from a single cause: the biopolitical subjectivization of hysteria. Whether hysteria resulted in a particular woman becoming a shrewd and successful businesswoman or destined her for a life inside a brothel, both were seen as contributing to Japan's imperialism. Regardless of the opposed ways imperial men morally coded these effects, they overwhelmingly concurred that both the "civilized business" (*jigyō*) of market consolidation and the "ugly business" (*shūgyō*) of prostitution and human trafficking were essential for Japan's advance in Asia.

Colonial Sexology Comes Home

Along with Habuto Eiji and Sawada Junjirō, Tanaka Kōgai (1874–1944) is considered one of the central sexologists of Taishō (1912–26) Japan. Tanaka began his influential sexology journal *Modern Sexuality* (*Hentai*

Seiyoku) in 1921, and along with the longer versions of his arguments published annually in his books, he quickly became one of the main sources of popular information on hysteria, S/M, and autoeroticism in Japan.[13] Beginning in 1929 he wrote exclusively metapsychological essays on the history of sexuality which took up themes such as the intermarriage between colonizer Japanese and colonized East Asians, the East Asian tradition of powerful and intense women he called "female supremacism" (*josei yūetsushugi*), and histories of Japanese vampirism, S/M, ESP, and cannibalism. His intellectual investment in these issues can be explained in part by his tenure in colonial Taipei as the doctor in charge of Taiwanese students in hygiene from 1897 until 1900 or 1901, where he worked under Gotō Shinpei. His return to Japan didn't interrupt his lifelong advocacy of Japanese colonial imperial policies he learned from his boss, including that Japanese ethnoracial formation is a composite concoction of several Asian elements and that Japanese colonialists must be skilled enough in biopolitics to respect local "life principles" while improving them through the imposition of hygienic practices and scientific infrastructure. Like almost every male Japanese official during the first three decades of the twentieth century, Tanaka was adamant that respecting life principles in East Asia meant celebrating and modernizing the grand Japanese tradition of commercial sex. As a Japanese elite working in colonial Taiwan, this meant enthusiastic support for its licensed prostitution system.

Paralleling the essentialization of sex workers inside Japan beginning in the 1870s, hysteria was frequently linked with sex work, and the men initially responsible for that linkage were the sexologists and doctors working in the colonial peripheries. I've already referenced some of the writings of Mori Tsuyoshi, the main Japanese neurologist working in colonized Korea, but to my mind the doctor most responsible for coding Japanese sex workers in Asia as hysterics was Tanaka Kōgai. Although very little of Tanaka's writings survive from his years working in the Taiwan colony, he would emerge as a major popular sexologist inside Japan after the First World War.

Like the chief physician of the Japanese army, Mori Rintarō, Tanaka was a persistent critic of European sexology and what he called its "Christian moralizing." In his popular text *Women and Passion* (*Josei to aiyoku*), published in 1923, Tanaka began his long discussion of prostitution (*baishō seidō*) with a stinging critique of Krafft-Ebing's famous de-

Imperial hybridity. A composite of the seven Asian ethnoracial donors to the Japanese phenotypical face. From the popular science magazine *Kagaku Gahō*, December 1927.

日本人の顔

近代日本人を構成するところの要素的人種は此處に掲げたる七人種である。寫眞はその代表的な顔である。（１）はアイヌ、（２）はネグリト、（３）はビルマ地方に住むインドネシヤ族、（４）はモンゴリヤ族、（５）はマレイ族、（６）は原住民のツングース族、（７）は支那人（ペイ）である。後者以上七人種の正面寫眞を合はせて作った人種の顔。これを近代日本人の典型的な顔と見てからう。次頁に載るものはその擴大顔にして西村眞次氏の日本人相の顔について見らるゝ。尚此寫眞も西村氏の發案であることを附記して置く。

nunciation of sex work as the "thorough poisoning of civilization" (271). Rather than classifying sex work as erotophobic abjection, Tanaka contends that a regulated system of prostitution has supported every major empire in world history, and Japan's should be no different. He argues that even the origin of the Christian empire defended by Germans like Krafft-Ebing can be traced back to a system of prostitution (296), and that Jesus Christ himself hired sex workers. According to Tanaka, this proves the "hypocrisy of Christian countries" all over the world that have the nerve to "curse Japan as the number one country in the world for prostitution" (292). In so doing, Europeans perpetuate a "deluded sense of the animalistic sexual instinct [*honnō*] of humans" and a distorted view of "the erotic drives, that in their increasingly incited state, are largely the products of modern culture" (308, 297). Because "behind all humans are drives that can't be repressed," he claims that "the more the state attempts to silence these drives, the wilder they'll become" (304). He finds proof of this in his historical reading of the unsuccessful attempts to eliminate sex work in ancient Rome and Syria and in early modern Japan with the Tempo Reforms. In finally refusing the repressive hypothesis (whose calculus holds that the level of civilized development depends on an equivalent level of sexual repression), Tanaka calls for the "scientific management of the sex drive," claiming that without erotic pleasure there can be no "joy in life" and therefore no hope for "modern civilization."

In a popular text of 1925, *Sex Maniacs* (*Aiyoku ni kurū chijin*), Tanaka provides an overview to his thinking on hysteria and sex work, a culmination of some two decades of research on the subject undertaken both in Taiwan and during one research year in Germany. The first three chapters of *Sex Maniacs* deal with the "difficult question" of the kind of women who do sex work. Tanaka claims he has "no reservations at all" about promoting licensed prostitution. This is owing to his medico-philosophical belief that human eroticism is not mainly about reproduction and because he thinks sex work serves several functions in advanced capitalist societies: "Regardless of the fact that modern society despises sex workers, they generate lots of revenue for businesses while they satisfy the sexual urges of young men" (7). As in all of his texts published in the 1920s, Tanaka is openly critical of monogamous marriage, claiming that it is structurally unable to satisfy the sexual desire of all men and some women. He grants a certain social role to marriage in raising children, but because of his commitment to critiquing the Euro-centric repressive hypothesis, his main concern is to investigate how Japan's empire might be structured to take into account fundamental anthropological truisms with regard to sexuality.

Tanaka is no different from other Japanese sexologists in privileging male heterosexual desire. But since his work is so concerned with de-stigmatizing sex work, he devotes the first two chapters of *Sex Maniacs* to rationalizing how licensed prostitution might not be such a bad thing for women. He concedes that the vast majority of women become sex workers for "socioeconomic" reasons. Modern capitalism causes huge discrepancies in wealth and poor families often have no other option than to send one of their daughters off to work in a brothel. Further-more, in Japan there is the problem of kidnappers who prey on young innocent girls and send them abroad like chattel slaves (1925, 36–37). These are all "external" reasons for women turning to sex work. Tanaka prefaces his discussion of "internal" (*naiteki*) reasons with the caveat that the "assumption that prostitutes become prostitutes because that simply is their nature" is an unfortunate "bias of modern society." He nevertheless thinks there are some women who are "innate prostitutes" (*sententeki baishōfu*). This kind of woman is sexually insatiable, he writes, and has a psychosomatic need for daily sexual contact with mul-tiple men. In other words, this type suffers from "classic nymphomania" (22–23). Furthermore, their restless and insatiable qualities are "similar to the condition called hysteria": "With hysteria or nymphomania it is impossible for women to be satisfied psycho-sexually with one husband. Because of her extremely high sex drive, this kind of woman is forced to leave the house daily in order to find sexual satisfaction" (23).

Even though he doesn't frankly advocate the career choice of sex worker for the hysterical nymphomania type, he strongly implies that the brothel is her ideal home. Moreover, although Tanaka states twice that "there is nothing pathological with women possessing a strong sex drive," in his chapter titled "Innate Prostitution" he cites several sur-veys of brothels to make the argument that 30 percent of sex workers suffer from "pathological" (*byōteki*) nymphomania and hysteria (1925, 36–37). In other words, although a healthy sex drive is simply a modern condition for many women, when this condition becomes demonstrably pathological, under hygienically biopolitical conditions the brothel is as good a place to shelter mentally ill hysterico-nymphomaniacs as any other. He advises that these women will be doing the kind of service work necessary to maintain a more enlightened, non-Christian civilization. The brothel is therefore offered as a more progressive option for serious hysterics than the psychiatric hospital (39).

Although Tanaka pays some attention to women's eroticism in two of his texts (unfortunately his most detailed account of female masturbation and orgasm was completely censored in *The Shadowy Aspects of Human Sexuality* [*Ningen no seiteki ankokumen*, 1922]), for the most part his obsession with women's erotic power doesn't translate into much concern with the physiology of women's pleasure. His most sustained discussion of "female sexuality" is in *Women and Passion* (1923). Predictably, half of the text takes up the theme of female hysteria. He leads into the long discussion of hysteria with two points: the first is his pronouncement that men and women are "democratically" aroused through the stimulation of erogenous zones (*hatsujōtai*; 11); the second is his concern to oppose this kind of unbiased "scientific" discussion of hormones and erogenous zones to popular misconceptions of women's physical and emotional weakness, many of which originated in European sexology: "It's erroneous to regard women's sexuality as weaker than men's" (10–11). Then he dedicates the next ten pages of *Women and Passion* to clarifying the fact that there is no direct relation between women's reproductive function and sexual desire: "Even among women forty-five and fifty years old, sexual desire remains very high. . . . Even where there is no reproductive capability there is an excess of sexual desire" (15, 18). He goes so far as to demonstrate that marriage is debilitating for women's erotic lives and that unmarried women have better sex lives: "Most women feel nothing at all sexually towards their husbands" (23). He explains that the "dreadful situation" of marriage best explains the recent rise in nymphomania, whereby frustrated wives end up visiting male sex workers, called *ryokan no bōi*, and frequently carry out acts of "perverse sex" (*tōsaku seiyoku*).

Despite the fact that Tanaka's work features a strong opposition to the erotophobia and misogyny of European sexology, it's clear that this antagonism serves mainly to establish Japan's non-Christian deployment of sexuality as more modern, scientific and enlightened. Beginning with the forced and free emigration of Japanese women to China and Southeast Asia in the 1880s and 1890s to work in the sex business, followed by the consolidation of licensed prostitution in Japan's colonies in Taiwan, Korea, and Manchuria, the sexological discourse of hysteria in Japanese was mobilized to justify the massive imperialistic deployment of sexuality. In the colonial periphery, lacking the *kokutai* regime of alliance discourse of "good wives, wise mothers" to act as the opposite pole to hysteria, the depiction of hysterical women as rebellious, nonreproductive, and economically and erotically independent from men contributed to the partial valorization and even role-model status for such Japanese women living in the Asian continent. The purported emotional instability and hypersensitivity of hysteria were not infrequently valorized as conditions that were paradoxically perfect for the shifting emotional state that facilitated "sympathetic identification with the colonized" (*KN*, 8 September 1921) and therefore was recognized as a positive contribution to Japan's imperialism.

4

STUBBORN FARMERS AND GROTESQUED KOREA

Whether it's intentional or not, the Oriental Development Company is frankly sucking blood.

KOREA AND MANCHURIA, JUNE 1912

The theft of Korean land by Japanese capitalists was so widespread and occurred on such a large scale within such a short period of time that it was without historical precedent.

KIM YONG-SOP, "THE LANDLORD SYSTEM AND THE AGRICULTURAL ECONOMY DURING THE JAPANESE OCCUPATION PERIOD"

The expropriation of the direct producers was accomplished by means of the most merciless barbarism, and under the stimulus of the most infamous and odious of passions.

KARL MARX, *CAPITAL*, VOLUME 1

Colonialism is not a thinking machine, nor a body endowed with reasoning faculties. It is violence in its natural state, and it will only yield when confronted with greater violence.

FRANTZ FANON, *THE WRETCHED OF THE EARTH*

Karate Kids

Most Japanese imperialists had personal experience with what they called "stubborn Koreans" (*futei senjin*), although each dealt with them in their own class-specific ways. For example, in the early 1880s Japanese thug merchants (*tekiya*) used their martial arts skills to physically force Koreans into buying shoddy Japanese goods. With group protection offered by their *ikka* (gangster clan) bosses and by the Japanese consulates, these market machos were the first Japanese capitalists to penetrate into Korean rural areas after the Treaty of Kanghwa in 1876 allowed Japanese free trade into Korean ports. They were quickly joined by human and drug traffickers and sex workers. After gaining full access into the Korean countryside in 1885, hustling and laissez-faire-ing Japanese set up chambers of commerce to collectively pressure the consulates and politicians back home to provide more protection and, therefore, easier profiteering (Takasaki 2002). The Japanese consulates were usually eager to support almost everything their merchants were doing, but they drew the line at the credit scams that Japanese predator lenders (*bakuto*) were forcing on defenseless Korean farmers. In the early 1890s the consulates were unwilling to defend financial fraud, concerned as they were with legitimizing Japanese merchant hegemony over Korean and Chinese merchants (Kimura 1989, 95–97). But in addition to their tacit approval of Japanese using judo against "stubborn Koreans," imperial consulates publicly supported a large group of arms-wielding Japanese merchants called the Keirin Shōgyōdan, who threatened at gunpoint Koreans in the countryside refusing to pay top dollar for their cheap goods and bogus sex enhancement pills. In the face of widespread Korean protest, the Japanese government was forced to step in and dissolve the group in 1898, when the consulates refused to act (Uchida J. 2005, 39).

When martial arts meet market artifice we come across an apt illustration of Rosa Luxemburg's insistence that capitalism always "employs force as a permanent weapon." Capital accumulation itself is the quintessential martial art. Japanese merchants resumed their activities in full force after Japan's victory in the major war with Qing China in 1895 won for it not only the Taiwan colony, but the bigger prize of banishing Chinese merchants from Korea. Not only were the Japanese consulates unwilling to restrain Keirin Shōgyōdan and other practitioners of business as a continuation of war by other means, but they began relaxing their earlier restrictions against credit scams. Older techniques of extra-economic force like judo and karate were now being joined to modern forms of expropriation like credit baiting and financial fraud (*kakeuri*). With the arrival of the new century, Karate Kid colonizers were replacing their *dōjō* martial arts clothes for the British suits of respectable imperialists and morphing into capitalist creditors and legal landlords.

Unsettling Settlers

The first generation of Japanese settlers in Korea resembled Muraoka Iheiji, poor hustlers biopolitically deconfined to fare for themselves in the new treaty ports in East Asia. As the Meiji government had designs on Korea from the beginning, imperial elites were disappointed that the only Japanese eager to settle in Korea after 1876 were disreputable carpetbaggers, traffickers, and scam artists. Still, elites did everything in their power to attract hardworking farmers to contribute to one of their main rationalizations for imperialism: the development of Korean agriculture. The Japanese government secured land for agricultural settlers as close as possible to Korean treaty ports and then made a concerted effort to provide free passports to Japanese farmers. Authorities also moved to preempt the migration of hustlers and other followers of the Japanese capitalist code of "making a quick buck and instant success [*ikakku senkin*]" when they issued the Regulations Concerning Japanese in China and Korea in 1883, which facilitated the deportation back to Japan of undesirable hustlers. However, as Kimura Kenji points out, new laws passed in Tokyo did nothing to stem the tide of unsettling settlers into Korea, where all Japanese newcomers were embraced by the consulates (1989, 24–25).

The appearance of Japanese landlords outside the treaty ports began after 1885, when Karate Kids and predator lenders claimed Korean land as collateral against outstanding debts. Taking full advantage of the "usurer-friendly" imperial milieu, Japanese accumulated capital by running up interest rates for Japanese products so high that former Korean landowners ended up as tenant farmers. With increasing frequency after the Sino-Japanese War, many Japanese hustlers became rich absentee landlords (Uchida J. 2005, 35). The situation continued right up until Japan's victory in the Russo-Japanese War of 1905, when Korea became a protectorate of Japan. With many calling for outright colonial annexation of Korea, imperial elites got serious about a systematic policy of increasing agricultural settlers from rural Japan. At that time most Japanese settlers looked down on Japanese tilling Korean soil as derisively as eighteenth-century British imperialists did their own settler countrymen, calling them lowly "earth scratchers" (Williams 1944, 4).

In February 1907 Katsura Tarō, former governor general of Taiwan and three-time prime minister, began to flesh out the idea for a financial enterprise to help agricultural settlers emigrate to Korea. Since the end of the Russo-Japanese War in Manchuria, Katsura had grown increasingly frustrated with the military's insistence on playing the central role in colonial governance. Military expenditures were draining too much of Japan's domestic resources, he thought, and in the colonial empire military men tended to downplay the importance of business and hard work. This attitude was hampering Japan's ability to profit from its new territories; what was needed was a renewed emphasis on commercial and human capital. After all, once the military had brutally crushed the resistance in Taiwan and was sidelined there after 1898, Japan's colonial program had proven wildly successful. Wouldn't it be wise to copy and paste this proven Kodama-Gotō program onto Japan's next colonial endeavors in Manchuria and Korea?

Katsura presented his ideas to the general meeting of the main policy group for Japan's imperialism, the Taiwan Society (Taiwan Kyōkai). Speaking in front of the central imperial dramatis personae—resident general of Korea and former prime minister Itō Hirobumi, Army Minister Terauchi Masatake, and SMR president Gotō Shinpei—he revisited the previous decade of successful activities sponsored by the Taiwan Society. Congratulating his audience for their support of business and professional training of colonial officials at the Society's school in Tokyo, Katsura invited his listeners to imagine the riches awaiting them if these same programs were downloaded for use in Northeast Asia. While Chinese coolies were working long hours building the infrastructure for Japan's colony in southern Manchuria, Katsura began the crucial redirection of attention with what Jacques Lacan called the "labor of the signifier" and henceforth changed the name of the group to the Oriental Society, Tōyō Kyōkai (Yamane 1976, 201–2; Lone 2000, 140).

The Society immediately began implementing some of its ideas. They were able to open a second school in Seoul in October 1907, fulfilling a huge demand for Korean-speaking Japanese officials and businessmen. A smaller school was set up in Port Arthur, Manchuria, and a fourth, larger school opened in Dalian in 1910. Regardless of its sterling accomplishments in Taiwan, Katsura and Gotō thought the Society could do much more on the Asian continent. After all, despite salient military and business successes, hardworking Japanese nationals who could potentially be modernizing role models to subaltern Koreans were still largely unwilling to migrate. As a financial and propaganda vehicle to encourage them to do so, the Oriental Development Company (Tōyō takushoku kabushiki kaisha, ODC) was conceived.

Britain's East India Company was put forward as the model for the ODC, as it had been two years earlier in the case of the SMR (Kimijima 1973, 41).[1] No one seemed concerned with the apparent contradiction of setting up an emigration assistance agency on the model of an extractive colonial enterprise, which was what the East India Company essentially was. Sure enough, after the Korean resident general Itō Hirobumi expressed strong reservations about large-scale Japanese agricultural settlements in Korea, when the charter of the ODC was approved by the Japanese Diet in March 1908 the company's focus was split between extracting profits and assisting groups of Japanese farmers wishing to settle in Korea.

This tension between profit taking and people placing became the fundamental aporia in Japan's colonialism, particularly in Korea. The ODC morphed in just two years from being the agency responsible for settling Japanese farmers in Korea into one of the largest landlords in East Asia. They were the directorate responsible for, in Kim Yong-sop's phrase, the massive theft of Korean land. Although scholars have tended to represent the ODC's activities in terms of bureaucratic incompetence in a time of crisis (Duus 1995; Kurose 2003), I have identified an ontological desire that drove imperial capitalism to grotesque in historically specific ways. In Korea, anticolonial resistance waylaid the plans for a large settlement of Japanese farmers and instead powered a shift in colonial policy that greatly pleased Japanese investors and land-grabbing capitalists.

The dramatically altered political landscape after the Russo-Japanese War provided initial support to the Katsura-Kodama-Gotō emphasis on immediate Japanese migration to Korea and Manchuria, where colonizers were needed to fill the spaces of Japan's newfound strategic advantage. While Kodama wanted five hundred thousand settlers sent to Manchuria to discourage the Russian military from starting another war, Gotō envisioned Japanese farmers instilling sound business sense into "backward" Chinese Manchurians and Koreans. By the fall of 1908 the Japanese government had adopted a policy of "channeling overseas migration to Manchuria and Korea [*Man-Chō imin shūchūron*]." However, impediments on the ground in Korea would prevent this from ever taking place.

In May 1907 Komatsubara Eitarō, the secretary general of the Oriental Society, toured Korea to investigate the possibility of promoting Korean agricultural development by settling Japanese farmers among Koreans. His findings did not bode well for the policy of channeling migration to Korea. Komatsubara reiterated the common view that the treaty restrictions made it difficult for Japanese to buy land, but he also noted forebodingly that those Japanese who had been able to purchase land demonstrated no interest in developing it; they were quite happy just to live off rent extracted from Korean tenants. As he surveyed the endemic corruption of Japanese merchants and the parasitism of Japanese landlords, he was dismayed that the colonization of Korea had gotten off to such a bad start. He urged both colonizers and officials to get with the program, keeping in mind that Japan's goal remained "the improvement of agricultural development, which will deepen the existing amity between the Japanese and Korean people" (Duus 1995, 305).

Desiring Decolonization

Despite seeing the warning signs, Komatsubara and other ODC officials were confounded by news of the first major Korean uprising against Japan's occupation after they returned to Tokyo in the spring of 1907. That guerrilla offensive stretched on until February 1909, intensifying in the summers of 1907 and 1908. The ODC plans to flood Korea with Japanese farmers would be a casualty of this first flush of militant Korean anticolonialism. The organized and resilient resistance shocked Japanese military elites, smug in their sense of superiority after the thrashing of Russia in 1905. The uprising itself has been depicted in detail elsewhere (Kim C. 1967; Kang C. and Iinuma 1982; Shin 1991); here my emphasis is on the ways this anticolonial desire drove Japan's imperialism to assume more complicated forms of political capture and surplus extraction. In chapter 1, I showed how the grotesqueing of the desiring production of Chinese immigrants led to the widespread use of cheap labor and the shunning of immigrant Japanese workers for the purposes of rapid capital accumulation. In Japan's largest colony, the ontological force of decolonization similarly induced the transformation of the ODC into a monstrous, vampiric landlord of Korean tenants, as the Japanese monthly *Korea and Manchuria* decried in the epigraph to this chapter.

From the moment the ODC began operations, capitalists in Japan and in Korea denounced it. The free trade advocates at the *Tokyo Economic*

Magazine (*Tōkyō keizai zasshi*) were philosophically uncomfortable with government meddling in markets and consistently attacked the SMR and the ODC on these grounds. By the spring of 1910, when it was evident that the ODC was dragging its feet on settling Japanese farmers in Korea, the editors blamed the lack of trust in market forces and absence of business acumen. The management of the ODC was, according to the magazine, "the primary reason for their failures": "It is run by military men and bureaucrats" (16 April 1910, 648).[2]

Mainly consisting of indefatigable, amoral merchants who had managed to carve out market access in Korea since 1876, the bloated ODC was also castigated by the Japanese business community in Korea. The business community's interests were embedded in many colonial publications; one of them was the popular Seoul-based monthly *Korea and Manchuria* (*Chōsen oyobi Manshū*). From the time it started publishing in 1908 its writers denounced the ODC operation. In a two-part series introducing the corporate leaders of the company, a staff writer with the nom de plume "Himalayan mountain man" ("Himaraya yamabito") writes, "Although there sure has been lots of hype about the ODC, nobody involved in the company is actually doing anything. As far as this reporter is concerned, this is a worthless and wasteful [*mui munō*] operation. . . . The only concrete evidence of 'development' anyone can find here is in the name of the company" (January 1910, 80–81). When the writer introduces us to ODC corporate leaders the descriptions are acidic. The first president, Usagawa Kazumasa, is said to be "surprisingly incompetent for someone with thirty years experience in the Army. Vice-President Yoshihara is basically a horrible man. Beginning with Usagawa and moving down the corporate ladder, they are all addicted to their big money salaries" (81, 84). In the second part of the installment the reporter expands on the class differences among Japanese settlers and the corporate military types at the ODC: "Different from all the regular Japanese in Korea hustling just to make an honest buck, these ODC fools like Usagawa and Yoshihara don't have anything like the typical settler mentality—they really do live in their own world. I'm very suspicious about the claim that these people are the so-called 'heroes of Korean development'" (*COM*, March 1910, 60–62).

The other main colonial monthly in Korea, *Korea Review*, was connected to the governor general's office and couldn't afford to be as openly critical as *Korea and Manchuria*. But even it felt compelled to address the widespread frustration toward the perceived "failures" of the ODC. The theme of its May 1913 issue was "the present state of disorder at the ODC," and after praising the SMR and the ODC as corporate beacons for Japanese imperialism in Asia, the reporter admitted, "The recent focus of the company's business operations is betraying the people's expectations of what the mission of the ODC was designed to be. As everyone understands, their primary mission is to bring Japanese agriculturalists to Korea. Our most important objective in colonizing Korea is assimilation, and without settlers this won't happen" (May 1913, 2–3). After prefacing their critique by asking Japanese colonizers to lower their expectations somewhat, two pages later the editors tackle the ODC's failures head-on. Confronting the company leadership with the charge that it is "disregarding the great immigration plan it was designed to carry out," they claim that the ODC has regrettably "proven itself a disgrace to the colonial mission": "We can only speculate on the various reasons for this, but the work of immigration assistance involves dealing with people. Unfortunately, the company leadership is drawn mainly from the military and banking" (5).

In several portraits like these of the ODC, there is a strong bias against militarists being involved in business. Although the Japanese army was praised for its great successes on the battlefield, it was regarded by the public as unreasonably dismissive of merchant and finance capital. From the time the ODC set up its corporate headquarters in Seoul in January 1909, Usagawa's five-year tenure as CEO with thirty years of experience in the army was shadowed by this sentiment. The ODC was disregarding its mission of "directing migration to Korea" and, consequently, must not be doing anything at all.

Grotesqued Korea

The fact is that the ODC was anything but inactive during its first few years. Moreover, there's a strong consensus in the scholarly literature on exactly what the ODC was doing, becoming, in Karl Moscowitz's phrase, "Korea's largest tenant landlord" (1974, 3) although scholars disagree on why. The literature is consistent in depicting a dramatic ODC shift in the mode of colonial grotesque, from emphasizing Japanese settlement to focusing on the extraction of Korean surplus in the form of ground rent and interest-bearing capital. The effects of this reversal are well documented (Kang C. and Iinuma 1982; Weiner 1994; Kurose

2003). Most important was the fact that Korean tenancy increased dramatically. The colonial governor general's land survey concluded in 1918 showed that 40 percent of Koreans had no land holdings at all; when you include those who owned tiny plots while renting the larger part of the land they worked, this figure increases to 55 percent. Although there is considerable debate on the numbers, most scholars agree that by 1930 the Japanese governor general eventually became the owner of approximately 55 percent of all land in Korea. The second important effect was the de facto abandonment of the immigration policy and resignation to a situation whereby absentee Japanese overlords would reside in urban areas and live comfortably off their extractive enterprises, leaving the countryside to Korean renters and pro-Japanese landlords. Connected to this was the shift in the understanding of what Japanese agricultural settlers would be doing, if the ODC was to sponsor any at all. The most detailed proposal drafted in late 1907 projected 10,000 immigrants during the first year of operations, 20,000 the second year, 30,000 the third year, and 10,000 each year after that. In 1908 Noda Utarō of the Oriental Society told a Japanese Diet committee that by 1920 the total number of Japanese agriculturalists would be between 350,000 and 500,000 (Aoyagi 1923, 659).

However, in 1911, out of a mere 1,235 applications for emigration, 160 were accepted by the ODC. By 1920 only 3,921 ODC-sponsored farmers were settled in Korea. In 1914 the same Noda, now ODC vice president, told a reporter that his company didn't feel any need to respond to criticisms about the supposed "failure" of the ODC's operations. The only constituency they were beholden to, he stated coldly, was the ODC stockholders; if dividends weren't plentiful, stockholders would invest their money elsewhere. Noda conceded that promoting emigration to Korea was an important activity, but it just wasn't profitable enough for the ODC stockholders: "In a newly developed territory like Korea, the first principle is, above all, to produce a return on investment. . . . If profits are not greater than at home, then Korea will never develop" (cited in Duus, 301).

A Korean scholar working on the ODC's failed immigration program has identified the reasons for the shift as having much more to do with Koreans' antagonism toward being colonized and their desire for freedom. Kim Hyun-kil notes that the sustained, everyday hostility of Koreans toward the Japanese colonizers doomed the dreams of Japanese agricultural settlement from the beginning (1971, 73). The ODC was not the first official sponsor of agricultural settlers; the first took place in 1907–8, before the ODC even had a name. The negative reports from these attempted settlements would have been difficult to ignore (Aoyagi 1923, 668–72). When the Japanese settlers weren't being physically attacked, they were ostracized by the Koreans living in the villages they had only recently given up everything back in Japan to settle in. This forced a rethinking of the assimilation strategy in Korean agricultural villages as groups of Japanese settlers were transferred from predominantly Korean villages into areas closer to Japanese army and police bases, or to urban enclaves. There are vivid portraits of this in the colonial press.[3]

In May 1912 two reporters for the *Seoul Daily Report* conducted interviews with ODC-sponsored settlers in different parts of the country, published on 21 and 22 June; selections came out first in *Korea and Manchuria* in an article called "Visiting the ODC Settlers." The Japanese settlers provide testimonials to their "miserable" lives. They speak of living in constant fear of their Korean neighbors and describe their relationship with the ODC in unflattering terms, referring to it as the "cold-hearted ODC [*Tōtaku no reitan*]." The reporters brag that this will be the first opportunity for Japanese readers to discover the real deal about the settlers' lives, in testimony not screened by the "pretty rhetoric" handed out by the ODC spokespeople in Seoul, lies that are "almost the exact opposite of the truth" (*COM*, 15 June 1921, 13). The settlers live in clusters of five to seven Japanese families isolated spatially and linguistically from the Korean farmers. They complain that the houses they live in are no better than animal shelters, that the property taxes are much higher than in Japan, and that the stubborn Koreans actively refuse any of the "tutoring" (*shidō*) in modern agriculture techniques that these Japanese insisted they came to Korea to provide (14). Several of the Japanese families admit that they just gave up on farming and started renting out their large farms to Korean tenants, becoming landlords just like the ODC. They tell the reporters that they don't consider this shift from farmer to landlord anything particularly "underhanded" (*kanshudan*), but when it is time to collect the annual taxes there are major conflicts with the Koreans, who "simply refuse to pay." The piece ends with several settlers relating their frustration both at the Koreans and at the ODC. One settler complains that the ODC is making money off them from the 5 percent interest collected on most of the settlers' mortgages and doesn't do anything at all for this profit—just like a bank (14).

There's a peculiar doubling of the situation of the Japanese settlers with that of the ODC: not being able to make enough profit to justify a huge move to Korea in the case of the settlers, and the ODC's not being able to satisfy the demands of the stock portfolios of their investors, they both abandoned the modernizing and civilizing mission and turned to explicitly expropriating land and living labor from Koreans. Aoyagi Tsunatarō's descriptions of Japanese settlers undertaking this shift reflects some of the same ambivalence palpable in the interviews in the *Seoul Daily Report*, wherein settlers felt the need to point out that there was nothing sleazy in their having become landlords; they were just trying to make an honest buck and doing what they could to survive in a harsh, alienating colony (Aoyagi 1923, 33–37). The Japanese settlers felt more secure financially and psychically within the contours of a legal and contractual relationship of landlord and tenant. Of course, these contracts were nothing more than what Marx called "legalized robbery," handing the landlords between 45 and 75 percent of their total crop. Korean tenants often ended up paying three-fourths of their production to landlords because of the new tenancy policies installed by the ODC, whereby agreements were made before actual crop harvests. Some estimates of rates paid under ODC landlords were as high as 90 percent.[4] Obviously when the rate of exploitation ran as high as it did, Korean tenants were often forced to turn to Japanese banks or Korean and Japanese loan sharks; the cumulative effect of this was to ensnare them even more inextricably in the grasp of imperial capitalism. Tragically, with indebtedness constantly threatening half of Korean farmers, some were forced to sell off their daughters to brothels or send their sons to Japan to find work; occasionally entire Korean families became enslaved to Japanese landlords (Kim Hyun-kil 1971, 104).

Of course, many resisted the Japanese occupation, taking up arms in guerilla movements or conducting covert acts of sabotage. Militant subaltern resistance is always undertaken for multiple reasons, but interrogation reports of captured Righteous Army guerillas reveal a common motivating factor: rid Korea of the invaders intent on pillaging its common resources and profiting from the sweat of its laborers (Kim 1967, vol. 1). When asked why he was risking his life, the thirty-two-year-old Kang Sa-mun responded that Japanese officials were illegally running the Korean government and stealing "Korean forests, rivers, and land for themselves" (Duus 1995, 226). Korean rebels even managed to communicate their focused indignation in Japanese army propaganda like *A History of Our Subjugation of the Korean Riots* (*Chōsen bōto tōbatsushi*) (Chōsen Chōsatsugun Shireibu 1913). It shouldn't be surprising that none of the captured rebels appear to have been persuaded by Japan's claim that the invasion of the peninsula was undertaken benevolently to develop, civilize, and modernize Korea; rather, they seemed to believe, in the words of Marx from this chapter's epigraph, that capitalist colonization "was accomplished by means of the most merciless barbarism, and under the stimulus of the most infamous and odious of passions" (1977, 928).

It might be useful to return to Foucault's notion of biopolitics here to help us configure both the large-scale immiseration of Koreans and the desperation that impelled some to wage guerilla war against Japanese machine guns and modern artillery with pistols, swords, and their bare hands. It is axiomatic that colonial biopolitics improved the lives (*faire vivir*) of many poor Japanese settlers after they were laissez-faired to emigrate to Korea, some of whom then withdrew from their agricultural villages into the cities to live comfortably off extractive rents as landlords. It is also evident that the lives of the Japanese stockholders and managers of the ODC were enriched as a result of the land grabs and property takeovers that produced, on the colonized side, what Ken Kawashima calls the "breakdown of social relations in the Korean villages" (2009, 26–27). In detailing the desperation of Korean peasants who "increasingly became a floating, rural population with nothing but its capacity to work as its only remaining, sellable commodity" (27), anti-colonial scholars like Kawashima and Kim insist that we not neglect the other half of Foucault's biopolitical command: *laisser mourir*, or let them (Koreans) die. Although Japanese colonizers tried to buy off a select minority of Korean aristocrats with "improved lives," the overwhelming effect of colonial biopolitics in Korea after the brutal subjugation of the various righteous armies in 1909 was to enhance the lives of the Japanese colonizers while laissez-faire-ing colonized Koreans and depleting bodies, often to the point of death (laisser mourir), for many peasants. Space allows only two corroborating examples. Insong Gill has confirmed that Japan's endeavors in Korea not only provided more sustenance and enhanced lives for Japanese (especially from 1920, when the colonial government transferred most of Korea's rice production to Japan, eventually supplying it with 40 percent of its demand), but that colonizer profiteering actually started to eat away at Korean bodies. Gill uses anthropometric data to show how, simultaneous with the improved lives of Japanese, Korean bodies actually began to shrink in the mid-1920s because of the reduced intake of calories beginning with Japan's occupation (1998, 124–26). What Chung Young-Iob calls after reviewing the data the "absolute decrease in food consumption by Koreans under Japanese rule" resulted in Koreans only regaining their pre-1910 height in the 1960s (2006, 291).

The second example is that of declining real income for wage laborers. When the relatively small group of urban professionals is factored out, there was an actual decline of waged income over the colonial period, to that of 87 percent of the 1910 base. Although wages rose 3 percent on average each year, inflation rates wiped out these gains. In contrast to the shrinking real wages, annual labor productivity gains of 7 percent fed right into the profit columns of Japanese businesses, many of which made 30 to 40 percent profits each year (Chung 2006, 276–80). As the colonized floating population of un- and under-employed increased each year, the surplus labor market joined hands with ethnic discrimination to hold wages down, while Korean desperation and repressive colonizer labor management drove labor productivity up—Japanese lives were improved in a direct biopolitical economy with the laisser mouriring of Koreans.

It shouldn't be controversial to point out that the military leaders responsible for policy decisions at the ODC in its first years had arguably the most informed understanding of the anti-Japanese movement in Korea in 1907 and 1908. Some of the closest confidants of the ODC president Usagawa had direct experience in counterinsurgency operations. Rather than maligning them as military men constitutionally lacking in business sense, as the Japanese press did, I want to underline the fact that the military had arguably the best grasp on the security environment in Korea and the violent hostility directed against Japanese settlers. The civilian leaders were still operating on the basis of the old strategy of encouraging immigration established in 1907 and could only react to the deteriorating situation with lies and propaganda. The reality was that Koreans were beginning to understand, in Fanon's words, that the "colonized can only find freedom in and through violence," and a reclaimed "life can only spring up again out of the rotting corpse of the settler" (1968, 86, 93).

The militant anti-Japanese resistance began in the spring of 1907 and ended in late 1908 or early 1909, after several of the guerrilla leaders were arrested (Iwanami Koza 1992). The ODC set up its corporate office in Seoul in January 1909 and began preliminary investigations about the best way to move ahead with settling Japanese farmers in Korean villages all over the country. However, the ODC was not greeted with a gradually improving security environment. Instead, the army reports and the colonial press reveal a resistance that was diversifying and expressing militant opposition to the Japanese occupation in more ways than before. Although the armed guerrilla opposition led by the Korean Righteous Army (Ŭibyŏng) had been largely defeated, the frequency of what Japanese called "mob" (*bōto*) resistance against imperial rule held steady throughout 1909. In response Japan's frustrated military launched a scorched-earth campaign against the remnants of the Righteous Army in Chōlla province in October 1909, known as the *Namhan Daetobul*, or "crackdown on the South." Reading the Japanese army and press reports of the Korean resistance, the ODC must have been alarmed to discover how multifaceted that resistance was.

In response to the organized resistance against the new Seoul-Pusan railroad, the newspaper *Seoul Report* (*Keijō Shimpō*) began reporting monthly on the damages caused by the Korean "mob." Citing police briefs, it revealed that levels of resistance held steady from the end of January 1909 until the beginning of May ("Bōto shutsubōchi higai ichiran," 11, 12, and 27 May 1909). One month later the newspaper expressed some surprise that the capture of key guerrilla leaders didn't result in any relaxation of militant resistance against Japanese rule (26 June 1909). In fact, nonguerrillas started to become more engaged in militant activities, as when five hundred dispossessed tenant farmers staged a demonstration at a Japanese military police (*kempeitai*) station in Seoul, threatening to burn down the building if their grievances weren't addressed (*Keijō Shimpō*, 8 July 1909). Months later, in its Sunday editorial of 31 October, *Seoul Report* called for an immediate and ruthless crackdown against Koreans. Claiming that the "system of peace and security" was in danger of breaking apart irreparably, the editors stated, "We aren't surprised that Westerners and Koreans lack the dignity and grace of our Japanese citizens, . . . [but we didn't expect] anything like the reactionary, stubborn violence that is endemic in today's Korean countryside. . . . Not only are the riots against our Empire not decreasing, they are clearly expanding."

Formal Subsumption of Desire to Colonial Capital

The subjectivization of Korean peasants as hot-headed and stubbornly clinging to their feudal past is standard colonial discourse. Although there is a longer history of the production of Koreanness in this way by Japan's rule,[5] the consolidation of this subjectivization happened in the first years of the protectorate (1905–10). One facet of a brutal counterinsurgency designed to wipe out a transforming Korean resistance was to see Koreans as everything Chinese coolies were not: unjustifiably proud, violent, and stubbornly holding on to their proud past. Given the production of Koreanness in these terms, imperial rule responded by imposing an order of "proper place" (*taigi*), within which Koreans had to recognize two things: first, they shared a racial and cultural history with Japanese; second, the fact that Japan was the only non-Western country to have modernized successfully meant that Koreans must understand their subordinate status. Rather than being resentful, they should be grateful to have their Japanese brothers as their disciplinarians and teachers in the political arts of modern government and in the martial arts of modern capitalism.

Hardly an issue went by in either of the two Japanese-language monthlies based in Korea when the question wasn't asked: Can Koreans be assimilated into the Japanese Empire? *Korea and Manchuria* and the *Korea Review* differed on the best way to do this; the former thought contact between Japanese and Koreans should be kept to a minimum and abhorred the practice of mixed marriages (*sōgo kekkon*), while the *Korea Review* favored the earlier authoritarianism of military rule and in the 1920s became a cheerleader for mixed marriages between Japanese and Koreans. Yet they both realized that after the unexpectedly tenacious resistance to the first years of Japanese colonization, the tactics were going to have to be significantly altered.

The ODC leadership quickly adapted to the Korean resistance and grotesqued it. Dropping their plans for an expansive, modern overhaul of Korean agriculture directed by Japanese farmers, they decided to leave the framework of the Korean agricultural village basically intact. The path toward expropriating as much Korean surplus as possible led the ODC to impose what Marx called an "alien regime" of excessive rents and high-interest loans on the preexisting social structure of the Korean village. In Kim Hyun-kil's words, Japanese colonizers "studied Korean land . . . and working within the structure of the existing Korean government and village, [were] able to obtain a maximum of profit from investment" (1971, 7).

Formal subsumption to colonial capitalism in Korea therefore entailed the intensification of early modern power relations in the countryside, exploiting the nascent class antagonisms that had become visible in the late nineteenth century via the struggle by the traditional *yangban* aristocratic elite to maintain their landowning privileges against popular peasant movements (Matsumoto 1998, 25–26). According to Kim Yong-sop, "Feudal agricultural practices came to operate under capitalist management principles. . . . Therefore, the landlord-tenant system effectively functioned as an institution that greatly increased the landlords' and capitalists' exploitation of the peasantry in comparison with the past" (quoted in Pang and Shin 2005, 146). What the ODC did was channel the class antagonism that was already developing in the countryside into a colonial capitalist grotesqueing. As Asada Kyōji argued, relying implicitly on Marx's formal subsumption to frame his position, Japan's colonization turned an incipient class struggle in the countryside into a sharp colonizer-colonized structure of capitalist domination (1968, chapters 1 and 3). Bruce Cumings concludes that the continuing land grabs by deterritorializing Japanese settlers combined with the sudden land privatization legislated by the governor general in 1912 had the effect of concentrating "landownership in the hands of the few," a situation that left a miserable tenancy situation "with few parallels in the world" (1981, 43).

Again, it is important to see the two-headed monster grotesqueing Korea—consisting of the Oriental Development Company handling financial and biopolitical power through land surveys and the census, and the Japanese army, who garrisoned a threatening military throughout the colony—as basically responding after the fact to the desires of the Korean masses for independence and justice. Foucault's suggestion that "populations are aware of what they want, yet unaware of what is being done to them" illustrates this biopolitical tendency to grotesque Korea (2007, 105). But there was yet another, more complex grotesqueing. The deterritorializing desire of Japanese Karate Kids hijacked the modus operandi of the colonial state, where the corporate capitalist ODC eventually articulated the project of the lower-class Japanese settlers to their own hegemonic one, becoming in the end indistinguishable.

In the second decade of the twentieth century, as Japanese pharmaceutical companies were profiting handsomely by selling desperately needed morphine and heroine to the European powers fighting in the First World War, a new type of grotesqueing emerged in the colony. Although surplus morphine began appearing on the streets of Seoul and Pusan in 1916 and 1917, peddled by entrepreneurial Japanese, after the end of the war Japanese drug companies such as Taisho Seiyaku needed to find new markets for their profitable morphine product. So the governor general of Korea stepped in to supply the requisite "extra-economic force" to open new drug markets in the colony. In early 1919 they suddenly began to crack down on opium selling and smoking and legalized morphine sales and use. In a few short years, 100,000 Koreans were addicted to morphine, a tactic that served the dual purpose of pacifying and incapacitating the colonized while making huge profits for the colonizers (Kurahashi 2008, 24).[6]

A KOREAN IS BEING BEATEN;
I, A JAPANESE COLONIZER,
AM BEING BEATEN

The 1 March 1919 mobilization for Korean independence was the single largest threat to Japan's imperial rule in its half-century of existence. Referred to reverently in Korean as the Sam'il Undong (March 1st Movement), the protest was initially centered in Seoul but quickly spread into towns and villages. After ten years of brutal military colonial rule (*budan seiji*) that had seemed to pacify the Koreans, and after a decade of easy expropriation of surplus from Korean land, labor, and life, Japanese colonizers were caught off-guard by the mobilization. As they had ten years earlier during the brutal scorched-earth crackdown in the south, the Japanese army responded mercilessly, smashing the peaceful demonstrations, arresting up to forty thousand people, and killing an estimated seven thousand before the smoke cleared (Pak 1920; Kim 1967).

In reacting to the demonstrations, Japanese elites dusted off the imperial binaries (civilized/savage, rational/irrational) they had deployed earlier in Taiwan and Korea to dismiss the protests as "barbaric" (*yaban*) and "blindly reckless" (*CK*, April 1919, 4–8). A new phrase that signified the Koreans' unwillingness to accept Japan's civilizing mission was "ignorant people" (*gumin*). Gumin were not the same bratty children and wild savages that Japan had dealt with sternly and parentally in the first decade of the twentieth century; they were now grown adults who were stubbornly refusing to recognize the great sacrifices that Japan was making in trying to drag Korea into the modern world (33–34). After it was clear that the mobilization was going to be repressed by the Japanese military regardless of the damage to Japan's international image, the editors at the *Korea Review* began to home in on the real *gumin*: the male Korean ringleaders of the demonstrations. In their lead editorial of May 1919, "The Korean Riots and Improvements in the Governor General's Policies," the monthly profiled this recalcitrant male elite: "Although we wouldn't go so far as to call them modern, these intellectuals provided the ideas that led to the riots. Others participated because they felt truly threatened by this group. . . . The male intellectuals resorted to a kind of hypnotic, psychological crowd control. Before anyone with any sense could stop it, violent, illogical ideas were transmitted to otherwise good, law-abiding people [*ryōmin*]" (2–3). According to the *Korea Review*, this hypnotic idea was the Euro-American notion of "national self-determination." Originating in Europe, recently pitched by U.S. president Woodrow Wilson, and now uncritically parroted by Korean male intellectuals, it poisoned the otherwise decent, Japan-loving Koreans: "[National self-determination] has resulted in the type of theater of the absurd we witnessed here in Seoul. . . . It's the primary cause of all the troubles in our colony and is distracting Japanese from our sole reason for being in Korea—to guide and enlighten [*zendō kyōka*]. We need to refocus on this mission so the derivative, foreign ideas of the violence-prone Korean intellectuals no longer influence the good Koreans who recognize all the positive things that we've done for them" (3–4). The opinion pieces in the *Seoul Daily Report* also make clear that Japanese elites identified Korean women and children as those most in need of "rescue" from these deluded male intellectuals. The demonstrations themselves proved their point that Korean women, children, and illiterate men needed Japanese paternal protection and pedagogy more than ever (*KN*, 7 and 8 March 1919). Some colonizers even went so far as to justify the murderous repression of the peaceful mobilizations as necessary to "save [*kyūshutsu*] the good women of Korea from the uncivilized behavior of Korean men" (*KN*, 19 August 1919).

The panicked sense of disavowal in these colonial texts is easy to deconstruct. By all accounts, the independence demonstrations were orderly and peaceful, and it was generally agreed that violence was the exclusive prerogative of the *colonizer side* (Moriyama S. 1992). Daily pictures of the peaceful and orderly protests in Japan's colonial press during the demonstrations belie Japan's accusations that Korean male intellectuals called savagely for Japanese blood and that Korean men forced women to participate in the protests against their will. Moreover, it is well known that Korean women played crucial roles in the anti-Japanese movement,[1] which contributed to the beginning of the Korean women's movement. The fact that several thousand Koreans were murdered in the following month of "pacification" points to the real savagery in this encounter between colonizer and colonized. Nevertheless, because these texts spoke the common sense of Japan's imperialists, I want to pause and look at what they were doing. How can we account for this psychic operation of disavowal and inversion in the Japanese editorial, where Japanese repression and violence are substituted for male Korean violence, and the courage of the Korean women mobilizing against Japan's colonization is reversed and transformed into a desperate plea for help addressed to these same colonizers?

Gayatri Chakravorty Spivak identifies a similar structure of disavowal and inversion in nineteenth-century British colonialism in India. In what might be the most famous essay in colonial discourse analysis, "Can the Subaltern Speak?" (1988), she dismantles the British discourse on widow sacrifice (*sati*) in colonial India, arguing that the paternalism of British colonizer opposition to the tradition of widow sacrifice should be configured as "white men saving brown women from brown men" (297). Moreover, as she analyzes the ideological violence of imperial paternalism which insists on saving Indian women from brown male-controlled traditions, she provocatively suggests that this colonial discourse be networked with Sigmund Freud's analysis of the rather slippery sentence "A child is being beaten" (296). What I think Spivak is getting at with this leap is that the structure of the colonial address is homologous to the work of fantasy in Freudian theory.

In psychoanalytic theory fantasy emerges when an original object is displaced and lost to the subject and, later, is reproduced when a traumatic antagonism (such as unexpected protests against colonial occupation) threatens the subject. The psychological function of fantasy is to translate, reverse, and eroticize this traumatic antagonism that contains the power to annihilate the subject's psychic integrity. Fantasy dissimulates this trauma by substituting a "scene" of desire that allows a psychic recovery and rearticulation of threatening loss, albeit in a more reassuringly erotic way for the (male) subject. This mise-en-scène operates by ignoring the normal distinctions between subject, object, and verbal act of desire, so that the subject can appropriate and inhabit any of the positions of the fantasy.[2]

Freud's essay "A Child Is Being Beaten," published in 1919, the same year as the 1 March uprising, describes several of his patients' fantasies of a child being beaten, which under the pressure of analysis reveal three different identifications for each patient: (1) My father is beating the child whom I hate; (2) I am being beaten by my father; (3) A child is being beaten (Freud 1963). In their influential reading of this essay, Jean Laplanche and J.-B. Pontalis (1986) insist that fantasy doesn't entail an identification with a single position within the fantasy; rather, identification is distributed among the three positions of active, passive, and verbal action of the scene: "Fantasy is not the object of desire, but its setting. In fantasy the subject does not pursue the object or its sign; one appears oneself caught up in the sequence of images. . . . As a result, the subject, although always present in the fantasy, may be so in a desubjectivized form" (26). Fantasy thus is not something "possessed" by a subject, but is a place where the subject *becomes predicate* in the staging of the proliferation of identifications and desires. Slavoj Žižek argues that through its role of mediating between symbolic law and material objects "fantasy constitutes our desire, provides its co-ordinates; that is, it literally 'teaches us how to desire'" (1997, 7–8). Laplanche and Pontalis claim that fantasy "provides the possibility of experience" (1986, 24).

Laplanche and Pontalis follow Freud in identifying the psychic operation of fantasy as that which enables the subject to deal with external threats to its sense of sovereign integrity. Fantasy comes to dominate other psychic operations because only it can provide mechanisms to defend the subject against serious splitting and potential dissolution. These mechanisms include the attempt to receive the threat masochistically so as to generate pleasure from it; inverting the threat completely through projection and negation; voyeuristic third-person detachment; and, as I've already suggested, eroticizing the threat in a way that reassures the subject that the external threat is actually a misplaced appeal for love and recognition. From the psychic perspective of Japanese colonizers responding to the 1 March demonstrations, fantasy works to invert the anticolonial threat from the Korean independence movement by miraculously transforming anti-Japanese Koreans into those who really desire the Japanese presence. Spivak suggests that both the slippage between different positions (the logistics of fantasy) as well as "primary" defense reactions and reversals are similarly present in the "civilizing mission" rhetoric of British imperialism in India.

In Laplanchian and Lacanian theory, the mise-en-scène of sadomasochism (different from the erotic *practice*) has sometimes been privileged to dramatize these improbable reversals of power. In turn, the reversals of active and passive and colonizer and colonized that we saw earlier were not limited to crisis situations in Japan's imperial rule. Because of the ever-present threat to Japanese imperialists and the generalized lurking danger that characterized the daily experience of many Japanese living in the colonial periphery, these threats were managed phantasmatically in different ways. Beginning in the early 1920s the colonial newspapers were puzzled by sex scandals that involved bondage, role-playing, and S/M. A *Manchuria Daily Newspaper* column titled "Was It Just Another Pickpocket? Or Was It Perverse Sexual Obsession?" described an incident in which a bourgeois Japanese woman named Kadozaki Haruko was either the victim of a pickpocket at the upperclass Yamato Hotel or "involved in an erotic game of pickpocket sadist and victim masochist" (*MNNS*, 18 March 1924). Although it would be unusual for a common thief to have access to the well-policed Yamato, the article states that Kadozaki was apparently tied up by a thief who entered her room and stole her purse. The article also reported that Kadozaki was not fazed at all by the incident but "actually was in very good spirits," and hypothesized that it could just be another incident of sexual role-playing involving threatening robbers and helpless victims, games that "[had] become increasingly popular at the hotel." The *Seoul Daily Report* of 11 June 1922 investigated a similar incident of roleplaying involving light bondage and "play" of soldiers and victims, this time at the upper-class Chōsen Hotel in Seoul.

We've already looked briefly at some of the writings of the *Korea Review* tabloid journalist Ishimori Sei'ichi. Referred to as the most popular journalist in the colonies, Ishimori's texts are filled with elements of ideological fantasy that encode the seething contradictions in Japan's imperialism. First, Ishimori exemplifies the primary function of ideological fantasy, which allows the imperial self to identify with and imagine itself immunologically imbricated with various forms of alterity, grotesqueing them at the phantasmatic level. Ishimori was famous for using masquerade and drag to get at the "real stories" of colonial life. Some of the disguises he adopted (suggesting identifications with the individuals) were those of a North Chinese coolie in Dalian, an elderly Korean male drifter in Seoul, a Japanese sex worker in Seoul, a French detective tracking Russian criminals in Manchuria and Russia, an elderly Russian man in Dalian, and a poor Japanese migrant worker in Seoul, where the journalist puts on blackface (*kao ni kuroi de sumi*) to convince the locals that he is a lower-class Japanese (*CK*, August 1915, 150). Second, although he was an ardent supporter of Japan's bright "civilizing" presence in Korea and Manchuria, he delighted in showing its Janus face and reverse "dark side" (*ankokumen*). He promised to show readers the "dark underbelly" (151) of the new colonial world, a world where he claimed the "overworked bodies are weak, but the erotic appetites are strong" and where people behave like "sleazy characters in Russian novels" (January 1914, 122, 123). He boasted that he would show the "real people" of Seoul, Pusan, and Dalian in all their "decadent glory" and "immoral scenes right out of a Flaubert novel" (October 1913, 107). These real people of Japan's colonial imperialism included the liberals in the colonial bureaucracy who turn into "sex fiends" (*shikima*) and prey on women at night (September 1915, 111); destitute Chinese and Korean sex workers who are so bold that they will "have sex with you right in front of their parents for money" (August 1915, 114); the modern colonizer working women who insist on doing everything in a rejection of tradition (April 1914, 90); cross-dressing Japanese and Russian women sex workers (October 1915, 97); pretty-boy gigolos (*danshō*) whom colonizer women pay for sex (June 1914, 117); notorious Japanese poison women who catch in their mosquito nets "horny little devils" (*irogaki*) and masochists of Korean, Chinese, and Japanese heritage (July 1914, 109); and thrill-seeking Japanese youth (*tsūkaiji*) who become wretched (*santantaru*) sacrifices to the dark side of Japan's colonial cities (October 1913, 81). Third, Ishimori's serial feature, "Strange, Uncanny Illusions That Appear and Disappear," emphasized the hallucinogenic character of the colonial world (April 1914, 87; see also October 1914 and December 1913). The introduction to the installment of October 1914 insists that because the writer himself resorts to a kind of dream logic, readers should be encouraged in a similar way to let their "imaginations run wild."

In Ishimori's feature series the reader of Japanese is solicited to identify with a truly universal conglomeration of gendered and ethno-racial speaking subjects: French, Russian, Korean, Japanese, Chinese. The homology with the mise-en-scène of multiple and contradictory identities in ideological fantasy is obvious. However, as ideological fantasy

The Japanese investigative journalist Ishimori Seiichi undercover as a vagrant North Chinese coolie in Dalian, China; a Japanese sex worker in Seoul, Korea; and a middle-aged man in Pusan, Korea. From the Japanese colonial monthly *Korea Review*, January 1914 and August 1915.

is an eroticized response to something that threatens the subject with dissolution, Chinese and Koreans are the identities most often incorporated by Ishimori. The ideological role of fantasy here would be to cover over, transform, and substitute threats from the colonized. Or rather, ideological fantasy *eroticizes by grotesqueing* acts of subaltern antagonism. This eroticizing capacity of ideology should be understood as a grotesqueing *response,* a secondary and parasitic eroticization meant to confine and contest the ontological desire for freedom coming from colonized subjects. Ideological fantasy is beneficial for imperial subjectivity both because it works to contain explicit antagonism—allowing Japanese imperialists to continue believing that the Korean colonized desires them and their superior society—and because it expands the available identifications for imperial subjects, producing a truly universal set of identifications for Japanese.

One of among thirty sketches of colonizer-colonized relations was Ishimori's two-part "A Story of Love Drenched in Blood" (*CK*, March and May 1915). This one describes the young Korean entertainer Li Hyungi's love affair with a Japanese businessman named Shirai Kenzaburo, a "good friend" of Ishimori's. An enthusiastic advocate of mixed relations between Japanese and Koreans—"the most effective and pleasurable road to colonial assimilation [*dōka*]," he joked (November 1917, 117)—Ishimori speculates philosophically on the first page about the erotic: "Erotic desire [*seiyoku*] transcends all boundaries of race and power. It shouldn't matter to anyone if I'm in love with a Korean or a beggar" (March 1915, 105). Ishimori strongly defends new colonial erotic relations, insisting that romantic love is "truly free" only in Korea, where people aren't burdened by those "feudal marriages between families in Japan, where there's never any passion at all" (106). But even more than the "free" eroticism in the Japanese colonies, Ishimori depicts the relationship between Li and Shirai as "liberated from any notion of common sense as it's usually applied to love affairs" (107), claiming that their relation is "way off the beaten path [*jōki o hazureta*]." The rumors about it involved Shirai sometimes becoming very violent toward Li, and at other times being excessively soft and passive. The reports of these reversals between "extreme cruelty" and supine softness "really excited" Ishimori when he first heard them, at which point he decided to write it up as a story.

Shirai was "gorgeous," but it was his insatiable sexuality and "animal-like" libido that made him famous in the sex districts in Seoul. Li was a perfect partner for him—just as beautiful and just as obsessed with sex. However, Ishimori reports that she was particularly attracted to Shirai's cruelty and was often seen with bruises on her face and arms the day after they had spent a night together (March 1915, 108). Together with the physical attractiveness of Shirai and Li, the "strange, cruel" quality of their eroticism was what qualified this as a story of "blood-drenched love" (108).

In the introduction to the final installment of May 1915, Ishimori relates that Shirai reluctantly agreed to an arranged marriage back in Japan. Once a year Shirai returns to Korea, whereupon he and Li resume their "hallucinatory world of pleasure" (109). But she doesn't spend her time waiting around for him; this is a Korean "who [doesn't] resemble Korean women at all" (98) in that it is "impossible to repress her sexual desire." In this regard she is more like "a decadent eighteenth-century Tokyoite" (98). But because the Japanese colonies seem to re-create this "flavor of Edo," in the end Li is "not really that exceptional" (99). Consequently, the annual reunion romp with Shirai is not enough to satisfy this Korean desperate for erotic relations with colonizers, and she continues a pattern of obsession with Japanese men. The last installment describes her abusive relationship with a Japanese sumo wrestler whom she "threw herself on" (99). The article depicts an incipient "hysteria," as she is found screaming at people in bars, "I'm not a woman who does it for money! I'm not that kind of woman!" (99). It quickly becomes clear to all that the burns and cuts on her body have been inflicted in acts of "sado-masochistic sex." The installment ends with Li's suicide, the final act of "love drenched in blood" (101).

Many of Ishimori's features worked to naturalize Korean women's obsession for Japanese men, inverting what was objectively the situation between colonized women and male colonizers. He also frequently staged Japanese men's masochistic passivity in the face of Korean sovereignty and sadism, both phantasmatic reversals of hegemonic practice in the colonial milieu. His celebration of relations between Japanese men and Korean women not only displaced and grotesqued fundamental colonial antagonisms, but also elided the historical fact that in the first decade of colonialism in Korea they would have had limited interaction outside the red-light districts. The overwhelming majority of interactions happened between Japanese *women* and colonized men and women.[3] Nevertheless, Ishimori represented a colonial space populated by Korean and Chinese women constantly enchanted and willingly seduced by Japanese men. These reversals of the actual conditions within which eroticization and antagonism take place are essential for the kind of dream work that ideological fantasy undertakes. It's important to point out that this operation of turning an oppositional antagonism into something very different is similar to what Tanabe Hajime (1963) meant by "absolute dialectics," whereby the Japanese imperial state magically transforms all resistance into positive identity.

On several occasions Ishimori performed passivity in relation to powerful colonial women. This was both a titillating game undertaken from a position of money and power and the inscription of a desire to give up power. In several places this was linked to sadistic and masochistic tendencies coexisting in one person, sometimes the writer himself. I've been arguing from a psychoanalytic perspective that central to the workings of ideological fantasy is the slippage between sadism and masochism, where the subject slides between the masochistic position of being beaten, the sadistic position of beating, and the voyeuristic position of detached identification with the act of beating itself. Owing to the overdetermined nature of power dynamics in Japan's colonial imperialism, the discourse of s/m in sexological circles inside Japan had clear colonial precedents. Perhaps this is why the person who became recognized as the expert on the phenomenon was none other than Tanaka Kōgai, the neurologist who worked under Gotō Shinpei instructing Taiwanese medical students for four years in colonial Taipei. Although Tanaka's writings from that period are scarce, his colonial experience strongly impacted his later writing.

Tanaka's best-selling book *Sex Maniacs* begins with his signature criticism of modern civilization: "Today, although one could say that externally, modern humans appear cultivated and refined, at the level of instinct and sexuality we are completely subordinated to elements that used to be called primitive. Because this erstwhile primitive in the modern will not go away, modern people have to do their best to disguise it. This book will attempt to remove that disguise" (1925, 1–2). Tanaka explains why he begins the disrobing by emphasizing nonreproductive sexuality: "Although most work in sexology is focused on gynecology, my opinion is that most sexuality has little to do with reproduction" (6).

First and foremost is that which subsumes all other nonreproductive erotic acts: sadism and masochism.

Tanaka develops his discussion by looking at cruelty in the animal world. There he sees a world where "cruelty and sweet love" exist side by side (1925, 12). Because sadism and masochism can be found in the lowest forms of life, he asks, "As the sexual drives have not been civilized at all in 5,000 years, why should sadism and masochism be any less present in humans than in animals?" (12). In fact, they're not; sadism and masochism can be found in "almost every human relationship between men and women" (13). He finds it in common quarrels, in physical fighting, and in passive-aggressive silences and avoidances. As for actual sadism, "although most people view it as horrifying, sadism and cruelty are nothing but a kind of erotic game that actually sustains relationships between men and women, and the powerful and the powerless" (13). Tanaka elaborates: "Cruelty brings the highest amount of sexual pleasure. Different from the common wisdom on this, partners don't despise each other when there is cruelty. This is a perfectly normal way for men and women to interact. Instead of living in a bashful harmony, men and women live in a state that should be called an *affectionate antagonism* [*mutsumajii yō na hantaikoto*]" (13).

Tanaka tempers this eroticization of imperial power hierarchies—men over women, the powerful over the powerless—with the warning that when desire can be satisfied only through violent abuse and cruelty (sadism) or only by being tortured and raped (masochism), there is a danger for the couple and the household. That is to say, when a relationship solidifies into a pure and fixed polarity of sadism and masochism, there will be problems. Be that as it may: "Men are alternately both masochistic and sadistic and if women don't get used to this state of affairs, then men will be forced to go outside the house for satisfaction. We should no longer deny the obvious fact that men have tendencies towards decadent and perverse sex lives that include elements of sadism and masochism" (16). He concludes the opening chapter thus:

> Rather than looking at humans as moral, bourgeois, and civilized, we should regard them as sex maniacs. In the constrictions of civilized life the instincts are repressed and forced to diverge from their savage state. The particular nature of humans is to constantly look for new adventures and stimulations and this is why I employ the definition

"sex maniac." Humans must be provided outlets for these natural impulses, for they are nothing but normal expressions of the perverse [*hentai hyōgen*]. (17)

In chapters 5 and 6 Tanaka references Freud, the texts of Sade, his own medical notes, and classical Chinese and Japanese literature, but his advocacy of s/m is tempered somewhat by his own consultation with actual couples. Although his survey leaves him convinced of the fundamental reality of s/m, his paeans to it as the cure-all for the problems of heterosexual marriage have somewhat subsided. He wonders, "If a man is a sadist or masochist and the woman is the opposite, then why can't they have a happy sex life?" (1925, 91); in practice, however, because the nature of sadism is to always "inflict more and more cruelty and pain" it will "eventually lead to the sadistic partner going outside the marriage for sexual satisfaction" (92). There have also been cases where either a male or a female masochist demands "so much pain that they have to go outside the relationship for satisfaction, and this sometimes leads to their death" (93).

In other words, civilized society isn't structured in a way that allows "natural desires" to express themselves. Excepting the temporary solution of war, where erotic violence can express itself freely, Tanaka can't imagine anything other than commercial sex to fill in the gap for modern civilization's repressiveness (1925, 94). Even if it had been possible, given the censorship restrictions, for Tanaka to openly advocate women sadists or masochists paying for sex with a male top or bottom, he doesn't even hint at it. Women have only two options: either suffer silently inside the home or become sex workers themselves, where the "opportunities for both sadism and masochism are readily available" (96).

When Tanaka was supporting the establishment of a licensed prostitution system in Taiwan in the early years of Japan's colony there, he hadn't yet developed the modernist sexology that he features here in the 1920s. In the late 1890s he, Gotō Shinpei, and others were more concerned with revenues and exciting consumer demand for Japanese sex workers. In other words, as important colonial officials they assisted in the production of biopolitical subjectivities for colonial capital. These subjectivities of Japanese women sex worker and hysteric, Chinese migrant laborer, deterritorialized Korean renter, and Japanese male pimp were the main ontological forces in producing value for the major Japanese capitalist concerns on the Asian continent. But parallel with these multiple grotesqueings of ontological desire, these subjectivities also drove the transformation to an entirely new regime of accumulation featuring a new dialectic of the eroticism of desire and the grotesque of political-economic capture and appropriation. We've already seen some foreshadowing of this new mode in Ishimori Sei'ichi's wild subjective splitting and in Tanaka Kōgai's manifesto calling for a widespread recognition in modern Japanese society of "normal expressions of the perverse." I call this new mode *neuropolitics,* and we'll turn to it now.

5

**ALL THAT'S
SOLID MELTS INTO
MODERN GIRLS
AND BOYS**

The metropolitan blasé outlook is at first the consequence of those rapidly shifting stimulations of the
nerves which are thrown together in all their contrasts. . . . Just as an immoderately sensuous life
makes one blasé because it stimulates the nerves to
their utmost reactivity until they finally can produce
any reaction at all, so, less harmful stimuli, through
the rapidity and contradictoriness of their shifts, force
the nerves to make such violent responses, tear them
down so brutally that they exhaust their last reserves
of strength.

GEORG SIMMEL, "METROPOLIS AND MENTAL LIFE"

My nerves are like overused sandpaper—all dull; only
the eye-catching, bizarre and grotesque can excite me
now.

TANIZAKI JUN'ICHIRŌ, 1918

The Department store owners use freshly killed bodies
for the mannequins; later on they sell the mannequins
to dicey human traffickers. The club owners use live
women for the sex shows, but they don't stay alive for
long. These days, even death seems to have a price tag
on it.

SAKAI KIYOSHI, *KŌREI MAJUTSU* (DEMON MAGIC)

Mannequinization

Beginning in the spring of 1928 rumors circulated wildly across the different levels of the metropolitan erotic-grotesque media that not only
live but also murdered and taxidermied women were being used as mannequins in department store window exhibitions. While the modernologist Kon Wajirō coldly reported in his *New Guide to Greater Tokyo* (*Shin-*

pen Dai Tōkyō annai, 1929) that the "mannequin girl" first appeared in the Ginza, and the anarchist feminist Yagi Akiko decried this newest tendency of the commodification of women's bodies in the feminist journal *Women's Arts* (Silverberg 2007, 61) that same year, the lower-brow erotic-grotesque construed the practice in somewhat more imaginative ways. Rumors published in erotic-grotesque collections such as Noma Jirō's *Researching Perverse Ero* (*Hentaiteki ero no kenkyū*, 1930) recorded that living show window mannequins were actually women who'd been kidnapped and forced into different types of slavery or women who freely sold their labor power and "willingly" stood motionless during the working day on orders from bosses. This tendency toward, in the words of Marx, "the inversion, indeed this distortion between living and dead that is characteristic of capitalism" (1977, 425) intensified after the Crash of October 1929, when profit margins imploded and new, invasive techniques of expropriating surplus were needed by capital in Tokyo's spectacle society.

In his 1930 illustrated book *The Floating World on Parade* (*Ukiyō on pare-do*) the well-known translator, painter, and essayist Sakai Kiyoshi read this figure of the mannequin girl as one of several new types of "hyper-girls" (*sentan ga-ru*) appearing in the parade of metropolitan capitalism. The others were the ubiquitous *moga*, the "chic girl," and "the Engels girl," this last a term pundits used to describe new-style leftist women (1930, 52). Sakai claimed that consumers quickly got bored with the older department store window displays, prompting more modern stores such as Mitsukoshi to feature a more convincing "life-like" look. Sakai quipped that using real women as mannequins represented the "most hyper mobilization to date of the sociological concept of 'women's work'" (3). However, the first mention of the practice of using real women as mannequins appeared in the Shanghai monthly *Kamashastra* of December 1927, edited by Sakai and the erotic-grotesque ringleader Umehara Hokumei,[1] where it was construed as the contemporary version of the long, continuous history in Asia of the "fetish worship of women's body parts [*join sūhai*]." Sakai's article identified the fascination with women's sex organs and body parts as a central element in "Eastern religions" in general and, as he learned from Minakata Kumagusu's writings, the focus of Tantric and other ritual sex practices in particular (*Kamashastra*, vol. 2, 1927, 116–54). He ended the piece by claiming that the ancient Asian practice of worshipping women's bodies in pieces continued with the logic of fetishism in modern capitalism: "With show-window mannequins, the practice of worshipping women continues into our modern era. . . . Although it might seem strange that real female corpses are occasionally used in these displays, it becomes understandable when we consider the long history of fascination with beautiful dead women and their sex organs" (164).

The best-selling novels of the erotic-grotesque writer Edogawa Rampo further sensationalized these rumors in works published between 1928 and 1934. In Rampo's novel *Blind Beast* (*Mōjū*, 1997), published in 1931, a blind artist stalks, seduces, and then mutilates the most beautiful *mogas* in Tokyo, turning their bodies into sculptures. Using his double identity as a sought-after masseur (*anma*) to gain direct access to the women (his massage business becomes wildly successful after he incorporates alternative methods into his practice, including oral massage, mild s/M, and hypnosis) he first intrigues the Asakusa stage actress Mizuki before seducing a café owner and a young, bored widow looking for thrills. After several great massages he gets Mizuki to visit his sculpting studio, then lures her, in her neuropoliticized condition of stimulation and stupefaction, into his "special room." Modeled on the funhouse exhibits of movable, tilting floors that first appeared in the late 1920s in the amusement park in Asakusa, Tokyo's consumer district, the room is filled with huge, artificial body parts of women constructed out of plaster and rubber and filled with water (47–49). Completely dark, the tactile experience of the room was designed to double the prespecular "phenomenology of perception" of the Blind Beast, as the actress discovers. When she's forced into this introceptive space (Merleau-Ponty 1964, 129) she can do nothing but step on, fall into, ingest, and swim around in the uncannily large primary objects: detached breasts, lips, and navels. The sightlessness of this tactile and auditory experience situates Mizuki in a narrative of developmental regression from her achieved success in the entertainment world. This psychic devolution back into the state of what Lacan (1966) called the dis-organized "body in pieces" becomes a flashback to the sensual experience of the hypnosis-massage she received earlier, as well as to the primal unity with the mother before the subject-object division.

This staging of regression to a kind of zero-degree humanity in the first room prepares Mizuki for what will take place in the special room, a dungeon replete with the paraphernalia of ritual s/M. After the rich

Japanese subculture language of painful flowers and whimpering obedient dogs proceeds for twenty pages or so, the final quasi-contractual degradation of Mizuki concludes with her pleas for mutilation and dismemberment, which Blind Beast agrees to. Following her murder Mizuki's body parts are reassembled by Blind Beast, who "makes a killing" selling them as department store models and show window mannequins; store managers and consumers alike marvel at their "life-like" appearance. The profits from the mutilated women—by the end of the novel seven women murdered by Blind Beast in this way have ended up on display—are invested by Blind Beast in the technological improvement of his special rooms. In this way femicide produces "modernizing effects" (see Bowlby 1985 on the gendered violence in commodification).

Several of the murdered women have worked hard to get to metropolitan Tokyo from poor rural areas. As Vera Mackie (2000) and Miriam Silverberg (2007) have demonstrated, the public visibility of these independent women was transforming urban spaces. *Blind Beast* documents the way a new regime of metropolitan capitalism possessed the capacity to denude these independent bodies through stimulation and stupefaction and then remake them according to its needs. It also narrates the opportunities and dangers for new migrants to the metropolitan center. As Tokyo's population doubled from 2.5 million to 5 million between 1913 and 1928, new arrivals often passed directly from formal subsumption into a new and overwhelming real subsumption. This invasive subsumption demanded more than the occasional subservience to capital that characterized the mere formal subsumption of living labor to capital in biopolitics.

To replay some of the discussion from my introduction, Marx defines real subsumption as the saturation of all aspects of life by capitalism. Not only are humans required to sell their labor on the market, but our leisure time is similarly dominated by commodification. As Antonio Negri (1991) argues, in real subsumption society itself is subsumed by capitalism. The invasion of a capital logic into heretofore uncontaminated zones means that the human subject itself will be stalked, stimulated, mugged, and robbed by capitalism in new ways. Moreover, as the whole of society is subsumed by capitalism, the working over of the subject will contain, in a fractal form, society itself. The mugging of the hapless subject will contain the DNA traces of the culprit: commodity capital. Therefore, real subsumption newly submits the neural network of human cognition and the nervous system of human sensation to capitalism in a regime of capture I call *neuropolitics.*

In the short story "The Human Chair" (Ningen Isu) published in 1924, Rampo intuited this neuropolitical invasion of the body and the de-anthropomorphizing effects that ensue. In the story a worker in a small factory becomes so engrossed in producing a chair that he "skipped food and sleep": "Really, it would be no exaggeration to state that the job became my very life, every fiber of the wood I used seemingly linked to my heart and soul" (1956, 7). Eventually he is so attracted to the stimulating possibilities provided by the commodity that he decides to immerse himself completely in it, becoming a "human chair." Mere contact with the commodity sets off such an intense neurological response that he wonders if he isn't going "slowly insane" (8). But he gradually loses the ability to differentiate anthropocentric reason from what Walter Benjamin called the intoxicating "rush of the commodity," and he eventually becomes so taken over by it that he willingly becomes a commodity himself.

The Nervous System, Grotesqued

Asakusa was a Tokyo entertainment district full of movie houses, theaters, amusement parks, peep shows, and fast-food establishments. Adjacent to it was the early modern center of commercial sex, Yoshiwara. Asakusa's pleasures were the effects of two methods of accumulating capital: through the surpluses expropriated from the colonial periphery and through accumulation by dispossession inside Japan, culminating in the huge profits made by exporting to the European countries engaged in the slaughter of the First World War. These accumulations propelled urban spaces in Japan into technomedia stages matched only by London and Paris. Along with Osaka's entertainment district, Shinsekai, Asakusa was the privileged *neurotopia* of metropolitan Japan, where new stimulations were purchased on the cheap by petit bourgeois and working-class consumers. In his well-known introduction to *A Record of the Underbelly of Asakusa*, the anarchist poet Soeda Azenbō chronicled the invasion of the body by new commodity forms (*Asakusa Teiryūki*, 1928; see also Silverberg 2007, 184–89). He depicts Tokyo's neurotopia thus:

In Asakusa, all kinds of things are exposed in their raw form
All kinds of human desire are dancing naked.
Asakusa is the heart of Tokyo; it's a marketplace of humans. . . .
The Asakusa of the masses is a foundry where all old forms are
    melted down and transformed into new forms.
A huge stream of all classes and races of people, all mixed up
    together.
A strange rhythm lying at the base of that stream—the flow of
    nerves. (Soeda 1982, 3–5)

The jerky movement of the poem in Japanese captures the neurasthenia of Asakusa, where the new technological media—radio pioneered in Tokyo in 1925, the phonograph and electric loudspeaker in 1927, the "talkie" film in 1929—clashed with advertising for the consumer's attention. If labor was only formally subsumed under capital in biopolitics, where workers were paid a wage lower than the exchange value of their labor, the regime of neuropolitics demanded that they *pay back* capitalism with their stimulated curiosity and stupefied attention in leisure time. In the movie theater, at the peep shows, in the cheap cabarets, riding the amusement attractions, and even just walking the streets flooded with advertisements and hawkers, their desire is organized to *pay attention* to new media commodities (see Beller 2006).

One of the most important theorists of this new shift in capitalist expropriation was the sociologist Akagami Yoshitsuge (1892–1953). Akagami's *The Face of Erotic-Grotesque Society* (*Ryōki no shakaisō*) was issued by the commercial publisher Shinchōsha in July 1931 to accompany the well-known guide to the erotic-grotesque-nonsense, *The Illustrated Guide to the Contemporary Hyper-Bizarre* (*Gendal ryōki sentan zukan*), and is an incisive introduction to what was called the new "immediate society" (*chokusetsu shakai*). Akagami details the various ways print and visual media draw consumers into capital almost immediately by offering new and fascinating images for sale designed to colonize human attention (1931, 80–94). While consumers' "most intimate thoughts and dreams" become indistinguishable from image commodities, "capitalist owners take advantage, and profit from it" (265). As I explain at greater length in the next chapter, Akagami shows how "advanced capitalism" (*sentantaru shihonshugi*) works to expropriate swaths of the attention that consumers direct to stimulating new commodities. As it does so, real subsumption substitutes stimulation and ideological instruction for the wage of formal subsumption. Human desiring production in its neuro-political mode of fascination and enthralled stupefaction is sold to the worker-consumer for the wage substitutes of pleasure, pleasure which now comes with ideological instructions on how to be an obedient pur-chaser in this new regime. Whereas human labor as erotic production was expropriated and grotesqued in biopolitics, here in the more in-tensive form of neuropolitics, the erotics of human stimulation and stupefaction are expropriated and grotesqued. Riding parasitically on waves of desire and visual attention, frantically grotesqueing these and exchanging them for cheap thrills and ideological inculcation, capital *really* subsumes the entire nervous system under a new neuropolitical regime. Akagami theorizes that this invasion of image commodities into the human sensorium is like "chemical warfare" which deteriorates the human nervous system as it "makes us addicted to its poison gas. . . . Is there any kind of protective gas mask effective against such on attack?" (267).

Similar to *Blind Beast* and Akagami's poison gas attacks, Soeda's poem shows how what could be called the "Asakusa effect" strips alien-ated humans down to a zero-degree state before hammering them into pulp and casting them into a new mold, a new image. Like Mizuki in *Blind Beast,* the consumers in *A Record of the Underbelly of Asakusa* get pleasure both from the process of consumption itself and from the prom-ise of transformation. Just as the foundry or factory (*chūzōba*) takes commodities such as iron and steel and "melts them down and trans-forms them into new forms," now neuropolitical capitalism inserts human flesh and nerves into this serialized industrial process. More-over, although the arduous productive labor driving the operations of the foundry was heretofore located far away from the world of leisure and consumption, in neuropolitical expropriation production is directly imbricated in pleasure and consumption. In Soeda's analysis these "new forms" are not shipped from a distant foundry to the site of consumption in the entertainment area of Asakusa; they emerge from the conflation of production and consumption in the "marketplace of humans," where the desiring production of human attention and stimulation is expropri-ated. While living energy as labor power was the source and substance of value in the formal subsumption of biopolitical expropriation, here the source is deeper and overwhelms the human nervous system. What

Soeda calls the "flow of nerves" or neuropower is the energy that drives the matrix of neuropolitics.

Nineteenth- and early twentieth-century neurology posited that neuronal activity is overloaded when the human organism finds itself unusually stimulated. At these moments neurons will try to divest themselves of what is called "quantity" (Qn) in order to maintain their standard equilibrium. A system tries to rid itself of Qn because constant or excessively high levels of excitation are destabilizing to the organism. However, in ridding itself of Qn the organism strips itself of something that neurons need to protect themselves against further destabilizing excitations. Therefore, an inextricable double bind is established for the human organism when it finds itself saturated by external stimulations. Technological media exacerbate this situation, producing new psychosomatic effects in humans living in metropolitan spaces. In one of the earliest intuitions of neuropolitical invasion, Georg Simmel argued in 1903 that the technomedia environment of the modern metropolis was indelibly transforming human nervous systems, eliciting wild affective swings from blasé boredom to hyperstimulated violence.

The sociologist and ethnographer of Asakusa, Gonda Yasunosuke, was one of the first in Japan to analyze this transformation in capitalism with respect to the ways it was transforming human bodies and pleasures (Harootunian 2000; Silverberg 2007; Yoshimi S. 1995). Gonda realized early on that urbanization and fixed-capital concentration in Japan after the First World War meant a displacement of the centrality of production from metropolitan areas. While previously the most important aspect of society had been the anthropocentric production of things oriented toward human use-value, Gonda theorized in 1923 that in Asakusa, "under this new form of capitalist economic rationale, human needs or human-centered demands have completely vanished [*shittsui*] . . . leaving only the criterion of profit-making. In contemporary society ruled by the law of profit, 'people' don't determine the value of 'things'; 'things' choose 'people.' Or rather, that which authorizes 'things' to decide whether 'people' possess value or not is in effect capitalist profit" (1974, vol. 4, 66). Gonda recognized in 1920 that the cheap, mass-produced pleasures in Asakusa were the work of capitalist conglomerates who profited greatly from offering homogenized, "factory-like pleasure" to workers. Nevertheless, he insisted that despite the homogenization and commodification of pleasure in Japanese capitalism, the new working-class and petit bourgeois consumers gathering in Asakusa were constructing a new kind of people's pleasure, one that was specific to the urban entertainment districts. He suspected that out of this new conglomeration of mass-produced commodities new use-values were being created. The research project that would preoccupy him for the next fifteen years was concerned with identifying the precise content of a "people's pleasure" and locating utopian transformations in the constitution of the masses that might arise from the commitment to pleasure in consumer spaces like Asakusa.

Gonda's main work and one of the most important texts of progressive social theory published in Japanese before the Pacific War, *A Theory of People's Pleasure* (*Minshū gorakuron*, 1931), is driven by the need to identify a central agency of popular pleasure. Gonda sees the late 1920s in Japan as an unprecedented era of national wealth, "the completion of the previous stage of capitalism" (1974, vol. 2, 183). Although there are positive elements to this, Gonda laments, "On the other hand, there is a widespread sense that the people are oppressed by the effects of this new stage in the form of 'things and money.' What are we to make of human life, buried as it is underneath all these commodities?" (184). Similar to his evocation of "a suicided human inside the consumer" (cited in Harootunian 2000, 170), Gonda was struggling to understand how the purchase price of pleasure in this new stage of capitalism seemed to be human life itself. The act of giving up one's life was the user fee required to enter this strange capitalist world that provided Japan with unprecedented wealth as it simultaneously robbed consumers of "life," defined as grounded in unalienated pleasure and production solely for use. From within this conjunctural contradiction of unprecedented wealth bringing about palpable losses the urgency arises to rethink the whole notion of "people's pleasure" in terms of advanced capitalism and its impact on consumer spaces. As a strange counterpoint to the wealthy present of 1931, Gonda begins *A Theory of People's Pleasure* with a recollection of what Tokyo life was like for most people after the Great Tokyo Earthquake of September 1923, when 75 percent of the city was destroyed and 160,000 people died. Characterizing the ensuing two-month period as one of a generalized "perverted, abnormal state [*hentai jōtai*]," Gonda claims that its most deplorable aspect was that people descended into a condition of "existence without pleasure." As we'll see, these same depictions of a postapocalyptic Tokyo bereft of authentic pleasure will be redeployed to reference the *hentai* subjectivities of the *moga* and *mobo* (modern boy) as they come to dominate Tokyo's street life and media-scape in the late 1920s.

The next section of Gonda's book introduces the three main tendencies in scholarly discussions of "people's pleasure." For the most part glossing liberal European social theory, Gonda locates the theory of the "objectiveness" of pleasure first, followed by the "theory of excess energy," and concludes with the "theory of pleasure as recreation" that reproduces healthy laborers for capital (1974, vol. 2, 188–90). He gives short shrift to the first two before lambasting the idea of pleasure as recreation, arguing that this theory "supports the capitalist emphasis on production for production's sake," something that actually robs the people of any real pleasure as it enriches "big capitalists" (190). He concludes with his signature historical anthropological claims that "play is older than work" and "historically, art preceded economic productivism" (202–3). Arguing that most activity in contemporary capitalism is done for "ulterior motives" and not because it is in and of itself meaningful or pleasurable, he wonders if there isn't a way to realign desire and satisfaction as the sociologist imagines they were before the myopic obsession with accumulation hijacked earlier forms of economic organization.

He concludes this section with a warning that readers must not interpret his argument as advocating the kind of zero-degree humanity we saw earlier, homologous to what the philosopher Giorgio Agamben (1995) has referred to as dehumanized "bare life" (*vita nuda*). Gonda clarifies that it was this naked primitiveness that most accurately characterized Tokyoites in the weeks after the earthquake in 1923. Referring again to that "state of perversion" that took over the people like a contagion, he decries human life reduced to pure impulsive acts driven by "desperate, animalistic reflex movements [*hansha undō*]" as one not deserving of a place in a rational, civilized society (1974, vol. 2, 204–5). In a barely disguised critique of the popular sexologists Tanaka Kōgai and Nakamura Kokyo, who were attempting to understand this very "state of perversion" as the universal psychosexual condition of metropolitan subjects living under real capitalist subsumption, Gonda sarcastically dismisses their "illogical school of perverse psychology" that tries to rationalize and even celebrate such primitive reflexes as nymphomania and fetishism: "We certainly don't want to fall into that trap!" (205).

He concludes this section by reiterating his well-known maxim that the masses should reformulate pleasure not as something done "for capitalist production or to expand the realm of commodification," but as that which directly "produces human life": "Pleasure precedes society, and pleasure's excess is that which gives birth to the world" (211). But his disavowal of the influence of the abnormal psychologists is registered clearly here: this a priori designation of desire and pleasure for human society is startlingly close to the thoughts of the central figures of Japanese sexology, the very same Tanaka and Nakamura.

In the next section of his text it's clear that Gonda is incapable of locating any new agency of popular pleasure with the capacity to avert his stigmatization of *hentai*. The various leisure activities established after the earthquake, which helped wrench Tokyo denizens out of their states of perversion (bridge societies, shamisen groups, tanka poetry circles, etc.) certainly don't qualify. Thus when we get to Gonda's discussion of the full-blown appearance on the streets of Tokyo of the sole heroes and heroines of the new capitalist order who have managed to break "free from the constraints of productivism"—the *moga* and *mobo*—his text is frozen. Admitting that he is both "seduced" and "horrified" by these "monsters" (*kaibutsu*; 1974, vol. 2, 241), he nonetheless proceeds to abject them as primitive, instinctual *hentai*. The *vita nuda* of 1923 is (living) the *vida loca* by 1931.

Gonda was rare among leftists at the time in taking seriously these new subjectivities. The Marxist critic Ōya Sōichi summarily dismissed the *moga* and *mobo* as driven by superficial desires for cheap new sensations (*shigeki*) without feeling "deeply about anything at all" (1930, 192). In perhaps the most well-known section of Gonda's book, titled "So-called Modern Life and Pleasure," he asks rhetorically, "If we pose the question of where we should locate the subject of modern life, it's clear that this subject is found in its purest form in the species of humans completely severed from a life of production and a life of labor" (1974, vol. 2, 243). His concrete definition of truly modern subjects—the rejection of a productivist life combined with the restless search for a liberated life within capitalism—could be applied only to the *moga* and *mobo*. Gonda intuited that these subjectivities represented the brave new world of mass culture's imbrication with pleasure and that it would be, he chided more doctrinaire leftists like Ōya, "a pity" for social theorists to reject them out of hand.

H. D. Harootunian's authoritative reading uncovers in Gonda a belief that "modern life created the streets that produced patterns of living that were neither ordinary nor regular, composed of the time of an unconnected, diverse humanity and the time of leisure separated from production when consumption ruled" (2000, 172). It's evident that Gonda is afraid that these new human subjectivities are mere homologues of the contemporary commodity form itself, in Deleuze's and Guattari's words, "infinitely decoding flows" and traveling well outside the fixed boundaries of the erstwhile centers of entertainment like Asakusa. What had previously been embedded in a space, and therefore determined topologically, now becomes unleashed and unhinged in modern capitalism: all that's solid melts into modern girls and boys. Yoshimi Shunya identifies Gonda's project as confining and conflating "people's pleasure" with the entertainment centers (1995, 36–41). For the decade of the 1920s Gonda's social philosophy was certainly unwilling or unable to locate popular pleasures anywhere else; modern pleasures are best elicited in technologized sites of fixed capital. But the tendency of the new *hentai* subjectivities is to transgress spatial boundaries and spread everywhere, what Guy Debord called the "becoming-world of the commodity" (1983, 66). At great pains to overcome his dispositional romantic populism when faced with these ultramodern subjectivities, Gonda denigrates the *moga* and *mobo* as "duped" by commodification and doped up on the rush of consumerism (on *moga*, see Sato 2003; Silverberg 2007; Saitō M. 2000).

Always a great stylist for a social scientist, Gonda's depiction of the *mobo* and *moga* comes close to modernist poetry. In his final verdict he goes to some length to provide historical reasons for his harsh sentencing of them. Acknowledging that there were Japanese precursors to these modern subjectivities who had "completely rejected the ideology of productivity" in the eighteenth-century version of Asakusa—the commercial sex district of Yoshiwara and the romanticized "floating world of Edo"—he nevertheless claims that all the different classes of early modern Japanese society were "equal" while they were partying within Yoshiwara's confines (1974, vol. 2, 246–47). With a strong gender blindness he contrasts this democratizing effect of consumption in eighteenth-century Tokyo (Edo) with what he sees as the rigid hierarchy of consumerism circa 1930, when the modern ideal of life completely devoted to play and pleasure is available only to the wealthy. Although he had been consistent in inserting the *mobo* and *moga* into the class position of the petit bourgeoisie up until now, this move to identify the hypersubjects of modernity as rich aristocrats functions as a preface of sorts for his condemnation of them as a "necessary evil." But in his only serious attempt to understand the *mobos* and *mogas* he can't quite let himself conclude in such damning fashion. So he gives us more poetry: "In contemporary Japan, the feudal class structure has collapsed and all residues have been erased by this new tide that calls for a liberated expression of life for all people, at all times, in whatever place. This call no longer needs anything like a 'Yoshiwara' to promote the perverse [*hentai*] predilections that sprout from a mode of being that rejects anything resembling a normal, productive life. The perverse desires of modern life shamelessly strut their stuff everywhere" (247).[2]

Gonda now understands that the subjects of this "perverse predilection" have attained the super- and subhuman capacity to "liberate themselves from spatial confinement" because they have managed to become indistinguishable from commodities. If commodities could speak, a phrase Gonda would know from his reading of Marx, they would do so through the mouths of these modern boys and girls in the Tokyo street pidgin of English phrases, trashed Esperanto, and de-Sinified Japanese. This is why they are de-anthropomorphized in his moral universe as "monstrous commodities [*kaibutsu no shosan*]." Furthermore, the whole moralizing rhetoric of "perversion" and "abnormality"— *hentai*—is deployed as a synecdoche for modern life in capitalism in that this one quality of *hentai* stands in for the whole of the modern. In this way Gonda returns to his initial depiction of Tokyo after the earthquake as "perverse [*hentai*] conditions." You'll recall that people then were driven by "pure instinct" and lived an "existence without pleasure" that he couldn't bring himself to call "human." Then as now, this kind of "modern primitive" instinctual existence lived superficially is bereft of authentic pleasure. It excites what Theodor Adorno and Max Horkheimer (1972) later called the "fetish character" of the commodity, whereby modern primitives worship reified things as deities. Finally, although Gonda had been insisting throughout his *Theory of People's Pleasure* that he would not fall into the trap of advocating policy to instruct the masses in proper pleasure, he concludes his text by suggesting that very thing. I think it's fair to say that when he did so a great opportunity to contribute to anything like a popular front left in Japan was forfeited.

Gonda was capable of articulating this kind of subjectivity—with clear utopian aspirations for "pleasure beyond capitalist productivity"—to a leftist politics, but he falls back on essentializing pleasure as that which has a necessary relation with production. He also refuses to recognize that contemporary capitalism, riding on the commodified pleasure of the *moga* and *mobo* in melting all solids, has liquefied and displaced Asakusa as a privileged site for the creation of popular pleasures. Instead, all metropolitan streets have been Asakusa-ized. In part I, I showed how the de-confining, laissez-faire-ing of life in biopolitical capitalism quite literally made Japan's imperialism. Here, we will see how the liberating of, not life—which had previously committed suicide as the price of entry into this new capitalism—but an alienated "second life" produced by commodified desires and consumerist dreams deepened Japan's imperialism.

Modern Sexology

The two projects that took seriously the impact of the new forms of commodification on the nervous systems of metropolitan Japanese were not projects of the left. Although the sexological work of Tanaka Kōgai and Nakamura Kokyō (which Gonda consistently maligned) is neutral in relation to capital, Kon Wajirō's ethnographic and market research project, referred to as *kōgengaku* in Japanese, *modernologio* in Esperanto, and *modernology* in English, celebrates the new interfaces shortening the distance between image commodities and human beings. Kon believed that capitalism had a positive, civilizing influence on tradition-bound Japanese. The supply-and-demand law of capitalism, together with the deterritorializing effect it had on traditional social forms, petitioned and pressured older cultural practices to reform or die out. I take up modernology in the next chapter; here I want to return to these two important sexologists.

The most complex treatment of the new subjectivities of metropolitan capitalism took place in mass culture sexology. The main journals were *Abnormal Psychology* and *Modern Sexuality*, in which the neuropolitical expressions of fetishism, sadism, masochism, voyeurism, necrophilia, and hysteria were introduced, investigated, and finally normalized as predictable effects of commodity capitalism. What I find most intriguing is that in these two central journals, but also in much of the mass culture sexology published in Japanese (beginning with the first issue of *Modern*

Sexuality in 1922 until 1935 or so), the signifier *hentai* was not deployed as a stigmatizing depiction of individual subjects. People were not profiled and policed as perverse, and erotic aspects were rarely linked to essentialized identities in Japanese sexology. Rather, they were considered effects of a modern condition that Gonda was struggling to understand. Unfortunately, these subjective responses blasted right through the only categorical frameworks available to Gonda to configure them: economistic Marxism and liberal sociology. However, in the hands of Nakamura, Tanaka, and other non-Eurocentric Japanese sexologists, the framework was much wider, and the subjective effects that will be personified by 1930 as *moga* and *mobo* were analyzed in a nonstigmatizing fashion. Drawing on a deep reservoir of global knowledges of the sort we saw in Minakata Kumagusu (who was a huge influence on Tanaka and Sakai Kiyoshi), the liberal expansiveness of mainstream Japanese sexology was the discursive foundry that manufactured, or in a more Foucauldian register, *produced* these subjectivities by naturalizing them as logical effects of the modern capitalist metropolis in Japan, beginning just after the First World War.

New Affects and New Pleasures

Before expanding on some of the ways Tanaka tried to normalize the new erotic states of hysteria and S/M, it's important to point out that the origin of modern Japanese sexology is most properly located in the work of the colonial doctors I discussed earlier, including those working under Mori Rintarō, the surgeon general of the Japanese army, from 1907 to 1916. In Japanese literary history Mori Ōgai (1862–1922) is considered one of the pioneers of the modern "I-novel." However, under his family name of Rintarō, he performed double duty as a chief scientific and medical expert. After four years studying hygiene, medicine, and psychiatry in Germany in the 1880s, he quickly advanced in the military's scientific hierarchy, finally serving as its surgeon general. Michel Foucault has argued convincingly that sexuality should not be considered the master signifier for a solid mass of immutable chromosomal determinants, but rather the "set of effects produced in bodies, behaviors, and social relations by a certain deployment" of a "complex political technology" (1980, 127). One of the early contributions Japanese sexology made to this political technology was Mori's definitive text on modern hygiene, *The New Hygiene Compilation* (*Eisei shinpen*).

Beginning with the edition issued in 1908, this text featured material previously published in Mori's own medical journal, *Eisei shinshi*, which included independent studies done by him and army researchers (many of these studies were undertaken to enhance the Japanese army's immunological pathogens in Asia, including recommendations for establishing "comfort stations" near garrisons), together with translations of the newest European hygiene research. In *The New Hygiene Compilation* he used these translations to introduce European scientific theories, only to critically examine and provincialize them using intellectual sources that deftly moved from the Ancient Greeks and Romans, through Hindu and Zoroastrian science and philosophy, and inevitably concluding with Japanese and Chinese science and medicine. Mori drew on his ability to read Latin, German, Chinese, and English to offer a startling synthesis of global knowledge on hygiene and sexology. In my analysis, Mori's work done for the Japanese army should be considered alongside the writing of Minakata Kumagusu, as both are confidently critical of erotophobic European sexology and both set the standard for the next decade of work in Japanese sexology.

Like Mori and Minakata, Tanaka was a vigilant critic of European sexology and what he called its "Christian moralizing." In *Women and Passion* (*Josei to aiyoku*, 1923) he argued that this moralizing rhetoric was the basis for Europeans' perpetration of a "deluded sense of the animalistic sexual instinct [*honnō*] of humans" and a distorted view of "the erotic drives [*shōdō*] that modern civilization and material culture have increasingly incited" (308, 297). Tanaka called it the height of hypocrisy for modern states to attempt to repress that which their advanced capitalism constantly stimulates: new affects and new pleasures. Rather than shamefully pretending that modern nation-states don't excite basic desires—a pretence that led directly to disasters such as the First World War in Europe—Tanaka recommended that the Japanese state provide outlets for erotic satisfaction and urged Japan's leaders to be tolerant of modern sexual expressions and urges. As it was also axiomatic for him that "behind all humans exist drives that can't be repressed," he thought that as a non-Christian country Japan was in a perfect position to lead the world in embracing new erotic sensibilities. He claimed that it was an obvious lesson of history that "the more that the state attempts to repress them, the more wild these same desires will become" (304). Therefore, in *Women and Passion* he called for the immediate adoption in Japan of a liberal scientific attitude toward "the sexual drives," claiming that without erotic pleasure there could be no "joy in life" and no civilization deserving of the name (305). The recommendation to nurture the erotic drives also informs his earlier book, *The Shadowy Aspects of Human Sexuality* (*Ningen no seiteki ankokumen*, 1922), which sold over twenty thousand copies. Here, he takes up the challenge of identifying aspects of modern sexuality, including sadism, masochism, fetishism, and necrophilia. Modern individuals, he writes, should be expected to embrace each of these erotic expressions at different times in their life (6).

Advising metropolitan subjects to involve themselves with S/M, necrophilia, and fetishism as a *natural facet of modern life* was the raison d'être for Tanaka's journal *Modern Sexuality*. He claimed later that the constant harassment of the Home Ministry censors was the reason *Modern Sexuality* had a relatively short life, running monthly from May 1922 until June 1925. But its brief publishing life didn't prevent it from quickly being recognized as the most important scholarly source of popular information on the new modes of erotic and neurotic expression; Edogawa Rampo, Minakata Kumagusu, and Umehara Hokumei were all fans. Tanaka's second career as a popular sexologist began with his contributions to Nakamura's journal *Abnormal Psychology*, which ran from 1917 until 1926. He was one of the two writers focusing on the new theme of *hentai seiyoku* (modern sexuality), but he went beyond the work of Kitano Hiromi by invoking superior medical credentials and by exploring the connections between the central aspects of modern sexuality of the 1920s and certain erotic states in Japan in the eighteenth and nineteenth centuries.

Nakamura's *Abnormal Psychology* was one of several new sexology monthlies that started publishing after the end of the First World War and constituted the "popular sexology boom" in metropolitan Japan. The others were Kitano's own monthly, *Sex Research* (*Sei no Kenkyū*), started in December 1919 after he left Nakamura's journal; Akiyama Yoshio's and Sawada Junjirō's *Sex*, which kicked off in January 1920; and Sawada's writing partner Habuto Eiji's monthly *Sexuality and Human Nature* (*Seiyoku to Jinsei*) that began publishing in October 1921. We need to be attentive to unbridgeable differences in the positions of these journals, especially with respect to their rendering of *hentai*. The cultural historian Kanno Satomi has designated the Eurocentric, erotophobic branch of modern Japanese sexology as the "Ebing school" (*ebingu-ryū*), after the German sexologist Krafft-Ebing (Kanno 2005, 82). Although Kanno doesn't identify the main followers of Krafft-Ebing in Japan, the main opponents of Eurocentric sexology were Nakamura and Tanaka.

Tanaka respected the liberal scholarship that appeared in Kitano's *Sex Research*, as writers with whom he worked at *Abnormal Psychology* were responsible for most of it. However, he and Nakamura were openly critical of the journals *Sex* and *Sexuality and Human Nature* and pulled no punches in dismissing them as prurient, sensationalizing, and moralistic (Saitō T. 2002, 8–9). From the moment of its first publication the contributors to *Abnormal Psychology* were also critical of Habuto's and Sawada Junjirō's best-selling *Theory of Perverse Sexuality* (1915). This text is basically an explication of Krafft-Ebing's *Psychopathia Sexualis*, building on two earlier Japanese translations. Habuto and Sawada published together until the late 1920s and, along with Tanaka, are often considered the most important popular sexologists in Japan during this period. Habuto (1878–1929) went to medical school in Germany in 1912, became licensed as a doctor, and immediately returned to Japan to put his knowledge of German sexology to use as a practicing gynecologist in Tokyo's Nezu area (Frühstück 2003, 106). This star of the Ebing school published several best-sellers after his hit in 1915, including *Popular Sexology* (*Fūzoku seiyokugaku*, 1919), *Standard Sexology* (*Ippan seiyokugaku*, 1920), and *Research on Perverse Sexuality* (*Hentai seiyoku no kenkyū*, 1921). Although his work is firmly opposed to the anti-Eurocentric sexology of people like Mori, Tanaka, and Nakamura, Habuto became noticeably less Ebing school beginning in the mid-1920s, when he appeared to take seriously some of Tanaka's criticism. He ran into trouble with the medical authorities in the spring of 1929, when they suspended his medical license for distributing the "King of Kings," a bogus male sex-enhancement medicine in which he had invested most of his savings. He committed suicide ignominiously in August 1929 before an impending investigation—a sensational culmination to a career of sexual sensationalism (Saitō H. 1997).

The other big player in the Ebing school, Sawada Junjirō, was known to lie about his credentials to sell his books and journals, falsely claiming to have studied neurology and biology in medical school. He studied literature in college, but his later training is unclear. Tanaka often mocked him and called him a *petenshi*, or fraud. Although he claimed in several places to be a physician, there are no references to any of his own patients in his sexology journal or in his books. Scholars who have tried to make an argument about Japanese sexology using solely the Ebing school leaders Habuto and Sawada do so on sketchy ground.

Many writers of the period attested to how aspects of mass culture were hegemonized by *hentai* and sexological literature beginning right after the First World War. The journalist Okada Mitsurō published a long essay in three parts in Tokyo's *Yomiuri* newspaper beginning on 29 April 1921 attesting to this new moment, called "Signs of the Sudden Explosion in Sexology Literature." Stating that one is "not only overwhelmed by the presence of sexology books and journals in the bookstores, [but] it's impossible to avoid the advertisements for them in the newspapers as well," Okada compares the contemporary situation to that of "five or six years" earlier, when there was only the Habuto and Sawada text *A Theory of Perverse Sexuality*. In 1919 Nakamura's *Abnormal Psychology* would stake out an opposing position on *hentai* and modern erotic expression; Tanaka was from the beginning a featured contributor. To further Nakamura's message of the universality of *hentai* and intending to thoroughly desensationalize it, Tanaka began publishing *Modern Sexuality* in May 1922. As Tanaka explained in his editor's introduction to the first issue, he pledged to "take up the research of sexuality in a serious and scholarly fashion": "We will engage each issue in an open-minded way and do our best to avoid the misunderstandings and moralizing that characterizes much of contemporary sexology. Sex research should not stigmatize certain people, but must enlighten and clarify all aspects of sexuality" (*Hentai Seiyoku*, May 1922, 2).

Building on the influence of Nakamura's *Abnormal Psychology*, Tanaka's new journal featured an unflinching look at an imperial society that was producing new neurological states and erotic expressions possible only within an almost universal condition of *hentai*. Here, for the first time, it's plausible to render *hentai* as simply "capitalist modernity." In Tanaka's journal and in his books Japanese readers are introduced to the new kinds of pleasures, passions, anxieties, and exhaustions elicited by modern capitalism in Japan's metropolitan sites. Joining a chorus of sexologists, sociologists, and doctors writing in Japanese, the deterritorialized pleasures that frustrated, froze, and finally pushed Gonda into fascism are treated complexly and sympathetically in the pages of

Modern Sexuality. Rather than configuring *hentai* as particular and de-viant—the position of the sexology journal *Sex* in particular and Habuto and Sawada in general—the journal posits the assemblage of neurotic responses to metropolitan capitalism that would be personified as *moga* and *mobo* as a *norm* of the imperial metropoles. Especially with respect to the *hentai* aspects that Tanaka privileged—sadism, masochism, hys-teria, and fetishism—these should be understood as standard and even banal within the affective conditions established by modern capitalism.

Tanaka universalized the four aspects of *hentai* most clearly in a col-lection of essays first published in *Modern Sexuality* and then collected as a book in 1928. His *Popular Science of Taste* (*Shumi no taishūkagaku*) attempts to ground the aspects of *hentai* by claiming that there are homologues in the animal world. As he would throughout the 1920s, he introduces the discussion of taste and pleasure with his standard warn-ing about situating humans where they belong, among the anthropoid genus (*ruijinen*): "Biologists never stop reminding us that we humans are animals and have not progressed psychologically very far beyond that condition. We have to recognize that with respect to our psychic func-tioning, the traces of our ancestors the apes remain very strong" (1–2). This means that instead of acting rationally most of the time, "humans respond to external stimuli as animals would, negotiating the force of the stimulus through either flight or fight." Although humans share a capacity for sheer force with other apes, they occasionally flee from threats, as orangutans do. Chimpanzees and gorillas are different: in most cases they strike out aggressively against the threat (3–4).

What differentiates us from our ancestors is that the two fundamen-tal responses of flight and fight form the basis for a series of secondary responses that are direct elaborations of them at a higher neurologi-cal level: hysteria and masochism are expressions of fear, while sadism, fetishism, and voyeurism are more complex expressions of the funda-mental function of aggressive fighting. In other words, all the modern expressions of neurotic subjectivity are simply the "reappearance of human's animal nature [*dōbutsu no seishitsu*]." As a result of this, there is really no such thing as civilized morality that can be clearly differen-tiated from the behavior of the lower life forms (1928, 14–15). Although the ostensibly normal interactions characteristic of modern life delude people into thinking the world is orderly and logical, when this order is interrupted during times of social crisis or war—commonplaces in the modern world, according to Tanaka—people act like the "instinctual animals [*honnō no hito*] that they really are. . . . For instance when a soldier enters enemy territory, it's natural for him to rape women and murder people" (15).

I want to talk now about Nakamura Kokyo, the second major figure in the sexological project to normalize *hentai*. Before I do that, though, it's crucial to clarify a point about the limits to the universalization of *hentai*. Although important popular intellectuals like Minakata and Rampo were much more open-minded about homoerotic theory and practice, there is absolutely no doubt that Tanaka considered homoeroticism perverse. Like Nakamura, he didn't register his homophobia by describing it as *hentai*; instead the code for homoeroticism was reserved for the main signifier of "perversion" in the dominant anti-Ebing wing of mainstream Japanese sexology, *tōsaku*. In Tanaka's major books, *The Shadowy Regions of Human Sexuality* (1922) and *Sex Maniacs* (1925), the signifier for perversion is largely applied to contingent acts and not essential identities. It should be pointed out, though, that in most of the cases of homosexual acts and in many of the cases of hysterical acts, as we saw in part I, these contain the potential to anticipate identities as "homosexuals" and "hysterics." This was not the case with sadism, masochism, or fetishism; these are all erotic aspects irreducible to identities.

Like many of the Japanese pioneers in psychology and psychiatry in the 1920s and 1930s, such as the Freud scholar Otsuki Kenji, Nakamura Kokyo (1881–1952) studied English literature, graduating from Tokyo University in 1905. Attending Natsume Sōseki's lectures inspired him to try writing, and he published a novel and worked as a journalist at the *Asahi* newspaper for four years after finishing his degree. It took him almost a decade to finish university because he spent a great deal of time at home caring for a younger brother with severe psychological problems. While nursing his brother, who died in 1908, Nakamura studied his various psychic ailments, especially multiple personality disorder and somnambulism. Frustration with the lack of information available in Japan in the area of what was then called *hentai shinri* (abnormal psychology) led him to organize the first psychiatric society in the country. With help from the well-known psychiatrist and university lecturer Morita Masatake and the neurologist Kono Ryunosuke, Nakamura became president of the Japanese Psychiatric Association in June 1917, and in October of that year the organization's internal journal, *Abnormal Psychology*, started appearing monthly (Oda 2001, 9–17).

Concurrent with the start of the journal, Nakamura opened up the first facility for psychotherapy in Japan in a small house in Gotenyama, Shinagawa, then a suburb of Tokyo. The next year, 1918, Morita himself opened a second center in Setagaya, Tokyo. It took Nakamura several years to get his center off the ground, but beginning in the winter of 1917 he claimed some successes in helping several patients with hysteria and severe neurasthenia. Using what became known as the "Morita method" in the 1920s, when psychotherapy centers spread throughout Japan, Nakamura employed a combination of dream analysis, group discussion, and self-help through journal keeping and growing one's own vegetables (Oda 2001, 18–19). The clinic was completely focused on rehabilitation, and Nakamura's method remained basically the same after he finished medical school and obtained his doctor's license in 1928. He was able to open a large hysteria treatment and research center in Chiba in 1931, connected to the Chiba University hospital, where he taught for a decade.

Through the journal, a monthly lecture series in Tokyo, sponsoring speakers to go into rural areas to give lectures, and an influential international annual conference, the Japanese Psychiatric Association quickly attracted the most influential psychiatrists, psychologists, sexologists, criminologists, historians of sexuality, and cultural anthropologists in Japan. It became the intellectual home for Minakata Kumagusu, who was invited to participate in the group's activities and publish in its organ. *Abnormal Psychology* is often credited with introducing German psychoanalysis to Japan, along with the techniques of hypnosis and dream analysis. The journal's first two years pioneered academic discussions of schizophrenia, telepathy, sadomasochism, sleepwalking crimes, vampires, the third sex, and the plausibility of channeling the dead. Almost every thematic that appeared in the erotic-grotesque novels of writers such as Rampo and Yumeno Kyūsaku appeared a decade earlier in the pages of *Abnormal Psychology*.

Barely two years after Habuto and Sawada kicked off the debate about *hentai* with their introduction of Krafft-Ebing to a popular Japanese audience in 1915, *Abnormal Psychology* would stake out a very different position on *hentai* and argue it for nine years, until Nakamura decided to go to medical school and shut the journal down in September 1926. Absolutely opposed to Habuto's and Sawada's phobic assignation of *hentai* to select individual identities, Nakamura claimed in his editorial introducing the first issue, "The abnormal is in everyone [*dare nimo aru ijō*]. . . . We will be using the word *hentai* as that which is relative [*sōtai shite*] to the normal—as an exception is to the rule; or as the special is to the standard. We absolutely don't intend for *hentai* to mean 'pathological'" (*Hentai Shinri*, October 1917, 1–2). In this war of positions in the debate about *hentai*, Nakamura explains that he is starting the journal in part because of his own frequent experiences of *hentai* in the form of depression and neurasthenia. In other words, this first scholarly investigation of all the *aspects* of *hentai* will not take the othering position that *identities* of abjected subjects, such as those stigmatized in Habuto's and Sawada's book, will be referred to as *hentai*. Aspects of abnormal psychology impact all modern people indiscriminately, beginning with the editor himself.

Normalizing *Hentai*

The journal *Abnormal Psychology* was more representative of the liberalism that characterized Japan after the First World War than the work of the Ebing school. And one of the goals of that liberalism was to enlighten the public. To this end, the journal and the Japanese Psychiatric Association put on countless lectures both in the cities and in the countryside; in the early days these usually included some demonstration of hypnosis, in which audience members could get hypnotized for the first time. The message here was that succumbing to hypnosis was evidence of the existence of *hentai* phenomena: *Hentai* are us! But more than mere showmanship, the lectures and demonstrations were enlightenment projects designed to instruct the public in new ways of thinking about good and evil, right and wrong, and criminals and innocents. Especially with regard to criminality, the Japanese Psychiatric Association shared the widespread sense in metropolitan society that crime was multicausal. Rather than looking at genetic and racial causes for crime, as was the case in European criminology, the Association took the progressive position that the world of capitalist industrialization as well as the specific site of urban Tokyo were the primary causes of crime.

Nakamura often made presentations to the Tokyo Metropolitan Police, and two years after the Psychiatric Association was founded he became one of their paid consultants. In the following years several of the sexologists connected to *Abnormal Psychology*, and to its spawn *Sex Research*, were paid to act as consultants on criminal cases. In this way Nakamura's and Tanaka's insistence on de-essentializing *hentai* spread well beyond a mass culture readership. It's difficult to say how much of an impact it had on juridical ideology, but the message to depersonalize crime and the abnormal led to a heretofore unrecognized acceptance of the fundamental criminality and injustice of urban, capitalist society. Nakamura's Association pioneered an analysis of the ways that humans, as fundamentally social and worldly beings, expressed aspects of *hentai* because Japanese and global capitalist society were themselves fundamentally *hentai*. As a contributor to the ten-volume series put out by the Japanese Criminological Society in 1930, Nakamura defined every modern subject as split to varying degrees between the three modes of *hentai* he called individual, social, and universal (*ippanteki*; Nakamura K. 1930, 5).

Similar to Rampo's and Gonda's identification of a "primitive" subject stripped of all "normal" characteristics of humanity and defenseless against further reification (owing to commodity capitalism's encroachment into the human nervous system), Nakamura insisted that it was absolutely ordinary for modern subjects to experience some form of personality splitting. What the journal referred to as "split-personality disorder" (*bunretsubyō*) was normalized in Nakamura's work beginning in the mid-1920s as simply "multiple personality" (*nijūjinkaku*), without the pathologizing *byō*, meaning "disorder." In a collection of his essays on multiple personality published in 1937 he warns that bourgeois ideology alone tells us that we are "unified at the levels of knowledge, affect and intentionality. . . . However, all scholars and doctors agree that each and every human experiences some degree of splitting" (2, 328). Although this can result in some people being completely split into three different personality types, "more often, it leads to two different kinds of personalities in modern people" (3). Nakamura discusses several case histories of people with "severe" splitting, all of them women. Here, in his major treatment of the projected "universality" of *hentai*, a global and Japanese phenomenon that produces effects of splitting and other neuroses in all humans, he neglects to mention one male patient.

Although I've offered a revisionist reading of what I think can be called the dominant stream of popular Japanese sexology in the texts of

Tanaka and Nakamura—firmly opposed to the sensationalizing eroto-phobia of the Ebing school of Habuto Eiji and Sawada Junjirō—there are clear limits to their liberal expansiveness. As we saw in part I in the discussion of Tanaka, the strong tendency in their work is to isolate women as objects of splitting. In many instances, despite their insis-tence on *hentai* as something that doesn't discriminate and universally impacts all modern subjects, their work treats women alone as the privi-leged subject split by modern society. When Nakamura emerged in 1930 as the main theoretician and therapeutic expert on hysteria in Japan, there was a gendered sensitivity that led him to recognize that women suffered the effects of modern life more than men did. We saw a similar sense in Tanaka as well. However, the overwhelming tendency in their work is to treat women as objects of splitting and men as subjects and authorities on splitting. The naturalization of this binary opposition was widespread in mass culture's reflection on the neuropolitical effects of imperial society. Even in liberal sexological and psychological discourse there was an acceptance of women as splattered and shattered irreme-diably by modern *hentai*; men were split only on occasion. As I suggest below, men and *mobo*s contain and manage their subjective splitting by themselves splattering women. It is not only a generalized modern and universal *hentai* that causes the neuropolitical shattering of women, but a very specific kind of modern male subjectivity that is frequently the cause of women's pain.

6

REVOLUTIONARY PORNOGRAPHY AND THE DECLINING RATE OF PLEASURE

The remarkable phenomenon of the increase in women readers in recent years has influenced popular writing in much the same way that the discovery of a vast colony might influence the country. The sudden development of women's magazines had an effect on the literary establishment not unlike that which the growth of the spinning industry's targeting of the China market has had on Japan's financial system.

ŌYA SŌICHI, *BUNGAKUTEKI SEIJUTSURON*

Film is the art form corresponding to the pronounced threat to life in which people live today. People need to expose themselves to shock effects in their adjustment to the dangers threatening them. Film corresponds to profound changes in the apparatus of perception—changes that are experienced on the scale of private existence by each passerby in big-city traffic.

WALTER BENJAMIN, "THE WORK OF ART IN THE AGE OF ITS TECHNOLOGICAL REPRODUCIBILITY"

The Killing Kapitalist Konglomerate

In the previous chapter I began to argue that a new type of economic logic featuring invasive ways of expropriating surplus from desiring bodies was evident in metropolitan spaces in Japan after the First World War. Before developing that argument here, I address two potential queries. First, wasn't this shift to a new capital logic merely a global phenomenon having little to do with the specificity of East Asia as a region and with Japan as its hegemon? Second, as modernizationists would emphasize, didn't the change to a more advanced form of capitalism merely reflect the awesome improvements in the technoscientific *relations* of production and have very little to do with the *forces* of production expressed in the contradiction between capitalists and workers?

By way of a positive response to the first question and a negative response to the second, my argument continues in a tradition of Marxist philosophy originally developed in the 1950s and 1960s by Frantz Fanon and other revolutionary theorists of subaltern agency and more recently by the "autonomous theory" of Antonio Negri and others. They argue that human energy in the form of labor and human expression in the form of desiring production are the fundamental motor elements in capitalism. All the other phenomena so insistently propagandized by liberal capitalist ideology and modernization theory as incontrovertible advances—machine technology, scientific progress, and so forth—are secondary and parasitic effects of the constituent and ontological force of living labor. It should be evident prima facie that without the labor of Chinese coolies, paid what Marx called the miserable "Chinese wage," there would have been no Japanese colonial presence in Northeast China beginning in 1905. Almost the entire built space was their doing, the ontically constituted evidence of their constituent labor. Similarly, without the remittances sent back to Kyushu and other places in Japan by the one hundred thousand women sent to do sex work and their kidnapper pimps in East and Southeast Asia beginning in the 1880s (along with another one million Japanese sent to work in the Asia-Pacific), these areas in Japan would not have been able to pay the price for imperial development: schools, hospitals, legislative buildings, police, and more. The causality here is direct. Somewhat more abstractly, without the invisible surplus sucked out of these and other laboring biopolitical subjectivities, Japanese capital would not have been able to advance to a higher stage which demanded more consumerism and more complex ways of commodifying things and people. A fortiori, without the violent expropriation of surplus value from living labor in biopolitical capitalism, there was nothing pushing imperial capital to intensify and expand into new areas, colonizing not just Taiwan, Korea, and the Guandong Lease in Northeast China as it had by 1910, but also, as the Marxist Ōya diagnosed in 1930 (this chapter's first epigraph), the very sensoriums of the rapidly expanding consumer readership in metropolitan Japan.

As a way to explore Ōya's provocation, I want to examine the erotic-grotesque print media, which not only hegemonized consumer stimulation (and therefore desire), but also pioneered the movement to saturate and subsume the whole of society under the commodity form. The erotic-grotesque writers, translators, and artists not only refused the standard posture of art for art's sake, but reversed the utopian position often assumed by aesthetes that a more beautiful world could be created only away from the vulgarity of market exchange and massification. For the most important of the erotic-grotesque cultural producers, Umehara Hokumei,[1] the ideal of a utopian transformation of Japanese society toward the goal of liberating people from sexual, ethnoracial, and class oppression could be achieved only *inside* capitalist media, immanent to reification. Umehara reasoned that the new printing and distribution methods developed after the Tokyo earthquake of 1923, concomitant with the explosion in mass readership as middle-class households regularly subscribed to one daily newspaper and three or four monthly magazines (Nagamine 1997; Frederick 2006), offered new opportunities for leftists and liberationists to popularize their opinions. His position, which would become de rigueur among leftist cultural producers into the 1930s, was that the mass media offered heretofore unimagined possibilities for creators to get their ideas across to the masses of consumers hungry for them. If these ideas could be put into provocative new forms designed to capture modern curiosity—to get metropolitan subjects to *pay attention* to and consume their commodities, inadvertently *paying back* to the capitalist system the wages they were (under)*paid* for their labor—then there was no limit to how far they could spread. For example, when Umehara wrenched control of the editorial direction of the new arts journal *Arts Market* (*Bungei Shijō*) from his coeditor, Kaneko Yōbun, in November 1925, he declared war on those who considered art too elevated for a world saturated by commodification:

> In the real world, art is a commodity whose value is determined by the abacus. However, all around us are artsy types who continue stubbornly to inflate the power of art and literature, claiming that it is the only thing left in this reified world with the power to transcend dirty money. Here is a message from *Arts Market* to those people: we kick off this magazine with the dual purpose of destroying that idiotic belle-lettrist superstition, while we push forward with the hypercommodification of art and literature. This is not a blasphemy [*bōtoku*] against the arts. Rather, it's to state the obvious: in advanced capitalist society it's impossible for something to exist that's not a

commodity. . . . However, the Japanese art world is dazzled by old-fashioned labels. It should be obvious that this violates the law of market commodification that rewards newness. Whether a commodity is good or bad, superior or inferior—Let the Market Decide! (*Arts Market*, November 1925)

To make certain that his readers didn't forget his crusade, Umehara included this declaration to embrace the power of the capitalist marketplace on the inside front cover of almost every issue of *Arts Market*. His political wager was that leftist and liberationist content didn't have to be compromised by sensationalized media forms guaranteeing quick profits. Because of the speed and efficacy of the new image commodities, it was quickly becoming axiomatic for him that liberation = commodification. It was also clear to him following the Tokyo earthquake in 1923 that modern sex and catastrophe—the displacements wrought by commodification and nature—were where the money and message were. This awareness is documented in his first novel, published in 1924 and immediately censored, only the beginning of what would become a lifelong struggle with the Home Ministry censors. Using the literary codes of the Japanese "I-novel," *The Killing Kapitalist Konglomerate* (Satsujin kaisha) tells the story of a young, impoverished freelance writer desperate to come up with something that will sell.

The novel begins with the first-person narrator detailing his writer's block caused by intense neurasthenia (*shinkei*). He's well past a deadline to rewrite his present manuscript and has to redo everything (Umehara 1924, 3). On the second page of the novel, the narrator thinks someone has come by to visit him, but it turns out to be only a telegram delivery, and the telegram's foreboding neuropolitical message is: "All over your body, your nerve endings are raw and stimulated" (4). The narrator bursts out laughing and admits, "Even I had to laugh at this." But the laughter doesn't last long: "All this sucks, really sucks [*saitei*]. My head—in other words, this manuscript—is killing me; but this Goddamned evil desire [*motto shinkaku ni akumateki jōnetsu*] of mine is the worst. I thought that tormenting myself like this would help me write something, any-fucking-thing. But what? I-novel? Young girl's first love? Film script? Translation?" (6). In this pioneering erotic-grotesque novel (Jō 1993, 108), we are offered a world wherein heretofore external media (in the form of the telegram etiologizing the narrator's frazzled neurasthenia) and internal neurological states are collapsed into one. Moreover, the sensorium of the writer ("my head") is conflated with the manuscript he's writing, as well as the one we are reading in Japanese. Commodities have literally deterritorialized the boundaries that previously separated people from people and people from things. Umehara depicts an invasion and hostile takeover of the very neurological operations of humans.

The narrator's block is overcome by a sudden visit from an old school friend named Santarō who has stopped in Tokyo on his way to Shanghai. Santarō bursts into the narrator's room and looks terrible; he has blood-shot eyes and is thin and strung out from an opium habit. Santarō explains that he's on the way to Shanghai on business with his company, the Killing Kapitalist Konglomerate. Repeatedly, Santarō challenges the narrator that he won't believe the "huge incident" that is going to take place there, something similar to what the company has pulled off in other places. As Santarō begins to tell his friend about the company, the narrator realizes that his friend's erotic-grotesque testimony has answered his concerns about what genre to use in order to make money: the tale of the bloodthirsty, sex-obsessed, and profit-mad company overwhelms all other narrative possibilities.

Santarō has been an employee of the Killing Kapitalist Konglomerate for several years, working in Japan and the United States. He relates that when he was first brought to the company's corporate headquarters in San Francisco, he realized right away that even though it was a huge hotel with many services, "they actually murder between three to five people each day, steal all their money, and then drain their blood into a huge pool" (20). He describes some of their methods, leading the narrator to write that he can't believe what his friend is saying: "This guy's completely twisted [*hentai*], what the hell is he talking about?" (21). Still, he urges him to continue.

Santarō explains the corporate capitalist philosophy of his company in the following way:

> Usually when people think of secret societies, they think of a group with a particular philosophy, but our group doesn't think about abstract crap like capitalism and nationalism; our deal was about pure profit-making. Killing Kapitalist Konglomerate existed for the sole purpose of extracting surplus and killing people. . . . At other com-

panies workers organize strikes and make political speeches, but our company is just about killing and money. What other people call revolution or proletarian liberation is like the nonsense of mentally retarded children. If you take money and women away from us, there's nothing left—zero. . . . Most people think like I do that it's totally fine to kill humans; there's no way around this. Intellectual types like you probably call behavior like this "abnormal psychology" [*hentai shinri*]; and maybe you're right, it's *hentai* all right. But it's all second nature. When I first started with the company probably half of what I did was done out of curiosity; I was fascinated with all the killing and free sex. The other half I was forced to do. But now the devilish part has completely taken over and burned its way right through me, now it's my life. And this much is life too: the more the world is civilized, the more its dependence on murder increases. That's the dirty secret to the whole civilization deal. (23–30)

Santarō recalls that before he began to work with the company he was forced to go through a neuropolitical initiation involving drugs and a kind of electroshock therapy. This is how he becomes what he calls a "Jap hitman [*jappa jobuman*]." He describes a typical initiation into a secret society replete with hooded men, guards with rifles, loud military music, and a group of judges deciding whether or not to accept the person into the society. Santarō is terrified they will just kill him (53). After answering some questions he is given the company name S 403 and told to swear an oath, which he repeats. After some chanting he realizes that he has been accepted, and a huge man he refers to as Monster (*kaibutsu*) shows him around the company's huge hotel compound (64–71). Monster appears to have a fairly morbid sense of humor, as the huge rooms are given the title "The First Block of Hell," the "Second Block of Hell," and so forth. The First Block is where the daily killings happen. It seems that the company kidnaps rich people, fleeces as much money as they can, and then murders them and mutilates the bodies, draining all the blood out of them. Company members consume some of the blood and body parts in the dining area, the Second Block of Hell. The leftovers are sold to various places, including to natives colonized by Japan in the South Pacific (*Nanyō*). There are two full pages here (74–75) that have been almost completely deleted by the censors, pages in which the scenes of cannibalism seem to have been depicted fairly explicitly.

The next large room they visit is the "hostess room," filled with beautiful women from all over the world, where the men in the company can go and do anything they want to them. The next day Santarō is ordered to go to New York City to commit his first murder for the company (at an African American gathering in Madison Square Garden). First, though, he is told to go to the hostess room for some fun before he departs. He describes the scene to the narrator this way:

> When I walked into the room, everywhere I looked there were half-naked women; there were even people having sex right in public! But it was all perverted sex, probably way too weird for you [*Kimi, zenbu hentai seiyoku bakari taerarenai*]. As soon as I sat down in a seat about ten women were all over me, embracing me. Let me tell you I was pretty happy about that. . . . There was one woman in particular who unleashed a beastly desire inside me and I couldn't get enough of her. But even so, it was obvious I could do anything I wanted to any of these women; they were all my possessions [*shoyūbutsu*]. (81–82)

The narrator interrupts to confess that he's totally envious of Santarō's experiences and that "all the readers are jealous as well" (82).

Santarō says that he fell head over heels for a Spanish woman who is the daughter of a rich merchant from Chicago. She starts speaking to him in Chinese, thinking that because he is so short he must be Chinese. (Santarō wears a mask and is dressed completely in black, like all the other company men whenever they are on the premises.) She tells him how much she wants him over and over, and then confesses that she was kidnapped and brought to the company in San Francisco. Apparently, she was forced to service company men sexually for a whole year, right in the same room where she is having nonstop sex with Santarō. She says, "Men would come and see us anytime they wanted. At first it was horrible, then I stopped thinking about it. After I refused to let it enter my head, it gradually became just a way of life for me" (87). Then she graduated to being a dancing girl, so she had to have sex with men only every once in a while.

Santarō returns to San Francisco after going to New York to murder an African American advocate for black independence; after the murder he has the body sent to the company branch in Shanghai, where they'll undertake experiments on it. After his first murder for the company he becomes obsessed with a Polish woman who left Eastern Europe during the First World War hoping to send money back home to her sick father. After the company lends her money she's forced to be a sex slave. Apparently, the company has performed a sort of lobotomy on her because all she does is alternately laugh and scream, while she is forced to have sex with men in the company. At some point a new company member is ordered to cannibalize her, and Santarō tells the narrator, "He had no choice but to go through with it" (131).

As Santarō notices women disappearing from the hostess room, he goes to investigate and finds a man defiling freshly killed corpses (pages 138–40 have been heavily censored). This is too much for Santarō, and he asks the necrophile why he doesn't just go up to the hostess room for sex with live women rather than having sex with dead ones. The man responds that he "despises all those women up there" (142). He explains to Santarō, "You probably think this a pretty outrageous type of sexual perversion [*hentai seiyoku*], but let me tell you that the necrophilic desire to violate women is a desire just as human as any other. Given that, there are ethical considerations [*dōtokushin*] that I'm dealing with here just like in any other kind of sexual encounter." Santarō remains incredulous and repeats, "If you think you want to molest why don't you go to the hostess club upstairs where all the women are our slaves and you can do whatever you want to them?" But the necrophile just laughs. At this point Santarō turns to the narrator and confesses, "You're probably one of those guys who thinks that this is the perverse of the perverse [*hentai no hentai*]. You know, before I joined the Company I would have thought that as well, but now I just don't know anymore" (143).

The activities continue at the company, with murders and abductions happening on a global scale. Santarō's affair with the Spanish woman ends after she is murdered and eaten by a new employee. The operations of the company put severe psychic stress on Santarō. He starts to explain to the narrator that about a year ago (he has been in the company for five years) he began to feel that he was different people living inside one body (282). At this point he starts to unravel somewhat and tells the narrator that before he left for the United States he worked as an editor for one of the new women's magazines in Tokyo. It's because of that experience and the feelings that he's developed since being in the company that he says, "When I die, I want to be remembered as a woman" (306). Abruptly he asks the narrator, "Do you want to commit suicide with me on Sunday?" He explains that there is a Suicide Club at the company where members, guests, and sex slaves can go and kill themselves. At the end of chapter 28 the narrator exclaims, "This guy is off the hook! I realize now what a small world I've been living in; I've never heard anything like this. What a scary company he belongs to" (309).

The last chapter is set at the Club, where there is a formal ball taking place called the "Dance of Death" (*shi no buyō*). It is a classic decadent club scene replete with a jazz band consisting entirely of topless women; other women dance naked on huge cakes, while still other women lie bleeding on the lushly carpeted floors. Santarō relates that the most beautiful women are Chinese and that there is at least one Japanese woman who has been "passing" as Caucasian. Club members sexually fondle these dying and dead women, while women who lose at blackjack are immediately murdered (314). Santarō has discovered the Suicide Club. Losing at cards leads to immediate death, and it seems that Santarō is trying to lose. After a few hours playing and not losing, he gives up and pulls a Chinese coolie worker outside and asks the man to kill him. The Chinese man gives Santarō chocolate, telling him that it is laced with a poison, but it turns out to be opium and, just his luck, Santarō becomes hopelessly addicted to the drug and is forced to do more killing for the Killing Kapitalist Konglomerate in exchange for his regular opium supply (315). This last scene took place two years before Santarō's meeting with the narrator, and he has been conducting business for the company in the interim, moving back and forth between Shanghai, Tokyo, and the United States.

The form and content of the novel are so overwhelming that I think it's best to let the text speak for itself. It was immediately prohibited from being sold publicly, although approximately a hundred copies were distributed privately. There are few comparisons to it in world literature; Ferdinand Céline's work in the late 1930s and William Burroughs's and Dennis Cooper's work are a few that come to mind. For our purposes, it's fairly obvious from the portions I've translated that there's a positing of the modern capitalist world as *hentai*; the word appears over twenty times in several different signifying contexts. From this generalized modern condition of *hentai* there's an eliciting of even more intense instances of *hentai*—what Santarō refers to as the "hentai born from hentai"—necrophilia, cannibalism, and so forth.

As I try in this book to locate a new neuropolitical regime, one that expropriates human attention and transmutes desire, I find that the central characters in the biopolitical regime I identified in part I all appear here, abstracted in neuropolitics as well: coolies, kidnapped women forced to do sex work, pimps, and inhumanly greedy capitalist corporations like the Oriental Development Company and the South Manchurian Railway Company. The subaltern subjectivities spawned from the imperial periphery return to the metropolitan center as spectral reminders of the bodies whose stolen labor pushed capital to this new stage, where all elements of human life are submitted to and subsumed under capital. They appear here right at the start of this new neuropolitical regime, and they will be featured characters in the erotic-grotesque media from the mid-1920s until the mid-1930s.

I wanted to begin the discussion of erotic-grotesque media by giving readers a sense of some of the representative texts; we have already looked at Edogawa Rampo's fictions. In Japanese cultural history the period from 1926 to 1934 is often allegorized as the "erotic-grotesque-nonsense age" and is compared to Germany's Weimar cabaret culture or the flapper or jazz age in the United States. It is either celebrated as a continuation and intensification of the liberal cosmopolitanism of Japan after the First World War (Yonezawa Yoshihirō and Jō Ichirō; Silverberg 2007), or its cynicism and hedonism are linked to the fascism of the late 1930s by both offering cultural conservatives something to rail against and eventually providing drifting and directionless *mobo, moga,* and salarymen with some deeper cultural national purpose (Minami Hiroshi; Kanno Satomi). Although my analysis draws from both positions, I am going to argue something different.

Contemporary critics in Japan were equally divided over the erotic-grotesque as a social phenomenon; it was dismissed as a superficial, media-driven fad by leftists like Ōya and Gonda and taken seriously as the expression of the most advanced form of capitalism by Akagami Yoshitsuge and, in a different way, Umehara. In chapter 5, I read several important sexologists together with the sociologist Akagami to develop the idea of "neuropolitics." Here, I return to Akagami's *The Face of Erotic-Grotesque Society* (1931), the introduction to the popular *The Illustrated Guide to the Contemporary Hyper-Bizarre* and arguably the most widely available contemporary introduction to the erotic-grotesque.[2] It dutifully depicts the different aspects of this ultrabizarre capitalist society using the general framework of the "erotic-grotesque-nonsense," three words that, by late 1930, were commonly deployed together.

While it is a titillating introduction to the phenomenon, *The Face of Erotic-Grotesque Society* is much more, filled with references to and critical readings of contemporary social, psychological, biological, and political economic theory. It represents one of the few attempts in Japanese before the Pacific War to understand how the shifts in contemporary hypercapitalism were impacting all aspects of human society, down to reprogramming the wetware of human neurology. For Akagami, the phenomenon of the erotic-grotesque is best understood first as the effect of the acute division of labor (*bungyō*) in capitalism. This produces increasing abstraction away from an intuition of how things are produced and toward the fetishistic consumption of things driven by the reification rampant in modern capitalism (1931, 6–8). Rather than being able to see society as a whole, humans are frantically trying just to keep up with the exhausting and brutal pace of metropolitan society, inducing wild swings of affect, from "melancholic depression to drunken excitation" (7). However, these wild oscillations from slackness and exhaustion to breakneck speed and frantic chaos aren't simply human responses; they are isomorphic with the technical operations of machines everywhere evident in modern metropoles and are switched on and off randomly.

His observation that the wetware of the human nervous system is becoming more like the hardware of machine technology impels Akagami to urge the application of "the theory of the dialectic to the level of psychic functioning" (1931, 13). Employing the dialectic to understand the new relation between machinic technical media and human psychic functioning will be the first step in "identifying new modern forms of economic value production" (13). He notes that the recent dominance of credit and financial speculation is obviously one new type of value extraction in capitalism. But the newest form of value mining—the one that Akagami will be primarily concerned with specifying under the rubric of the erotic-grotesque in modern Japanese capitalism—is the extraction of value through the extension of the pathways of capital and control into the human body, pathways that "directly touch on the nervous system [*kanjō no kinsen fureru*]." The neuropolitical invasion of the body by factory technologies at work and by the abstract violence of the commodity form threatening humans "while we are in the movie theater, shopping, reading magazines, or simply in the streets," means that humans don't respond to external stimuli as they did in the nineteenth century. Akagami's dialectic applied to the human psyche demonstrates that a central aspect of hypermodern capitalism is that humans now appear both "super- and subhuman" at the same time (22).

Although human neurasthenic transformation is evident among the "stars of modern capitalism"—the salarymen, students, and proletariat (1931, 9)—Akagami warns that the sole beneficiaries of this inhuman system are the superrich who remain impervious to the shock and awe of modern capitalism. They act in a cool and rational fashion within the logical parameters of the profit motive. When they aren't on "skiing holidays in Hokkaidō" or vacationing on the "beaches of Southeast Asia," these supercapitalists are scheming about new ways to extract surplus from the masses, such as "forced labor" (kyōsei rōdō; 10). Their most successful recent scheme is figuring out how to expropriate value directly from the human nervous system.

Akagami's second and third chapters, "Primitivism in the Modern" and "Curiosity," expand on several themes introduced by the sexologists Tanaka Kōgai and Nakamura before him. For Akagami the "second nature" or "second life" of modern capitalism, referenced frequently in the sexology discourse as well as in Umehara's erotic-grotesque work, has the powerful effect of returning humans to a stage of development before the establishment of civilized societies with codified legal systems. As Gonda theorized around the same time, more grand and grounded ethical commitments to family and nation are absented in the contemporary metropolis dominated instead by fleeting novelty and stupefied fascination. Like many others in Japan at this time, Akagami deploys the metaphor of the "modern primitive" to depict this state wherein a historically specific second nature or second life of hypercapitalism appears to regress alienated humans to a state dominated by pure instinct. Instead of human deportment taking place through the ethical determinations of good and evil and the affective determinations of pleasure and pain, the rewiring of human nervous systems has stripped metropolitan humans of all ethical and sensual reasoning, remaindering only raw "Pavlovian" humans as modern primitives (84–85). These primitive subjects of metropolitan Japan possess only the most basic instincts for sex and survival; "higher" civilizational concerns for development and community are glaringly absent. Modern capitalism has pillaged all human civilizational progress, leaving societies ruled solely by the "law of profit" espoused by a tiny elite, with the rest of humanity transmuted by capital into idiot receptacles on life-support systems, like the human biopower left to subsist as carcasses in the film *The Matrix* (1999). Even the instincts that humans are left with by this expropriative system are continually "obliterated in the boiler of capitalism" (Akagami 1931, 33). In producing primitive metropolitan subjects incapable of ethical adjudication, advanced capitalism installs what Akagami calls the "rational system of the irrational [*higōriteki*]."[3]

The one thing that remains constant throughout the scalding assault on erstwhile human instincts is the condition generated from these attacks: curiosity. Akagami writes, "The instinctual impulse for newness producing curiosity is the sole thing that is allowed to progress in modern capitalism" (1931, 78–79). He reserves the signifier *nonsense* to describe the logic of unreason that codifies what counts as curious for modern urbanites. Unlike morality, physical science, or industrial organization, nonsense "respects no rules or laws." It is even opposed to language itself, being ruled by and attracted to images only (58). The evanescence and speed of images is perfect for responding to and stimulating curiosity. Although capitalist domination is carried out by a tiny directorate through planning and mathematics (60–61), this is mystified by the capitalist elite. However, on the receiving end of capitalist domination is a space "beyond words and rational logic," where nonsense rules the world of the subaltern through the force-feeding of "gestures and images" (58–59), similar to Walter Benjamin's capitalist "phantasmagoria, which a person enters in order to be distracted. [Therein] he surrenders to the manipulations of the commodity while enjoying his alienation from himself and others" (2008, 101). The contemporary media environment of "sports, dance halls, advertising, and film" is proof enough for Akagami that the image commodity is what is most important for Japan's advanced capitalism.

While the poet Soeda depicted capitalist real subsumption as a "foundy" (*chūzōba*) that pounded and grinded human nerves and flesh into new forms, Umehara and Akagami likened the process to a "slaughterhouse" (*tosatsujō*) for humans. Describing how capitalist slaughter transforms humans unrecognizably by cutting them off from their previous ethical and affective understanding, Akagami moves into a complex discussion of the precise function of the erotic and grotesque in this neuropolitical regime. Within the movement of the curiosity instinct, what Akagami calls *ero* becomes sovereign. However, the signification of *ero* by some of the central erotic-grotesque social theorists and cultural producers is not quite the same as the elaborations on modern sexuality by Tanaka, Nakamura, and other physicians and sexologists. The Sino-Japanese compound dominating the sexology discussions was *seiyoku*, "sexual desire." Although it grew out of Tanaka's discussion of *hentai seiyoku* as "modern sexuality," what comes to be widely referred to as *ero* is less human and more shot through by the logic of the commodity. Neither *ero* nor *hentai seiyoku* is condemned as the personal failure of this or that individual, and both are understood as the logical effect of metropolitan society newly dominated by the invasion of nihilistic commodities into heretofore inviolable human realms such as the rural farm, the bourgeois home, and private psyches. Also like *hentai seiyoku*, *ero* bridges the distance between the external world of image commodities and the internal world of fantasies and singular sexualities; it is the sign of the conflation of the two. However, beyond *hentai seiyoku* and similar to the Möbius strip of recent postmodern theory, *ero* is the proof that human interiors have been invaded, expropriated, and projected onto the screen of the sum total of the image commodities, what it took Guy Debord until 1967 to identify as the "society of the spectacle." As human psychosomatic interiors are invaded and occupied, they are intimately and directly subjected to the stimuli of image commodities, now with their defenses against these external threats eliminated. Akagami theorizes that the only thing the compromised human organism is able to do in this situation is to *become one with the invading agent*, gradually emptying out erstwhile vitalist, authentic pleasures and desires and replacing them with alienated, commodified *ero*. Akagami's extraordinary chapter "A Sociology of *Ero-Guro*" offers a detailed discussion of this that is worth quoting at length.

> As Plato says in his philosophy of *ero*, by means of their imaginations, humans are able to visualize the perfect idea of the Beautiful as it exists in the heavens. Male readers out there, merely through the after-image [*ushiro sugata*], you feel you possess a woman. But do you really think that this adequately represents some really fantastic woman? Why do you think that only by means of the after-image you've captured the real woman? . . .
>
> There is a beautiful woman, but she was made beautiful through the filter [*kami*] of the imagination, a beauty that is previously modified [*modefuai*] by the Idea. All this takes place because *ero* filmically

projects her as an after-image. Therefore, when you look again at the real woman your gaze will pass right through her and you'll be disappointed by reality. Your *ero* will become scrambled [*muchakucha*] as you face the real world without the comfort of your imagination. However, this disappointment will fade as *ero* discovers substitute commodities.

When humans search for the most stimulating things driven by curiosity, they make use of their pupils and their vision; this is where we are able to feel the strongest sensation of *ero*. Concretely, this is where we are most immediately exposed to *ero*, and if we experience *ero* without thinking critically about this register, this will only result in *ero* remaining savage and primitive. However, no matter how critically distanced humans become, the pulse of modern life is so feverish that everyone seeks out the most intense and ferocious shocks and stimulae. The end result of this is an *ero* that is beastly, sexually perverted, bizarre and *hentai*. Advanced capitalism puts these modes of *ero* to work for it [*shokugyōka*], and reaps profits from them [*eirika*]. In cafés, in bars, in dance halls, in movie theaters, in peep shows, in casinos, modern capitalism is mobilizing and taking full advantage of *ero*. (1931, 150–51)

In offering this most incisive analysis of the new centrality of alienated desire to advanced metropolitan capitalism, Akagami is clearly struggling to find the language to describe what he thinks is happening when modern capitalism "puts *ero* to work for it." Nevertheless, he succeeds in outlining the contours of a system of value production that goes beyond the expropriation of surplus labor (central to the previous mode of formal subsumption of waged labor in biopolitical capital) to work directly on human perception and attention. *Ero* works for capital by directing the curiosity of humans to image commodities, which humans are solicited to *pay for* as their increasingly stripped-down primitive curiosity impels them to *pay attention to*. Intuiting what the media critic Jonathan Beller (2006) insightfully calls the "attention economy," Akagami understands that the image commodities of *ero* capitalism must become increasingly more bizarre, strange, and *hentai* to continue to elicit stimulation and stupefaction and guarantee the human investment of money and attention. Through the dialectic of image commodities and human psyches that Akagami called for earlier—where what had previously been Two distinct entities are sublated into a more complex One—human cognitive deportment becomes a homologic extension of a process whose "end result is beastly, bizarre and *hentai*." Akagami's language here appears to intentionally collapse the distinction between the contents of the image commodities and human actions; the teleology of modern *ero* capitalism runs in the direction of the dialectical synthesis of the two.

As Akagami is sketching out the tendency for modern image commodities, it makes sense that his description pushes in the direction of film. The talkie was introduced to Japan in 1929, the year before Akagami's book was written. As capital needs to continually elicit human attention, the description of this process converges toward moving images, the image commodity that is most successful in capturing human curiosity. Although magazines similarly bulldoze commodities directly into the human sensorium, the moving image is so powerful that it leads humans to misrecognize phantasms as real things. Akagami warns men not to confuse "after-images" of women—pictures "taken" by men and montaged through their image-commodified imaginations so as to make them more *ero* and curious—with actual women. But he seems to realize that these warnings about confusing the image commodity with the physical referent are too little, too late. The neuropolitical invasion of humans' most intimate recesses by the image commodity is an irreversible process, permanently wiring the neural networks of human cognition with the hardware and software of modern capital.

> This dreadful [*osorobeki*] *ero* is expanding its intensity beyond all limits with astonishing speed. For while the nervous system of modern people is becoming more complex through the intensity of this new capitalism, at the same time it makes nervous systems weaker [*fueburu*] and more dependent on capitalism. Because of this control over the human nervous system—constantly making humans more vulnerable and manipulable—we are solicited to seek out the most intense *ero*. The ugliness of capital's operation is such that it puts a price on this subsumption of our desire to it [*kondō ni atai suru*]; because its cruelty makes us break out in a cold sweat, the elements of humanity that we have left make us realize that we desperately have to escape or our overloaded nervous systems will be driven to insanity by the system. However, because most of us were raised with

an older, traditional moral sensibility, we just don't possess the means to resist this new invasion when it attacks us. (1931, 152)

The relentless neuropolitical invasion of the body leaves humans weaker and weaker. With each assault we are less able to prevent the invader capital from eating away at more and more of our nervous system. Akagami's rhetoric—hideous, ugly, bizarre, *hentai*—attempts to capture the "perverse" and dispossessive violence of this new kind of capitalism, a system so monstrous that while its very existence is indebted to the theft of human energy and *ero*, it insatiably penetrates further into the neuronal core of this energy, intensifying human addiction to capital. These addicts become so dependent on this system that, as the system puts a price or user fee on all pleasures to be had within it, they pay again for their continued exploitation. The more we desire, the more extractive surplus neuropolitical capital is able to suck out of us. The more we consume in this system, the more our personal urges and dreams are substituted for reified, homogenized *ero*.[4] The more we live life itself in this system, the more we contribute to our own death and humanity's destruction. We should recall here Walter Benjamin's analysis that in fascism "humanity can experience its own annihilation as the supreme aesthetic pleasure" (2008, 42). The only appropriate thing to call such a scandalously *hentai* imperial system is "erotic-grotesque."

Akagami concludes the chapter by explaining the exact connection between *ero* and *guro* ("the grotesque"; 1931, 152–53). Whereas modern people are unable to resist the intensity of the shocks and stimuli (on the contrary, they can only embrace this overload), they are at pains to camouflage their increasingly immoral and perverse behavior. Here, we come across the cunning (*kōkatsu*) of moderns, a cunning that in contemporary society culminates in a *guro* expressed in nonsense, gags, and puns. Therefore, "by means of the capitalist stooges and paid clowns [*hōkansei*] of *guro*," *ero* is overloaded again and invades the body with a renewed and refreshed intensity.

Those hired by capital to propagate *guro* (which Akagami elsewhere identifies as violent professional sports, car racing, *sumō* wrestling, film, and striptease) don't do a very good job of hiding the dispossessive operations of *ero*. Instead, they redouble *ero* by expanding the range of what is experienced as curious and stimulating, producing what Debord called an "abundance of dispossession" (1983, 30). *Guro* or the grotesque elicits *ero*, but in a different way from that discussed by sexologists; the *guro* of high-tech car racing now unleashes in modern people an *ero* never seen before. The effect of an *ero* multiplied and mediated through *guro* leaves humans more frantic and ferocious. Very different from the standard rendering of the erotic-grotesque as an aesthetic phenomenon, *guro* plays a crucial ideological role in Akagami's analytic. It both covers over the neuropolitical invasion of the body which substitutes personal desire for the alienated *ero* of the capitalist image commodity, and as it does this camouflage work *guro* expands the affective range of *ero* by adding grotesque elements to it. When *guro* bleeds into *nansensu* (nonsense), it destroys whatever social significance language may have had; the *guro* of a comedian's sight gags or of high-speed car crashes pushes media signs to transcend written language in the direction of the pure image, toward film.

Umehara and the Revolutionary Kids

Six years before Akagami developed this critique of the ways the image commodity expropriates surplus by inciting consumer curiosity and soliciting human attention, Umehara was hoping that a similar function of curiosity could help direct consumer attention to progressive messages. He wagered that the proletarian journal *Arts Market* might work to make the content of the image commodity, and therefore its semiotic significance, trump its power as image. The anticapitalist and antiracist contents in *The Killing Kapitalist Konglomerate* were the first examples of this new media politics. He did win over several proletarian cultural producers to this new way of getting their voice out, including Nakano Shigeharu and Murayama Tomoyoshi, the central figure in the MAVO visual arts movement (Weisenfeld 2002).

Umehara Hokumei studied European literature at Waseda University in Tokyo from 1919 until 1921, when he dropped out to become involved in journalism and liberationist politics on a full-time basis. According to his son Umehara Masaki, at this time in his life "liberationist" meant freedom from what Hokumei called all the "feudal elements" that he saw dominating Japanese society in the early 1920s: sexual repressiveness, rigid ethnoracial hierarchies, and class domination (Umehara M. 1968, 1978). Hokumei (this pen name means "revolution in the north") began his radical political activities as a junior high student, helping out with strikes and radical union activities in his hometown. His time at Waseda was spent reading, attending strikes (often marching with the workers in his trademark tuxedo, a proto-Dadaist move), and doing research on white supremacist groups like the Ku Klux Klan. His son argues that through his research on racist groups, Hokumei quickly acquired a sensitivity to ethnoracial discrimination in Japan (Umehara M. 1968, 224). While supporting himself as a freelance translator, in 1922 he spent six months in western Japan working with oppressed *buraku* outcaste groups.[5] Returning to Tokyo after falling out with *buraku* leaders over his wild schemes for publicity, Umehara focused on writing the *Killing Kapitalist Konglomerate*.

After finishing the novel he found himself drawn to a text he had studied at Waseda, Boccaccio's *The Decameron*, which became one of the Ur-texts for the erotic-grotesque writers and editors over the next decade, made possible by Umehara's pioneering translation.[6] The situation around the publication of Umehara's translation of Boccaccio set the precedent for the spectacles and media events that he and his friends would stage through the early 1930s. Years earlier Togawa Shukotsu and Ozawa Teizō had tried to publish a full translation of the Boccaccio text, but it was banned by the Home Ministry. Umehara realized that he needed to resort to different measures to get his translation OKed by the censors. First, after finishing a draft by working intensely through late 1924 with available French and English translations, he invited officials from the Italian embassy in Tokyo, along with several prominent Italian writers, to attend a gala he organized in Asakusa to honor the five-hundredth anniversary of Boccaccio's death. The Italian ambassador and his wife, several other minor Italian officials, one Italian writer, and several of Umehara's friends, together with a few geisha hired by Umehara, arrived in Asakusa for the event. One week earlier Umehara had placed advertisements in two Tokyo papers announcing the event and declaring that he was just about to publish his translation of the first half of *The Decameron*, basically daring the Home Ministry censors to ban it in the face of all the buzz generated in the art world and at the Italian embassy. On the evening of the successful event, Umehara was presented with a special cultural award by the Italian ambassador, thanking the Japanese translator for his deep appreciation of Italy's cultural endowment. Very drunk, Umehara immediately gave the award to a café waitress he was hitting on (Umehara M. 1968, 227).

With political cover and financial support from the Italian embassy,

Umehara's *The Complete Decameron* (*Zenyaku Decameron*) was published in March 1925 and sold out its first run of six thousand copies in one month. Critics and the high-brow reading public were ecstatic over its appearance, and the reviews in the main newspapers, the *Asahi* and the *Yomiuri*, expressed both delight and shock that it was approved for publication by the Home Ministry censors. The *Yomiuri* exclaimed, "This rare book [*chinpon*] appears in Japan for the first time. Usually the authorities sternly judge this kind of pornographic text [*waihon*] and after scrutinizing it will immediately ban it. However, in this rare instance, Mr. Umehara Hokumei's *The Complete Translation of The Decameron* has quietly received a 'pass' from the strict censors" (13 April 1925).

Four months before the second half of *The Decameron* was released, Umehara published another popular text, E. L. Williams's *History of the Great Russian Revolution*, translated with the communist Sugii Shinobu, which was a celebratory interpretation of the events surrounding the Soviet victory. Umehara was astonished that it too got past the censors. In his inimitable style he wrote exactly that in the "Translator's Introduction": "Cut the . . . ! well what can we say, we translators are completely floored by the pass. Just what the hell is going on these days with the censors is anyone's guess. Wouldn't just an ecstatic scream be the most appropriate reaction here? [*Nantoitte, zekkyō shitara iindai?*] Yaaaawhooooo! Our *History of the Great Russian Revolution* got a 'pass' after all" (Umehara H. and Sugii 1925). Umehara himself speculated that the censors were caught off-guard and never anticipated that a straight history of the new Soviet Union would generate large sales. Whatever the reason, the censors, angered at the popularity of both of Umehara's translations, were now itching for some payback. In October, when the second half of *The Decameron* was perfunctorily submitted to the Censorship Bureau before the first printing of six thousand was sent off to stores, the Home Ministry abruptly ordered the book banned. In Umehara's words, "Thirty cops burst into our printing factory in broad daylight and hauled off all 6,000 books on six trucks" (*Arts Market*, November 1925, 2).

Umehara began using his power as the editor of *Arts Market* to popularize his new confrontational style against the censors. On the back cover of the November 1925 issue, he reports that the continuation of his eagerly awaited translation has been unfairly prohibited from public sale and its "publication has been ordered stopped! Revised version to appear soon." As he would do on several other occasions in the following years, in provocations that resulted twice in his imprisonment, Umehara deliberately publicized and sensationalized the banning of part 2 of *The Decameron*. His main vehicle for this was paid ads in newspapers. Alongside news of the censorship he put an ad in the entertainment newspaper *Bungei Jihō* on 21 December 1925 coldly describing what had happened and calling the censors "hypocrites." His strategy was to publicly embarrass the government's censors, hoping to incite consumer interest in his and his friends' books. But his schemes weren't limited to this. After the publication of the first half of *The Decameron* he arranged through the Italian embassy to have signed copies sent to the Taishō emperor and his son, Hirohito, who would assume the throne in two years.

Umehara complained to his embassy friends of the government's decision to ban the second half of *The Decameron* and threatened to hold a second Boccaccio bash in December 1925, which got his picture displayed prominently in the *Yomiuri* newspaper of 22 December 1925. After negotiations with the Home Ministry he agreed to resubmit a slightly altered version, which was approved by the chastened censors. In February 1926 both halves of Umehara's translation were published as one volume, and, owing in no small part to the politicization of the censoring, it sold well. Aside from purely commercial factors, several accounts have testified to the impact of this translation on the mass culture of the period (Yamaguchi 1994, 344–54). Umehara himself wrote about the intense investment he and his friends had in the text and the reasons he went to such lengths to make it commercially available. In the special issue of *Arts Market* published in October 1927, called "World Decameron" ("Sekai Decameron"), he explained why he put so much energy into getting the book into Japanese: "Along with other revolutionary kids [*kakumeiji*] working in religion and art, during a time of danger and emergency Boccaccio succeeded in exposing the darkness of the world of the Middle Ages to the bright light of the Renaissance. We intend to shine the same kind of light on the 'darkness of Japan.'"

Umehara, the uncontested leader of the pack of "revolutionary kids," waged war against the censors for the next seven years, until the pressure got too great. In 1932 he went underground, retreating to western Japan. Two years later he resurfaced as a fairly overt supporter of Japan's imperialism, returning to Tokyo with help from some longtime subscribers in the Japanese military to assume a position as the in-house historian and archivist at the nationalist Yasukuni Shrine. In addition to the constructed media sensations like that surrounding the publication of *The Decameron,* Umehara pioneered other techniques for getting his books and journals safely into commodified forms for mass consumption. Arguably the most effective of these was his adoption of a little-known system established to facilitate scientific and scholarly publications in Japan, the *kaiinsei,* or "members-only subscription system," as mentioned earlier. According to Yonezawa, "The members-only system was the best way to get pornographic books published in Japan during the early Shōwa period" (1999, 66–67). Umehara used the members-only system to distribute the second monthly journal he edited during this period, *Hentai Shiryō* (Perverse/Modern Documents). He used the pages of *Arts Market* and newspaper ads to attract subscribers. Umehara's son claims that circulation of *Perverse/Modern Documents* peaked at three thousand in 1928 (Umehara M. 1968, 234), while Yonezawa guesses that the number was closer to sixteen hundred (2001, 32–33).

As Umehara often exaggerated the number and influence of subscribers to intimidate the censors, we should be cautious about his claim that by its second year more than 250 doctors had signed up (*Arts Market,* March 1927, 2). His son identified three main groups of *Perverse/ Modern Documents* member subscribers: university professors, high-ranking military officers, and public prosecutors and judges. A number of prominent writers and publishers probably constituted a fourth group. We know the identities of some subscribers from Umehara's published pleas to subscribe to yet another book or magazine of his; each new title required a new list of members to be registered at the Home Ministry. One high-ranking military officer and subscriber to *Perverse/ Modern Documents* in 1925 was the Guandong army field marshal Ogasawara Naganari; Umehara drops his name twice in print (Abel 2005, 271).

The third journal that Umehara edited during this period was the legendary *Grotesque* (*Gurotesuku*), but he was unable to get it approved for members-only publication because the Home Ministry could find no academic or scholarly merit to it. So, like all the other mass culture publishers, he took his chances with the censors and made the first *Grotesque* available for purchase in bookstores in November 1928. Yonezawa claims that six thousand copies quickly sold out, and it's not difficult to see why. In addition to Umehara's notoriety, a glance at the graphics (topless women are prominent, as in *Perverse/Modern Documents*) and the table of contents reveals eye-popping features on fetishism and sex crimes. For those wondering how such explicit eroticism escaped censorship, we should remember that the censors had their hands full as mass culture magazines began to feature more and more articles on sexuality, *hentai* and otherwise. More important, the censorship codes of the time say very little about sexuality, only that representing sexual relations between married people was forbidden. Yonezawa argues that the lingering Confucianism of the prewar censorship civil codes led to an exclusive focus on the sacrosanct patriarchal home, so only explicit relations between husband and wife and adulterous sexuality were illegal. Thus everything short of, or in pleasurable excess of, intercourse between married men and women, with either their spouses or adulterous partners, was not strictly considered sex in the prewar censorship code (Yonezawa 2001, 4–5).[7]

Jō Ichirō and Yonezawa advance an analysis of the historical shift away from *ero* toward *guro* by insisting that the censors had much less to legally ban when images and words came to focus on things merely *grotesque*, which could include almost anything. This was clearly Umehara's hope when he titled his new magazine *Grotesque* (Kanno 2005, 157). This strategy marked the beginning of the widespread deployment of erotic-grotesque as a single phrase. Umehara's magazine was, it's fair to say, the first strictly erotic-grotesque medium. From this point on, predecessor texts were retroactively identified as *ero-guro*, including some of the sexology journals I discussed in the previous chapter, and popular fiction by writers Tanizaki Jun'ichirō and Edogawa Rampo. This retroactive assignment is largely owing to Umehara's bridging of popular sexological concerns with modern nonreproductive sexual practices, together with modernist graphics and a new focus on eroticized violence. *Grotesque* most successfully accomplished this and was at the center of the explosion of what Umehara Masaki called the "sex journalism" of the period. Both Kanno Satomi and Jō credit this magazine with having a large impact on the pulp, *ero-guro* monthlies that succeeded it in the early 1930s, such as *Criminal Science* and *Criminal Digest* (Kanno 2005, 159–68; Jō in Yonezawa 1994, 131). Kōdansha's *King*, a monthly published in runs of up to a million copies, was another pulp monthly influenced by the graphics and focus on eroticized violence pioneered by Umehara's *Grotesque*.[8]

Umehara's new focus on *guro* at the expense of *ero* highlighted the ways eroticism was present in otherwise nonsexual acts, such as war and crime. Moreover, the centering of *guro* reflected the pressing need to mobilize curiosity as a way to get consumers to pay attention to and thereby pay for fascinating commodities. To be sure, this was also over-determined both by his desire to avoid the censors and his entrepreneurial desire to remain one step ahead of the publication market increasingly flooded with sexological magazines and books. His interest in how *ero* is excited by *guro*, especially in the example of war, appeared to intensify with his trip to Shanghai in 1927, where he produced the first issue of *Grotesque*.

Umehara took several works in progress, the subscriber's list for *Perverse/Modern Documents*, and his close friend, Sakai Kiyoshi, with him to Shanghai to escape the powerful centrifugal force of censorship (Yamaguchi 1994, 349). In collaboration with Sakai, he planned to map out the first issues of *Grotesque*, continue working on translation projects, and put out a second monthly that would include articles written in Chinese. This was the famous *Kamashastra*, a vehicle through which they promised to bring the "sexual revolution [*seiyoku kakumei*] to China" (*Kamashastra*, vol. 1 1927, 2). According to Jō Ichirō, another reason for going to Shanghai was to consume women and drugs with their Japanese purchasing power. Jō quotes Umehara describing their second night in Shanghai, when Umehara's friend Tanaka Giichirō initiated them into the Shanghai nightlife: "When we arrived at the devil's den we took a seat in a back room and waited until they finally appeared: one girl who was still just 16 or 17 together with a middle-aged woman who had already ridden some rough waves in her life. It would be definitely stretching things a little to tell you how breathtakingly beautiful they were, but they gave a sense of Chinese style—perfect white skin all made-up, a little fleshy" (quoted in Jō 1993, 125–26).

In addition to buying Chinese women inexpensively, they took advantage of cheaper printing costs to finish several projects, including a pornographic German novel set during the First World War called *Balkan Krieg* (1926). The author's name is Wilhelm Meiter, but Umehara surmises it is a pseudonym and that the German text is a translation from a Turkish original. In any case, *Barukan kuri-gu* was published in May 1928, and its four hundred copies were sent from Shanghai to subscribed members. Umehara introduces the Meiter text as portraying the "loose moral atmosphere prevailing during wartime." His translation represents the first clear linking of war and erotic excess in Japanese modernism, where enemy women beg to be raped by victorious soldiers and troops resort to necrophilia, and it does so in Umehara's cavalier fashion that would be repeated often in popular discourse of the 1930s. It should also be recognized as a crucial mass culture precedent for the eroticized violence that characterized Japanese militarism in Asia. For these reasons, I'd like to translate a few pages to give readers a sense of it.

The novel is divided into two halves, the first titled "War Is Just One Big Orgy" and the second "The Debauchery and Cruelty That War Brings." The text begins with a warning about how different soldiers' psychology is from noncombatant civilians.'

> Different from the paths the rest of us take, soldiers only briefly march along to the sounds of military music. . . .
>
> Inevitably they are sent off to war. Everybody, themselves included, expects dreadful things to happen to them; but instead, while they trudge on towards their and their opponent's annihilation, they end up having one hell of a good time [*yorokonde iru no da*]. When it comes time for the final battle to completely destroy the enemy, they discover they enjoy all the aspects of war. They especially enjoy the freedom that war offers, prancing around like horny devils with their eyes all aflame. It's said that soldiers forget this wartime freedom during times of peace, but actually the instincts of that wartime freedom remain with them after the war, in their interactions with wives, servants, and daughters. (Umehara H. 1928, 10, 9)

The first full paragraph introduces us to a young female servant named Eterka, working for the Hungarian Baroness Helena. Helena's mansion is described as a decadent love nest (*kanzen na ai no su*). A second maid is named Veronica. When she enters, she reminds Helena that they agreed to frequently console each other over their departed lovers on the sofa, and Veronica asks Eterka if she understands precisely what that means. Before the younger servant can answer, Helena masturbates herself to orgasm while she makes the two servants watch. After she climaxes, Helena reports, "Right now I'm so excited that . . ." (15).

After some persuading, Helena succeeds in getting the maids to talk about their sex lives with their boyfriends, a discussion which leads to cunnilingus among the three and mutual masturbation; they are having a "Parisian threesome [*mitsupari*]." The scene ends when dildos (*jinkō no inkei*) are brought out and "love juice is flowing out of all three of them." The last line of the first chapter reads, "Both on the battle field and at the home front, war transforms human instincts and free will in improbable ways. I want to tell you other stories about some of the ways that it does this" (19). The stories featured in the first half of the book range from an oversexed Austrian woman who resigns herself to having sex with dogs when she can't find any soldiers to sleep with (chapter 5), to a narrative about a superhumanly endowed Esteban whose "gun" is seventeen inches long. While having sex with the "lascivious" wife of the commander of the Romanian army, who "sleeps around with differ-ent men [*otokogui*]," Esteban's sexual prowess is said to be equal to that of a "stallion" (14–17).

The second half of the novel, "The Debauchery and Cruelty That War Brings," depicts the sexual violence ensuing from the occupation of an unnamed Balkan city by a victorious army. Rape and other sexual atroci-ties are described in some detail. The first chapter offers this establish-ing shot:

> Soldiers flooded into the city. All the troops remaining behind to guard the city were killed and the victorious soldiers rampaged freely in all the houses of the city. Although there were elderly, children and some sick people alive, pretty much the only fit humans left living were women. The victorious enemy officers and soldiers conducted themselves in the standard manner of the rulers of an occupied city [*senryōshita machi no shihaisha to shite furumatta*]—each woman was raped; virgins were raped repeatedly. And if any of the women complained about this treatment it only served to further excite the sexual desires of the men.
>
> However, it should be said that none of the women tried in any way to resist the invaders. Rather, the women were burning up with sexual desire [*josei no nake ni taezu, jōyoku ni mi o kogashi*]. Even if a soldier only so much as looked at a woman, she'd immediately give him her body; they were loose, shameless women all right. Not only had these women crossed way over the civilized line into complete degeneracy, but with a heightened sense of pride there were many women who decided that they wouldn't let themselves be sexually satisfied by the military conquerors. So the women fearlessly flew

off into a drunken orgy of sex [*nikuyoku no tōsui ni tobikomu*], and they became the kind of sex partners that these men had only ever dreamed about. . . .

When the soldiers needed to move on to a planned invasion of Turkey, the women of the city pleaded with them to stay longer. Ignoring them, the soldiers left the city only to discover that several of the insatiable women had cross-dressed as men to stay a little longer with their rapists. . . .

Several of these women witnessed a similar atrocity when the victorious army marauded through northern Turkey, raping over four hundred women in one village, included 100 black women. (202–3, 302, 324)

It's important to have a sense of what Umehara and *Arts Market* were doing with *Balkan Krieg*, as this kind of cavalier treatment of erotic violence and war atrocities appeared later in the pulp erotic-grotesque magazines *Criminal Science* and *Crime Digest*. It also showed up several times as the featured thematic in *Perverse/Modern Documents* and in Umehara's *Kamashastra*. For example, in the inaugural issue of *Perverse/Modern Documents* Umehara printed four pictures of splattered and rotten corpses from a collection of German antiwar photography called "War against War" by Ernst Friedrich, published in 1924. As Kanno Satomi argues, Umehara "disregarded the political message of the original book by inserting sarcastic captions underneath each picture" (2005, 161). A similar jokey approach is featured in his captions to eight horrific photographs (decapitations, rotting corpses) from a collection of photographs from the First World War published in *Kamashastra* in 1928. I insist that Umehara's frivolous approach to the violence in war influenced a similar attitude in the popular pulp monthlies that followed in his wake. I've included a picture of an advertisement for a special second anniversary issue called "War and the Sex Inferno" in the June 1932 pulp monthly *Criminal Science*.

Look! At this unprecedented amazing Publication! The underbelly of war is exposed by the raw, naked images in bold style! The exquisite contents should not be overlooked by researchers in popular sex habits. Do the horrors of war and the sexual decadence that it causes necessarily have an explosive effect on the instincts that are normally repressed? Do those same horrors revive the animalistic longing of

Grotesque photos
designed to capture
and colonize readers'
attention. From the
erotic-grotesque
monthly *Kamashastra*,
January 1928.

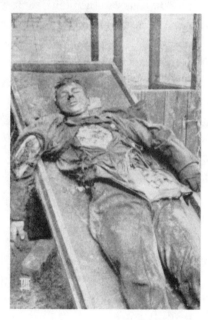

War Is a Sex Inferno! Advertisement for forthcoming second anniversary issue of the erotic-grotesque pulp monthly *Criminal Science*, June 1932.

young virgins that rips off the mask of repression? Your eyes will pop out with all the sadism, orgies, prostitution and bastard kids running rampant [*chōryō*]!

Beginning just after the Manchurian Incident of 18 September 1931 that kick-started Japan's invasion of China, military officers began writing regularly in the pulp *ero-guro* monthlies. For example, in the November 1931 issue of *Criminal Science,* half of the writers are high-ranking Japanese military officers, dutifully explaining the necessity of Japan's invasion to the magazine's readers, accustomed to more salacious fare. Similarly, in the pulp monthly *Crime Digest,* military officers were featured contributors in 1931 and 1932, appearing right alongside articles on sex crimes, homoeroticism, and fetishism. Although the standard scholarly interpretation of the relationship between erotic-grotesque modernism and military fascism assumes a mutual hostility, I'm arguing that there were many overlaps and continuities. Some of the articulations of erotic-grotesque modernism to imperial necropolitics are evident in Umehara's attempt to get the most sensational images in print so as to profit from them. But erotic-grotesque modernism was more than Umehara. The presence of military officers writing on the logistics of war with China alongside articles on *hentai* sexuality in *Criminal Science* and *Crime Digest* should alert us to other connections, which I explore in part III. As a taste of that argument, I think it's symptomatic that in the first years of *Crime Digest* the inside table of contents page was framed by silhouettes of topless and completely naked women. This pornography literally framed articles written by military men on army supply lines and Japan's air force capability. Kanno writes that in providing a forum for the Japanese military these pulp erotic-grotesque monthlies "didn't betray readers looking solely for obscenity" (2005, 162). In other words, readers who paid money to excite their curiosity were repaid with the advanced capitalist lesson that armed conflict was sexually stimulating. Warfare was fundamentally porn rawfare.

Akagami's favorite examples of the grotesque were demolition derbies, sumo, and professional sports; Umehara became fixated on eroticized war as his signifier for the grotesque. The assistant editor of *Kamashastra,* Sakai Kiyoshi, preferred opium and other drugs as grotesque's master metaphor. While in Shanghai he and Umehara had many opportunities to visit the opium dens.[9] Although they included caveats about how "horribly addictive" the drug is when they wrote up their various ethnographies of the Shanghai opium dens (*Grotesque*, January 1929, 19–33; *Kamashastra*, vol. 1, 1927, 29–46), the attraction to the drug is clear. For Sakai this combination of easy addiction and unspeakable pleasure crystallized his understanding of the grotesque as something inextricable from desire. Opium smoking is a constant feature of his essays in Umehara's journals and in his own journal, *World Decameron*. Sakai was influential in establishing opium use as a staple of the images of the erotic-grotesque, and *Chinese* smokers can be found leisurely toking in the main *ero-guro* collections published from 1930 until 1934.

Sakai published a two-volume history of ritual sex and drugs with *Arts Market* in 1928 and 1929 based on research he did in Shanghai. The second volume is an exquisitely designed objet d'art intended to match the languorous sensuality of its topic, drugs as sex aids. Using materials gathered in the used bookstores in Shanghai's French concession, *Sex and Drugs* (*Rabu hiruta-*) describes the laudatory effects opium smoking has on sexual intercourse. Along with illustrations and over three hundred pages on other drugs that enhance sexual desire, Sakai writes, "In Asia, when men and women have sex they often smoke opium. Although opium makes the sex better, when it's over and the drug wears off, this can produce a real sadness. Furthermore, the man often has fantasies of having had sex with a woman much more beautiful than his real-life partner" (1929, 20–21). Although it makes sex more "sensual and intense," opium always makes the smoker desire more and better sex. "When opium smoking is combined with buying prostitutes," Sakai warns, "it can make a rich man poor in a month" (211).

Akagami theorized that car racing and professional sports were grotesque both manifestly and in the ways they masked the neuropolitical extensions of capitalism directly into the inner core of modern consumers, substituting a commodified *ero* for personal, subjective desire. The "revolutionary kids" Umehara and Sakai found different examples of the grotesque in eroticized war and opium. But images of warfare and narcotic commodities similarly hide the neuropolitical process of the expropriation and substitution of personal desires for commodified *ero*. As they work as a smokescreen (or big hit) hiding the predominant way value is produced and surplus extracted in advanced capitalism, they also further excite the consumer's curiosity, enmeshing attentive desire deeper into neuropolitical *ero*. This process, Akagami warned,

ultimately makes humans complicit in their own death, a process dialectically inextricable from neuropolitical capitalism's frenzied need to attract consumers' curiosity with increasingly bizarre and violent images
(1931, 144–45). We've seen glimpses of this in Rampo's masochists in
Blind Beast, in the Suicide Club to which Santarō invites the narrator
in the *Killing Kapitalist Konglomerate*, and in the teleology of death implicit in the consumption and content of Umehara's commodification
and *eroticization* of warfare.

Mitsukoshi Department Store, Neurotopia

In 1931, when pressed to reflect on his participation in disseminating
necrophilic images, Umehara responded that as a good capitalist he
was simply giving consumers what they wanted. He was just "responding" to consumer demand and "reflecting" the real world and therefore
shouldn't be accused of "selling" the erotic-grotesque: "I never intended
to do something labeled 'erotic' or 'grotesque.' . . . All I did was boldly
put into print what the world gave me" (Umehara M. 1968, 233). This is
a long way from his early hope that progressive political thought would
become more available through the capitalist market; in 1931 he claimed
to be merely *reflecting* the capitalist reality around him, not transforming it in any explicit way. The world, or at least the "world" bracketed as
the increasingly grotesque image commodities driving advanced capitalism, had finally caught up with the revolutionary vanguardist. So much
so that the final issue of *Grotesque* applauds imperialism in Manchuria
(June 1931, 2–19). It also contains the first image I can find in metropolitan mass culture of a colonial "comfort woman." The article about this
"new kind of colonized woman" is designed to stimulate heterosexual
curiosity and desire and promises easy access to such women for Japanese men brave enough to go to the Asian continent (123).

Readers who might be unconvinced about the ways the real subsumption of neuropolitics functioned to rewire human nervous systems seamlessly into a capitalist mediascape eager to sell images of war and death
for profit may be persuaded by a quick look at a social science invented
in Japan during this period: Kon Wajirō's modernology. Modernology
labored to understand the curiosity pricked and produced by the *ero-
guro* media but was designed less to criticize neuropolitical subsumption than to observe and categorize it. Taking a similar approach to
Umehara and most of the erotic-grotesque producers in granting sover-

eign authority to the capitalist marketplace, it celebrates the new interface shortening the distance between market commodities and human beings. In this sense and others, it is like Umehara's endeavor to introduce "revolutionary" erotic, antiracist, and pro-war messages via capitalist image commodities.

Kon burst onto the Tokyo mediascape in the spring of 1925, when a team of his researchers undertook an extensive investigation of the behavioral patterns of consumers in the popular Ginza shopping area of Tokyo. Published in 1926 as "A Description of the Manners and Customs of the Ginza District of Tokyo" (Tokyo Ginzagai fūzoku kiroku) in the popular women's magazine *Fujin Kōron*, it launched Kon into the public spotlight. The bourgeois shoppers of the popular Mitsukoshi department store were reportedly astonished by the team of statisticians asking them questions and cataloguing—in notebooks and with photographs—the minutiae of their everyday habits of dress, their particular way of walking, their body angle when squatting, the various modes of sneezing and scratching themselves, their degrees of excitement and disappointment, and other trivia. It was not the first time that bourgeois Tokyoites had been exposed to this type of obsessive classification, but this was their first experience as the object of an empirical gaze aggressively calling itself a new "archaeology of the modern," a social science intervening directly into their psychosomatic worlds. After that, upper- and middle-class consumers could hardly avoid presentations on contemporary customs and manners drawn from Kon's research with graphs and charts in the large Tokyo department stores like Mitsukoshi or Maruzen. Made up of equal parts of what we would today call semiotics, market research, and anthropology, this new science, Kon claimed, infiltrated and synthesized the classificatory disciplines of "anthropology, sociology, neurology, efficiency analysis [nōritsugaku] and geography" (1973, 20). Finally, a social science was appearing in metropolitan Japan that both reflected upon the neuropolitical imperatives of commodification in real subsumption and fed back into and redoubled the process.

Kon's challenge was that for modernology to transcend previous sciences of observation, it needed to situate itself firmly within the chaotic transformations of material space and be immanent to the speed and motion of a contemporary capitalism ruled by what quantum mechanics called fluid dynamics (ryūrikigaku). What would count as objectivity under the protocols of modernology wouldn't resemble the objectivity characterized by the "dead stasis" of nineteenth-century science. Informed by what would be called in postmodern social theory "self-reflexive objectivity" and the critical ethnographic insistence on partial truths, the situated knowledge of modernology would be always conscious that it takes place both "within the spaces between subject/object, researcher/researched, doctor/patient, judge/criminal *and* on the left side of those binaries." Kon continued:

> When there isn't a clear awareness of this complex relation the advances of modernological objectivity will become once again the procedures of empty bureaucratic ceremony. . . . As investigators, each one of us has a heart-felt idealism with respect to popular commodities, so that as we construct modern life from within, it's best to confess in advance our own desires. Only when this is our epistemology as investigators, can anything like objectivity be possible. (1973, 17)

The sense of an outside, whether in the form of critical distance or in a detached objectivity, is relentlessly fading here. Although objectivity for Kon still carries the traces of a circuit between material space and a temporary transcendence above that space as subject, researcher, doctor, and judge, the magnetic pull of modern capitalism is shortening the circuit and melting the older binaries in its neuropolitical vortex. Similarly, the modernological methodology of objective classification assumes a teleology where the outside gradually implodes into the inside riding on real subsumption. From the beginning of the first theoretical flashes of modernology, acknowledging the fact of the collapse and conflation of the older binaries was the foundation for transforming the epistemology of the pre-modernological social sciences.

Although Kon didn't explicitly praise commodity capitalism, he was forced to admit that modernology's insistent apoliticality—he said on several occasions that modernology was beyond "red, black or white, like modern science" (Kon and Yoshida 1930, 15)—was helping consolidate the status quo of consumer capitalism. As a defense of sorts, he claimed that it might have been proper for previous researchers to criticize capitalism's tendency to dissolve older traditions and customs. But opposed to the defense of familiar traditions and customs in Yanagita's folk studies, Kon claimed, "[Modernology was exclusively] concerned with the new, as it was taking place in front of our eyes" (1930, 27). To critics who castigated modernology for chasing the new in its "bizarre," extreme form, Kon replied that modernology was comfortable with this charge. Modernologists, like consumers of commodities, "must always be in a state of surprise and curiosity" (30). However, he warned that these critics should not confuse modernology with amateurish research in popular culture (*fūzoku*) that might otherwise share modernologists' affect of excited curiosity. Although the invested interest in the object on the part of the researcher might be the same, the operation of record- ing it was completely different: "*Fūzoku* scholars are too impressionistic, while we use the most modern techniques of observation" (33).

These scientific techniques included photography, business account- ing, sketching, and documenting with words. Modernologists would often resort to each of these techniques in their research. For example, women and men shopping innocently in the Mitsukoshi department store could at any time be secretly "tailed" (*bikō*) by one of Kon's researchers. On a return visit the following week, these objects of modernological research might see photographs or sketches of themselves in presenta- tions of activities conducted in the department store while shopping. These would frequently include "scientific" observations of how the shopper expressed surprise or disappointment when first encountering a commodity, the specific items finally purchased, and neurological re- sponses such as the degree and intensity of twitching, scratching, or wiping (1930, 37). The quality and quantity of physical tics such as foot- tapping and hair-pulling were neurological indices that led Kon to claim that his modernology was unprecedented both in Japan and the West. Also unique to modernology was its largely positive attitude toward the commodity form's invasion of the human nervous system. The scratch- ing and twitching were both rational responses to the exciting stimuli of department stores and show windows and signs measuring the relentless infiltration of humans by neuropolitical capitalism. Looked at through a study of the new forms of attention, modernology's concern with the "bizarre" activities of human deportment was not bizarre at all.

Both the exterior and the interior of human subjectivity were being transformed by the new world of commodity capitalism, and although the effects of this might seem bizarre to the untrained eye, the moderno- logical gaze considered this process a rationalizing one. In the place of "traditional custom" of the premodern world or the nineteenth-century world of imitation, capitalism had ushered in a world where fashion and style were now about "rational freedom" (Kon and Yoshida 1930, 20). Customs in the twentieth century made sense for modern life in ways that earlier customs, which served only empty ceremonial purposes, did not. Capitalism made twentieth-century customs rational, Kon believed, by giving agency to individual consumers. As Harootunian explains, "Buying and consuming was an act of conferring social meaning on the thing, and this recognition disclosed a conception of subjectivity—people occupying a position of knowing what they wanted and why, and thus capable of acting on this knowledge" (2000, 181).

To modernology's critics, this "knowledge" was barely distinct from superficial "desire" for the new and curious produced by commodity capitalism. Although Kon deflected the criticism that he was just chasing after the new and bizarre, he and other modernologists were known to lose their cool in the face of this dismissal. As early as 1926 Kon declared that modernology preferred to "avoid the bizarre and abnormal," and focus on the everyday of society (1929, 5). However, by 1930 modernologists' attempt to keep some distance from modern customs was clearly failing, as several practitioners turned to collecting erotic curios. For example, in a collection edited by Kon and his collaborator Yoshida Ken'ichi, Yoshida is extremely concerned to demarcate his work from that of voyeuristic "hobbies of the modern bizarre [*ryōkiteki shumi*]." In an essay titled "The Modernology of Love," Yoshida follows six couples on evenings out. Claiming that he could have pursued at least one of these couples right up to the point of watching them have "sex in public," he shies away because this would be no different from erotic-grotesque journalism (Kon and Yoshida 1930, 57). This shying away allows Yoshida to claim scientific distance for modernology, at least with respect to the cheap voyeurism of erotic-grotesque *fūzoku* researchers like Umehara's friends. Although it might appear that modernologists were unknowingly submerged in the new commodity world, Kon insisted that there still remained a gap between observer and observed, subject and object.

This small differential, invisible except to those with modernological perception, allowed for what Kon called its quality of "fluid permeation to infiltrate every minute part of the cosmos," down to the very "molecular level of the structure of contemporary society" (1973, 22). This liquid, molecular permeability of modernology allowed for the heretofore unprecedented speed of its deployment. At once materially situated and "utopically ideal," "contingent and necessary," and immanent and transcendent, this new science was alone capable of simulating and doubling the speed, fluidity, and transformability of modern capital itself. Most important, by continually foregrounding its situatedness as a material practice and its immanence to the commodity form, modernology contained the potential to outrace and expropriate the modern itself, similar to the grotesqueing capacity of capital. At this point of optimal functioning, the deployment of modernological methods, Kon suggests, is capable of classifying even the speed of modern boys and girls as temporally late, detecting in their place "modern primitives" (15, 37). The time lag positioning modern life itself as "late" in relation to the hyperspeed of modernology-becoming-capital is an effect of modernology's capacity to make "every distinct thing in the world clearly understandable, as if it had been detected by the eyes of God" (23). As a divine gaze, modernology would not kill, judge, and condemn like the Christian God or like leftist social science of the sort practiced by Gonda, but would magnanimously give birth through its representational power. As divinities of classification, modernologists declared their First Commandment: that living things, commodities, and machines are interchangeable and equivalent.

However, a different political lens sees a world where the human has become collapsed into things and all value transferred to the rationality of capital as the complete irrationality of the world. This is the world of the leftist erotic-grotesque ethnographers (people whom Kon Wajirō never failed to dismiss as nonscientific impressionists). In their popular works we can see some of the ways neuropolitical capitalism worked rationally all right, but, to borrow a phrase from Murakami Rōroku's introduction to Nakayama Yuigorō's *User's Guide to Modern Hentai* (*Hentai shoseigei*), it "worked rationally to intensify the irrational" (1929, 3). In one of the main texts in this genre, Noma Jirō's *Researching Perverse Ero* (*Hentaiteki ero no kenkyū*), the author responds directly to the modernological dismissal: "Many people make fun of us for conducting research on *hentai* and *ero*, but we're certain that we conduct our affairs in good faith. We feel in fact that this is the most important research topic as *hentai* lies at the source of all our lives" (1930, b). Promising "thorough research" on issues such as rape, bestiality, necrophilia, and promiscuity, Noma insists that the final outcome "will be a major contribution to human culture" (2)

Nakayama's more modest text is one of several in this genre (reprinted over ten times within two years) that scrutinizes the different aspects of *hentai* in detail. At over thirteen hundred pages in length, it is a *tour d'horizon* of every possible deviation from an assumed norm of human deportment. Addressed to newcomers to Tokyo, as well as to readers in the countryside and in the colonies curious about goings-on in the imperial center, the main message is that nothing is as it seems. Behind every advertisement, film, and newspaper is a con. All the rip-off artists of the modern city—loan sharks, hustlers, thieves, finance capitalists— compete for ways to expropriate whatever the unassuming new arrival to Tokyo has of value. If the newcomer decides to hire a go-between to find a spouse, this will only be an elaborate scam to steal money by "manipulating people's deepest desires" (Nakayama 1929, 2–4). The same thing with job advertisements, as these are actually ways to kidnap people and make them do slave labor; without fail the reality of the job turns out to be the opposite of what is promised (48–64). Prostitutes are the worst, however. Although their ubiquity might lead one to think they are regular people, they are really the worst kind of swindlers (845). In fact, the whole visually fascinating mediascape of the city— peep shows (*karakuri*), sideshows (*misemono*), film, and pornographic stereoscopes—adds up to a huge spectacle of *hentai* designed only to frustrate and fleece (352, 560, 718). Relying on metaphors that doubtless made modernologists cringe, for the first time in Japanese readers are warned about the newest kind of urban monster: the blood-sucking demon or vampire (*kyūketsuki*). *Vampire* in its original signifying sense in Japanese meant "capitalist extortionist" with demonic powers.

Nakayama introduces readers to the newest type of expropriative entity by depicting a vagrant who moves into a poor workers' tenement in the Kanda district of Tokyo. He doesn't appear to have any friends in the housing complex and is said to have been seen coming into his small apartment late at night carrying large coffins. Other residents in the tenement think it's strange that he isn't either doing day labor or out hustling for better jobs (1929, 485). One night there is a party at the tenement and his image changes dramatically; he apparently possesses enormous charm and flirts with everyone. While seducing men and women alike, he informs them of the fabulous, inexpensive things he has for sale. The coffins that he was seen carrying into the tenement complex turn out to be loaded with cheap consumer items, such as worthless soaps and tonics to turn one's skin white and cheap electrical items. The next day there is a sign outside his apartment announcing the formation of his own company, called the National Prosperity Firm (486). All the women and a few men who "can't identify a thief when they see one" (487) buy up the vampire's commodities. The first section ends by identifying the vampire's goods as "totally strange" and the consumer electric goods as "electric witchcraft" (487).

Nonetheless, it seems that the people are pretty happy with their new consumer items, and the "vampire" is seen carrying more and more coffins into his apartment at night. He next sets up his own small bank and loan business thanks to what Nakayama calls his "sorcery at accumulating capital [*chokinma*]," and he hires some people to run his business for him in the tenement as he himself relocates to a more middle-class neighborhood. At this point in the narrative Nakayama asks, "But who really is this strange man that has been set up as a great innovator by these unknowing women?" (488). The man's name turns out to be Takayanagi Junnosuke, and after he moves out of the Kanda tenement his loan company starts to really take off.

With his profits made from "swindling surplus cash" from almost everyone in Japan by extracting human "sweat and blood," he sets up twenty or so enterprises described as "spectral companies" under his original National Prosperity Firm, which is by now a huge *zaibatsu* capitalist conglomerate. His success seems unlimited, and he decides to run for the Japanese Diet, being assured of easy victory by his political advisers. This section ends with Nakayama intervening to tell us that this man "is a rare phenomenon which was brought into being by the modern age" and must be referred to as a "cold-blooded hunter of capital [*reiketsu na ōgon tsūkyūsha*]" (1929, 489). As the vampire is beginning his campaign, we are told that it is marked by lies and evil deception; nonetheless he is very charming and seductive and he seems to possess the ability to make the people's "blood hot." Here again, the repetition of the signifier blood—sweat and blood, cold and hot-blooded—draws readers' attention to the vampire's expropriative process of subsuming it.

In the last four pages the rhetorical force is intensified and the execrations against the vampire increase. Nakayama militantly mourns the fact that "by his bloodthirsty means, working people who don't understand the depths of the vicious greed of financiers are becoming unable to eat or clothe themselves" (1929, 499). Later we are warned that his financial instruments were "real murder weapons, knives in his hands" (499). Finally, Nakayama reveals that the "evil financiers wouldn't hesitate at the chance to devour us and drain us of our life substance until we died to increase their profit margins" (500), relating that all over the country the vampire's *zaibatsu* sucked up capital and people alike. The vampire capitalist is surely the "biggest monster to have ever possessed our society." When the law catches up with the vampire he's arrested and sentenced for fraud. But even this "victory for the people from the heavens" proves to be ineffectual, for his *zaibatsu* keeps growing and making a profit even when it was supposed to have stopped operating. The vampire seems to have the ability to escape from the jail during the night, so that prison for this monster is no hindrance at all (501).

In these and other legends of advanced capitalist Tokyo, Nakayama depicts what Murakami calls in the introduction not the customs of a primitive society but "that of the most advanced modern civilization": "Like savages, each one of us competes to the death with the next" (1929, 2). Nakayama's book ends with two hundred pages of "grotesqueries" about modern Tokyo: kidnappers, pimps, corrupt prostitutes, and capitalist counterfeiters. The food you eat (1238), the sex you have, the very thoughts you think to yourself privately (1387) actually belong to someone else, usually a capitalist sucking the very life out of you. The message that this book gives to newcomers to Tokyo is that the only way to survive in such a world is to start thinking like these rip-off artists and capitalist hustlers. Nakayama depicts a world so corrupted by commodification that the only solution is to quickly figure out how to become a "savage" oneself. At this moment there is no escaping the fangs and succubae of imperial neuropolitics.

Like most erotic-grotesque media, Nakayama's book is haunted by the biopolitical subjectivities that drove Japanese capitalism to an advanced stage and regime of capture I'm calling *neuropolitics*. In this macro shift where commodification infiltrates all aspects of metropolitan life, it really subsumes not just labor as in formal subsumption, but the whole of society. As we saw, it operates by capturing human attention and curiosity, thereby "putting the erotic to work." Through this mobilization of *ero* and the grotesque masking of it, neuropolitics approaches the absolutizing of the erotic and grotesque—absolutizing in the sense that there are no other paths or solutions available to them in neuropolitics. Although neuropolitical incorporation centered on consuming and being consumed, the biopolitical subjectivities that drove capital to this regime of accumulation are present as dematerialized image commodities themselves. As such, their existence as undead media will help push Japanese capital once again to a new regime of accumulation, what I call *necropolitics*. But we're getting ahead of ourselves. First I want to undertake more vampire hunting.

Intertext II

NEUROPOLITICS
SPROUTS FANGS

Capital is dead labor that, vampire-like, lives only by sucking living labor, and lives the more, the more labor it sucks.

KARL MARX, *CAPITAL*, VOL. 1

Believe me, the zombies are more terrifying than the settlers; and in consequence the problem is no longer that of keeping oneself right with the colonial world, but of considering three times before urinating, spitting, or going out into the night.

FRANTZ FANON, *THE WRETCHED OF THE EARTH*

In fall 1929 the vampire made its first appearance in Japanese metropolitan media. Beginning with the vampire essays in popular erotic-grotesque collections, followed by Edogawa Rampo's popular novel and Jō Masayuki's story, both called *Vampire*, in 1930, vampire media quickly captured the attention of the mass reading public. The fantasy critic Sunaga Asahiko writes that this early Shōwa (1926–89) period came to be dominated by what he calls "vampire eroticism" (1993, 152). Sunaga locates this eroticism both in the consumer's masochistic desire to be engorged by this kind of image commodity and in a vampire image that constantly seduces. As the most crystalline version of the neuropolitical invasion of human interiority by the real subsumption of capitalism, the vampire is the most terrifying totalization of the dialectic of erotic and grotesque. With the arrival of the vampire, neuropolitics sprouts fangs.

Philosophers and writers on the left, such as Tosaka Jun and Nakayama Yuigorō, decried this vampirization and zombiefication (which Fanon would later engage) of invaded humans using gothic and grotesque tropes. They intuited that vampirization both allegorized a consumer subject that needed to ingest image commodities *for life* and revealed the violent expropriation of human insides essential for advanced capitalist accumulation. Placing this process within a capital logic submitted to real subsumption, *The Japanese Ideology* (*Nihon ideorogiron*, 1935), Tosaka Jun's major attempt to theoretically dismantle this system, relies heavily on the rhetorical force of gothic and grotesque images. He mobilized tropes of bloody dispossession to expose the lies of a self-proclaimed harmonious and noncontradictory Japanese capitalism. Composing the essays that made up *The Japanese Ideology* at the precise moment these vampire texts appeared, Tosaka argued that the political critique of exposing the "contradictions of the idealist cover-up perpetrated by Japanese liberalism" always "leaves a trail of blood [*ketsuro*]" (1967, vol. 2, 228, 234). Employing the same signifier used as the title for the last vampire novel published in Japanese before the Pacific War, *Dokuro-kengyo* (*The Skull of Death's Stranger*, 1938), Tosaka writes, "Through liberalism's ideological camouflage, the skull of death which is idealism stripped naked, receives a soft baby-like flesh covering" (230). The mask of baby-faced idealism, which Tosaka identifies as one of the supports for the hegemonic pull of fascism in the early 1930s, hides what he referred to elsewhere as the veritable "demon child" of a rabid and bloodthirsty capitalism.

For Tosaka, in certain historical moments the bankruptcy of liberal capitalism cannot but lead to the abdication of critical analysis by politicians and intellectuals, deceived and deluded by the necromantic "black magic [*majutsu*] of a harmonious social totality" (1967, vol. 2, 349). *The Japanese Ideology* insists on locating the drift toward fascism in the inability of bourgeois intellectuals to grasp the tendency toward a seamless suturing of society latent in liberal capitalism (see also Žižek 1991).[1] In Japan this tendency was most visible in the ways liberalism conflated and connected the three elements of everydayness, philistinism (*zokubutsushugi*), and common sense, through what Tosaka calls a "Mephistophelean" contract that legalizes an "act of Satan": "Satan and Mephistopheles try to seduce . . . while real common sense possesses the capacity for critique" (251). The dialectics of *The Japanese Ideology* posit that "the aspect of common sense is nothing but that which is negated right from the beginning" (260). The harmonizing coerciveness in liberal capitalism negates class-specific common sense, leaving not the critical common sense of a lived proletarian everydayness, but an undead version Tosaka calls mere "averageness." He reminds his readers that this negation of class consciousness is "not a simple or naive process at all," but is forcefully "solicited" by an operation that constantly "works to promote averageness itself" (262). The end result is a "common sense having nothing to do with the common or the rule of the majority, but rather is an idealist fiction which has to be worked up [*hataraku*] by pressure and force" (263). Writing at the same time as Antonio Gramsci in Italy, Tosaka lamented that true subaltern and proletarian common sense based on "existential everydayness" had been "forced underground [*chikashitsu*], overwhelmingly crushed" (266).

Vampire eroticism and Tosaka's "Satanic and Mephistophelean seduction" were given a mass culture voice in Edogawa Rampo's popular 1930 novel *Vampire* (*Kyūketsuki*, 1987). As the first vampire novel published in Japanese, it consolidated the prototype for the vampiric in Japan. We already saw in Nakayama Yuigorō's erotic-grotesque account that the vampire in Japan is very different from what I've called the "invader-from-without" mode popular in Euro-America (Driscoll 2000, 176). Totally othered as the Jew, queer, or monstrous infrahuman in Bram Stoker's novel and European films such as *Nosferatu* (1922), the vampire in Japanese mass culture is a seductive humanoid creature who arises immanently from within metropolitan capitalism. This kind of "incorporator-from-within" vampirism confirms Tosaka's sense that the monstrosity of fanged power must mask itself as baby-faced and softly seductive to succeed in destroying subaltern and proletarian common sense and to extract their lifeblood. As we saw in chapter 6, and as is evident throughout the media of the early 1930s, the vampire image commodity in Japan's metropoles was fascinating and worked through seduction and Tosaka's sense of "solicitation" to lure subjects into neuropolitical capture.

The erotic-grotesque writer Sakai Kiyoshi penned the clearest expression of this. In *Demon Magic* (*Kōrei Majutsu*, 1931) Sakai argues that, unlike European examples of vampirism, in China and Japan vampire stories are marked by the absence of animosity toward the vampire: "In Eastern vampire legends the victims of vampire attacks actually like the vampires. In Japan we have many vampire-like legends where werewolves turn into women and have sex with men, and bats turn into men and have sex with women; while it's terrible, the process is actually very pleasurable at the same time" (27–28). Sakai then claims that vampirized humans "take on some of the powers of vampires and are said to be sexually alluring, making it easy for them to populate other areas and multiply their power" (34).

At first glance, Rampo's *Vampire* seems to follow the Eurocentric invader-from-without mode. His introduction profiles vampires as creatures that arrive during the night to attack people asleep in the security of their home. He writes that his novel's main character should be compared to the monstrous characters in "Balkan legends," and like them, "the most evil person in the world" (1987a, 2). After a page of explicit description of the mode of sexual appropriation of vampires, he concludes gruesomely with the hypothesis that desperate vampires, who can't find fresh kills, resort to robbing graves. These creatures don't die, of course, so it seems that until they are properly disposed of, even the dead aren't safe. This introduction suggests an invader-from-without lineage, but it will prove to be only the first of Rampo's famous narrative tricks. A clearly identifiable vampire in the European mode won't appear again; in its place we are given a series of vampire effects, drawing from the external invader-from-without mode only to critique it. For example, in the third chapter, after the first sign of the appearance of the vampire, a wooden stake is found in the room of a mysterious guest. The ostensible purpose of the strange stake escapes the maids, but the novel hints that it's to drive through the heart of vampires. Later in the same chapter another mysterious figure is described as very strange because he possesses "neither a shadow nor a reflection in the mirror [*kagemo katachimo nai*]" (67).

The novel begins in a scene of upper-class consumption in a resort hot spring outside of Tokyo. Two men are having a duel; their weapon is a deadly invisible poison that has been placed in one glass by a waiter, while a second glass is filled with plain water. The youngest dueler, Mitani Fusao, goes first. He is described as a beautiful youth of about twenty-five who looks fifteen, a Japanese version of the Hollywood actor Richard Bartholomew. His partner is a successful artist and photographer named Okada Michihikō, who is around thirty-five and also good-looking. It seems that the two men are both lovers of the same woman, a widow named Yanagi Shizuko, who is described, *moga*-like, as, "25, but appearing 20." Mitani goes first in the duel over the poisoned glass, and selecting what seems to be the unpoisoned drink, claims victory. Okada refuses to drink from the remaining glass and leaves the resort humiliated. Immediately, Mitani and Yanagi get down to it, their "love-making like vomiting blood" (13). Mitani is described as being drawn to Yanagi in a "violently erotic way."

In the next scene we learn that Yanagi's husband, a convicted jewel thief and white-collar criminal, died in prison only six months before. The figure of the jewel thief extortionist exposes a trace of colonial appropriation, as many of the jewels in this period were looted from Japan's colonial periphery. In the scene that follows we witness the opulence of the dead extortionist's home, now his widow's property. Then the widow's six-year-old child is kidnapped under suspicious circumstances. While searching for her child, Mitani and a butler discover the partly decomposed body of her husband, who was ostensibly buried two months before. The body is described as having strange marks and bites, suggesting that the vampire apparently at work could not find a fresh kill and resorted to exhuming the jewel thief.

Two scenes later the narrative returns to the opulent residence as the mansion staff and two police are shown searching for clues. Here, we are introduced to one of Rampo's signature themes, already familiar from chapter 6: sculptures or mannequins incorporating freshly killed people. The police are horrified to discover that the extortionist had made statues in the mode of traditional Japanese art using recently taxidermied humans, which leads to more suspicion about his vampirism. Rampo's master detective Akechi Kogorō is brought in and gradually figures out after seven murders and instances of quasi-vampirism that the only person connected to each of the seven murders is Mitani, the beautiful boy who won the duel at the resort.[2] So the dragnet is set up as Akechi utilizes the same tricks that the vampire had employed throughout the novel: high-tech photographic tampering, cosmetic surgery employing medical and theatrical technologies, and elaborate film techniques. The beautiful Mitani turns out to be nothing at all like the hideous invader from the Balkans. He is charming, seductive, and righteous; the penultimate scene is dedicated to his justification for all the murdering and blood sports.

Rampo's novel narrates how a vampire-like entity robs the life substance from several disparate figures. At first glance, the vampire attacks don't appear to transform victims into vampires, as they do in the Bram Stoker invader-from-without mode. But as the stories recount the excited media attention, vampirization does seem to offer the dead victims a kind of half-life in the press and in rumor circuits. The attacks redouble the power of the vampire, and they also provide an expanded media identity to the victims as the newspapers and police register and disseminate information about them medialogically. In other words, the act of vampirization doesn't simply repress and eliminate these people, but *subjectivizes* them, giving them a kind of second life in the capitalist media as it sustains and expands the vampire's own horizon of life. Through the multiple vampire attacks, his victims—*moga*, high-stakes colonizer jewelry thief, and proletariat—are all granted notoriety and social identity. *Vampire* demonstrates some of the ways a sexy vampire-like entity works through seduction to incorporate humans. While the entity appears to need the victims to survive, the victims are also complicit in their own deaths through their Mephistophelean transference onto him. Although they seem to recognize the danger in intimate contact with the vampire entity—a danger that excites the pleasure of the contact—their potential death doesn't deter them from deepening this relationship. It's apparent that in the event of their murder, the ex post facto sensationalizing of it by Tokyo's society of the spectacle will guarantee them *life in death*. Recalling Akagami Yoshitsuge's analysis of the way capitalism substitutes vitalist human desire for a commodified *ero* whose contents include pleasure in suicide and murder, it would be difficult not to see this dramatized in Rampo's *Vampire*. A process that Akagami showed was taking place formally in advanced capitalism is substantialized here in the contents of Rampo's erotic-grotesque novel.

If you'll excuse the metaphor, what is fundamentally at stake here and what I'd like to drive into your hearts is quite simple: the victims all know the quasi-vampire Mitani Fusao, and their desire to participate in a process of seduction leads directly to their own deaths. Although I can't yet make the claim that their desire was for some kind of auto-annihilation—morphing it from something neuropolitical into what I call *necropolitical*—we can note some of the tendencies in metropolitan mass culture that so alarmed Japanese Marxists. To wit, in order for advanced capitalism to continue to capture and feed off attentive human curiosity, it must constantly up the ante in terms of the content of image commodities to be consumed, and I would argue that the sensationalized image commodities in Rampo's novels of this period are exemplars of this dynamic. Because of what Akagami referred to as the "declining rate of pleasure" (1931, 172) in the consumption of fascinating and bizarre commodities, the tendency of capitalist media was heading quickly toward the outright celebration of violence, criminality, and death, what he called the "telos of the grotesque." Dialectically Akagami pointed to the way this destination of the grotesque had the effect of networking with what Benjamin called the "distractions" in capitalist media space to achieve an emptying out (what we might think of as a materialist version of the philosopher Nishida Kitarō's 1928 concept of the "space of nothingness," or *mu no bashō* [1970]) and erasing of the previous programs determining human desires and deportment. Benjamin was clear that distractions caused by capitalist media led to the consumer being "ingested" (*Einverleibung*) by the vampiric image commodity (2008, 56–57). One of hundreds of mass culture erotic-grotesque images from 1928 to 1933 illustrating this process of being stupefied and ingested by a monstrously seductive succubus, figure 5 is an image commodity that, like Rampo's *Vampire*, both criticizes and contributes to this operation of ingestion and extension of a capital logic. In Akagami's analysis this process of infiltration remaindered "bare Japanese" as human zombies highly susceptible to the perverse pedagogy of capitalist neuropolitics.

Akagami intuited the unbounded nihilism of the capitalism of real subsumption to replace pleasurable use-value with exchangeable *ero*, and predicted that the process of the expropriation of human desire, which goes so far as to instruct consumers to act against human life itself, would culminate in a "festival of necrophilia" (1931, 178). In a prescient analysis, given that right-wing terrorism in the form of the Manchurian Incident would very soon dominate Japanese politics, he warned, "Today's erotic will flow into tomorrow's Satanic; our contemporary *guro* prepares us for tomorrow's *tero*. [. . . Advanced capitalism] possesses the capacity to make blood flow from the flowers of human culture" (179). Using a play on transliterated words that almost works in English (*guro*, or grotesque, anticipates *tero*, or the "terroresque") the sociologist warns that contemporary capitalism takes the fundamental operation in commodification from the beginning—the substitution of living, desiring labor for dead commodities—and tracks the transformation of this dynamic into metropolitan Tokyo circa 1930–31. Here, authentic human desire in consumer capitalism has been wrung through so many neuropolitical substitutions and takeovers that, as *ero*, it can be ideologically instructed to find pleasure in death. To return to the title of this book, the absolutizing of the erotic in advanced capitalism spirals into drives toward death; the absolutizing of the grotesque leads

Stupefied and stoned spectators being devoured by a vampiric demon image. From Sakai Kiyoshi's erotic-grotesque illustrated book *Arabian Nights*, printed in Shanghai in 1927 and sent by post to Umehara Hokumei's subscribers in Japan, Korea, and Northeast China.

to taking life in the forms of political assassination, systematic rape, and imperialist war.

The fact that the novels of the most popular detective writer, and arguably the most important writer in Japan from 1925 to 1934, dramatized neuropolitical expropriation has gone unrecognized. But in Rampo's fiction, serialized in large newspapers and pulp monthlies like *King* and *Modern Boy* before coming out in cheap editions, there is a clear exposition of the formal outlines of the same system that Akagami was attempting to map. The substance of the expression of erotic-grotesque fiction confirms the form of the content of Marxist erotic-grotesque social theory. As we already saw in his 1931 *Blind Beast* (*Mōjū*), in *Vampire* the desire of the main characters is shown to be complicit with their own undoing, their own death. With a misogynist literalness in *Blind Beast*, the women are ideologically instructed to desire their own annihilation, and this desiring-death is shown to be profitable for capital via Blind Beast's accumulation by dispossession. Similarly, the outrageous Pygmalionism in the 1927 *Strange Tale of the Panorama Island* (*Panorama Tō-kidan*) and *Black Lizard* (1933) is shown to be a quasi-contractual agreement between two parties: the taxidermied and "perfectly preserved" humans on one side, and the mad colonizer Hitomi Hirosuke and the *yakuza* villainess Black Lizard on the other.

In *Strange Tale of the Panorama Island* Hitomi, the neurotic addict of erotic-grotesque fiction, fakes his own suicide before substituting his own body in the coffin of a look-alike wealthy scion of the owners of a desolate private island (1987b, 28–29). When he miraculously "rises from the dead [*sosei*]" after having been buried for eight days, the family is so happy that they write him a blank check to refurbish the decaying island. Even though Hitomi's new wife suspects something is strange after their first erotic "little death" subsequent to the faked "big death" that widowed her for a week, he proceeds unfazed with his diabolical scheme to turn the natural ecology of the island into several linked images with an expanse "like Manchuria" (84). The main feature of Hitomi's own private Manchukuo is having successfully recruited unemployed actresses, actors, and other bored and depressed beautiful people to experience the "ultimate curiosity" and willingly suicide themselves into statues or surgically hybridize with animals à la *The Island of Dr. Moreau*. After installing this capitalist second nature, Hitomi takes his seat in the middle of the island to enjoy the visual pleasure of watching the panoramas (using lights and movement to simulate cinematic "dissolves" and "fades" [93]), which is said to surpass even the most lavish of Hollywood spectacles. He is apprehended in the end, but not before his "obscene production" has elicited the "heights of curiosity" in consumers thanks to his nihilistically "playing games with death and life" (113).

Rather than construe Rampo's novels as social critique, as I do here, some might ask, given the genre of horror detective fiction: Aren't the figures Blind Beast and the quasi-vampire Mitani Fusao merely criminals? If these are just depictions of criminality, couldn't the novels simply be othering criminals as deviant, inscrutable, and, yes, *hentai*? Wouldn't this lead one to assume that their message is strongly conservative and pro-police, especially given the fact that the detective Akechi Kogorō ends up capturing the criminals in the end? Contemporary leftist critics of Rampo frequently voiced these same suspicions. Immediately after his first commercial successes, the Marxist critic Maedakō Hiroichirō (1888–1957) lambasted Rampo's detective fiction in the December 1924 issue of *Shinchō* for siding with the police against the proletariat. For someone who had already published a kind of critique of money in "Two-Cent Coin" (1923) and an analysis exposing the deanthropomorphic effects of commodification in "Human Chair" (1924), this understandably angered Rampo. In a debate with Maedakō published in *Modern Boy* in May 1925 (see also Nakajima 1994), Rampo insisted that although it was primarily an intellectual game, his detective fiction was not at all "bourgeois literature," but contained a salient "spirit of resistance [*hankō seishin*]." Rampo, always careful to mask his real politics so as to keep the police off his back, defended his right to produce mass culture texts for no other reason than to stimulate his and his readers' curiosity, while he assured Maedakō that the politics of his detective fiction were not something that Marxists should waste their time "complaining about" (*Shinseinen*, May 1925, 151, 152).

My reading of Rampo locates him as a consistent, if increasingly abstract and muffled critic of contemporary power. In addition to the humanist Marxist themes in the short fiction I just mentioned (stories praised by the Marxist critic Hirabayashi Hatsunosuke and other leftists), there is *Imomushi*, a well-known antiwar fiction written in 1928 that got him into trouble with the police, and at least two novels that explicitly criticize overseas Japanese colonization: the rewrite of H. G. Wells's

Island of Dr. Moreau (*Kotō no Oni*, 1929) and the popular novel *Strange Tale of the Panorama Island*, twice made into films. To my knowledge the novels critical of colonization have not been read that way by critics, but Rampo scholarship has for the most part refused to read his work politically.[3] This is surprising given the pervasiveness of a Japanese intellectual habitus in the 1920s "dominated," as Miriam Silverberg has argued, "by Marxist conceptions of society" (2007, 39). As far as the novels of colonization are concerned, there's evidence that the two months spent with his family in colonized Korea in 1911 when he was sixteen offered him some insight into the oppressiveness of Japan's colonial occupation. Several novels incorporate colonialism from within, as readers often followed his detective Akechi Kogorō back and forth between the imperial metropole and the periphery in East and Southeast Asia. For example, in *Spider Man* (1929) Akechi has just returned from several years on the Asian continent, revisiting stopovers in colonial cities first reported in Rampo's earlier detective novel *Dwarf* (1926). When I bluntly queried Rampo's son Hirai Ryūtarō on the question of Dad's politics, he confided that his father held mainly socialist positions in the 1920s, although these wavered significantly in the mid-1930s (personal communication, 1996). We don't have to obsess over this to move ahead, but I did want to present evidence documenting Rampo's critical stance with respect to the multiple faces Japanese capitalist power assumed in the 1920s and 1930s.

Rampo was equally thin-skinned about attacks launched by the political right that he was overly identified with the criminal mentality and that his work propagated violence and social chaos. Beginning around 1928 with the novel *The Monstrous Feminine* (*Injū*), serially published in *Modern Boy* that fall, the most important debate in Japan prior to the Second World War concerning the nature of the detective novel erupted around his work. Among several others, including the editor of *Modern Boy* from 1920 until 1927, Morishita Uson, the critic Kōga Saburō expressed his disappointment over the fact that, after showing some early promise, Rampo's fiction in particular and Japanese detective fiction in general lacked the kind of scientific objectivity and logical clarity found in Euro-American detective fiction. Repeating a moralizing dismissal of Japanese literature popular in the late nineteenth century, Kōga proposed dividing Japanese detective fiction into "wholesome" (*honkaku*) and "perverse" (*henkaku*) types. Using the same *hen* cognate as *hentai*,

Kōga inserted most popular Japanese detective fiction into the perverse category (Kawana 2003). This debate over wholesome and Eurocentric as opposed to perverse and Japanistic fiction passed through several iterations, with the supporters of wholesome fiction holding a clear minority. From 1924 until 1936 the "unwholesome" side dominated intellectually and commercially; the reading public overwhelmingly supported it with their wallets. Even intellectual giants like Tanizaki Jun'ichirō and Satō Haruo defended the perverse pens of Rampo and Yumeno Kyūsaku and thanked these unwholesome writers for producing a body of mass culture work artistically superior to most high-culture literature in Japan at the time.

Despite loyal fans and intellectual supporters, conservatives continued to point the finger at Rampo when sensational crimes occurred in Tokyo. The most well-known instance was the discovery in October 1932 of a dismembered corpse in the Tamanoi district of central Tokyo (Kata 1985). When no substantial leads appeared after the first two weeks, one reader of the *Yomiuri* newspaper wrote a letter to the editor speculating that, since the murder coincided with the break Rampo was taking from writing, wasn't it obvious that Rampo himself was the perp? Having recently undergone an unpleasant investigation by the authorities, Rampo took the police attention that the letter incited so seriously that he wrote a defense of "perverse" detective fiction for the same *Yomiuri* daily.

Rampo's defense, "The Detective Novel and Catharsis," published in May 1933, signifies on several levels. Manifestly, he provocatively conflates Greek tragedies such as *Antigone* and *Oedipus Rex* with erotic-grotesque detective novels:

> The reason for the existence of detective novels is to provide catharsis to society; catharsis in the sense deployed by Aristotle in his *Poetics*. . . . The unprecedented grotesque of classical Greek tragedy is communicated through beautiful poetry, but it pulled in audiences through the technique of catharsis. For the purposes of maintaining the spiritual and psychic health of the community, the immorality of Greek tragedy utilized fear and terror to evoke catharsis in audiences. (1994, 115)

We should be careful before taking seriously the claims of concern for a sound Japanese *kokutai* (the organic national body) from the author of *Blind Beast* and *Black Lizard*. Isn't this more like an ironic version of

Marx's famous line from the *Eighteenth Brumaire*: the first time as (Greek) tragedy, the second time as (Japanese detective) farce? But Rampo continues, somewhat more seriously, to develop this point, drawing on his close friend Minakata Kumagusu's theory of totemism—no doubt filtered through his recent study of Freud: "From the beginning of human society, totems and taboos forcibly prohibit [*kinatsu*] robbery and murder . . . but they can't eliminate immoral and criminal feelings—these remain latent deep inside even the most morally upstanding humans. Buried therein lurks the so-called 'criminal instinct'; psychoanalysis would say that the more moral these people are, the more horrible are their unconscious desires for criminality" (115–16). Thanks to the gore and necrophilia in popular art forms like Greek tragedy and the erotic-grotesque novel, whose affect simulates a repertoire of immoral instincts, the latter are exercised and excised safely. The end result of consuming either classical or modern erotic-grotesque work is the curative "'act of sublimation' [*shōka sayō*] dear to psychoanalysis" (117), which guarantees that criminal impulses won't be actualized in the real world. Especially given the contemporary condition in Japan of "widespread neuroses" like S/M, necrophilia, and hysteria, these antisocial desires need to be given room to breathe, and "dreams and works of art are most effective for this" (116). Because of the psychosocial equilibrium inaugurated by this hydraulic relation between sublimation and the controlled acting-out of perverse affect, Rampo bashes back at conservatives by insisting that "writers of detective fiction are the least likely people in society to commit crimes." The firewall of sublimation positions "writers and readers of perverse detective fiction to be the best-adjusted members of society" (117).

There's much to discuss in this essay, but I'll focus on only two points. The first is that Rampo's irony makes it difficult to discern any clear political stance. Did he actually think that the erotic-grotesque detective novel was aesthetically comparable to Sophocles and Aeschylus? Probably not. Did he think that the inscriptions of S/M, necrophilia, and fetishism in his work functioned cathartically for Japanese metropolitan society? Probably so. Although he acknowledged the force of social critique in Greek tragedy, did he identify a similar critical power in his own work? Based on two interviews with his son and a perusal of Rampo's published positions in the major debates over the Japanese detective novel, I would argue that Rampo felt relatively confident about the critical sensibility—against the state, the ideology of science, the commodification of life in capitalism—that informed his early work, but that he worried that this was getting sidelined by commercial pressures in the late 1920s. We know that he was increasingly torn about the kind of psychosocial effects emanating from his erotic-grotesque fiction (Kawana 2008, 74). Deep ambivalences about the depictions of necrophilia in his work led to writing hiatuses in 1927 and 1932. In a quite literal way, commercial and other pressures leading to an increasing reliance on murder and erotic violence in Rampo's fiction corroborate Akagami's theory of a "declining rate of pleasure" for consumers of image commodities in advanced Japanese capitalism. As a dramatization of media capitalism's need to supply more and more sensational content to attract the attention-deficited curiosity of what Simmel called blasé metropolitan consumers, Rampo's novels relentlessly up the ante on—but also the ambivalence about—violence and outré modern sexuality.

His 1930 novel *The Culmination of the Erotic-Grotesque* (*Ryōki no hate*, 1930) both *critiques* consumers' demand for more sensational image commodities and *contributes to* it as a bizarre consumer commodity. The story is centered on the life of a young sensualist named Aoki Ainosuke, one of the throngs of nouveaux riches whose families benefited from Japan's economic takeoff concurrent with the First World War in Europe. Although he married the most beautiful woman he had ever seen three years before the story begins, neither this nor the pursuit of consumer pleasures in every realm imaginable was enough to cure his ennui; he was the new type of capitalist consumer who constantly "needed more and more stimulation" (1987c, 3). Out of a blasé sense of desperation he vows to become a "student of perversion," dedicated to searching out "strange shocks and stimulations to every part of the body and mind" (3). The specificity of Aoki's erotic boredom relays us back to the discussion of fantasy in intertext I; it turns out that his need for increasing levels of stimulation isn't satiated by either active or passive sexual positions. Even though he's turned on by "being a cruel aggressor" and a "helpless victim" (*higaisha*), "he was doomed to an eternal state of dissatisfaction because, although he both received and inflicted pain, he was above all a third person [*daisansha*], or a detached spectator" (4). Although Rampo establishes Aoki as seamlessly sutured into ideological fantasy—"the type of man who loved fantasy and illusion"—

his consumerism led to his "confusing texts with reality . . . and his obsession with commodities led him to retreat completely from reality for days on end" (6).

One December day Aoki decides to attend a local festival at Yasukuni Shrine, an important Shinto site in Tokyo. Festival days at Yasukuni bring out the Siamese twins, shamisen players, and circus acts reminiscent of early modern Japan. Bored with modern revues, cinema, and horse racing, Aoki takes in a different kind of "curiosity hunting [*ryōkisha*]." In the crowd he runs into a dead ringer for his close friend and Tokyo University classmate Shinagawa Shirō, who now works as a salaried worker for a science magazine. Surprised to find his square friend at such a dicey event, he confronts the man and is disconcerted when the double has no idea what Aoki is talking about. Distraught, Aoki, "detective-like," tails the man and is shocked when he turns out to be stealing wallets in some kind of identity theft scam. Several days later, while shopping on the Ginza, Aoki meets a well-heeled pimp (*ponbiki shinshi*) who takes him to meet the man who is impersonating his friend Shinagawa. At a sleazy flophouse on the outskirts of Tokyo, the pimp invites him to join a special thrill-seekers club (*tsūkai kurabu*) which combines sex and costume play as members pay for information about people they want to double and stalk. The enterprise is like a massive private detective organization. Now a hybridized detective consumer, Aoki immediately gets involved in a standard orgy (1987c, 37–38) before deciding that he prefers to watch other club members' modern sexual practices, including hard-core S/M and, later, necrophilia (*satsujin inraku*; 86–89).

Discovering that Shinagawa's double is a member of the same thrill-seekers club, Aoki brings the real Shinagawa to watch his double have intense sadomasochistic sex. The experience of voyeurism is too much for Shinagawa, who has to leave the club, tormented with anxieties about what kind of crimes his double has been committing. This leads Aoki to fixate on the idea that Shinagawa and his double are the same person. The use of documentary film and photography in the club contributes to blurring the image commodity with reality. After an intense three days hitting the peep shows and films and checking out the pretty boy sex workers in Asakusa (1987c, 72–75), Aoki begins to wonder whether his wife is not a member of the sex club as well, something that "incites his curiosity" intensely (92). After a second murder in Tokyo implicates club members, the detective Akechi Kogorō appears on the scene. It turns out that Akechi has been impersonating several people (including using Shinagawa's identity for a while) over the past six months while investigating and *participating in* the activities of the club, including the hard-core S/M scenes as Shinagawa's double. Akechi discovers that a mad Japanese doctor named Ogawa specializing in human improvement technology (*ningen kaizōjutsu*) has been using the club as a front for extreme cosmetic surgery. Using such surgical technologies as an "epideascope" to change skin molecules, Ogawa has taken advantage of the tendency of neuropolitical capital to plunder the human body and the vanity of some of the club members to change their appearance completely. Making copies of Shinagawa and others has made it easier for Ogawa to get members to commit crimes and murders as part of the "thrill package" the club offers, resulting, in at least one case, in the death of a club member.

In order for Akechi to eventually apprehend Ogawa he's forced to copy the criminal's tactics; it is only after he decapitates a female club member that readers find out that Akechi has faked them out. Nevertheless, Akechi has been paying to consume the club's cosmetic surgery, S/M, and blood sports. Different, in theory, from the other members, Akechi maintains a minimal distance on all the pleasures the club offers its members. Nevertheless, similar to Akagami's analysis and anticipating Walter Benjamin's definition of fascist aesthetics, the "culmination of the erotic-grotesque" here leads to individuals desiring an end of sorts to their own lives, as well as willfully participating in the murder of other humans. What begins as a desire to overcome the declining rate of pleasure ends up as an orgy of human annihilation. At the last minute, after enthusiastic participation in all the extreme thrills, the detective leaps out of the circuit of the neuropolitical substitution of useful living desire by exchangeable, necrophilic *ero* to become "the savior of the whole world" (1987c, 167). But Akechi admits that he barely escaped from the circuit, exclaiming that for the whole time he was involved in the S/M scene at the club, he couldn't decide whether he "loved it or hated it" (141).

Rampo's detective Akechi Kogorō emerged from within the tightening contradiction joining complicity with neuropolitical capitalism to a critical distance from it. His utilization of the detective, I would argue, provided a temporary suspension to his dilemma. Although there's much more we could say about the detective figure in Japanese mass culture of this period, at the very least, Akechi is a subject who is both immanent to and transcendent of the operations of capitalist power in *The Culmination of the Erotic-Grotesque*. The featured star in Rampo's best-selling novels of the 1920s and 1930s, Akechi is seemingly the only person in Japan impervious enough to neuropolitical capture to pull off a partial escape from its entrapment. Like Kon Wajirō's bragging that an optimally functioning modernology could outrun commodification, and Umehara Hokumei's doomed hope that capitalist media could be used for antiracist and even anticapitalist purposes, detective Akechi encodes a fantasy of noncomplicity with capitalist power. However, Akechi remains less vulnerable to complete neuropolitical capture because he, more than anyone else in Japan, understands both affectively and intellectually how it works. To understand and stay attuned to the frenetic transformations of advanced capitalism, he must give himself over to the seductions of power and the pleasures offered by fascinating images. To critically expose the operations of neuropolitical capture and expropriation, he needs to immerse himself in it by *paying full attention*. Without a transference of his own desiring fascination onto neuropolitics, Akechi knows that he won't be able to affectively understand how the ciphers of neuropolitics ensnare victim consumers.

Before Akechi became established as Rampo's fictional double — and as someone both in and out of power — he was prefigured in the famous story "The Flâneur in the Attic" (Yaneura no sanpostia) (1925), but as a *criminal*. In this story the protagonist, Gōda Saburō, feels that his inherited wealth and boundless free time guarantee a buffer between his private desires and social reality. However, when boredom drives him to experiment with all the diversions listed in a consumer guide for the wealthy, "The Complete Compilation of Pleasure," the discovery of a crawl space just above a room in his apartment building incites his passion for voyeurism. Voyeurism offers Gōda distance, transcendence, and pleasure. His voyeurism also guarantees a nontransitivity with respect to the outside world, until his surveillance of one of his neighbors reveals the unbearable situation of the neighbor's public identity equaling his private identity, so Gōda must kill him (Rampo 1987d). Something similar occurs in Rampo's story "The Phantom Lord" (1925), in which the main character feels that escaping into secret rooms and closets provides a space safe from capture.

In this earlier work the illusion of an outside to power leads to murder, while in the Akechi novels the minimal sense of an outside is what (barely) distinguishes crime from the law. This sense of a separation between complicity and critique, or crime and the law, probably enabled Rampo to continue writing. However, the uncanny indistinction marking the relation between and the shared tactics of the detective Akechi with the archvillains Spider Man, Lupan in *Mask of Money* (1930), and Black Lizard established a moral ambiguity that captured readers' curiosity, made large profits, and brought increasing police surveillance.

I've been arguing that the specific operations of neuropolitical expropriation drew consumers deeper and deeper into relation with image commodities, what Marx called real subsumption. In the late 1930s Theodor Adorno theorized that advanced metropolitan capitalism was leading image commodities to assume a powerful "fetish character" that was substituting for what was previously considered objective reality. See the contents of Rampo's novels, as they become more and more fascinating, beginning to take on the kind of fetish character that Adorno, Tosaka Jun, and others were attempting to analyze. As they do so, they take on the qualities of film.

The becoming-filmic of the image commodity functioned in two ways in Rampo's work. First, in a quite literal way, he starts to write so as to facilitate screen adaptations. The car and boat chases, smoky club scenes, and backdrops of consumer luxury like the Ginza coffeehouses and huge department stores that become increasingly prominent in his novels are clearly influenced by his desire for the novels to be put on film. Second, as a doubling of the movie camera the gaze of the omniscient detective Akechi became isomorphic with film. This doubling wasn't just a mechanical extension, however; it provided a sense of technological neutrality to Rampo's texts. It grounded his imagined transcendent safety from the neuropolitical seduction that he seemed to need as his writing became more and more invested in necrophilic spectacles. In other words, the filmic elements in Rampo's novels helped secure some deluded sense of an outside to commodity capitalism. Yet at the same time this dialectical dynamic offered twenty-four-hour access into immanent complicity. One senses a real terror in Rampo with the closing of this gap. To return to the issue of tragedy, maybe this terror of being engulfed by neuropolitical expropriation speaks to the tragically modern in the erotic-grotesque novel. Like Aeschylus's heroes battling against fate and destiny, Rampo and his detective are vainly battling against the catastrophic rush into a capitalist deathworld, with private consumers' desire becoming indistinguishable from the public world of alienated *ero* and necrophilic, grotesque spectacle.

Neuro- becomes Necro-politics

Although the erotic-grotesque detective novels of Rampo exemplify the kind of critique leftists like Akagami were trying to advance, it would take an entirely different fictional genre to prove their dark prophecies about the tendency in neuropolitical capitalism to invite consumers to desire their own death. Sharing the same mass culture pages with Rampo's novels in monthlies like *King*, the older literary genre of the "glorious soldier" (*bidan*) was refashioned in 1932 to push the tragic ambivalence exposed by the erotic-grotesque detective novel into the full necropolitics of a spectacularized desire for personal death. These *bidan* became ubiquitous overnight in metropolitan society after the first bloodlust of the Manchurian Incident. On the screen and radio, in the theater, and in large circulation monthlies we find thrill-seekers like the erotic-grotesque antiheroes Gōda Saburō and Aoki Aonosuke now dressed up in Japanese army uniforms and airlifted to the front lines in Northeast China, mobilized for imperial war. Exactly like Aoki and other Rampo characters, the heroes that appear in these neuropolitical *bidan* are much less concerned with military strategies and tactics than they are with a single-minded pursuit of their own eroticized annihilation.

For example, in a set of *bidan* called "True Stories of Human Bullets from Japan's Manchurian Army" (Manshūgun nikudan jikki) published in *King* in March 1932 and written by Japanese covering the Manchurian Incident, each of the main characters is fixated solely on his own annihilation, regardless of the impact this will have on the outcome of a battle. Although the heroes are tangentially linked to the larger strategy of Japan's military occupation of Northeast China, the heroes' expressed reason for committing themselves to battle with Chinese is their own private "decision to die [*shi o ketsu*]." And in each case this death wish is opposed to the cowardly Chinese, who are depicted as wanting only to go on living. This craven desire for life impels the narrative logic of the *bidan* to depict Chinese behavior as "shameful" and "slavelike" (*do-*

reiteki). By contrast the necropolitical logic of these new *bidan* represents the suicidal deportment of the Japanese as "heroic" and "glorious" (*hisō na*).

Mizuguchi, the hero of the first *bidan*, isn't even a soldier, but a civilian accountant responsible for materiel. Even here, in the figure of the accountant, in whom we might expect to find the strongest commitment to calculation and risk-avoidance, the story centers around his single-minded dedication to privatized annihilation. We join Mizuguchi when his unit's munitions supply truck is run aground in a botched supply effort. Fifteen Japanese subsequently come under fire from 150 Chinese infantry and 400 "bandit" cavalry, forcing the Japanese into a small safe house. When the Chinese bombard the house and set fire to the back porch, Mizuguchi delights in the realization that his only option is to rush through the front door into the enemy's machine-gun fire. The safe house is described in *Inferno*-like terms, everyone bleeding profusely and agonizing like "raging demons" (*King*, March 1932, 115). As Mizuguchi hurls himself through the gauntlet of machine-gun and rifle fire like a "mad bull," the soldiers left behind are brutally butchered, everyone "cut up into pieces [*kirijini shita*]." Riddled with bullets and bayonet wounds, Mizuguchi manages to make it through the gauntlet to fall dead on a small hilltop, holding the Japanese flag in one hand and his sword in the other. With a backdrop of severed body parts and bloody corpses so gory as to make one's "hair stand up straight," Mizuguchi manages to scream out, "I took it! [*Shimeta!*]," which, written in the Japanese katakana script as it is in the text, could also mean "I killed myself!" or "I choked the life out of myself!" (116). When Mizuguchi dies alone the text represents the Chinese as "withdrawing from his fury," but rather than the Chinese retreating as a result of his attack, it's more likely that they withdrew because the outnumbered Japanese, refusing to surrender, were "wiped out." The only aspect of this behavior remotely resembling "heroism" is the fact that Mizuguchi was able to fly the Japanese flag on the small hilltop for a few seconds.

"When the Flesh Dies, the Spirit Lives" features First Sergeant Chinohara, who we find right in the middle of a fierce battle with Chinese troops. "Punching, kicking, and lashing out with his blood-covered sword," Chinohara is engaged in hand-to-hand combat, his men outnumbered by superior Chinese forces. The Japanese are being bombed from the air and dodging a "hail of machine-gun bullets" on the ground, as they wrestle with and bite the Chinese enemy (*King*, March 1932, 117). The soldiers are waving their swords wildly, screaming, and being blinded by flashes of gunpowder and grenades—all "pumped up." The only referent that readers would have for this synesthesia of total war would be the blitz of sounds, sights, and smells from the commercial media they would encounter walking down one of the main streets in Asakusa. Here again, not even thinking about retreating or surrendering, the seriously wounded Chinohara sets out on a one-man rampage, eventually stumbling onto a small hill. With "blood pouring down over his face and waving his sword, seriously damaged from all the people he had stabbed," Chinohara finally topples over on the ground dead, slicing his head with his own sword as he falls (118). Minus a limb and unrecognizable from the knife and bullet wounds bloodying his whole body, Chinohara's body releases his spirit, proudly transmitting his honorable "battle death" (*senshi*).

In the only monograph on the historical transformation in military *bidan* from the 1890s until the end of the Second World War, Nakauchi Toshio does not think to link the startlingly new kinds of stories that appeared immediately after the Manchurian Incident to erotic-grotesque modernism. Read with Rampo and Umehara, however, they clearly inscribe the effects of commodification and de-anthropomorphism following from the neuropolitical invasion of human interiors. At the level of content, the *bidan* imagery is lifted right from erotic-grotesque fiction in its foregrounding of gratuitous violence and gore. For example, each of these *bidan* contrasts the white snow of Northeast China with the red blood and splattered body parts of Japanese. Nakauchi astutely points to the reversal in these new soldier hero stories with respect to individualism. He claims that the late nineteenth-century *bidan* were ideologically indebted to the notion of a "group self" (*ikkoku banmin*) and expressed the "erasure of the individual by the social groupism of Japanese patriarchy symbolized by the Emperor system" (1988, 36–37). But after the Russo-Japanese War of 1905 a "new heroism," involving elements from ideological individualism, began to transform the contents of the *bidan* (105). After the First World War the Japanese army was caught between having to acknowledge the importance of privatized bravery (*yūki*) and still emphasizing loyalty (*chūgi*) to emperor and nation. The huge volume of Manchurian Incident *bidan* (selected by the Ministry of Education in consultation with the army to be distributed to schools) tries to resolve this contradiction in its title: *Manshū jihen chūyū bidan* (Kyōiku-sōkanbu 1933). Joining *chūgi* and *yūki* in the rare expression *chūyū* ("loy-alty" and "bravery"), this collection nevertheless couldn't avoid includ-ing many *bidan* like the ones described earlier, appearing first in popular monthlies like *King* and Kōdansha's *Kodan kurabu*.[4]

Louis Young has identified the Guandong army cavalry commander Koga Dentarō as representative of what Nakauchi calls the "new hero" of the 1930s *bidan*. The leader of the pacification operations after the bombing runs conducted personally by Ishihara Kanji and others against the surrendered Chinese army in Jinzhou, Koga used the nearby old walled city of Jinxi, Manchuria, as his regiment's base. When Chinese regular and guerilla forces tried to retake Jinxi, Koga disobeyed orders from Guandong army headquarters and foolishly pursued the approxi-mately 1,000 retreating Chinese, leaving only 21 Japanese to guard the whole city. Despite the fact that his pursuing force of 130 quickly found themselves pinned down, when Koga heard that the Japanese flag at Jinxi was under attack, Koga, in Young's description, "split his forces again, taking half to rescue the flag and leaving the rest to 'hold off the enemy'" (1996, 108). The result of this intransigence and what several *bidan* refer to as his "arbitrary self authorization" (*dokudan*), was the useless slaughter of Koga and all his officers. Despite this, his suicidal tendencies and personal willfulness made him into the most celebrated Japanese hero of the Manchurian Incident; countless *bidan*'s were writ-ten about him in the monthlies, and this nihilistic new hero was resur-rected in two major films, on several music recordings, and in the popu-lar theater. It didn't matter that Koga and his eleven officers died for nothing, or that Jinxi was retaken by Chinese forces. He had acted reck-lessly with the apparent end of his own private death on the battlefield in mind. This resonated with Japanese metropolitan consumers inside the capitalist slaughterhouse splattered with erotic-grotesque image-commodities.

PART III   **NECROPOLITICS**

THE OPIATE OF THE (CHINESE) PEOPLE

The sale of opium was both a huge source of capital to support our military imperialism and a means to weaken and kill Chinese people. . . . The way we accomplished this was through the market, where we used our military strength to buy opium as cheaply as possible and then sold it at astronomical prices to desperate addicts.

KANEDA SEI, FORMER MANCHUKUO MINISTER,

TESTIFYING IN CHINA, 1954

Why, the slave trade was merciful compared with the opium trade: We did not destroy the bodies of the Africans, for it was in our immediate interest to keep them alive. But the opium seller slays the body after he has corrupted, degraded and annihilated the unhappy sinners.

ENGLISH REFORMER M. MARTIN, CITED IN KARL MARX,

"THE OPIUM TRADE," 1858

Japan's imperialism built on the sacrificial base of the accumulation by dispossession tactics of bio- and neuropolitics, but it changed significantly with the military invasion and colonization of Northeast China after the Manchurian Incident of 18 September 1931. The new logic of imperial rule was institutionalized in the establishment of the Manchukuo state on 1 March 1932, and the Manchukuo template was then forcefully applied to North and Central China in the mid-1930s, before being used to set up military governments in areas liberated from Euro-American colonial rule in the Greater East Asian War (Katō Y. 2007). The Manchukuo-ization of Asia was therefore anticolonial colonialism, much like the pimp Muraoka who freed women only to traffic them himself. It was a war waged to liberate in order to then recolonize. For

Japanese policy planners imagining a Greater East Asia after the Second World War, only the relatively resource-poor Philippines and Burma would be allowed to maintain true liberation as independent nations. All the other areas were targeted for longer-term resource extraction by Japan (Kobayashi 2007a).

Japan needed resources to stoke its depression-stalled capitalist engine and would soon need more to wage total war. Many war planners shared the assumption that anticommunist Japan would go to war first against the Soviet Union and then against the United States in what the mastermind Ishihara Kanji called the "final war" leading to the post-apocalyptic Japan-controlled peace. Huge parts of East and Southeast Asia were identified as resource extraction areas to support these wars. As we saw in part I, Korea, Taiwan, and the Guandong Lease in Manchuria were all used as platforms to send resources and stolen surpluses back to Japan. Because of this pillaging and profiteering, imperial elites on occasion needed to biopolitically buy off select segments of colonized populations with "improved lives" (*faire vivir*) aided by hospitals and modern hygiene while "letting the rest fare for themselves and die off" (*laisser mourir*). I don't doubt that many Japanese were sincere in wanting to replace China as the country best suited to guide Asia into a non-Eurocentric future. But it's equally important to recognize that during Japan's fifteen-year war (1931–45) Japanese elites believed they were living in a time of emergency. Their most urgent task was to conquer and hold resource-rich areas in Asia so as to secure development inside Japan and to prepare for future wars. Recalling my discussion of ideological fantasy in intertext I, these two contradictory positions (civilizers and looters) continued to coexist in the same epistemic field of select imperialists, with the Asianist Ishihara being only the most prominent (Abe 2005). However, the ideological elements of ultranationalism combined with the renewed sense that capitalist profiteering was beneficial to Japan, which emerged in the 1930s, sidelined most of the sincere plans to develop Asia. Furthermore, the displacement of bio- and neuropolitics by necropolitics impelled Japanese elites such as the fascist "new bureaucrats" to forgo earlier Pan-Asian interpellations.

Northeast China became the most important new resource area for Japan's empire, frequently metaphorized in neuropolitical terms as Japan's "life-blood" or in biopolitical terms as a "lifeline" (*seimeisen*). However, as a lifeline, Manchukuo was biopolitical vampirically and *imperialistically* in that the easy theft of Chinese labor, land, and life was primarily intended to improve the lives (*faire vivir*) of a certain population or *class* of Japanese: rich capitalists, powerful militarists, and the emperor's family.[1] Certainly the overwhelming majority of Chinese were left to die (*laisser mourir*), as were many Japanese. Therefore, because the emphasis during the fifteen-year war is on taking by armed force areas designated as crucial for Japan's elites, I find biopolitics to be insufficient to describe the dominant tendency in late imperial rule. In an important corrective to Foucault's First World bias, Achille Mbembe (2003) proposes *necropolitics* to more precisely depict the existential predicament of subaltern populations living in colonial and postcolonial spaces. Mbembe suggests that when the political accent moves through modernity—or in the terms I've established here, bio- and neuropolitics—to return to the sovereign's right to kill and murder (*faire mourir*) while leaving the rest in the condition of "living-dead," modernizing biopolitics is best thought of as the secondary and tertiary effects of a necropolitical order whose main focus is on killing and plundering, not on enhancing people's lives.

Mbembe's important intervention takes us only so far, however. It becomes clear that with the Great Depression of 1929 elites such as Ishihara and Kishi Nobusuke began to configure imperial war as the most efficacious way to revive Japan's capitalist system. Elites in the 1930s reversed Gotō Shinpei's policy of business as a continuation of war by other means to prioritize war as a continuation of capitalist business by other means. Similar to the Bush administration's justification in 2004 of imperial war in the Middle East as "good for American jobs and the economy," Japanese elites understood military occupation as the best shortcut to extracting surpluses. War as a continuation of business by other means was intuited as the emerging tendency for Japan's rule in the erotic-grotesque Marxism of Akagami and Nakayama. They identified new modes of value extraction and grotesqueing, including forced labor, induced drug addiction, and violent consumer spectacles such as car crashes. When these marginal aspects of neuropolitics are transferred to an Asian theater of war as a continuation of business—in other words, when the political accent is on killing and violently incapacitating—they move centripetally out of the margins into the matricial center of necropolitical capitalism.

This turn to necropolitics entailed a displacement of the real subsumption of human attention and desire to capital. Distinct from the formal and real subsumption that characterized bio- and neuropolitics, a new mode of subsumption I call *deformal subsumption* arose in 1932, defined by its relative unconcern with systemic reproduction. In the necropolitical capitalism hegemonic in Manchukuo, drugs, forced labor, and sexual slavery were not intended to *reproduce* labor power and consumer investment; they were directly and indirectly linked to their death. Therefore, we need to think outside the framework of Marx's formal and real subsumption. In a fairly explicit way Japan's necropolitical capitalism begins to take on what Mbembe calls a "murder-suicide" logic: not only in killing off workers and consumers by forced labor and pushing life-threatening commodities like heroin, but in the commitment to total war the whole apparatus of Japan's imperialism is placed in danger. We can render the Japanese term *hentai* into "deformal" here to reference the mode of subsumption characteristic of necropolitical capitalism in an attempt to highlight its deviant unconcern for the biopolitical maintenance of human life and to underline its diversion away from the reproduction of the system in the direction of full, systemic annihilation.

My notion of the deformal subsumption of life to capitalist death might help explain the extensive reliance on the system of "comfort women," forced sex workers institutionalized by the Japanese military and civilian elites in Asia. The 150,000 to 400,000 comfort women supported war as a continuation of business by other means to the extent that some military and private proprietors of comfort stations, or rape rooms, profited handsomely on women's and girl's forced labor, but they profited by preparing the consumers of their commodities for death in war. Factoring in that women were often raped twenty-five to thirty-five times a day (endangering their health and life) and occasionally committed suicide, we can see the tendencies of sexuality in imperial necropolitics deformally subsumed because they led directly to death. Unlike the regime of sexuality in imperial biopolitics that expanded Japanese markets, maintained the health of many sex workers, and elicited an improvement of life (*faire vivir*) for male consumers, sexuality in necropolitics directly produces death (*faire mourir*) by preparing soldiers for death in war and putting the lives of forced sex workers at constant risk.

It should go without saying that the two previous modes of imperial rule continued to operate residually alongside emergent necropolitics. To fight the total war Japan embarked on in 1937 obviously required massive biopolitical mobilization. Select populations in Taiwan, Korea, and Manchukuo were bought off with such techniques as education or modern medicine so they would be less prone to resist imperial rule and more willing to go off to die in Japan's wars or be worked to death in its capitalist factories. However, in the necropolitical period Japan's inconsistent biopolitical commitments were just as often simulacral scams. For example, in 1944 the Manchukuo state required almost two million Chinese opium addicts to report to detoxification clinics, a mobilization pitched to local Chinese leaders as part of a drug eradication campaign. Designed by the new bureaucrat Furumi Tadayuki (1901–81), it literally shuttled Chinese addicts directly out the back door of these clinics, where they were transformed into forced laborers (*RDQDZX*, vol. 14, 820–21). As I tried to demonstrate in part II, building on the ways laborers are dehumanized and objectified, the commodity-driven instrumentalization of human life in neuropolitics had the effect of transmuting consumers from subjects into objects, what Marx in *Grundrisse* called the reversal of the anthropocentric "connections between humans" to the capitalist privileging of the "relation between things" (1973, 157). The penetration into and modification of the human nervous system (constructing what Tanaka and other erotic-grotesque theorists called a "second life") had the effect of ideologically instructing consumers to turn against a more authentic first life, even when it was their own. Although indebted to neuropolitics, the vanguard form of necropolitics was consolidated first in the colonial periphery in Manchukuo, and then—similar to the ways in which Césaire (1955) and Fanon (1968) track the genealogy of European fascism—moved back into Japan's homeland, where Japanese subjects were killed off just like North Chinese laborers, seven million of whom, by 1941, had only a 50 percent chance of surviving one year of forced labor (Ju 2007, 211).[2] Japanese nationals thus became "coolie-ized" through the centripetal diffusionism of necropolitics from Manchukuo back into Japan.

This coolie-ization of Japanese subjects culminated in the Matsushiro Plan, devised by the Japanese Army High Command at the end of the Second World War. While six thousand of Japan's top elites withdrew to a huge underground facility built by Korean and Chinese forced labor in the small castle town of Matsushiro in northern Nagano, Japan, all other adult Japanese were ordered to defend them with rocks and swords against the high-tech North American invaders. As Ōhigata Etsuo has argued, "The plan was to fight the Americans until the last Japanese was alive—with the exception of the elites hiding out in Matsushiro" (*Rekishi kyōikusha kyōgikai* 1995, 77–78). On 3 August 1945 the necropolitical order actually went out from headquarters directing all "volunteers" in eastern Japan to take up positions in coastal mountains and on beaches in preparation for the North American landing (527).[3]

War Machines

Mbembe singles out traffickers and mercenaries as central subjectivities in necropolitics, calling them "war machines." He follows Deleuze and Guattari, who classify them as being from a "different origin, a different assemblage" than nation-state institutions like the military and police. War machines are deterritorializing forces of nomadic origin, and therefore "one of the biggest questions is: How will the State appropriate the war machine?" (Deleuze and Guattari 1987, 418). To understand Japan's imperialist necropolitics we will focus on war machines in the form of human and drug traffickers in Northeast China, spawn of men like Muraoka Iheiji, who were left to fare for themselves (*laissez faire*) in biopolitics and ended up winning market hegemony for Japanese capitalists over Chinese merchants.

In chapter 2, I showed how these pimp, war-machinic "men engaged in ugly business" refused to be appropriated when their number in Manchuria increased to several hundred in 1918. Instead, the imperial state, through the Japanese consulates, allowed itself to be appropriated to some degree by *them*, providing legal cover through extraterritoriality and police protection to support their competition with Chinese merchants. The Manchukuo regime became similarly appropriated as the military invasion of Northeast China was completed by February 1932. At this point Japan's Guandong army desperately needed revenue to establish the new state, in addition to requiring useful intelligence from on-the-ground Japanese sources with experience in dealing with Manchuria. The only Japanese in control of these two precious commodities of intelligence and drugs were the hustlers and traffickers, who were now joined by opportunistic *yakuza* groups like the Kokusuikai, who ran a large operation in Fengtian, Manchuria, providing strikebreakers trained in martial arts to Japanese-owned factories in North China "threatened" by Chinese labor organizing and boycotts (Arahara 1966). Fortunately for Manchukuo state formation, both the traffickers and the *yakuza* were willing to deal with and deal to the two other power blocs: the Guandong army and the elite new bureaucrats who began arriving from Tokyo in July 1932.

Building on Meyer (1998) and Yamada (2002), I argue that the key to understanding Manchukuo, and consequently Japan's military imperialism during the entire fifteen-year war, is in following what these traffickers were doing—with the exception of South Manchurian Railway Company employees, the only Japanese actors in Northeast China operating outside the Guandong Lease colony at the time of the Manchurian Incident. Although they were class enemies, the hustlers and traffickers would eventually form alliances with the military leaders Amakasu Masahiko and Itagaki Seishirō and with the civilian new bureaucrats. By mid-1932 their combined power, bolstered by a working relationship with a second *yakuza* group newly relocated to Manchukuo, the Seigidan, was too much for the army and new bureaucrats to ignore. In September 1918 the Japanese consul in Fengtian wrote to Gotō Shinpei warning about the Japanese traffickers, and an almost identical cable was sent ten years later, in December 1928, from the same Fengtian consulate with a similarly alarmed warning for the Japanese prime minister Tanaka Giichi. In it, Consul Hayashi complained that the activities of the numerous traffickers were undercutting Japan's claim to be a civilizing power and infuriating local Chinese. As their criminal actions were routinely ignored (when not aided and abetted) by the Japanese consular police in the nearby Guandong Lease, Hayashi recommended that if Tokyo wanted to improve its image, it should do everything in its power to extradite the traffickers (FMA, "Collections of Improper Business," vol. 1, 4.2.2.34).

Tokyo refused to rein in the traffickers after the First World War. With their connections to politicians and criminal *yakuza* inside Japan and their working relationship with the Guandong army and *kempeitai* (military police) in Manchuria, their number had ballooned to ten thousand or so by the time the communiqué in 1928 identified them as *rōnin*. *Rōnin* referenced this diverse group of decommissioned soldiers, veteran drug dealers, second-generation pimps and traffickers, and *sōshi*, or private bodyguards, a group I designate as "hustlers" and whom Katherine Meyer calls "soldiers of fortune." At the level of class, these Japanese mainly hailed from a humbler one than the military college graduates Itagaki and Amakasu, and lower still than the new bureaucrats Hoshino Naoki (1892–1978) and Furumi Tadayuki, who were elite Tokyo University grads. Owing to class and gender formation, this hustler assemblage's sole raison d'être in Manchuria was, according to the historian Tsukase Susumu, "to make as much money in as short a period of time as possible" (2004, 171–72). In 1924, between the Fengtian consul complaints of 1918 and 1928, the Third Conference for Japanese Consulates in Manchuria was held in Tokyo, and report after report detailed the negative impact Japan's consular policy of protecting hustlers had on local Chinese (96–97). One official claimed that most Chinese in the area couldn't distinguish Japanese consular police from drug traffickers. From the Chinese perspective, all Japanese were a bunch of criminal war machines who had come to Northeast China with the single purpose of stealing and swindling as much as they could. By the eve of the Manchurian Incident their number had mushroomed to approximately thirty thousand. By spring 1933, with the new opportunities afforded to Japanese nationals by the occupation, the hustler assemblage population doubled to sixty thousand, with many newcomers settling in with the Kokusuikai and Seigidan *yakuza* syndicates (FMA, "Documents Related to Hustlers in China," 17 March 1933, D.2.5.0.1).[4]

The diary of a Japanese drug trafficker going by the pen name "Child of Gion" (Gionbō), written in 1924 or 1925, provides a rare on-the-ground account of the extent of Japanese trafficking in North China and Manchuria in the years preceding the Manchurian Incident. Called "The Result of Incidents of Opium Smuggling," the handwritten document details the activities of a major smuggler as he is wheeling and dealing in Tianjin, Beijing, Fengtian, and Harbin. Supported everywhere he goes by Japanese consulates and their police and military, his drug supply is transported easily and safely on SMR trains and ferries. We discover that there are more than one hundred Japanese shooting galleries for narcotics in Changchun, Manchuria, and that half of the Japanese in North and Northeast China are directly connected to drug trafficking (Gionbō 1999, 57, 168). He estimates in several places that, excepting SMR employees, *all* Japanese merchants in the region can be directly or indirectly linked to drug trafficking.

I argued in parts I and II that bio- and neuropolitical capitalism worked through a dialectic of a creative, ontological *erotic* and a parasitic, ontic *grotesque* that transformed and expropriated the erotic, what Akagami Yoshitsuge construed as capitalism "putting *ero* to work" for it. Here in part III, necropolitical capitalism was constituted first by "putting to work" the *ero* of hustlers and war profiteers who, while marginal to previous scholarship on the fifteen-year war, were the central constituent subjectivities of it. These key necropolitical subjectivities were also the principal agents of grotesqueing, allowing us to witness an intensification of the tendency—already present in neuropolitics—to shrink the gap separating *ero* and *guro*. In necropolitics the gap is conflated and absolutized. While the ontological drive for some escape from an unbearable present was answered by capitalists in the form of consumer commodities (and in the case of drug commodities, Chinese users' needy desire for opium and heroin certainly established Japanese dealers as capitalist oppressors), in this section I focus less on the ways in which subaltern and consumer desire drove Japan's imperial system. Rather, I zero in on how the vampiric and invidious *ero* of the hustlers and traffickers drove the Manchukuo state to assume the form it did, through a reciprocal grotesqueing and hegemonic coalition with the two opposing power blocs: the military leaders and the new bureaucrats. As I demonstrate in this last part, the ontological motor for Japan's imperialism passes from the subaltern laborer in part I to the mass consumer in part II, then finally to the hustler assemblage. When their *ero* becomes the Manchukuo state's *guro*, necropolitics emerges as the monstrous mien of Japan's imperialism.

Puppet Strings, Purse Strings

Much has been written about the puppet strings Japanese imperialists used to manipulate the Last Emperor of China and his circle of Qing monarchists after the establishment of Manchukuo in March 1932. However, much less has been written about the *purse strings* underwriting the huge occupation of Northeast China and their narco supply lines. The scholarship on drugs in Japanese imperialism largely focuses on the period after the beginning of full-scale war with China in July 1937. Eguchi Keiichi's (1988) argument that opium revenues financed the Japanese army after the Marco Polo Bridge Incident shows that without drug revenues, it would have been difficult for Japan to wage the kind of wars it did from 1937 to 1945. However, the Manchukuo colonial state's dependence on drug revenues began even before the 18 September 1931 Manchurian Incident, when the co-conspirators Itagaki Seishirō and Ishihara unsuccessfully sought Japanese financing for their various plans for the military occupation of Northeast China. Having no luck among right-wing industrialists, they did receive fifty million yen from the drug trafficker Fujita Osamu, who got his start selling heroin in Shandong province. There, in the late 1920s, Fujita met Yamauchi Saburo (who became a major Japanese heroin producer in Manchukuo during the 1930s [Meyer 1998, 188–91]) and many other *sensei* experienced in the trade, as over half of the Japanese living in Shandong's urban areas were "men engaged in ugly business." In the 1920s the Last Emperor Puyi resided in the Japanese concession in the nearby treaty port of Tianjin (close to Beijing), where he and his opium-addicted Empress enjoyed a regular supply from their trusted Japanese dealers. The percentage of the five thousand Japanese residents involved in trafficking was so high that the Tianjin consul Yoshida Shigeru claimed in 1922, "If we were to apply the letter of the law against the drug traffickers in Tianjin, there wouldn't be a single Japanese remaining in the city" (quoted in Senga 2007, 59). In the International Military Tribunal for the Far East (IMTFE) the United States and its allies concluded, "Successive Japanese governments . . . pursued a systematic policy of weakening the native inhabitants' will to resist . . . by directly and indirectly encouraging the increased production and importation of opium and other narcotics and by promoting the sale and consumption of such drugs among such people" (*Tōkyō saiban shiryō*, ii–iii, quoted in Jennings 1997, 106).

In his authoritative monograph on drugs in Japanese imperialism John Jennings paraphrases the IMTFE: "In the judgment of the IMTFE, Japan's guilt in conspiring to promote the drug traffic in China was beyond doubt. In Manchuria, Japan had sanctioned the traffic to finance her operations and to weaken the power of resistance of the Chinese people. The pattern was then repeated by the Japanese army, operating behind puppet regimes in northern and central China" (1997, 107). However, Jennings goes on to critique the Tokyo Trial's conclusions as simply victor's justice and claims it is exaggeration, verging on conspiracy theory, to say that Japanese elites deliberately plotted to subjugate China using drugs. Consistent with right-wing critics in Japan, Jennings implies that overestimating Japanese maleficence played into the geopolitical needs of the United States after the Second World War. While partly sympathetic to critiques of the U.S.-led IMTFE, I draw on Ōta Naoki (2005), Yamada Gōichi (2002), and heretofore ignored archival material in Chinese to argue almost the exact opposite in the case of drugs: that the IMTFE's conclusion seriously understated the importance of drugs both for Japan's financial viability and as a tool for counterinsurgency war. In fact, Ōta and Yamada also criticize the IMTFE, but for singling out civilian traffickers like Nitancho Otozō and Satomi Hajime and thereby ignoring the systematicity and centrality of drug trafficking for colonial occupation and war. Drawing on both internal documentation from the Tokyo Trial's International Prosecution Section (IPS) and Chinese sources, I estimate that between 50 and 55 percent of all the revenues earned from Manchukuo products came from drugs.

Although critics on the left and right are skeptical of the conspiracy theory disseminated by the United States and the IMTFE, Ōta, Yamada, and I find that the IMTFE opinions were consistent with those of most international critics of Japan's drug dealing in the 1930s and 1940s in seriously *underestimating Japanese imperialism's reliance on drug revenues*. In his long chapter detailing the saturation of Northeast China by drugs immediately following the Manchurian Incident of September 1931, Yamada cites a well-known report from the U.S. consul in Shanghai, M. R. Nicholson, written in 1933.[5] Nicholson documents an alarming increase in the commercial drug market in several cities in Manchuria and supplies the names of popular Japanese-run opium dens in Fengtian. He claims that before the Incident the four or five Japanese drug places operated discreetly, but by the beginning of March 1932 many previously straight Japanese businesses had turned to selling opium and heroin exclusively—and publicly. Nicholson calculated that by six months after the Incident there were six hundred of these "drugstores." Other startling increases are cited in smaller cities (cited in Yamada 2002, 193–94). In a second, more comprehensive report filed by Nicholson's office in May 1936,[6] he claims that there were only ten or so opium dens in Andong, Manchuria's Chinatown, before the Incident. By spring of 1933 there were 145 legal opium dens in Chinatown and almost 700 drug places in Andong's Japanese concession. In the town of Fengcheng to the east of Andong the five quiet opium dens operating before the Incident mushroomed to seventy-six by January 1932 (IPS Records, M1690, Roll 475, "Drug Conditions in Liaoning, Manchukuo," 147–48). Yamada suggests that these investigations, led by the U.S. consulate in Shanghai, "leave Japanese with the strong feeling that this information represents American enemy propaganda and is grossly exaggerated" (194). Then he spends two pages analyzing a report published by researchers at the SMR called "The Different Kinds of Opium in Manchuria." Looking at the situation in Andong around the same time as the U.S. consulate, the SMR researchers not only confirmed an urban landscape transformed beyond recognition by narcotics and opium, but they enumerated many more drug places than the Americans found, listing over four thousand establishments where the primary or secondary attraction was drugs. The conclusion so surprised the SMR research leaders that the principal investigator was sent back in August 1932 to confirm the numbers. Yamada sums up his comparison of the research by concluding, "It turns out that the American Nicholson was by no means exaggerating the number of drug establishments; in reality he was underestimating the extent of the problem" (195–96).

Fortunately for our understanding, there were others on the ground illuminating the degree to which the hustler assemblage and soldiers of fortune had deterritorialized urban Northeast China. The North American journalist Edgar Snow wrote that seemingly overnight they turned Harbin, Fengtian, and other Manchurian cities into "places of living death" (1934, 12). Amleto Vespa, an Italian correspondent who worked in Northeast China for two decades and was an adviser to the leading Manchurian warlord Zhang Zuolin, claimed to have been held hostage and forced to work for Japanese intelligence in Manchukuo for four years. Vespa's exposé was written just after he managed to escape Manchukuo and was published in 1938 as *Secret Agent of Japan*. It reads like nothing so much as Umehara Hokumei's *The Killing Kapitalist Konglomerate*. Among other pulp-like claims, Vespa insists that when Japan's Guandong army set out to conquer Northeast China, almost all of the Japanese civilians working in the region were "crooks and adventurers, smugglers, sellers of narcotics, brothel-keepers. This underworld gentry constituted 95% of the Japanese in Manchuria. Protected by their own flag and extra-territorial rights, they were beyond the reach of Chinese laws." He sums up his ethnography of Japanese intelligence with this denunciation of Manchukuo's drug dealing: "It is unquestionably a part of the Japanese policy to poison the whole world. The more Japan can undermine other nations through these body-and-soul-destroying drugs, the easier it is going to be to conquer them" (30, 90).

Leaving aside for now his claim of a 95 percent human trafficker and dealer population (although this percentage is uncannily similar to

Gionbō's estimate of Japanese connected to trafficking made a decade earlier, in 1924), Vespa provides portraits of Japanese hustlers in Manchuria that, unsurprisingly, match the descriptions of Muraoka Iheiji's henchmen (see chapter 2).

> Konstantin Ivanovich Nakamura was a Japanese, who, as his name indicates, had embraced the Russian Orthodox religion. . . . A barber by trade, he had a small shop at Nahaloika, a suburb of Harbin. . . . But the shop was only a front. His real business was dealing in morphine, heroine, and opium; and conducting a house of prostitution a short distance from his barbershop. . . . In 1923 Nakamura had contracted an illegitimate union with a Russian woman, a widow with an eleven-year-old daughter. After a few months he assaulted the little girl. As a result of a complaint by the mother, the police arrested him and handed him over to the Japanese Consul. The Japanese Court could not find him guilty of having done anything wrong because, according to Japanese law, he had "bought" her when he "bought" the mother.
>
> In 1926 the police had once more to deal with Nakamura. This time a Russian who had gone to his barbershop for a shave had been drugged and robbed of $500. When he woke up, he went to the police and made his complaint. As before, the Japanese Consul took a hand in the matter, declared that the Russian was not drugged but was just plain drunk. Nakamura was scot-free. (Vespa 1938, 32–33)

Vespa prefaces his sketch of "Kostia" Nakamura by claiming that he was an ideal-typical hustler, as criminal as 95 percent of the Japanese civilians living in Manchuria outside the Guandong Lease. What's important here is that after the Manchurian Incident, marginal hustlers like Nakamura took center stage in their roles as prominent businessmen— owning and operating the profitable opium dens and shooting parlors that mushroomed up overnight in the urban areas—and as coveted advisers to the Guandong *kempeitai*. The Japanese hustlers had sole possession of the drug and intelligence commodities desperately needed by the new regime. They also had crucial, on-the-ground information necessary to carry out a successful counterinsurgency war. Yamada writes that because of their local knowledge these hustlers were magically transformed post-Incident into "wise, patriotic teachers [*senkaku no shishi*]" (2002, 211). Nakamura himself became an important adviser to the *kempeitai* in Harbin immediately after the Incident, where his Russian and Chinese fluency and knowledge of the locals was in high demand. Doubtless surprised to find himself being addressed in the Confucian-like terms of "sensei" and "revered patriot," Nakamura merely took his hustling to a higher level, assisting the *kempeitai* in extortion and confiscation and leaving the small-time trafficking and shakedowns to newcomers. Finally realizing Muraoka's Iheiji's dream, his hustling was recognized for its important contribution to Japan's empire.

The prehistory of flooding Northeast China with drugs in the early 1930s was the breakthrough, just after the First World War, of Japanese capitalists introducing narcotics into local markets in China. As I mentioned briefly in chapter 4, Japanese drug companies such as Taishō Seiyaku had grown quickly during the war, responding to the demand for morphine and heroin from European armies. Some of their products were also smuggled into Korea and China, and as Japanese products they traveled quickly and safely on SMR railways from the port of Dalian deep into Northeast China, where they were marketed by Japanese and Korean hustlers (Kurahashi 2005, 127–30). Heroin joined morphine as a new, cheaper alternative to opium for Chinese and Korean consumers, and Japanese chemists working in small labs in Dalian were the main producers during the 1920s (Yamada 2002, 35–37). The hustlers were so successful at getting this product to market that the average annual consumption of morphine among residents of Japan's Guandong Lease was the highest in the world by 1932, matched only by cocaine consumption; the insatiable users in Japan's colony also consumed the highest per capita amount of that substance (Kobayashi, in Brook and Wakabayashi 2000, 154).

Discordia Association

Knowing that their Japanese nationality would grant them protection and risk-free profiteering, the hustlers pounced on the new opportunities available after the Incident. In 1954 the new bureaucrat Furumi testified while on trial in China that many hustlers took advantage of their newfound power, making "windfall profits" (*hengcai*) seemingly overnight (*RDQDZX*, vol. 14, 813). Marx similarly references Warren Hastings's East India Company drug trafficker cronies, calling them "cleverer than alchemists"; "[they] made gold out of nothing" and ironically revealed the limitless possibilities for British profiteering when colonial sovereignty combined with drug dealing in India (1977, 917). To give readers some sense of how Japanese drug dealers were "cleverer than alchemists" in Manchukuo, by the time the official Manchukuo Opium Monopoly was established in November 1932, on the occasions when Manchukuo authorities didn't simply confiscate poppy directly from Chinese growers at gunpoint they would purchase opium from Chinese farmers at a price that fluctuated between ten and eighteen Chinese yuan for a *liang* (3.75 grams), depending on whether the product was extraordinary, top grade, or middle or low grade. By late 1933, all this raw opium was turned into market-ready opium at one of three official Manchukuo opium-processing plants (*RDQDZX*, vol. 14, 822). About 50 percent of the market-ready product would then be sold officially through the Opium Monopoly by the fourteen hundred government-licensed dealers at a price ranging from twenty to forty yuan per *liang*. The remaining 50 percent of this opium was retailed on black markets by unlicensed Japanese and Korean dealers for prices that fluctuated between two hundred and six hundred yuan inside Manchukuo, with the price climbing even higher in Beijing, Tianjin, and Shanghai (819).

Adding together consular warnings, Vespa's exposé, Furumi's claims, the *kempeitai* reports, and the rare trafficker's diary, it's evident that these hustlers and *yakuza* underlings were frolicking giddily in the new market environment, which saw them making a profit of anywhere from 100 percent to 6,000 percent. Many of them may also have felt smug satisfaction that the selfish work they had been doing to control markets was paradoxically, through the "invisible hand" of necropolitical capitalism, making an important contribution to Japan's successful occupation. From their perspective, not only had their presence contributed to the Guandong army's justification that the Incident was about protecting "Japanese rights and commercial interests," but their local knowledge proved crucial when the Guandong army and *kempeitai* were forced to rely on them as advisers. Vespa's insistence that almost all of the Japanese civilian advisers in Manchukuo were originally hustlers trafficking in drugs and humans might seem implausible at first glance. But consider the diary of the Japanese hustler Hirota Yūji, which describes being forced to operate clandestinely for three years under the strict drug eradication campaign the modernizing warlord Zhang Xueliang initiated in late 1928. After the Manchurian Incident, Hirota and other hustlers could sell openly, with profit margins ballooning and their social status transformed unrecognizably into "honorable Japanese *sensei*" (*Kempeitai Shireibu*, vol. 6, 1987, 199–201).

The internal correspondence of the *kempeitai* high command and the international reports confirm the exuberant publicness of the hustlers. A *kempeitai* report from November 1931 complained that all areas of Manchuria had been "inundated" by Japanese hustlers taking advantage of their "pretty new cover as 'patriots'" (*Kempeitai Shireibu*, vol. 6, 1931, 196). Edgar Snow reported that in just two years the hustlers had made the large city of Harbin unrecognizable (1934, 13). Not one to pull punches, Vespa's horror at enumerating all the new Japanese brothels open for business by 1936 was outdone by his observation of the "diabolical" spread of drugs by the hustlers:

> Within a few months after the Japanese invasion, the whole of Manchuria, especially the large cities, was infested with this abominable evil. In Mukden, in Harbin, in Kirin, etc., one cannot find a street where there are no opium-smoking dens or narcotics shops. In many streets the Japanese and Korean dealers have established an effective system. The morphine, cocaine or heroin addict does not have to enter the place if he is poor. He simply knocks at the door, a small peephole opens, through which he thrusts his bare arm and hand with 20 cents in it. The owner of the joint takes the money and gives the victim a shot. (1938, 96–97)

The hustlers pioneered other "effective systems" just after the Incident. In Andong they turned parts of their drug establishments into pawnshops where poor Chinese addicts could sell the clothes right off their backs for drugs (IPS Records, "Drug Conditions in Liaoning, Manchukuo," 150). Outside the cities Japanese and Korean pushers handed out drugs to first-time users below cost, as free-trial offers for adults and special introductory "kids' sizes" for children (Pernikoff 1943, 105). Japanese sundry merchants were known to form business partnerships with drug dealers to sell cigarettes that had been secretly laced with opium (*Chinese Recorder*, October 1935, 606).

The reports of the U.S. Institute of Pacific Relations and the League of Nations Opium Advisory Committee on the situation in Northeast China before and after the Incident differ from Vespa's ethnography only in their rhetorical tone. Writing for the former group, Frederick Merrill observed that just after the Incident the cities of Harbin, Kirin, and Fengtian became "infested with drug peddlers and riddled with drug addiction" (1942, 96). This situation impelled novel forms of necropolitical management such as the infamous "ash heap" near the consumer area of South Gate in Fengtian, where many of the bodies of the four thousand dead and dying Chinese addicts found in the streets of that city annually were dumped. According to the Christian missionary monthly *The Chinese Recorder*, which published gruesome photographs of the Fengtian ash heap, many Chinese addicts were required to have a rope tied to their wrists before gaining entry to the more than two hundred Japanese shooting galleries near South Gate; if they weren't able to physically walk out of the drug establishment, they would be dragged out by the rope and deposited on the ash heap to die. *The Chinese Recorder* reported that there were ash heaps in other Manchurian cities as well: "The main motive of dumping dope victims on ash heaps is conscienceless profiteering in human life" (October 1935, 608). I've included an image of the Japanese drug area in Harbin, behind which the body of a dead Chinese addict was stripped of his clothing and dumped in 1940, awaiting disposal in the nearby ash heap.

Nothing captures the reality of the tsunami of drugs flooding Manchuria better than the market price and the explosion in the number of addicts. The price of a shot of heroin was three times higher before the Incident than the twenty Japanese cents Vespa claims was the going rate at needle joints in 1936. According to an SMR survey, before the Incident an hour in an opium den cost on the average two yen; after the Incident, in Fengtian or Harbin one could go into a similar type of establishment and get four grams of opium (good for an hour or two of fine smoking) for forty cents, plus an extra forty cents for the opportunity to flirt with a "young and pretty waitress. . . . With the house charge, [the total was] only one yen" (cited in Yamada 2002, 335). Not only did the rush of hustlers into the new Manchukuo lower the price of opium to one-third of its pre-Incident rate, but they took advantage of another of their trafficking commodities and began the Japanization of the Chinese opium den by introducing "waitress" service, a kind of work that was called in Chinese *yan ji*, or "opium prostitution" (*RDQDZX*, vol. 14, 822).

Kaneda Sei, the Manchukuo vice minister of welfare in 1944, testified at the Japanese war crimes trial held in the old Manchukuo in the mid-1950s that there were, "at the most, 200,000 opium addicts" in Manchuria before the Incident, owing to the eradication campaign begun

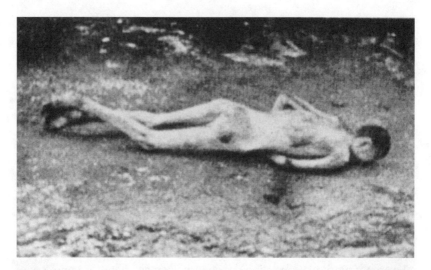

A dead Chinese addict dumped behind the Japanese consumer drug area in Harbin, Manchukuo (shown here), circa 1940. Most likely the body would have been disposed of with thousands of other dead addicts in the Harbin ash heap, about five hundred meters away. From *E de Yomu: Shien, Dokuen [Daitōa] Genei*, 2007.

in fall 1928.[7] Based on two Manchukuo surveys, Kaneda estimated that there were about *three million* opium addicts in Manchukuo by 1944, out of a population of just over forty million (*RDQDZX*, vol. 14, 822–23). The situation for heroin and morphine addicts was worse still. U.S. Consulate Nicholson's second report of May 1936 was based on surveys of narcotics addiction in several places in Manchukuo's Liaoning (Fengtian) province. He points out that there was almost no narcotics addiction before the Incident, whereas by 1936 the rate of addiction had risen from a low of 18 percent in Chunghe to a high of 35 percent in Fengcheng (IPS Report, "Drug Conditions in Liaoning, Manchukuo," 148–49). By 1944 there were about five million Chinese in Manchukuo addicted to heroin or morphine; when this is combined with opium addiction, roughly 20 percent of the colonized Chinese population was seriously addicted to drugs.

Shots in the Arm

It did not take long for Manchukuo elites to see the solution to all of their financial problems in drug trafficking. We know from several of their testimonies in China at the trials in 1954–56 that the colonial state was dependent on what was called its "secret fund." For example, Manchukuo's last chief of Administrative Affairs, Takabe Rokuzō, admitted that the Manchukuo state "owed its entire existence to this secret fund" (quoted in Mutō 1963, 36). Furumi Tadayuki testified that "Manchukuo was a gargantuan construction built with the secret fund of the Guandong Army" (*RDQDZX*, vol. 14, 816). Kaneda's testimony that at least 50 percent of the opium produced in Manchukuo was marketed "off the books" and outside the purview of the official Opium Monopoly clearly identifies the source of the fund as black market opium revenues (757–93). The urgent need for opium revenues grew from the disruption caused by the Guandong army's military occupation, which stalled regular export markets and interrupted tax flows throughout the region (Asada and Kobayashi 1972, 38). The army decided they wanted outside observers to recognize their regime as an independent state, so military elites moved from being war planners to being financial planners, with Ishihara Kanji drawing up the first budget for Manchukuo on 1 October 1931. Based on Japan's previous experiences in Taiwan and Guandong, the idea of drug monopolies as the main shot in the arm for the infant regime was put on the table immediately. Ishihara's budget itemizes revenues from potential opium and salt monopolies right at the top (Tsunoda J. 1984, 86–89).

When the League of Nations' Lytton Commission finished their investigation and left Manchukuo on 2 April 1932, elites got serious about the budget, and new bureaucrats from Japan's Finance Ministry were drafted to run Manchukuo's ministries. Hoshino Naoki was appointed head of the Finance Ministry and immediately began to get Manchukuo's main cash source, the Opium Monopoly, up and running. The customs duties, along with the extensive confiscations by the *kempeitai* of Chinese goods and bank deposits during the Incident, had generated some revenue, but this was less than half of what the first budget called for. Manchukuo received two loans from the Japanese government in March 1932, but they still needed financing. So Hoshino and Furumi were forced to go begging for loans to their Tokyo banking connections. They were quite successful, as over two-thirds of the investment total in Manchukuo for the first four years was in securities and direct loans, almost one billion yen (Kaneko 1987, 337; L. Young 1998, 213). What was the leverage they put up against these loan packages? Nothing but the huge revenue potential of drug sales (*RDQDZX*, vol. 14, 813). As Yamada Gōichi puts it, the Manchukuo propaganda that sold the Incident as Japan heroically saving the region from corrupt warlord rule and restoring the sage governmentality of the ancient Chinese kingly way (*wangdao*) quickly "gave way to Hoshino's need to balance the budget with the leverage of drug sales" (2002, 242). The kingpin's way would from this point on prove the lie of the kingly way.

It is increasingly difficult to question the fact that the Manchukuo Opium Monopoly had nothing whatsoever to do with restricting drug flows. Indeed, as Yamada states matter-of-factly, "it was about accumulating capital" (2002, 235), and the new bureaucrats were in agreement with the Guandong army that capital accumulation would be brought about in the most timely fashion by *expediting the circulation of drugs*. As the chief accountant for the Manchukuo state and one of three people responsible for setting up the Opium Monopoly, Furumi testified in 1954 that whatever Manchukuo's public blandishments on drugs, the army and civilian elite unanimously agreed behind closed doors that "the more the better [*duo duo yishan*]" (*RDQDZX*, vol. 14, 812). Hoshino Naoki was a Christian, and this led some international voices to accept at face value the lies that he peddled about Manchukuo's sincere efforts to suppress drugs. However, no one in policy circles at the time questioned that the Opium Monopoly was anything but the legal means to steal and sell as much as possible. Whether this means that "the Japanese" were deliberately trying to drug "the Chinese" into a comfortably numb colonization is a claim that requires more evidence. However, during the war crimes trial in 1954, among some forty pages of handwritten testimony about aspects of Manchukuo's finances, Furumi confessed, "To carry out Japan's imperial advance, the adoption of an opium policy was the most important of our usual tricks [*jōtō shudan*]. Legally, systematically, and with a refined rationality, along with securing our primary goal of fostering the physical ruin of the colonized people, our opium policy carried a secondary importance as a crucial source of revenue" (quoted in Arai and Fujiwara 1999, 123).

This in a nutshell is the conspiracy theory that Jennings and others have tried to debunk: the drug policy of Japanese imperialists that Furumi emphasized later was "from head to tail designed primarily to cause the debilitation and ruin of the Chinese people" (quoted in Arai and Fujiwara 1999, 129). In the much longer Chinese text that this Japanese translation is taken from, Furumi elaborated that the opium policy was deployed to "decay [*tuifei*] the bodies and degrade [*xiaoruo*] the spirit of Chinese resisting Japan's imperialism" (*RDQDZX*, vol. 14, 815). Given that everything else from Furumi's testimony has been confirmed, I see no reason to doubt what he says about drugs; many of the civilian elite were candid about their ethnoracial disdain for Chinese. Furumi detailed further that when Chinese elites living in Manchukuo expressed horror over the drug-induced social breakdown and demanded redress from Japanese leaders at a series of conferences in 1937, not one Japanese among the fifty in attendance supported the Chinese (814).[8]

The new bureaucrats were extremely anxious about stabilizing the "security situation" in Manchukuo (which would have entailed killing Chinese) so as to move ahead with economic planning and plunder in the hopes of attracting Japanese and international investment. This meant that those in the *kempeitai* responsible for confiscation and pacification operations inside and outside the large Manchurian cities would have unanimously preferred an enemy stoned on or overdosed from drugs. On the other hand, the more humane among the military elite, such as Guandong army commander Mutō Nobuyoshi, saw the regime's commitment to drug dealing as a necessary evil, as did Ishihara

Kanji. But even these reluctant traffickers understood that the very existence of Manchukuo, and therefore Japan's imperial endeavor in China, was dependent on drug revenues. In a top secret communiqué to Japanese Foreign Minister Uchida Yasuya sent on 5 December 1932, General Mutō wrote, "[Let us hope that there are] superficial [*hyōmen*] aspects of the Opium Monopoly that might lead some to believe that we are committed to the kind of prohibition advocated by the former Chinese leaders of the region, . . . [even though] we all recognize that the Opium Monopoly is in reality designed for the sole purpose of increasing revenue for Manchukuo" (FMA, "Documents Concerning Drugs in Manchukuo," D.2.5.0.1–3). Maintaining some degree of "appearance" (*hyōmen*) over and against the brute "reality" (*jijitsu*) of having to deal drugs to finance empire in China was important to proud army officers. For arrogant new bureaucrats like Furumi, for most of the hardened *kempeitai* leading pacification operations in the countryside, and for some of the hustlers, the importance of drug dealing for Manchukuo state revenue was *secondary* to its effectiveness in bringing about the necropolitical ruin of Chinese.[9] Kaneda, the civil affairs chief in Jilin province during the 1930s, doubtless spoke for most, if not all of the Japanese elites in Manchukuo when he testified:

> [Opium functioned as] both a huge source of capital to support our military imperialism and as a means to weaken and kill Chinese people [*Zhonghuo renmin ruozhong wangshen de gongju*]. . . .
>
> The dual purpose of our opium policy was to reap huge profits [*dali*] while eliminating [*miejue*] the citizens of Northeast China. The means to do this was through the market, where we used our military strength to buy opium as cheaply as possible [*zuidi de jiage*], and then sold it at astronomical prices to desperate Chinese addicts. Together with the huge sums we made smuggling opium outside Manchukuo, this gave us the luxury of turning quick profits with almost no investment [*yiben wanli*]. (RDQDZX, vol. 14, 815, 820)

"Cleverer than alchemists," Kaneda and other Japanese elites found in opium the ultimate necropolitical commodity, allowing Japanese to profit while killing Chinese. Their admissions suggest that Yamada and Ōta are correct in criticizing the IMTFE judgment in Tokyo, holding that, "successive Japanese governments . . . pursued a systematic policy of weakening the native inhabitants' will to resist," for demonstrably *understating the situation*. The judges suggested that opium was employed only to "weaken" Chinese resistance, while on the contrary, there was considerable support in Manchukuo for drugs to be used as murder weapons against Chinese. Japan's necropolitics indeed made a killing selling drugs.

A Chinese subaltern is shooting heroin; I, a Japanese imperialist, dealt it.

Scholars suggesting that Japanese would deliberately commit such atrocities have been accused of racism, so a final word is in order here. Unlike the operations of ideological fantasy I identified in Japanese colonialism in Korea, in Manchukuo the interpellative calls of the previous civilizing mission, such as development and coprosperity, were largely absent, establishing a Schmittian political theological distinction between Japanese friends and enemies (Schmitt 2005). Although this is not the place to detail how Japanese elites naturalized an ethnoracial disdain for Chinese out of widely held multiracial Japanese origin stories, we can quickly state the obvious.[10] Japan's military dispatched China's in the First Sino-Japanese War of 1895, and with its economic takeoff during and after the First World War Japanese popular discourse solidified an understanding of the Japanese nation-state as modern and developed, with China binarized against this as feudal and backward. Moreover, because of the recent history of civil war and internal uprisings in China, starting with arguably the bloodiest civil war in modern history in the Taiping Rebellion (1850–64), followed by the Boxer Rebellion of 1898–1901 (in which the Japanese army joined with European armies in China to crush the revolt) and the long civil war between the communists and Jiang Jieshi's Nationalist Party starting after the 12 April 1927 Incident in Shanghai, Chinese life was seen by Japanese elites as programmed for self-destruction. Beginning in the early 1920s and corresponding with the flooding of Japanese-made heroin into China (*Gendaishi shiryō*, vol. 12, 1986, lxiv), two new codes were consolidated to further rationalize Japan's imperial presence in China. The first was Manchuria as Japan's lifeline. The second code legitimated hustlers and elites alike: "Our Special Rights and Privileges as Japanese in Manchuria" ("Waga ManMon no tokushu keneki"). It was popularized in a book written just before the Incident by Shinobu Junbei, openly arguing that because Chinese were "corrupt" (*fuhai*), "arbitrary," and "anarchistic," Japanese citizens naturally had to take sovereignty into their own hands in Northeast China. The opposed ethnoracial profile of Japanese as "righteous" (*seigi*) and "civilized" meant that Northeast China would be much better off in Japanese hands (Shinobu 1932, 428–52).

A quick detour through Marxist cultural studies can advance my argument here and show how a version of Tosaka Jun's "Japanese ideology" worked to dehumanize ethnic Chinese. Gramsci renders ideology as the "principles, programs and goals" through which a particular class seeks hegemony and thereby imposes its own "values and attitudes" on a society (1971, 86). Hegemony is easier to consolidate when the dominant class can get a subordinate class to buy into or, in Louis Althusser's reformulation, be interpellated by its ideological vision. In 1937 Tosaka argued correctly that the specificity of Japanese fascism lay in the class alliance of the new bureaucrats and the imperialist military officers (1967, vol. 5, 4–6). I argue that ideological hegemony in Manchukuo became so seamless because it managed to articulate, or suture together, three different classes of Japanese colonizers: the new bureaucrats, the military, and the hustlers and *yakuza*. In other words, Japan's *colonial* fascism in Manchukuo is best understood when we add the hustler assemblage into the hegemonic alliance.

Gramsci and Tosaka would agree that ideological analysis must consider social behavior to be determined by consciousness of class or group interests. Moral decisions then evolve out of the interrelationships among self, class, and group. With respect to the hustlers, at least some of them would have been involved in murder. It's hard to imagine what moral censors would have been available for this class to oppose a program designed to "weaken and kill" Chinese through drug dealing. The hustlers were constitutionally amoral, concerned first with their self-interest as petty capitalists and second with their group interest as Japanese nationals.

Consider the case of Furumi Tadayuki, whose self-interest in advancing his career as a new bureaucrat would have impelled him to do almost anything, up to and including personally dealing narcotics for Manchukuo in Beijing in spring 1944 (*RDQDZX*, vol. 14, 819). As chief accountant and paymaster for the regime, the young (thirty-one when he arrived from Tokyo in July 1932) Furumi was responsible for the Manchukuo policy of paying Chinese in top administrative positions half the Japanese salary for the same job.[11] When pressure was put on the Japanese leadership to change this in the late 1930s, Furumi was incredulous that anyone would question the self-evident truth that *any* Japanese worker was worth double the salary of even the best Chinese (Zhonguo Fushun zhanfan guanli suo 2005, 26). As an elite graduate of Tokyo University, he had interiorized the common sense of Japanese ethnoracial superiority of the 1920s. Once in Manchukuo, Furumi's self-interest was directly linked to his class and group interest in consolidating Japan's imperialism. Like all of Manchukuo's elites, he understood that the state's drug policy was the crucial element in that consolidation. Leaving aside for now the fact that he ultimately confessed to having personally dealt drugs, it's also difficult in his case to imagine any moral scruples that might have interfered with a plan to profit from and kill Chinese.

It's probably easiest to demonstrate how commonsensical the opium policy's dual purpose of making a profit and eliminating Chinese would have been for the class of militarists. Some of them had participated in the brutal crackdown against Korean nationalists in March and April 1919. These same men led the pacification efforts in the countryside against Chinese in the months following the Incident, and *kempeitai* later also directed the kidnapping of Chinese men and women for forced labor, for use as test subjects in the biological experiments of the so-called factories of death organized by the Manchukuo-based Unit 731 (where some six thousand human subjects were killed in medical testing), and for use in "comfort stations" and rape rooms. More than even the new bureaucrats or the hustlers, there would have been an absence of moral censors in this class of militarists. The powerful Guandong army staff officer Tanaka Ryūkichi no doubt spoke for some of the Japanese militarists in Manchukuo when he told a Tokyo reporter in May 1936 that, "To be perfectly frank, the ways you and I look at the Chinese are fundamentally different. You seem to think of them as human, but I see them as pigs" (quoted in Hotta 2007, 152).

State of Exception, State of Extortion

It took fifteen months to get the single most important institution in late Japanese imperialism up and running: Manchukuo's Opium Monopoly. For six weeks beginning on 1 October 1932 Hoshino, Furumi, and the head of Manchukuo's Monopoly Office, Nanba Tsunekazu, test-drove a Temporary Requisition Law, which legally required unlicensed dealers to sell their drug stocks to Manchukuo agents. It failed miserably. After this debacle desperate bureaucrats had to figure out where they were going to get opium to sell. Although they assumed that they would be able to buy all the opium they needed from growers in northern Heilongjiang and Jilin provinces, the Manchukuo state still lacked full authority there. In direct violation of Japan's agreement with the League of Nations, Hoshino tried to arrange opium shipments from Iran and Turkey, but without any initial success. So they turned to their last option, seeking help from Japan's successful local representatives: the hustlers. Although there was no love lost between them, this unrecognized alliance between the new bureaucrats and the hustlers who controlled what Yamada calls the huge "free market in drugs" in post-Incident Manchukuo proved to be the salvation for Japanese imperialism in China—and sealed the necropolitical fate of approximately twenty to thirty million ethnic Chinese before the end of the Second World War, with as many as ten million dying of drug-related causes (Kurahashi 2008).

There were two crucial moments in this improbable marriage, and Amakasu Masahiko and other military police were the go-betweens each time. As is true regarding the involvement of the hustlers, the importance of the Guandong *kempeitai* in the operations of colonial war during the first year has been downplayed in the English- and Japanese-language scholarship, in strong contrast to the Chinese scholarship. We know from the massive compilations of material left behind by the Guandong *kempeitai* and translated into Chinese that they were the chief on-the-ground face of the oppressor in the early days, looting, murdering, and otherwise advancing colonial depredation (*RDQDZX*, vol. 5). Most important, they were ordered by the Guandong army to perform two crucial actions immediately following the Incident: "confiscate Chinese money and financial assets [*zaisei no sesshū*]" and "take over local government" (*Kempeitai Shireibu*, vol. 1, 1987, 9). During the ensuing months they handled some of the most difficult tasks: disarming Chinese police, confiscating property in the countryside, and taking over all the Chinese banks. As thanks for these efforts to get the state up and running, and for their ongoing work in arresting or killing all enemies of Japanese Manchukuo, the Guandong army allowed many military police to set themselves up as Japanese "lords of war" in local areas, operating their own drug, prostitution, and protection rackets (*RDQDZX*, vol. 4, 362–438). Although Manchukuo was a typical colonial state of excep-

tion in that the law was consistently suspended, it also acted from beginning to end as a state of extortion.

The first moment of the *kempeitai*-brokered marriage between the
new bureaucrats and the hustlers followed from the failure of the temporary confiscation order, when Manchukuo special militias were unable to collect any opium except for a bit fleeced from a few hundred
Chinese dealers (Yamada 2002, 245). The Opium Monopoly subsequently required all users and dealers to register with authorities, and
the *kempeitai* and Hoshino divided dealers into wholesalers and retailers (*RDQDZX*, vol. 14, 816–17). In consultation with the *kempeitai*, Nanba
and Hoshino designated one hundred of the biggest Japanese hustlers in
the free market as government wholesalers, who in turn were allowed to
select their own official retailers. This essentially legalized the de facto
free market system controlled by the hustlers. There was a heated debate among Hoshino, the *kempeitai*, and Nanba about whether any Chinese would be chosen as wholesalers. Like most of the civilian elite, Hoshino didn't like Chinese people and wanted only Japanese wholesalers
(or colonized Koreans who were legally Japanese in Northeast China),
while the *kempeitai* in local areas were eager to reward select Chinese
they had been working with in their own trafficking rackets. In the end
a compromise was reached and a handful of Chinese dealers became
authorized Manchukuo wholesalers. In turn, these wholesalers were required to report the names of their handpicked retailers to the Opium
Monopoly (although most operated openly without a Manchukuo license, paying bribes rather than more expensive business taxes). Kaneda
reported in 1954 that there were about fourteen hundred licensed Manchukuo opium retailers by the mid-1930s; however, we know that Fengtian alone had this many retail drug shops (*RDQDZX*, vol. 14, 816). One
of the investigations undertaken for the U.S. consulate in Shanghai reported in 1935 that there were one thousand underground opium dens
in Harbin not approved by the Opium Monopoly, and only seventy-six
licensed establishments (IPS Records, M1690, Roll 308, 623).

This first attempt at registering dealers proved ineffectual, as both
classes of dealers refused to follow the profit (a laughable 10 percent
for wholesalers and 8 percent for retailers) and price (usually twice the
market rate) guidelines set by the Opium Monopoly. This forced Hoshino and Furumi in late 1933 to reach out to the most criminal of the

nonregistered hustlers and offer them Manchukuo protection and support (*RDQDZX*, vol. 14, 812). Yamada Gōichi calls this the second crucial moment, when the new bureaucrats decided to "reverse their principled dislike for the underground hustlers" (2002, 520–23). Although the first attempt at confiscation had turned up little, the second attempt included paying the hustlers and low-level *yakuza* big money to spy on unauthorized Chinese dealers, who, robbed once during the first temporary period, were much more systematically despoiled in the second (438). Japanese hustlers became deputized advisers in Manchukuo (like Kostia Nakamura) or salaried employees working in the four provincial departments of the Opium Monopoly, whose activities centered around the legal confiscation of opium and narcotics from the 99 percent of Chinese traffickers not registered with the Opium Monopoly. The bureaucrats' embrace of many of the approximately sixty thousand Japanese hustlers finally allowed the Manchukuo state to start accumulating capital. Combined with the Guandong army's first foreign policy action—the military invasion of poppy-rich Rehe province, completed on 4 March 1933—this led the Opium Monopoly, after losing money at first, to earn ten million yuan (U.S.$5 million) in revenue for that year.

The Man Who Ran Manchukuo after Dark

By 1 March 1932, when the Manchukuo state was formally established, Japanese imperialists were already using the phrase that would become common parlance by the late 1930s: "The Guandong army runs Manchukuo during the day, Amakasu runs it after dark." To explain briefly how Amakasu Masahiko was in a position to run Manchukuo at night, I'll begin in fall 1929, when he arrived in Manchuria from France. He'd gone to Paris on the Japanese army's dime after serving less than three years of a ten-year prison sentence for the notorious murder of two famous leftists, Ōsugi Sakae and Itō Noe, in the chaotic aftermath of the Tokyo earthquake of 1923.[12] Having immersed himself in European research in international espionage, Amakasu was assigned, with Doihara Kenji, to organize intelligence and trafficking networks across Northeast China. He ended up hiring close to one hundred soldiers of fortune and by summer 1931 had consolidated his crack Fengtian-based Uchifuji syndicate, a second syndicate in Harbin, and an incipient drug and intelligence operation in Shanghai, which would be his base of operations for selling Manchukuo drugs and bribing his way into crime circles between 1932 and 1934. With support from Doihara's syndicate, Amakasu's investment in the Uchifuji syndicate paid immediate rewards, as they provided the crucial intelligence required for the successful surprise attack on Zhang Xueliang's troops on 19 September. Throughout that time Amakasu was busy multitasking; on 17 and 18 September he was in Fengtian preparing for the attack on Zhang, then he headed north to unleash the war machines of his Harbin syndicate on that city. In Harbin he personally assumed the lead and most dangerous role in cahoots with his hustler allies, kicking off a three-day reign of terror. Intending to create total chaos, they hoped to induce the Guangdong army to occupy Harbin, which they planned on justifying in the name of protecting the four thousand Japanese residents and businesses. Impersonating a Chinese coolie and driving a vehicle without number plates, beginning at 11 P.M. on the nights of the 22nd and 23rd, Amakasu set off on his rampage. Equipped with hand grenades and small arms, he drove around and around the city firing at people and property from his darkened vehicle. Because Amakasu had almost no functioning Chinese, his identity as a Japanese provocateur would be revealed immediately if he were arrested. So he carried a fake letter in his shirt pocket written in Chinese from the warlord Zhang authorizing him to conduct terrorism in Harbin. His plan, if apprehended by the Chinese police, was to blow himself up before his identity was revealed and hope that the police would find the letter on his splattered body (Mutō 1956; Tsunoda F. 2005).

In July 1932 army headquarters transferred the military leaders of the Manchurian Incident back to Japan. Only Doihara, Amakasu, and his drinking buddy, Itagaki Seishirō, remained, and they became the three Manchukuo founding fathers still in China. From the summer of 1932 until 1939 Amakasu was the de facto head of Manchukuo's Secret Police, for which he directed drug, human, and intelligence flows out of the infamous *teishūshitsu*, or "black operations room" inside Manchukuo's Civil Affairs Ministry (Sano 2008, 279). So when the new wave of the Manchukuo imperial leadership needed to embrace the hustlers in the fall of 1933, Amakasu was the obvious choice to act as go-between. In prison in Japan in 1924 and 1925, he had connected with *yakuza* who later migrated to Manchuria, and he had already embraced other hustlers when he set up his two syndicates in 1930, so he enjoyed business and personal relations with many of those the elites hoped to recruit. As a *kempeitai* captain in Tokyo in the early 1920s Amakasu had specialized in harassing labor organizations, and he relied on support from *yakuza* goons in the Seigidan syndicate. As the majority of the Manchurian hustlers were nationalistic rightists—to say nothing of the openly fascist elements in the Manchukuo *yakuza*—Amakasu's reputation, both as the murderer of the famous leftists and as the man who risked his life during the Incident, would have generated tons of respect from them. Many of them would have idealized him; the rest would have feared him.[13]

When it came time to negotiate the alliance, the new bureaucrats would surely have remembered the crucial role some of the hustlers and soldiers of fortune played—as the source of vital pre-Incident intelligence and brave terrorism throughout—in creating their very own colonial playground of Manchukuo. And in mid- to late 1933, faced with the difficulties of installing the Opium Monopoly without the active support of the hustlers, Hoshino likely authorized Amakasu to broker a very attractive proposal. This would have included legitimacy as paid Manchukuo advisers, cushy jobs as salaried workers in the Public Security Offices, or, even better, in plum positions in provincial Opium Monopoly bureaus, where they would have been deputized to do what they were already doing: confiscating drugs from Chinese dealers and extending their own trafficking and racketeering networks (IPS Records, M1690, Roll 475, "Opium Monopoly in Manchukuo and Its Connection with the Guandong Army," 196).[14] This all adds up to the hustlers being resurrected from the underworld to become the public face of Manchukuo in just two years. Also included in Amakasu's deal would have been the promise of unfettered border crossings into the nearby lucrative drug markets of Beijing and Tianjin. Although some scholars point to the elimination of extraterritoriality for Japanese as proof that Manchukuo was sincerely committed to its public Pan-Asianism (Duara 2003), years go by without a single arrest of a Japanese hustler moving drugs out of Manchukuo proper. When hustlers were nabbed the fines were negligible (Rehe Bureau of Security Report 405, in *RDQDZX*, vol. 14, 843).

When the Manchukuo borders lost some of their porousness starting in 1940 (after Japanese were caught bringing drugs *into* Manchukuo from North China) the Manchukuo hustlers adapted accordingly, eager to continue turning a ten to eighteen Chinese yuan investment per *liang* into a two hundred to one thousand yuan sale in Tianjin or Shanghai. A Japanese clerk working at the Rehe Bureau of Security in 1944 described some of their creative responses to the restrictions. Smugglers were known to "put up to 4 liang (15 grams) of opium in a condom [*biyuntao*] and then ingest it," then they would vomit it up or shit it out after crossing safely out of Manchukuo. This technique was dangerous, though, as about ten low-level smugglers died each year when the condoms broke and released the drug. Other techniques included flattening out processed opium and inserting it under horses' saddles, "causing it to flatten out even more as they rode," and placing opium in the "bases of quill writing brushes [*maobi*]." More imaginative still, "they would stick several liang (10–14 grams) in the anuses of babies or small animals" and then extract the opium when they got over the border (841–42). Except for the danger of leaky condoms, Japanese hustlers smuggled drugs across Manchukuo borders into China with near complete immunity. In a second report of 1944 called "Trends in Opium Smuggling," the clerk described the ethnoracial hierarchy dictating punishment for opium smuggling and debunked the rejection of extraterritoriality on the part of Japanese. If a group of Chinese traffickers got caught, the Japanese police authorities would merely confiscate all their opium, banish the group from Manchukuo, and proceed to sell the opium themselves on the black market. On the rare occasion when a Japanese smuggler was caught at a Manchukuo border check, "the Japanese police would lie in their report that the amount was tiny, making the required fine very small." No opium would be confiscated, and the hustler would be free to go. If Chinese police got caught smuggling, the Japanese police authorities would "report that the person was caught with 50% of the actual confiscated amount" (making this a considerable fine) and confiscate the other half. As far as Japanese cops were concerned, "it was never possible to disclose [*bu jiefa*] information about Japanese police caught smuggling; they were effectively above the law" (843).

The final element in the Amakasu-brokered proposal to the hustlers would have addressed future supply. Manchukuo had invaded Rehe province in March 1933 for the sole purpose of confiscating its abundant poppy fields. As for heroin and morphine, the Manchukuo Opium Monopoly began building its own large pharmaceutical factories in Harbin and in the capital of Xinjing in fall 1933 (IPS Records, "Opium Monopoly in Manchukuo," 197–98), and the Guandong army dis- and repossessed the huge Rehe heroin factory owned by the warlord Tang Yulin. Thus the hustlers were guaranteed a steady supply without having to rely on small narcotics producers (IPS Records, M1690, Roll 475," Heroin Manufacture in Chahar and Jehol," 2).

What did the hustlers offer the Manchukuo regime? The anecdotal evidence suggests that there was a quid pro quo. Although the huge free market in drugs that existed in Manchukuo for years after the Incident included opium and narcotics, the amounts of heroin and morphine surpassed the growth in opium, and based on the investigations of heroin (as opposed to opium) addiction rates, there is evidence that heroin addiction increased faster beginning in late 1933 (IPS Records, "Drug Conditions in Liaoning, Manchukuo," 147–50). I take this to mean that the expanding numbers of hustlers dealing opium offered to gradually shift into selling exclusively heroin and morphine. This does not mean that Manchukuo officials weren't selling heroin as well, but it does suggest a broad agreement to divide the drug market spoils between opium (henceforth controlled by the Manchukuo state and its licensed and unlicensed agents) and morphine and heroine (controlled by the hustlers and *yakuza*). In the end Hoshino, Furumi, and Amakasu got the verbal commitment of up to 120,000 additional ears for intelligence work and received assurances that the hustlers would gradually back off the opium market and shift into heroin and morphine. The fact that narcotics remained completely unregulated in Manchukuo until fall 1937, and then was inconsistently regulated until the end of the Second World War, could not have been accidental (Merrill 1942, 99).

Manchukuo, War Machine

It is an entirely different kind of grotesqueing when the Manchukuo elites allow themselves to be ingested by the hustlers, whose demeanor then dominates the modus operandi of the entire regime. However, we need to understand this more fully as, like many of Manchukuo's signature tactics, it was downloaded for use later on, particularly during the widespread looting of Chinese gold and artifacts by Japanese after July 1937. The Japanese Emperor Hirohito's own brother, Chichibu, grotesqued the operating logic of the lowest hustler when, in the wake of military conquest in central China, he directed the huge Golden Lily looting operation, stealing priceless Chinese gold artifacts and Buddhist relics (Seagrave and Seagrave 1999, 18–20). Something similar occurred in Manchukuo in 1937, when a new group of bureaucrats incorporated tactics from Muraoka Iheiji and other human traffickers and mobilized kidnapping and forced labor as official policy. In 1933, I want to underline, the vanguard of imperial politics was committed to necropolitical profiteering, whereby capital was accumulated in a direct relation with the ruin of a colonized and occupied people. New bureaucrats Furumi and Hoshino pledged allegiance to a criminal operating logic in which the hustle of the soldiers of fortune assemblage became the massive flow of money into Manchukuo's secret fund. A shadowy underworld of carpetbagging and trafficking thus became the public deportment of the newest form of colonial rule.

To what extent did Manchukuo rely on drug revenues for its official budget, separate from its off-the-books secret fund? The colonial state started mimicking the hustlers who were trafficking drugs outside Manchukuo just after the first full year of the Opium Monopoly. The Monopoly was limited by Manchukuo statute to distributing drugs inside its own borders, but they actually sold less than half of the appropriated opium back to registered Manchukuo wholesalers in the first year, while in the second year the amount was less than one-third. The Opium Monopoly reported that 4,763,000 *liang* of opium was sold from July 1933 to June 1934; the next year the amount doubled, to over nine million in sales (*Manshūkoku gensei* 1936, 98). However, the persistent U.S. consul in Shanghai, M. R. Nicholson, claimed that he was sent figures clandestinely from an employee at the Manchukuo Monopoly Bureau for opium sales inside Manchukuo. According to these internal figures, the amount of opium sold by the official monopoly *inside* Manchukuo's borders was under two million from July 1933 to June 1934 and under three million the next year (Yamada 2002, 521–23). The Opium Advisory Committee for the League of Nations used these numbers to conclude that Manchukuo was illegally selling the difference between its official Opium Monopoly sales and the actual sales inside the country (less than half in the first year, less than one-third in the second) on the global market, mainly through the trafficker Satomi Hajime in Tianjin and through Amakasu's drug syndicate in Shanghai.

Because of the intense scrutinizing of Manchukuo by the League of Nations Opium Board after 1933, the official opium revenue figures published by the Manchukuo bureau are thought to be only half or less of the actual total made by the state.[15] It's safe to assume that the true 1934–35 Opium Monopoly profits were double the official thirteen million yuan and twice the twenty million claimed for the next year (Manchukuo Ministry of Information 1940, 693). This represented about 15 percent of all revenues from the first year and 20 percent from the second year, which roughly compares to the early years of Taiwan's colonization. Yet this amount is but Monopoly money and represents only a fraction of the profits made from opium. Welfare Minister Kaneda testified that an average year in Rehe province alone in the early 1940s saw seven hundred million yuan (US$350 million) in profits earned (*RDQDZX*, vol. 14, 821), almost four times more than the total annual opium revenues from all four Manchukuo provinces for 1943 and 1944 (Myers 1982, 255). When these figures are combined with the annual loan packages leveraged on drug futures and the taxes generated from the licensed wholesale and retail markets, it's clear that the financial viability of the regime depended on opium; there were no other revenue sources as lucrative. And all this can be stated without factoring in revenues from narcotics, by all indications a more plentiful and profitable commodity than opium beginning in 1936. All told, in any one year in Manchukuo after 1935, approximately 50 to 55 percent of all earnings would have been generated from overt and covert drug sales.

Kingpin Ways and Means

It's easy to imagine the vast sums that circulated on the Manchukuo drug market around powerful players like Amakasu Masahiko. What Yamamuro Shinichi estimates as around twenty million yen at any one time at Amakasu's disposal (equal to the total Opium Monopoly revenue for 1935–36), this money went to fund both black market operations such as the Shanghai Incident of February 1932 as well as more public operations such as the Guandong army's invasions (2002, 17). The respected historian of Manchukuo Kobayashi Hideo claims that Manchukuo civilian elites such as Kishi Nobusuke and the CEO of Nissan, Ayukawa Yoshisuke, would have received money from Amakasu's secret fund as well as occasionally donating to it (2007b, 38). Although it's important to focus on the Opium Monopoly, it's crucial to understand that the shaping of the huge drug market in Northeast, North, and Central China by imperial elites and hustlers (or imperial elites *as* hustlers) was designed to both expand the circulation of drugs and transform what some French Marxists call the "mode of regulation" of the lucrative market from competition to monopoly. This allowed Japanese to make huge and safe profits from the growing number of Chinese addicts while irrevocably muscling out many of the Chinese dealers. With only 10 percent or less of the huge Manchukuo drug market controlled by the Opium Monopoly in some places, this allowed opportunities for hustlers to generate personal fortunes. Ultranationalists like Amakasu then plowed their personal fortunes back into extending Japan's imperial advance. As human traffickers like Muraoka Iheiji had done earlier, some hustlers became important Japanese financiers, with huge holdings and portfolios. As commodified *ero*, necropolitics in Manchukuo was driven by the desire of the hustlers, whether ultranationalist or not, a desire that the Manchukuo regime *absolutized*.

Walter Benjamin's recommendation to undertake a "curious dialectics" of opiate consumption can network the necropolitical greed as *ero* of Japanese drug profits in a direct calculus with the expropriation of the lives of colonized Chinese (2000, 220). Serious opium addiction overwhelmed nearly 10 percent of the Chinese in Manchukuo by 1944, when the Ministry of Welfare counted 2.9 million addicts (*RDQDZX*, vol. 14, 822). However, the colonial state never counted the largest form of addiction. The U.S. consulate in Shanghai hired a team of investigators to determine heroin and morphine addiction in several cities and towns in Manchukuo between 1933 and 1935. Still only a few years into the imperialist takeover, the rates of addiction to hard drugs ran from 10 to 20 percent, with overall Chinese narcotic addiction rates as high as 33 percent in some areas. The findings were so high that the report writers felt the need to brace their readers by appending this explanation: "This statement may appear to be exaggerated to people outside of Manchuria, but those who have seen the conditions with their own eyes and those who know the purpose for which Japanese carry out their narcotic policy will agree with the above estimate" (IPS Records, "Drug Conditions in Liaoning, Manchukuo," 153–54). In Beijing and Tianjin in the late 1930s addiction rates were even higher (IPS Records, M1690, Roll 475, "Japan's Narcotization Policy in North China," 20–22). Considering the fact that narcotics revenues outpaced opium revenues in Manchukuo from 1936 on, we can assume that the number of Chinese addicted to narcotics surpasses the number of opium addicts, leaving at least 20 percent of Manchukuo Chinese with serious drug addiction by 1945.

There was one more necropolitical effect of the Manchukuo elite's absolutizing of the hustler assemblage's *ero*. The feminist scholar Nishino Rumiko has confirmed accusations by international critics in 1938–41 of Japan's drug dealing by highlighting what she calls the "systematic" spread of drugs among East Asian women forced into sex work at "comfort stations" (Nishino 2007; Merrill 1942, 59). Both as a means of extracting even more surplus out of these women's bodies and as a means of control—addicts are unlikely to flee from a secure supply and when high, less likely to try—proprietors of comfort stations and Japanese *kempeitai* had a deliberate policy in many places to get comfort women addicted to drugs (Kawada, in Yoshimi Y. and Hayashi 1995, 163–64; Women's Active Museum Documentary Evidence, 7 October 2005). In her narrative of one year of hell as a forced sex worker in the Japanese navy's comfort station in Shanghai (where the first large station was set up in March 1932), Hana Kōhei describes several of the young women confined there as "addicted to opium," including a Korean woman who ended up committing suicide (Nishino 1992, 52–54).

Many of these women at the Shanghai comfort station were heavily indebted to the house for other things besides drugs, including makeup, kimono, and other daily necessities. Nishino has detailed the way military comfort stations charged women four or five times the market rate for basic items, creating a situation in which they couldn't leave because they knew the authorities would force their parents to pay off their debts. Nishino's study of the Korean forced sex worker Pak Yong-sim describes how drugs were used in the Nanjing comfort stations both for social control and as a way of squeezing out even more surplus capital; this system of control was institutionalized way back in the 1890s with pimps like Muraoka (2003, 29). Young women and girls regularly fell back on opium and heroin to get them through hellish days of sexually "comforting" multiple soldiers in wildly different psychological states. As Pak testifies, "Without opium it would have been impossible to go on living at the comfort station" (30). Drugs were the only way for the women to endure serial rape and physical abuse. An estimated 30 percent of these women never returned to their home country. For these women at least, to say nothing of the ten million or so of Chinese consuming drugs peddled by necropolitical capitalists, neuropolitical solace purchased by drug commodities often led directly to necropolitical death. This, I argue, was the dominant tendency in this third period of Japanese imperialism.

JAPANESE
LESSONS

There are many people who will disapprove of the whole scheme of a planning department to do the thinking for all the men. . . . Those holding this view, however, must take exception to the whole trend of modern industrial development.

FREDERICK TAYLOR, *THE PRINCIPLES OF SCIENTIFIC MANAGEMENT*

The implication or threat of force alone was sufficient to insure that the people would comply.

CIA DIRECTOR WILLIAM COLBY, TESTIFYING ON THE PHOENIX PROGRAM IN VIETNAM, 1970

In the first years of the Shōwa reign (1926–89) researchers of the capitalist erotic-grotesque, inspired by Marx, wrote thick encyclopedias enumerating all the economic, physical, and governmental "perversions" impacting Japanese people and society. Whether exposing Ponzi get-rich-quick schemes, new techniques of kidnapping, or pharmaceutical gimmicks promising miracle cures and better sex, their texts warned innocent readers about the predatory appetites of the new imperial capitalism. Nakayama Yuigorō's *User's Guide to Modern Hentai* provided an obsessively detailed description of human traffickers, loan sharks, blood-sucking extortionists (*kyūketsuki*), scam artists, and fake advertisers (*petinshi*)—the primary agents of dispossession emerging in Japan after the First World War. They sought to make money in any way possible, whether by "manipulating people's deepest desires" or "profiting from death itself" (Nakayama 1929, 3, 708). In the preface to his own huge collection, *Researching Perverse Ero*, Noma Jirō shuddered to think what kind of atrocities would occur if directors of capitalist *hentai* ever managed to get full control of a society (1930, 5).

Manchukuo in the 1930s was just such a place. There, arguably more than anywhere else in the world, the agents of *hentai*, here configured as capitalist "dispossession," enjoyed absolute hegemony. After eighteen months of ambivalence on the part of civilian and military elites, the Manchuria-based soldiers of fortune were embraced and deputized by the regime. Internationally known murderers such as Amakasu Masahiko became Manchukuo's public face, representing it on important diplomatic missions to its fascist allies in Germany and Italy.

Three subjectivities became constituent forces in Japanese-occupied Northeast China: the money launderer and new bureaucrat, the war profiteer, and the forced laborer. The first two are represented by two men, Kishi Nobusuke (1896–1987) and Ayukawa Yoshisuke (1880–1967), who were beneficiaries of the multiple modes of expropriation—*kempeitai* looting of money and valuables, state and nonstate drug trafficking, military land grabs—that were required to get the state up and running. It was the responsibility of the new bureaucrats Furumi and Kishi to launder the stolen treasure and drug money. Beginning in mid-1937, Kishi served in the dual roles of vice minister of industry and deputy chief of the omnipotent Office of Administrative Affairs. He was the most powerful figure among the civilian elite in Manchukuo for three years, from 1936 to 1939, and went on to serve as vice minister of commerce and minister of munitions in Tōjō Hideki's war-time cabinet. As founder of the Liberal Democratic Party (Jiminto) in 1955, he also created the one-party state in Japan and served twice as prime minister. After the Second World War he admitted to laundering lots of money during his Manchukuo years (Ōta 2005, 421–22). Ayukawa was one of the most important industrial capitalists in Japan beginning in the mid-1920s and the founder and CEO of Nissan. He moved its corporate headquarters to Manchukuo's capital in December 1937, mainly to profit from the Five-Year Plan for military industrialization necessary for Japan's total war (Kobayashi 1995a).

Kishi is often singled out as the exemplary "new bureaucrat" (*shinkanryō*). As a group these men played central roles in Japan's military imperialism after the Manchurian Incident and in the intensification of domestic fascism inside Japan. Moreover, he is credited with overseeing the first of Japan's massive Five-Year Plans in Manchukuo. While the new bureaucrats have received solid scholarly attention, only recently has the continuity between the role of bureaucrats in Japan's colonies in Taiwan and Korea and those, like Kishi, who cut their teeth in Manchukuo been addressed (Pauer 1999).

Namikata Shōichi's work on Gotō Shinpei's "enlightened autocratic rule" in Taiwan and young Japanese bureaucrats in colonial Korea shares my approach in trying to identify the ways Japan's colonial periphery was a stronger influence than Euro-America on forms of rule consolidated inside Japan in the 1930s. Namikata (2000) argues that when the colonies are reconfigured as "kingdoms of bureaucrats" in which paper pushers took the lead in writing the blueprints for colonial rule, the precedent for Kishi in Manchukuo is clear. Kōketsu Atsushi similarly argues that the main role for bureaucrats in Japan's colonial imperialism was to "maintain the colonial hierarchy of domination and subordination" (2005, 99). The consolidation of this hierarchy rested on the exercise of sovereignty in three distinct areas: administration, legislation, and justice. In Japan's colonial rule these three areas, normally divided among managerial engineers, politicians, and judges and police, respectively, were condensed into one: the new bureaucrat. Gotō Shinpei established a set of biopolitical axioms for colonial rule; overdetermining these was his conflation of liberal and mercantile capitalism with colonial expansion, which I rendered as "business as a continuation of war by other means." Gotō's *bunsōteki bubi* was offered as a solution to the main problem confronting imperialists after Japan's victory in 1905: how to solidify and extend imperial tentacles into continental Asian soil following successful military campaigns in 1895 and 1904–5. He saw the management of labor and immigration flows as one part of this solution, with fixed capital projects and business management as their complement.

Although Gotō is remembered mainly for his achievements in administration (the first of Kōketsu's three realms), he also established an important double-track legal structure: the colonized Taiwanese were to follow customary law, while the Japanese colonizers, when subject to any laws at all, were expected to abide by the more modern civil codes of Japanese imperial law.[1] Gotō installed a similar dual track in the Guandong Lease in 1906, bringing some of the bureaucrats he trained in Taiwan with him to Northeast China to manage the place.

It will help illustrate the difference between bio- and necropolitical rule if we examine the genealogical line of the colonial bureaucrat running from Gotō to Kishi. In contrast to Gotō, Kishi did almost nothing in the realms of the judicial and legislative when he was in Manchukuo. Kida Kiyoshi (1900–93), who worked under Kishi in Manchukuo before becoming the chief of personnel in Administrative Affairs, explained his boss's lack of concern frankly: "It's important to understand that Kishi referred to all Chinese as 'lawless bandits' [*hōhi*]" (quoted in Ōta 2005, 320). Kobayashi Hideo suggests that Kishi was merely the most public among the Japanese elite in his disdain for Chinese; all of them referred to Chinese in racist terms in private (Kobayashi 1995a, 196). Elaborating a raciological bias prevalent in all forms of colonialism, Kishi's subordinates Kida and Furumi agreed that their boss's profiling of Chinese as "anarchistic" and "incapable of governing themselves" meant that there was no point in creating much of a juridical system in Manchukuo because Chinese were constitutionally incapable of following laws.

Exactly what Northeast China meant to Kishi is fairly easy to establish. First, he normally referred to it simply as "Manshū," not bothering to attach the -*koku*, or nation-state, suffix to form Manchukuo in Japanese (Manshūkoku), as was fairly standard among elites at the time. This refusal to acknowledge the state-ness of the Manshū*koku* regime is symptomatic of Kishi's general vision of China as a static, reified thing, available for the taking like any other commodity he might purchase, say, on his regular trips to Asakusa, Tokyo (Ōta 2005, 46). China, like the Chinese, was to be taken and consumed as an inanimate commodity. Furumi told a reporter in the 1960s that his close friends Amakasu Masahiko and Kishi had the same philosophy for dealing with Chinese: make sure they understand that Japanese are the ones with the money and the power; when you communicate this firmly to them, Chinese won't cross you (41). In other words, despite the reality of Kishi's infrahuman racialization of Chinese as too barbaric to obey laws (consistent with the CIA's policy toward the Vietnamese expressed in the epigraph), he was certain that, like dogs and other animals, they were at least capable of apprehending brute force. Furumi was no slouch himself when it came to dehumanizing Chinese. In China in 1954 he testified to his comfort with the larger Manchukuo policy toward Chinese coolies: morph them into "machinic extensions of the Japanese Imperial Army; non-human automatons [*jixie*] absolutely obedient [*juedui fucong*]" (RDQDZY, vol. 14, 862). Elsewhere, he described how naturalized the "inhuman" (*wei-rendao*) treatment of Chinese laborers was among Japanese imperialists, recalling that ordering Chinese to act like robot slaves was considered the most appropriate "Japanese lesson" (*riyu yuyan*) for them (864).

In another sharp contrast to Gotō, Kishi's life in Manchukuo revolved exclusively around his Japanese associates at work and carousing with Japanese militarists and *yakuza* bosses at night. During his three years in Manchukuo he rarely strayed outside the capital, with the exception of trips to Tokyo and his monthly jaunt to Dalian, some six hundred kilometers south of his base in Manchukuo's capital of Shinkyō. According to Shiota Ushio, these excursions to the densest concentration of Japanese consumerism in China were to hunt for Japanese women. Like frat boys on spring break, he and Furumi would hop on the air-conditioned, high-tech SMR train Asia Express and soon find themselves "in Dalian, where all the available chicks were" (Shiota 2006, 107). Although Furumi had a Dalian house where he kept his young wife, he would merely check in with her briefly before joining Kishi out on the town. Even though Kishi did his most intense philandering in the Dalian brothels, he was no prude in Shinkyō either. Whether it was at his favorite Japanese bar-restaurant, Hachidai, near the Office of Administrative Affairs, or at the three other Japanese bars nearby, Kishi was known to contract for sex regularly with waitresses and prostitutes. Unlike some of the rowdier hustlers and militarists who would publicly leave through the front door with the woman they had bought that night, Kishi preferred to arrange for his chauffeur to meet him and his commodity at the back to whisk them off discretely to a hotel. For this reason his womanizing wasn't well known, but this doesn't mean that Kishi wasn't letting the good times roll. On the contrary, when he was locked up in Sugamo prison in 1946 awaiting trial, he reminisced about his Manchukuo years: "I came so much, it was hard to clean it all up" (quoted in Ōta 2005, 278).

War as the Continuation of Business by Other Means

I apologize for rushing right to the money shot before giving you much of a plot. This male stud is actually the physically unattractive career bureaucrat who joins Japan's Ministry of Commerce and Industry in 1921 and gradually works his way to the top. He is sent on an investigative six-month tour in the United States, England, and Germany in 1926, and when he returns he provides Japanese policy circles with the first in-depth look at Frederick Taylor's labor management, economic planning, and industrial rationalization. Amazed at the productivity gains driven by dehumanized, Taylorized workers in American factories, Kishi was even more impressed by the emphasis on production planning in

German industrial capitalism. Several years after his trip he urged Japanese elites to borrow from this German model: "Although Japan and Germany have about the same amount of resources, the Germans devise rational plans for economic development by using technologist-engineers together with business management and planning" (quoted in Hara Y. 2007, 39). Kishi was sent off on a second extended trip to the United States and Germany in 1930 and gave several speeches when he returned home.[2] These speeches were important for two reasons: they implanted the phrase "industrial rationalization [*sangyō gōrika*]" into the heads of Japanese elites, and, more important, they caught the attention of several important ultranationalist army officers, who then befriended him.

Kishi's "industrial rationalization" became a synonym for economic planning by elites and, through his deepening friendship with powerful figures in the army—just when many of them were arguing for a decisive military solution to the political stalemate in Northeast China—began to stand in for planning for large-scale war (Kobayashi 2005a, 36–42). Although Japan's military budget had been reduced after the First World War, before the streamlining so characteristic of the period of Taishō (1912–26) democracy began, the army was able to get an important law passed in 1918 that legislated the "immediate adoption of economic controls during wartime" (Bōeicho bōei kenkyūjo 1967, 36–44). Called the Military-Industrial Mobilization Law, it was later referred to by army leaders as the legislative lever that would help the push to total war in the 1930s. Another colonial bureaucrat, Miyazaki Masayoshi, worked in Dalian with the SMR for a decade before returning to Tokyo in mid-1932 to set up the committee to draft the first Five-Year Plan with the total war guru, Ishihara Kanji. For these two, and Kishi, economic planning was explicitly war as a continuation of business by other means. Miyazaki and other elites saw military expansion on the Asian continent as a way to end the economic deadlock in Japan caused by the Great Depression of 1929.

For Kishi economic planning in the form of war as a continuation of capitalist business meant that the emphasis on competition in liberal capitalism had to give way to integration among companies producing the same goods, ideally creating one or two huge monopolies. Integration should take precedence over the furious pursuit of profits. Profit would be allowed, and even guaranteed in many cases, but it would be generated exclusively through the top-down squeezing of labor—even tighter than liberal capitalism allowed for (Kishi 1932). As economic planning was configured in Manchukuo, what the Marxist tradition calls monopoly capitalism meant that businesses producing the same goods would be consolidated (*ichigyō issha*), new bureaucrats would plan and command, and wages would be forced down as low as possible. In the case of Chinese labor, wages would be allowed to fall below the line of "necessary social reproduction." In other words, workers' lives would not necessarily be reproduced in the first flushes of necropolitical capitalism as Kishi got it up and running in Manchukuo.

It's important to point out that, because of his reputation as an economic planner first and a right-wing autocrat who despised democracy and praised German National Socialism second, Kishi was heavily recruited by the Guandong army to run Manchukuo's economy. Up until the mid-1990s, scholarship on Manchukuo has seen the Guandong army enjoying overwhelming authority in all aspects of rule. However, the authoritative overviews in Chinese, studies on Miyazaki Masayoshi, and works emphasizing the power of Manchukuo's Office of Administrative Affairs (*ZDLSG*, 95–98; *RDQDZY*, vol. 3, 312–13; Kobayashi 2007b; Mimura 2002) have led newer scholarship, like mine, to highlight instead the authority of the new bureaucrats in Manchukuo. Kishi was forthright about this in interviews he gave after the Second World War, and although there are minor disparities in each version, in the set of questions put to him by the journalist Hara Yoshihisa in 1981 he responded that as long as it was understood that the long-term goal was for an economy geared toward total war, "the planning and management was left up to my discretion" (Hara Y. 1993, 35). At other times he remembered being more colloquial with the military; when he told them to leave the economic planning to experts like him, he phrased it as "Let the rice-cake makers handle the rice-cakes [*Mochiha mochiya ni makasetamae*]" (quoted in Ōta 2005, 271). He consistently claimed that his coming to Manchukuo to set up the infrastructure for total war was conditioned on the army's granting him complete control. The larger point here is that the economic preparation for a system of total war was put in place *first* by the civilian elite in Manchukuo before this colonial template was subsequently used in Tokyo (Kobayashi 2004; Kōketsu 2005).

When Kishi went to Manchukuo he brought a concrete idea of what economic planning for total war would entail: complete control over a passive and dehumanized Chinese workforce, the superhumanization of Japanese managers and planners, and the system of targets for key industries that he learned in Germany. When he got down to his schedule of work during the day and partying hard every night,[3] the details of the planned war economy were quickly filled in. Kishi soon realized that the milieu of Manchukuo was perfect both for hooking up with women and for experimenting with Taylorism; he must have been delighted to find a colonial milieu that for over three decades had stressed the importance of an obedient Chinese labor force trained to receive Japanese lessons from overlord colonizers. When Hoshino and Amakasu made a pact in 1932 with the Manchukuo-based *yakuza* groups Seigidan and Kokusui-kai—specialists in terrorizing Chinese workers and intimidating *batou* bosses—this only added to the tactics of "labor management" available to Kishi. He got personally close to several *yakuza* bosses while enjoying the Manchukuo nightlife, and they later became important donors to his political machine (Ōta 2005). As I argued in chapter 1, beginning in 1906 Japanese elites relied on almost free Chinese immigrant labor. Furthermore, the pioneering new bureaucrat Gotō Shinpei had installed research bureaus at the SMR that were basically planning agencies where, as Frederick Taylor advocated in the epigraph, "they do the thinking for all the men." So when Kishi merged the Euro-American codes of labor management and economic planning with the ingrained habitus of Japanese colonial rule (with the extra pressure of *yakuza* thugs intimidating and hustlers drug-addling Chinese labor), the result was an almost seamless system well lubed to join the means of industrial capitalism with the ends of total war and death. Gotō's biopolitics became Kishi's necropolitics.

*De*formal Subsumption

In parts I and II, I traced the shifts in capitalism from a biopolitics that operated through formal subsumption, to a neuropolitics that was driven by real subsumption, drawing on autonomous Marxists like Antonio Negri. Although there is much of value in autonomous Marxism, it reveals a strong bias toward modernizing processes, which, in agreement with Marx, are seen as having necessarily progressive outcomes. In fact, Negri frankly recommends the modernizing quality of real subsumption. Although he admits that the effects are always "bivocal," he insists that the revolutionary aspects of capitalism are irrevocable. Identifying the centrality of cooperation and the sharing of ideas in the post-Fordist worker, he locates the key struggle in real subsumption as "the problem of the expropriation of cooperation" (Negri 2005, 129). In other words, cooperation and socialization are givens.

However, Taylorist labor management needs to maintain a strict fire-wall between what Marx called "mental and material labor," and the colonial milieu in Manchukuo was Taylor-made to secure this separation. In addition to the colonizer-colonized relation of subordination, planners and bureaucrats conducted their own *horizontal* cooperation in Japanese, while *vertical* cooperation with Chinese labor was prevented by the Japanese-Chinese language differential. Nearly all workers in rapidly industrialized Manchukuo spoke Chinese, while all the elite managers and planners spoke Japanese. As autonomous Marxists can't account for these massive blocks to cooperation, we need to go beyond their analyses to configure the structure of domination reproduced there by Kishi. Consequently, in Machukuo real subsumption doesn't lead to the expanding of use-values and the production of new collective subjects; rather, it takes advantage of the absolute surplus extraction latent in formal subsumption (where there is a lack of concern for the need to reproduce workers so they show up rested for work the next day) with the relative surplus extracted from technomachinic inputs in real subsumption. I call this extensive, absolute surplus extraction—up to and including the death of the worker—combined with the expansion of intensive inputs into the production process *deformal subsumption*. Continuing to track the shift from colonial biopolitics to fascist necropolitics—while keeping in mind the ways the capitalist reification inherent in neuropolitics mediates this shift—we can now begin to identify Kishi's necropolitical "death principles" in contradistinction to Gotō's biopolitical "life principles."

For North Chinese immigrant labor in Manchukuo, deformal subsumption differed from the standard violence of formal subsumption in that it was overdetermined by the incursions of real subsumption driving neuropolitics. In part II, rather than discuss how neuropolitics works on labor, I chose to focus on the image commodity. However, technological inputs into the factory and the intensification of mechanization in farming meant that real was replacing formal subsumption in agriculture as well. When the Great Depression hit Japan, most farming families felt compelled to insert themselves further into real subsumption through loans or the selling off of daughters (Nagahara 1989).

In Manchukuo coolie labor was also subject to neuropolitical invasion in the new registration and biometric procedures required for all North Chinese workers in the Manchukuo Foreign Worker Control Law of March 1935, which gave widespread power to Amakasu Masahiko's labor management company Datong Gongsi (*MKS*, 1971, vol. 2, 1155–56; *RDQDZY*, vol. 14, 861). Based on their earlier studies, the SMR also strongly advocated fingerprinting and photographing of Chinese immigrants. Led by Wada Toshio, the SMR produced basic aptitude tests to "scientifically" adjudicate the physical strength and capacity for slavish obedience they saw as optimal for coolies. Using Taylorist measurement techniques and physiognomics—what Stephen J. Gould called the racist "mismeasure of man"—Wada's team produced typologies of Chinese workers based on body size, cranial shape, and structure of the nose and jaw. They came up with a system using data cards with specific qualities to be numerically ranked, and these were regularly used by Japanese employers and immigration authorities. The SMR studies classified coolies into three types: the Shandong type, the Hebei type, and the Manchurian type. Consistently making up over 70 percent of all North Chinese immigrant laborers, Shandong coolies were profiled as a "thick-skulled type representing a low level of culture and capacity," qualities confirmed by their "strong backs and powerful grip." Their biometrics of "large jaw, a cranial circumference of 55 centimeters, facial length from 1.35 to 1.4 times the line of the lower jaw, prominent cheekbones, stupidity, big teeth, a bridge of the nose that indicated docility, submissiveness, and barbarity" added up to a type "perfectly suited for physical labor." Hebei coolies were a little smarter than those from Shandong, thanks to their "anthropologically superior" cranial shape. Owing to this racial profile, Hebei coolies were seen as best suited for the semiskilled labor of carpentry, plastering, and bricklaying (Tucker 2005, 32–33).

When Hoshino Naoki became chief of Administrative Affairs in December 1936 he moved quickly to get Kishi to take his former position as deputy chief, which Kishi assumed at the beginning of July 1937. Maintaining his other position as vice minister (*jichō*) of industry, Kishi was granted almost unlimited power. When Ishihara's and Miyazaki's Five-Year Plan for Industrial Development started in April 1937 Kishi was personally responsible for implementing it. Although almost noth-ing has been said about Kishi's position on what was called the "coolie problem" in Manchukuo at this time, given the fact that the Guandong army granted him authority over all aspects of the Manchukuo econ-omy, it's safe to assume that he was worried about maintaining a reserve army of cheap Chinese labor. Both for security reasons and because the expectation was that millions of Japanese workers would rush into Man-chukuo, the Guandong army attempted to curtail North Chinese emigra-tion right after the Manchurian Incident. This policy lasted some three years, but by 1935 the restrictions were gradually relaxed as the army was reassured by the *kempeitai* influence in Amakasu's Datong Gongsi (the company claimed to have registered and photographed each of the 491,000 coolies entering Manchukuo in 1935) and by the expanded au-thority granted to *yakuza* fascists to intimidate Chinese workers.

Right after the Five-Year Plan began in April 1937 the official Man-chukuo policy on Chinese labor reversed completely, and there is evi-dence of Kishi's input. Although he doesn't single out any one bureau-crat, Kojima Toshio's overview of the Manchukuo labor policy identifies that reversal as a logical effect of the "gradual replacement of the Army by the civilian authorities as those responsible for North Chinese im-migrant labor policy" (Eda et al. 2002, 39). Representative of the shift is the crucial "Outline for Labor Control in Manchukuo," presented for rubberstamping to Manchukuo's State Council by Hoshino's and Kishi's Office of Administrative Affairs on 10 August 1937.[4] The policy (*hōshin*) includes several bills that concretize the shift that Kojima pointed to. The intro explains clearly, "A Manchukuo Labor Association is needed in this time of emergency to consolidate the groundwork for labor man-agement conducive to moving ahead smoothly with rapid industrial de-velopment. While not obstructing the policy of encouraging more Japa-nese to immigrate, the Labor Association will rationalize and nourish [*kanyō*] Chinese resources, while continuing to emphasize the control of workers inside the country and workers entering the country" (Minami Manshū tetsudō kabushiki gaisha keizai chōsakai 1937 [1980], 368).

The specific bills granted this new Labor Association authority over recruitment and transport of Chinese labor, as well as wages. Regarding conscription (*boshū*), the Association is charged with "rationalizing the unpaid labor of arrested bandits [*zokueki no gōrika*]," as well as "utilizing the labor of women and children" (Minami Manshū tetsudō kabushiki gaisha keizai chōsakai 1937 [1980], 368). In Manchukuo's colonial discourse *bandit* signified anyone who was not openly supporting Japan's rule. *Rationalizing* here is more than the mere forced labor of rebels and other "criminals"; from now on rationalizing will occur under the direction of the Labor Association and will no longer be the sole prerogative of the *kempeitai* and their *yakuza* shock troops. Children's and women's labor came under official policy because "expanding labor resources" inside Manchukuo meant not only increasing the influx of coolies, but required the "conscription" of Manchukuoan Chinese farmers to labor on the infrastructural projects under way as part of the Five-Year Plan. The Association would forthwith instruct Chinese women and children to assume all the responsibilities on family farms in the place of men forced from their fields and sent to the labor camps—in other words, to use Kishi's phrase, "rationalized."

The policy to unify wages is even more ominous. It should be seen as a threat to Manchukuo capitalists who refused Kishi's order to keep wages as low as possible, which was necessary to follow the prescriptions of Taylorism and Japanese colonial capitalism. Kishi's planned economy was geared toward production goals and profit taking, not competition with other Japanese firms; profit would come primarily from rationalizing labor costs as much as possible. The ne plus ultra of wage rationalization would be withholding pay altogether—that is, unremunerated, forced labor.

The last part of the policy proposal is called "Purpose," and the Office of Administrative Affairs provides a clear explanation as to why they are recommending a thorough reversal of Manchukuo labor policy, from one concerned with *restricting* the flows of North China laborers into Manchukuo in favor of Japanese flows, to one focused on *expanding* the Chinese labor supply. The consensus in 1937 in Manchukuo on the "coolie problem" underlined the urgency of mobilizing as much cheap Chinese labor as possible, using any means necessary to do so: "The reason for the new policy is to guarantee the growth of labor resources [*rōdō shigen*] inside the country and to intensify the ongoing training of workers in preparation for dispatching them to wherever they are needed" (Minami Manshū tetsudō kabushiki gaisha keizai chōsakai 1937 [1980], 369).

While the policy is attributed to Administrative Affairs, Kishi's personal involvement is clear. The language of "rationalization," "scientific management," and "labor control" is very similar to language in his earlier speeches and writings, and as the official in charge of all aspects of the Five-Year Plan he would have been alert to the danger of labor shortages. He often had to listen to local Japanese capitalists complaining about profit ceilings in the atmosphere of "control" that dominated business in Manchukuo. Considering that he was well aware that his career and future political ambitions were riding on his management of the Five-Year plan, it's not surprising he would take a personal interest in expanding the influx of North Chinese and consolidating the Manchukuo policy of forced and unremunerated labor. Using the same language as the Office of Administrative Affairs, the Office of Civil Affairs issued Manchukuo Directive 41 on 9 October 1937, which is the first official endorsement of forced labor in Japan's imperialism.[5] Building on the call for the dramatic "rationalization and increase of labor resources inside the country . . . in these times of emergency" in the policy of 10 August, Article 5 of Directive 41 authorizes Manchukuo agencies to utilize "methods of forced conscription [*kyōsei boshū no hōhō*] to satisfy labor demand" (*MKS*, 1971, vol. 2, 1160–65).

Even before Kishi's Office of Administrative Affairs wrote the first forced labor policy in August 1937, the coerced labor of "criminals against Manchukuo" was accepted practice. In the first few years of the state these were Chinese civilians and soldiers resisting Japan's invasion. After a successful military campaign the Japanese military would make prisoners of war do slave labor constructing the infrastructure necessary to maintain control of the newly subjugated area. Beginning in January 1938 a new category, called *furōnin* and *fulangzhe* in Chinese (vagrant, delinquent), provided Manchukuo provincial police and the *kempeitai* with dictatorial powers to sweep almost anyone off the street and into work camps. Chinese men faced the real danger of being categorized as "delinquents" and conscripted for the possible death sentence of permanent forced labor if they were caught without a proper residence card or were unable to provide proof of employment. After 1940 male residents of Manchukuo ages eighteen to fifty who did not perform unpaid labor annually and maintain official work books proving they'd fulfilled this duty faced the same consequences (*RDQDZY*, vol. 14, 875; Eda et al. 2002, 367).

On 10 September 1941 another Administrative Affairs policy was approved by the Manchukuo State Council, this one ordering all "Manchukuoan" men to serve six months of unpaid labor every three years; in 1942 this was extended to one year of labor every three years. The law stipulated that small subsidies were to be paid to remaining family members based on the size of the farm, but this rarely happened in practice (*RDQDZY*, vol. 14, 884). Beginning in 1938, when Chinese men were required to serve three months every three years, an average of 1.5 million men were required to do forced labor each year in this category, with the number reaching as high as 1.8 million in 1944 (820). The law's extension to one year in 1942 made it difficult for some of these "legal" forced laborers to return home after their year of service. We know from the testimonies of Japanese and Chinese corrections officers at the war crimes trials that many resident Manchukuoan forced laborers were never released; in effect, they were stop-lossed and compelled to work nearly to death (916, 924–26).

After the outbreak of full-scale war with China in July 1937 North Chinese were also kidnapped or swept up from POW camps and sent forcefully to Manchukuo to work. Although we have exact numbers from Ju Zhifen's authoritative work only on the years 1942–44, several Japanese elites testified that there were forced laborers taken in this way beginning in 1938. Furumi and Kaneda both estimated that one million captured North Chinese were press-ganged each year into Manchukuo as slave laborers. With the 2.4 million Ju has established for the 1942–44 period, and around 4 million for the period before that, the total is some 6.4 million North Chinese forced laborers (*RDQDZY*, vol. 14, 820; Ju 2007, 218). The fourth category of forced laborer included the large numbers of North Chinese tricked by Japanese labor recruiting companies like Datong Gongsi and the North Chinese Labor Association operating in Japanese-controlled areas of North China. Taking advantage of the social chaos and economic depression caused by the Japanese army's scorched earth campaign in the region, recruiters managed to lure many unemployed North Chinese to Manchukuo. Zhuang Jianping's groundbreaking work on this subject makes clear that most went to Manchukuo under false pretenses. Recruiters in the Japanese-occupied cities of Jinan and Qingdao were instructed to utilize neuro-political means such as film to implant false information. Datong Gongsi sponsored regular free film nights for destitute Chinese. These events normally included a feature in Chinese set in Manchukuo and produced by Amakasu's Manchurian Film Corporation (Manei) and starring Ri

Koran, the Japanese sex symbol attempting to pass as Chinese, followed by a documentary about the beauty and riches of Manchukuo, and concluding with a Japanese animated film. The theme of each of the films was invariably "the happy situation in Manchukuo" (Zhuang 2007, 233). Manei also sponsored free film showings in the countryside, distributing fliers made by Manchukuo labor recruiting agencies. Unemployed Chinese would often come back three or four times to these monthly events before deciding to ship off to Manchukuo. Zhuang claims that the number of Chinese workers brought to Manchukuo from the two largest recruiting agencies were 492,000 in 1938, 1 million in 1939, 1.3 million in 1940, and 1 million in 1941 (231). When added to the resident Manchukuoan (*guonei*) forced laborers, these numbers basically equal those provided by Furumi and Kaneda. However, despite the fact of being lied to about the happy situation, pay, and work conditions, the laborers were usually free to return to North China after their contract was up. A large number of forced laborers brought to Manchukuo outside this recruiting system were destined to die there.

Dirty Laundry

As a self-proclaimed "playboy of the Eastern world," Kishi kept the Chinese laundry women busy cleaning the stains off his sheets at the Yamato hotel and other Manchukuo rendezvous sites. But he didn't entirely excuse himself from all activities associated with laundering. Mutō Tomio, Manchukuo's Vice Minister of Communications and one of Kishi's and Amakasu's close friends, wrote in one of his memoirs that Kishi was always "throwing money around": "He personally gave me 200 yen every month in addition to my salary" (Mutō 1956, 71). Remembering how lavish Kishi's spending was—there were never any receipts or accountability—Mutō disclosed that many elites personally benefited from "his free use of money" (quoted in Iwami 1994, 77). Another civilian elite, Kida Kiyoshi, claimed that there was no need to have supplementary funds for off-the-books operations, as "money was always available, and Kishi threw tons of it around. . . . The atmosphere was more like that of the hustlers and small-time criminals" (quoted in Iwami 1994, 76).

Indeed, the Manchukuo state did appropriate the modus operandi of the hustlers and *yakuza*, and it became harder and harder to distinguish the two. When Kishi was transferred to Manchukuo in the fall of 1936, on just his second day on the job he had a meeting with Amakasu Masa-hiko. We have no idea what they discussed, but the two quickly became friends. We do know about Kishi's involvement with Amakasu's drug syndicates, as he benefited from Amakasu's largesse and at times made his own donations to fund Amakasu's operations (Hara Y. 2007; Ōta 2005). Moreover, a few months after arriving in Manchukuo, Amakasu introduced Kishi to the biggest civilian drug dealer in the world at the time, the Japanese-passing-as-Chinese, Satomi Hajime. When Kishi first met Satomi, probably sometime in early 1937, he was running the off-the-books opium operation for Manchukuo in Tianjin. In December 1937 Satomi was transferred to Shanghai were he directed the massive opium dealership for the Japanese military until the end of the Second World War, the revenues from which allowed Japan to continue fighting a two-front war in East and southeast Asia and against the United States in the Asia-Pacific (Sano 2005). It's interesting in this regard to recall that Kishi had two major concerns that kept him from going to Manchu-kuo earlier than he did, and almost kept him from going altogether. The first was his worry about what the state would use as guarantees against the huge loans needed to finance the Five-Year Plan. His second worry was the more basic one of industrial supply exceeding military demand. It's safe to assume that the second Sino-Japanese War begin-ning in July 1937 took care of the second worry, as war against China, together with plans for a second war against the Soviet Union, assuaged Kishi's anxiety about oversupply. The first worry was probably dealt with during his welcoming meeting with Amakasu. From this point on there is no indication that Kishi was concerned about financing. As I showed in chapter 7, huge opium profits become the security put up for the first loans to Manchukuo in 1932. By 1936 revenues from morphine and heroin sales would have been added security. Amakasu was one of only a handful of Japanese in China with insider knowledge about the enormous revenues from drug trafficking; it is hard to imagine that he didn't reassure Kishi with this information. Then again, Kishi might not have had to wait until his second day on the job to be briefed about the huge drug revenues. When he reported to Hoshino at the Office of Ad-ministrative Affairs on his first day of work he entered the site where, according to Welfare Minister Kaneda Sei, the "overall management of Manchukuo drug operations was directed" (*RDQDZY*, vol. 14, 821).

The photographs and written descriptions of Kishi during this period never fail to depict a giddy exuberance: laughing and joking while doling out money during the day and looking forward to his drinking and fornicating at night. By his second year in Manchukuo Kishi was the primary point man for an extraordinary shuffling of money. In fact, so much money circulated around him that Mutō Tomio, only half jokingly, suspected Kishi of practicing alchemy (Ōta 2005, 336). The less naïve among Kishi's assistants had a more concrete sense of what "alchemy" (*renkinjutsu*) really meant from some of Kishi's pet sayings during these years, one of which was "Only drink water that's been filtered."[6] Excepting Mutō, everyone understood that this was Kishi's code for "money laundering." One evening in the middle of October 1939, just before leaving Manchukuo for good, he gathered his friends together at his favorite Japanese restaurant. As described by both Mutō and Furumi (Ayukawa was in Japan, and Kishi had already said farewell to Amakasu), Kishi wanted to make sure that his closest associates knew about his personal political goals. In addition to asking for support he wanted to pass on some of the financial secrets he had mastered during his years of managing Manchukuo's Five-Year Plan. One of his "Japanese lessons" was "Political money should only be used after it's been laundered through a filter [*rokaki*]. Whenever questions arise about financing, the politician using the money can feel confident that the water he paid for is potable" (quoted in Ōta 2005, 421).

Kishi was a strong supporter of Kita Ikki's fascist 1919 *Fundamental Principles for the Reorganization of Japan* (*Nihon kaizō hōan* 1971), which called for a revivified emperor-centered *kokutai* through the repression of labor unions and banishment of political parties. Together with squeezing the lifeblood out of Chinese labor by Japanese managerial overlords, Kishi's insistence on squeezing impurities out of Chinese water and blood-stained wealth overturns Gotō Shinpei's emphasis on the biopolitical health brought about by the incorporation of immunities. Kishi's necropolitics opposes immunities within to the fascist non-contamination of being immune *from*. This *kokutai*-influenced phobia about contracting Chinese immunities was hegemonic among Japanese imperialists in Manchukuo, although it took Japan's most powerful gangster after the Second World War, Kodama Yoshio, to express it clearly. During his time looting and profiteering in Manchukuo and Shanghai in the late 1930s and 1940s, where he first met Kishi, Kodama expressed this necropolitical *"immunity from"* colloquially while giving marching

The new bureaucrat and head of the Five-Year Plan for waging total war, Kishi Nobusuke, wearing the uniform of the fascist Concordia Association and enjoying himself with his Japanese male subordinates in Manchukuo, circa 1938. From *Maboroshi no kinema: Manei*, 1989

orders to his syndicate of Manchukuo hustler spies and *yakuza*: "We Japanese are like pure [*kirei na*] water in a bucket; different from Chinese who are like the filthy Yangtze River. But be careful. If the smallest amount of shit gets into our bucket, we become totally polluted. Since all the toilets in China empty into the Yangtze, Chinese are soiled for eternity. We, however, must maintain our purity" (quoted in Meyer 2003, 210; see also Haruna 2000).

Kokutai Becomes *Hentai*

Whether the contaminating agent was his own semen, Chinese feces, or Manchukuo drug money, Kishi knew when it was time to call in the cleaners. Although there were many forms of laundering in Manchukuo, money laundering worked generally like this: even before 1 July 1932, when the Manchukuo Central Bank opened with assets looted from the four main Chinese banks in Manchuria, the Guandong army set up a Bureau for Special Financial Assets (Tokushu zaisan shikinbu) that was an official state institution. Later incorporated into the Central Bank, until

1941 this bureau operated independently as what Yasutomi Ayumu calls a "tunneling facility that shuttled money earned on the black market into Manchukuo's Central Bank" (1999, 90). The laundering of money from the black market was so systemic in the early 1940s that *Investment Monthly*, the Finance Ministry's monthly organ, openly reported on it (*Kinyū Geppō*, 31 July 1944; 31 August 1944).

But the laundering possibilities extended even further. As Kaneko Fumio (1995) has argued, the Manchukuo financial system was from the beginning meant to be independent from Japan's Central Bank. Not only did Tokyo Finance Ministry officials refuse external auditing, but these officials were themselves responsible for installing the financial system. This nontransparent system was ostensibly set up with money laundering in mind (Kaneko Fumio, personal communication, 9 November 2007). In the only monograph on Manchukuo's banking system, Yasutomi suggests that this laundering-friendly system was necessary because opium continued to be Manchukuo's main export until the end of the war (1999, 91). Although Yasutomi says nothing about the vast sums earned from dealing heroin and morphine, when these are added together with the revenues gained from the ongoing theft of Chinese property and possessions, it's clear that the Manchukuo Central Bank took full advantage of the nontransparency to protect the privacy of its depositors laundering opium profits and loot.

Driven a Nissan Lately?

More than a month after Ayukawa Yoshisuke moved most of his Nissan *zaibatsu* conglomerate to Manchukuo's capital, Kishi and the Guandong army threw a lavish welcome party for him at the Yamato hotel. Meanwhile, Japanese troops were concluding their atrocities in Nanjing, China (Hara A. 1976, 233). The date was 27 December, the day the Manchukuo State Council's Manchuria Industrial Development Act went into effect, welcoming Nissan to Manchukuo under its new name, Mangyō. There couldn't have been a more convenient place for Ayukawa, who settled into a second-floor suite of the Yamato hotel, home to two men who would soon become his close friends: Kishi and Amakasu. Mutō Tomio was one of the two hundred guests, all Japanese except for eight Chinese members of the State Council. The impressionable Mutō gushed that Ayukawa was one of the greatest men he'd ever met, and he remembers Ayukawa's first Manchukuo speech at this event as promising greatness: "Japanese technology and Chinese resources are the keys to our success. But we need even more Japanese technology and engineering, and some from abroad as well. When these are mobilized, we will enlist the huge supply of Chinese labor to our cause, some 40 million! I believe strongly that when you have a supply of Chinese numbering over 40 million, and bring in Japanese engineering and technology, in ten years we will be able to surpass the level of development inside Japan" (quoted in Mutō 1989, 136).

Although Ayukawa often metaphorized Northeast China as a "blank slate [*hakusho*] waiting to be written on" by Japanese imperialism (*Ayukawa Yoshisuke kankei bunsho* 331.4, 8/9),[7] his language changed somewhat after spending October 1936 admiring the achievements of Japan's imperialism in East Asia. Still depicted as a blank slate, now China was full of resources to be expropriated. It took Ayukawa about a year to decide to move most of Nissan to Manchukuo, in what was seen by many in Japan at the time as a huge risk. For his part Ayukawa publicly referred to the move to China both in terms of the ideological code of imperialism (the coprosperity of Manchukuo and Japan) and the civilizing mission of capitalist markets.[8]

The older leftist scholarship written in Japanese on Nissan represents the move to China in very different terms (Hara A. 1976; Suzuki 1992). Ayukawa formed Nissan in 1928 as a capitalist conglomerate (*zaibatsu*) that linked his myriad business interests in steel production and machine parts with the Mitsui Trading Company, together with the businesses of his brother-in-law, the industrialist and influential fascist Kuhara Fusanosuke (1869–1965). Nissan's portfolio ballooned during the post-Incident stock market bubble that compounded Japanese investment following the military occupation of Northeast China. The new *zaibatsu* Nissan differed from more established ones like Mitsubishi in that it did not have its own internal bank and was funded by stockholders; smallholders held over 50 percent of Nissan stock in the late 1930s. The most important difference, however, was Nissan's presence in the heavy industries in general and its subsidiaries, Nissan Motors, Nissan Chemicals, and Hitachi, in particular. Ayukawa was already profiting from military subsidies by 1932 by selling machine parts made by Nissan's Tobata Casting to three Japanese companies that produced military trucks. He started Nissan Motors in 1934 in part to attract more such subsidies. Although it's been difficult to determine the extent of direct state support, we do know that when Nissan's Model 80 truck came off the assembly line in its Yokohama factory in May 1937, Japan's military was its number one customer. The famous Nissan Model 90 bus was also popular with the military.

By 1936, however, almost all of Nissan's capital gains in Japan were wiped out by the imploding stock market. Despite the success of Nissan Motors and the popular Datsun car, Nissan's profit rate also dropped significantly between the second half of 1934 and early 1937, and Ayukawa's risky purchases of smaller businesses during 1930 had not paid off (Iguchi 2003, 44). The downward pressure he faced in all his businesses was compounded by two new changes inside Japan: increasing tax burdens and an intensified competition for skilled workers, leading to wage increases for the labor aristocracy that Ayukawa depended on.

Nissan Becomes Mangyō

It took about eighteen months for the army leadership in Manchukuo to realize that leaving the economy in the hands of the hustlers was, to say the least, not the best way to prepare for total war. They also realized they would have to sacrifice their bias against finance capital to their desire for rapid industrialization. Hoshino and Furumi, the elite bureaucrats sent to Manchukuo from Japan's Ministry of Finance, were instrumental in this shift (Asada and Kobayashi 1972). In June 1934, after Hoshino visited Tokyo, the Manchukuo State Council announced that for the first time it was encouraging private investment from Japanese capitalists (Suzuki 1992, 268). Up until then money had come from Japanese government channels, black-market loans, and the SMR. Despite this surprising invitation to Japanese money markets, no new investors responded, as private and government borrowers inside Japan were sucking up most available capital. We should be careful, however, not to attribute this inability to attract private investment to the Guandong army's supposed anticapitalism. Even the army's radical right quickly forgot their short-lived criticisms of liberal capitalism and recognized the right of capitalists to make a profit and own property privately. As long as the old financial conglomerates were kept out of Manchukuo— the code for this was *zaibatsu hairubekarazu*—capitalist enterprise was encouraged. Although the Guandong army's "Outline for the Foundation of Manchukuo's Economy" issued in March 1933 was clear that financial speculation was detrimental to the colonial state's future, the "revised capitalism" called for would feature a mix of "special companies" managed by the state (industries directly connected to military expansion), together with small and medium-size industries run by private capitalists. Moreover, the army went so far as to welcome foreign capital under its "open door" policy and promised to protect free enterprise (*MKS*, 1971, vol. 1, 382–83).

Frustrated with the slow pace of military industrialization and alarmed at the newly reported Soviet troop strength in Siberia, Ishihara Kanji took advantage of his new position as head of operations at the Army General Staff in Tokyo to speed things up in Manchukuo. He asked Miyazaki, his acquaintance from his Northeast China days, to chair a research group with the goal of installing a massive Five-Year Plan for military-industrial expansion in Manchukuo by early 1937. Ishihara and Miyazaki brought together the most important business, military, and government officials to participate. As Kobayashi Hideo argues, the goal of this "Miyazaki group" was nothing less than preparing Japan economically and financially for "total mobilization in wartime" (1995b, 115).

The Miyazaki group finished a draft of their visionary plan for China by summer 1936. Before they finished, however, the group realized that they lacked leaders with experience in industry and planning to actualize the plan on the ground. Based on his policy speeches for the planned economy, total war proponents like Katakura Tadashi and Ishihara saw Kishi as the ideal person to take charge of the infrastructure necessary for unlimited war. In the summer of 1935 army and civilian elites began the negotiations to get Kishi to Manchukuo. The Miyazaki group also needed someone with experience in setting up high-tech automobile and airplane facilities to team up with Kishi. It seems that Ishihara Kanji himself approached Ayukawa sometime around late January 1936 about creating factories in Manchukuo (Iguchi 2003, 40). By the time the plan was finished and agreed on by the Japanese and Manchukuo governments in late October, Ayukawa had accepted an invitation to visit Manchukuo. Once in China he met Kishi and Hoshino and had extensive meetings with the president of the SMR, Matsuoka Yōsuke—the same Matsuoka who orchestrated Japan's dramatic withdrawal from the League of Nations in 1933. Ayukawa was impressed with what he saw during his visit, although he had reservations about the lack of vertical integration with parts makers and other small industries necessary to establish car and airplane production facilities.

As soon as it became clear that Kishi would take charge of the Five-Year Plan, he involved himself in the recruitment of Ayukawa. But Kishi knew that two things had to change in Manchukuo before Ayukawa would agree to come: the reluctance of the army elites to allow financial and capitalist conglomerates whose raison d'être was profiteering, and the monopoly privileges enjoyed by Matsuoka's SMR. Through his partying and large slush fund Kishi had ingratiated himself with the Guandong army. Never shy when it came to taking credit for policy successes, he claimed in postwar interviews that he alone was responsible for getting Ayukawa to move (Ōta 2005; Hara Y. 2007). With Kishi pressuring him from Manchukuo and the proud Ishihara pouring him beer like a demure office lady in Tokyo, by June 1937 Ayukawa agreed to transfer a large part of Nissan to Manchukuo and submitted financial reports on 26 June (*Ayukawa Yoshisuke kankei bunsho* 331.4). Japanese business leaders called this "the financial world's February 26 Incident," after the famous fascist coup attempt of 26 February 1936 (Iwami 1994, 70).

The capitalist bias coloring much of this historiography has concocted an image of Ayukawa as the heroic businessman, constantly responding to challenges and overcoming them by taking brave risks and charting new territory. Leftist scholarship, again, provides a welcome clarity. Hara Akira writes that the two main reasons for Ayukawa's move were anything but heroic: Nissan's finances were approaching bankruptcy levels, and the growing tax burden inside Japan, compared to lower business rates in Manchukuo, made the profit environment quite appealing, even before it became more welcoming after Kishi took control in late 1936 (1976, 238–39). Moreover, the attitude toward liberal capitalism was changing inside Japan and moving relentlessly toward protectionism and capping business profits. Suzuki Takashi sums up his overview of the year leading up to the decision to relocate Nissan with the provocative conclusion that Ayukawa went in order to *escape* the confines of the planned economy (1992, 272). Extending Suzuki's analysis a bit, it seems that Ayukawa went, not necessarily to avoid the restrictions of economic planning per se, but because he wanted to be doing the economic planning—or at least living next door to his buddy Kishi, who was responsible for planning decisions.

In this light Ayukawa's move to Northeast China was anything but risky when Nissan Holdings became Mangyō on 17 December 1937. Hara Akira argues that the sweet deal he ended up with was far and away the "safest option for him" at the time: "Everything about his businesses was guaranteed" (1976, 236). The details of the generous package that Ayukawa negotiated are well known. First, he was given control over all the nontransportation businesses of the SMR. For this huge concession he promised to produce trucks for the Guandong army. Second, he demanded control over the entire process of industrialization in Manchukuo, from the extraction of resources, to the establishment of coal and iron ore processing, to the final installation of large industrial production facilities. Ayukawa's Mangyō would assume almost dictatorial powers with command authority over the major capitalist enterprises in Manchukuo. As far as the financial terms, the Office of Administrative Affairs guaranteed the entire principal and a 6 percent annual return on all investments related to Ayukawa's businesses for ten years. (This deal is uncannily like the "cost plus" contracts that private companies such as Halliburton had with the U.S. Pentagon.) As far as dividends were concerned, the Manchukuo regime let Ayukawa pay out as much as he wanted (Ayukawa 1937, 52–53). All told, Ayukawa got so much that Hara insists that the deal completely wiped away the previous commitments to regulating profit that had been the defining characteristic of Manchukuo's capitalism (1976, 238).

At least for the first year (March 1932–March 1933) the Guandong army bragged about keeping the "corrupt" conglomerates Mitsui and Sumitomo out of Manchukuo. The army and the general public perceived them as responsible for the 1929 Crash and blamed them for profiting from Prime Minister Inukai's decision in December 1931 to take Japan off the gold standard; the *zaibatsu* conglomerates had to work hard to reverse the public's negative impression. Although Mitsui and Sumitomo were centrally involved with the navy and army inside Japan in the armaments buildup of the early 1930s (when Japan doubled the percentage of the military budget from 25 percent to almost 50 percent of the national budget), the more radical of the army officers needed more convincing. In 1932 Mitsui collaborated with the Ōkura Group to build a huge new arsenal in Fengtian. Surprised at continuing overtures from the Guandong army after the signing in May 1933 of the Tanggu Truce, which granted Japanese merchants and soldiers exclusive rights to profit and pillage in the large DMZ in East Hebei, North China, Mitsui began to quickly expand both its portfolio and direct investment strategies in Hebei and Manchukuo in late 1933. Among the latter were the Japan-Manchurian Flour Company and the Japan-Manchuria Linen Weaving Company—"joint enterprises" Mitsui set up at the request of the Manchukuo regime (Fletcher 1989, 104). Mitsui benefited immediately from its eagerness to collaborate with the Guandong army when the Chinese government in Nanjing doubled tariffs for Japanese products in retaliation for military invasion; this would have been crippling if Mitsui hadn't been able to relocate business to Manchukuo and Hebei. Moreover, the chaos created by the hustlers and soldiers of fortune making incursions into North China created huge opportunities for smuggling Mitsui goods, mimicking the opium and narcotics trade. The signing of the Umezu-He and Doihara-Qin Accords in June 1935 facilitated a rapid expansion of the Japanese drug trade north and south of the Great Wall, and at this point Mitsui and Mitsubishi publicly diversified their product lines into opium, which they purchased from Iranian and Turkish sellers and marketed exclusively in newly occupied North China (*Gendaishi shiryō*, vol. 12, 190–91). The establishment of the so-called second Manchukuo in East Hebei in November 1935 further excited the illicit movement of Japanese goods from Manchukuo into North China. While trade regulations were put into place in January 1936, the second Manchukuo set tariffs on Japanese goods so low that it basically legalized all the smuggling (Nakamura Takafusa 1983, 35–36). After the Japanese Foreign Ministry promulgated its Amō Doctrine in 1934 almost all Japanese business and military leaders were preparing for some kind of bloc economy, with Japan's hegemony projected to extend throughout East and Southeast Asia. Together with the mobilization for total war went what Miles Fletcher calls "trade mobilization" (1989, 122). Saber rattling at China met portfolio and ledger brandishing at Chinese boycotters and Indian tariff officials as war trade became indistinguishable from trade war.

But none of the actions of big business to cooperate with Japan's military matched Ayukawa's. His Nissan Motors contract with the army continued inside Japan throughout the Second World War, so Ayukawa went to Manchukuo with the express purpose of consolidating the bloc economy and the Guandong army's "defense state [*bōei kokka*]." Business historians have expended time and energy speculating on what

Ayukawa thought he would achieve in Manchukuo: Was he trying to secure peace with the United States through soliciting investment? Was he hoping that the civilizing effects of global trade would apply the brakes to Japan's rush to total war? Whatever his personal beliefs on these issues, he was originally asked to go to Manchukuo by Japan's most powerful proponent of total war, Ishihara Kanji. As he was on friendly terms with Ishihara and was an inside adviser to the Miyazaki group, it's inconceivable that Ayukawa didn't know of Ishihara's and Miyazaki's necropolitical designs for war against both the Soviet Union and then the United States. Like other Japanese elites in Manchukuo, Ayukawa worked extremely hard for recognition by the United States. To my mind this is not mutually exclusive with the understanding that Japan might have to engage in an apocalyptic war with the United States to secure regional hegemony in the Asia-Pacific.

Always the opportunist, Ayukawa became a vocal defender of the militarized bloc economy. Here, it's important to recognize what another important war planner and new bureaucrat, Mōri Hideoto, called in 1938 Japanese imperialism's "Janus face" (Mōri Hideoto kankei bun-sho, 223). In the case of Ayukawa, when facing New York bankers he always insisted on free trade and the open door in China; to Japanese audiences he showed a face wholeheartedly committed to the totalitarian defense state. In the original version of an essay titled "The Reasons for Re-reconsidering Manchuria," written in September 1938 for the important mass culture journal of ideas in Japan, *Central Review* (*Chūō Kōron*), he seems to have forgotten his earlier commitments to the open doors and flat worlds of liberal economic theory.[9] A little less than one year after his move to Manchukuo, Ayukawa was still aggressively courting Japanese investment. However, he did so in the new language of economic blocs and strict controls over wages and prices. He proselytized that, unlike inside Japan, prices were kept extremely low in the colony, making land and other resources necessary for industrial projects "incomparably cheap."

> But for all that, we will be considering the most important resource — labor power. In Manchuria you can set up construction sites quickly, and enjoy large discounts [*kosuto o yasuku kōjishite*] by taking advantage of all the cheap workers. . . . As far as raw materials are concerned, the huge reserves of iron and coal have been talked about

previously, but in addition to those, industrialists need to reconsider the reserves of labor power lying on the Chinese continent as well. Again, the wages used as investment in this resource are extremely low [*teiren*]. (*Ayukawa Yoshisuke kankei bunsho* 911.5)

At this time in Ayukawa's main factories the phrase "extremely low wages" would qualify as an understatement. Taking full advantage of Kishi's and Hoshino's recommendation to rationalize the mobilization of prison and Chinese enemy labor, Ayukawa started using unremunerated labor early on at his Shōwa Iron and Steel Works (Shōwa Tekkōjo). One of the two largest enterprises in Manchukuo, Ayukawa's Mangyō assumed 55 percent majority ownership of Shōwa Iron and Steel in March 1938. As the labor historian Zhao Guangrui has shown in scrupulous detail, immediately after taking over Ayukawa began using Chinese forced labor at his Shōwa facilities under the category of *tokushu kōjin*, or "special worker" (cited in Eda et al. 2002, 340). Although there were only 144 Chinese special enough to have to work for no pay in 1938, by 1939 there were 690 in this category, of which only 373 survived until the end of that year. The numbers of special workers increased steadily until September 1941, when the Manchukuo regime announced the New Order for Labor, widening allowable forms of forced labor (*RDQDZY*, vol. 14, 866–69; *MKS*, 1971, vol. 2, 1177–78). With approximately four million North Chinese forced to Manchukuo to perform slave labor from 1941 until the end of the Second World War (approximately 40 to 50 percent of whom were worked to death), together with seven million to eight million resident Manchukuoan Chinese, there's no doubt that Ayukawa's businesses profited from this crime against humanity. We should note that Ayukawa also profited from energy costs kept low by the superexploitation of Chinese coal miners. Kishi designed the Five-Year Plan to operate through the SMR's Fushun coal mines, which provided cheap energy for most of Ayukawa's businesses. Here at the largest industry in Manchukuo, there was an annual death rate similar to the 55 percent at Ayukawa's Shōwa Iron and Steel. From 1938 until 1944 at the Fushun site, 25,000 of the 40,000 "nonforced" Chinese workers needed to be replaced annually, mainly as a result of death on the job and execution for perceived insubordination, in addition to a smaller percentage managing to escape alive (Taiheiyō Sensō Kenkyūkai 1996, 110).

As yet another aspect of this kind of dispossession, Zhao shows how

Ayukawa's Shōwa Iron and Steel was at the center of the Japanese colonial labor system, a system that specialized in a complete separation between engineering and planning (always done by Japanese) and physical labor (reserved for Chinese). Although Ayukawa often extolled the scientific "development" that Japanese imperialism was bringing to China, at his own factories a hierarchy was established to explicitly *prevent* engineering knowledge from being passed on to Chinese workers. There was no technoscientific transfer of knowledge, no "Japanese lessons" to guide Chinese out of civilizational darkness. Instead, there was what Zhao calls an "engineering knowledge blockade [*gijutsu fūsa*]" to consolidate the colonial hierarchies between engineers and physical laborers for decades to come. In the rare situations where Japanese and Chinese worked in the same occupation, Japanese earned three to four times more than Chinese (*Manshū kōgyō rōdō gaikyō hōkoku*, August 1939, 79–80). Even in the best of wage situations for Chinese, Kishi's wage controls meant that the rampant inflation impacting Manchukuo's economy from 1938 on brought Chinese workers to the brink of death—and pushed many beyond. Along with the business strategy of keeping costs as low as possible, Zhao concludes, the obsession with rationalization translated into widespread forced labor, starvation, and death for Chinese in Manchukuo (cited in Eda et al. 2002, 369). In the Marxist terms I introduced earlier, modern factories like Ayukawa's Mangyō industries benefited both from expanded technomachinic inputs characteristic of real subsumption and the squeezing of labor power beyond its capacity to reproduce found in the absolute surplus extraction in formal subsumption (what Deleuze and Guattari [1977] call "capitalist delirium")—the necropolitical hybrid I'm calling deformal subsumption.

In agreeing to move his main businesses to Manchukuo, Ayukawa profited from the rationalization of forced and other cheap labor in deformal subsumption. This was in addition to the guaranteed subsidies paid to him yearly by the Manchukuo regime to meet his profit margins. The extent of these subsidies is difficult to determine exactly, although looking at the official Mangyō business reports from 1938 to 1941 (*Ayukawa Yoshisuke kankei bunsho* 331.6, *Mangyō keigyō hōkokusho*) it appears that they came in the form of direct deposits and stock purchases. The 10 percent paid out on Mangyō's privately owned shares were due to large Manchukuo subsidies. F. G. Jones claimed that these subsidies constituted 70 percent of Mangyō's profits in the second half of 1940; based on Ayukawa's business reports the subsidies totaled around 60 percent of profits in both halves of 1939 (1949, 150). The war profiteer Ayukawa and his stockholders clearly expropriated riches by installing the industry necessary for total war. As far as the deposits from Manchukuo to Ayukawa's Mangyō are concerned, I showed in the previous chapter the extent to which Manchukuo relied on drug dealing and confiscation for its revenues. There should be no arguing with the fact that part of this money found its way straight into Ayukawa's pockets. Moreover, Manchukuo civilian elites have described the close friendship Ayukawa enjoyed with Amakasu and Kishi, his neighbors at the Yamato hotel (Shiota 2006, 111). Furumi describes regular meetings of the famous "odd society," where Ayukawa, Amakasu, Kishi, Furumi, and others would focus on Japan's "Asian strategy," and depicts Amakasu's and Ayukawa's friendship during this period, suggesting it is extremely unlikely that Ayukawa was unaware of Amakasu's drug trafficking (cited in Ōta 2005, 323). Ōta Naoki states frankly that the close working and personal relationship between the "Manchukuo Three" (Ayukawa, Kishi, Amakasu) was inextricable from the huge revenues taken from drug trafficking (322–24).

Although Mangyō would not become the great industrial giant that Ayukawa had hoped, thanks to his "cost plus" arrangement with Manchukuo his profit margins remained steady right up until 1943. However, to continue profiting from necropolitical capitalism in Manchukuo he was asked to pay the regime back by publicly praising Kishi and the Guandong army's policies. Even before his move to Manchukuo, Ayukawa had started to shift his public face in Japan toward lauding economic blocs and control, while in his efforts to attract North American investment to Manchukuo he spoke internationally of free flows of capital. What did he really think at this time? Furumi and other elites have written of Ayukawa's participation in special operations planning designed to eliminate British influence in Southeast Asia. Although it's impossible to determine the extent of this, some of Ayukawa's public speeches given outside Manchukuo to Japanese audiences during this period reveal a strong commitment to the ideological program of Japanese colonial fascism: a controlled economy centered on the Greater East Asian bloc, the rejection of personal freedoms, and the unquestioned authority of Japanese bureaucrats and technicians—the sum total of what Ayukawa referred to glowingly as "totalitarianism" (*zen-taishugi*).

In a speech called "Manshu as a Place for Working as an Engineer" delivered in January 1939 at a Japanese engineering school graduation Ayukawa urged all the students to go to Northeast China and experience what he called the "Manchukuo feeling" (totalitarianism). He confessed that if he were in the same position as the young men present at his talk, he would without question move to Manchukuo to contribute.

> If I were in your position I would be thinking 95% affirmatively about going to Manshū; if I were young like you all I would go to Manshū without fail. . . . But I need to tell you that the sense there is different from that inside Japan. As far as thinking about your own personal achievements [*jiko eitatsu*], up until now we Japanese have been taught not to do something that isn't going to further our personal goals—if you are going to benefit from it, then do it; if not, then don't. This is usually thought of as liberalism and individualism. However, the world we are in today is changing quickly, moving from liberalism to planning and control, what generally occurs under the rubric of "totalitarianism." Whatever you call it, what's most important here is that everything becomes unified from the standpoint of politics. As most of you know, by bringing about planning in the economy and totalitarianism in politics—meaning that all individual units become fused with the state—nation-building has been able to move ahead quickly and successfully in Manchukuo. (*Ayukawa Yoshisuke kankei bunsho* 911.5)

Ayukawa follows this introduction by expanding on the advantages inherent in such totalitarian societies. He says that the older bias toward self-reliance (*jikyūjizoku*) in the ideology of liberal individualism isn't suited to the contemporary world, where the production process requires many single parts working in harmony toward one goal. Each of these units (*tani*) needs to think of itself not as an isolated thing, but as a replaceable element of one grand totality. Moreover, in addition to the larger scale physical production, the element of time itself is changing in totalitarianism. In liberal capitalism individuals think of cost and benefit in the short term, but Ayukawa lectures that short-term profit is giving way to the "longer scale of time" necessary for the massive industrial projects in Manchukuo.[10]

To make sure he hasn't alienated any of the students, he reassures them that this new totalitarian "feeling" still requires human energy and commitment, in fact even more so than in liberal capitalism: "Totalitarianism begins from below and works upward to finally unify with the state." However, he warns the students that this necessary human energy can't be allowed to question or think critically: "Everyone involved has to believe fully in the project and mobilize for it; the end result will be the future development of Manchukuo, a model paradise in the East." Before concluding with a plea to the students—"From the bottom of my heart, please come to Manshū!"—he challenges them with the prediction that the way Japanese imperialism is expanding, "all the weak people will be left behind in Japan." In terms of the necropolitical command *Kill and leave to die*, Ayakawa's challenge was also a kind of threat: Either contribute to the killing in China or be left behind to die.

Conclusion

Yes, all of us are studying death, studying how to walk
  into a tomb.
But who could believe the lessons of death would be
  so difficult.

YANG XU, MANCHUKUO-BASED CHINESE POET, 1943

Comrade workers, peasants, merchants and students!!
     Under the gruesome rule of the Japanese bandits
for the past five years, we do not even know who of our
mothers, fathers and brothers have been butchered. We
do not even know if our wives, sisters, or sisters-in-law
have been raped or forced to become prostitutes, or if
our homes have been burned down. . . . We cannot even
count the dangers awaiting us: being burned to death,
buried alive, strangled, dying in jail, etc. Many among
us have also experienced the phenomenon by poverty,
freezing to death, and starving to death.

POSTER DISTRIBUTED IN MANCHUKUO BY THE PEOPLE'S FOURTH
REVOLUTIONARY ARMY OF THE NORTHEAST, 26 APRIL 1936

Amakasu Masahiko, chairman of Manchukuo's propaganda film company Manei, was considered the most powerful cultural broker in
Japanese-controlled China in the early 1940s. So it was no surprise when
he was invited to be a special judge for the Greater East Asia Writers
Congress, held in August 1943 in Tokyo. Amakasu declined the invitation. Three days spent handing out prizes for Chinese and Japanese fiction must have been the last thing on his mind as he was frantically
raising cash for Japan's war effort. And it is probably a good thing he declined, as the prize-winning novel, *Beike* (Seashells), would have made
the man, known by then as Manchukuo's "drug kingpin" (*mayaku ō*),
more than a little uncomfortable.

Seashells was written by the popular Manchukuo-based Chinese writer Li Keyi (1920–79; real name, Yuan Xi), already well known for his stark depictions of everyday life in Manchukuo. *Seashells* details the lives of young, bourgeois Chinese involved in drugs, casual sex, and alienated consumerism in Beijing and Qingdao. It centers around two sisters: Limei, a recent graduate of Beijing University, and her younger sister, Liying. Newly married to a forty-something professor, Limei finds out she is pregnant by her previous lover; the novel hints that she reluctantly terminated the affair *after* her marriage. Unsuccessful at finding a doctor willing to perform an abortion, she tells her new husband she is sick and flees with Liying to the family vacation house on the China coast in Qingdao (under Japanese control in 1914–22, and again in 1937–45). The thorough saturation of North China by Japanese drug markets is the underlying theme of the novel.

In Qingdao the attractive sisters fall in with a handsome party boy, Bai Ju, who introduces them to the city's nightlife and soon gets Liying to sleep with him. The sisters fall deeper into the consumerism that marked their lives in Beijing. Becoming disillusioned with their new fast crowd after discovering that Bai is sleeping with several women, Liying returns to Beijing, where she withdraws from contact with people. Limei gives birth to a boy and returns to Beijing, where the father of her child begins to stalk her. After this ex-lover is arrested for dealing heroin, a physician threatens to blackmail Limei by telling her clueless husband that the child is not his. The dénouement has Limei falling victim to tuberculosis.

Against a backdrop of drugs and illness in Japanese-controlled China, the main characters espouse personal philosophies impacted by the commodity form. The first conversation in the novel features Limei listening in on a debate between her husband, Zhao Xuewen, and a friend, with Limei swayed by the friend's Nietzschean insistence that "humans are creatures of instinct [*benneng*]; despite what modern morality says, indulging these instincts isn't a sin" (Li 1984, 9). When her husband accuses his friend of wanting to return humanity to the barbarism of "savages" (*yeman*) characterized by massacres and plunder, the man continues undeterred, claiming, "Civilized morality is a crime against the human spirit" (10). The playboy Bai later countersigns this capitalist modern primitivism by philosophizing that human happiness can be attained only through pure commitment to "vulgarity" (*beisu*) and radical philistinism: "Worldly happiness can only be carnal, base, and bought" (22).

Yuan deliberately set the spatiotemporal diegesis of *Seashells* just outside Manchukuo proper, in Beijing and Qingdao in 1935 (two years before these cities fell under Japan's military occupation), leading two of the Japanese judges at the Congress to read the novel as critical of *Western* liberalism and consumerism (Gunn 1980, 39). However, the Congress as a whole recognized Yuan, along with other Manchukuo writers Jue Qing (1919–81) and Mei Niang (1920–), for their explicit critiques of everyday life in Manchukuo (Smith 2007, 56). Yuan fled Manchukuo for Beijing in late 1941 because he feared arrest by the Japanese *kempeitai*. Better readers of anti-imperial Chinese writing than the Japanese literary judges, the *kempeitai* were growing increasingly irritated with Yuan's literary production—not for his critique of Euro-American decadence, but because they knew Chinese read his work as denouncing Japan's rule in Manchukuo. Writing *Seashells* in Beijing in late 1942, Yuan set the novel in 1935 to avoid further *kempeitai* harassment. However, several characters are metonymically linked to Japan. Combined with the fact that every Chinese reader would have had some sense of the direct involvement of Japanese in the booming Chinese drug markets, when opium and heroin appear in the text the criticism of Japan is clear. It was certainly not lost on the Japanese *kempeitai*, who arrested Yuan in Beijing just a few days after receiving his first-place prize for *Seashells*.

The Third Greater East Asia Writers Congress was held in Nanjing on 12 to 14 November 1944, and again a popular Manchukuo-based Chinese writer, Mei Niang, won the prize for her *Xie* (Crabs). Even more than *Seashells*, it depicts the effects of necropolitical capitalism in Manchukuo. The life of the young woman protagonist Cui is shown being stolen from her, exchanged, and then returned to her as a death sentence over the course of the novella. When her father, Sun Wangfu, moves to Manchukuo's capital city he obediently interiorizes imperial gender ideology by dehumanizing women as "ready sources of cash [*yaoqianshu*]." In *Crabs* trafficked North China coolies aren't even worthy of the mediated exchange assigned to women, only direct use and disposal (Smith 2007; Zhang 1996, 444–45). The novel concludes with Sun selling off his daughter Cui.

Mei's earlier ethnographic fiction set in Manchukuo, *Zhui* (The Chase,

1940), establishes an equivalence between North Chinese coolies and sex workers that inverts desire for life into a necropolitical absolute where there is no other solution open to or escape from certain death.[1] A corroboration of Yang Xu's poem in the epigraph above, *The Chase* was one of the "difficult lessons about dying" offered to subaltern Chinese in Manchukuo. After the death of her father, the young girl Guihua takes a job as a sex worker in an opium den (*yan ji*) in order to support her mother and brother, both seriously addicted to opium (Mei 1940, 134–36); having opium dens sell women's bodies was one of the market innovations introduced by Japanese hustlers after the Manchurian Incident, and one that ran parallel with the "comfort system" of forced sex work in China. The occupational demands of working as an opium prostitute lead Guihua to a new reliance on drugs (Sun 1993, 428). In no time, immersion in what Fanon called the "deathworld" of imperial domination robs Guihua of what she mourns as her "virginal body and soul [*chunüde sheng he xin*]" (136). At home on the evening of Chinese New Year, just as she is about to tell her mother about the new rich client whose favor she's won, her brother verbally abuses her, demanding all her savings. When she goes to dry her eyes in a mirror, she recoils in shock at her opium-desecrated face (135).

With no choice but to return to work, Guihua is verbally and physically abused by a male for the second time in a few hours. Right in front of her coworkers her boss insults her, steals her wages, and strikes her before throwing her into an alley behind the opium brothel, "tossed away like garbage" to join the ranks of other Chinese addicts deposited in the ash heaps (142). She lifts her battered and bloody face off the ground just long enough to see her fate allegorized a few feet away as a dog feasts hungrily on the flesh of a dead cat, leaving only its meatless skeleton (143).

Mei Niang's fictions about Manchukuo open the conclusion to this book because they portray a logic of equivalence between East Asian women forced into sex work and the approximately ten to twelve million Chinese forced to do slave labor in Manchukuo, as both exemplify a kind of disposability. *Disposability* and *superfluity* have been deployed in recent postcolonial theory to describe the dehumanization of subaltern populations (Mbembe 2004) and restrictive immigration and asylum laws (Khanna 2006). Disposability has also been configured through Giorgio Agamben's influential work on "bare life" (*vita nuda*). Uncovering a dehumanized form of life that "may be killed but not sacrificed," Agamben identifies the "fundamental activity of sovereign power . . . [in] the production of bare life as originary political element and as threshold of articulation between nature and culture, zoe and bios" (1995, 8, 11). At first glance, the logic of equivalence bridging male coolie laborers to women forced sex workers in Manchukuo might be best approached through this trope of bare life, constructed by the sovereign banishing of nature and zoe.

I've argued that coolies and sex workers were the most important constituent forces in consolidating Japan's imperialism in its biopolitical phase, and it is impossible to fully apprehend the final necropolitical phase without them. The historian Ju Zhifen (2005, 2007) has helped contextualize the situation of unremunerated forced Chinese laborers in the matrix of capitalist Manchukuo, where the feverish pace of Japan's total war placed heavy demands on industries, with labor shortages endemic after the start of the Pacific War in December 1941. Analysts of these shortages have attributed them to the unavailability of skilled labor necessary to meet the pace of military-industrial production, compounded by a frequently unspecified situation of abuses against Chinese workers. Rewinding to my discussion of colonial Taylorism, recall that Kishi Nobusuke's colonial labor policy promised to deliver nearly free Chinese labor and guaranteed revenue streams to capitalists and war profiteers like Nissan's Ayukawa. But apparently North Chinese coolies were balking at Manchukuo's industries refusing to pay decent— or any—wages. The children of Chinese laborers who had crossed into Northeast China from Shandong and Hebei annually since the 1880s now refused to do so willingly when wage floors were lowered like coffins into the ground by Kishi's necropolitics. Moreover, in 1936 Manchukuo law began restricting remittances sent back to North China, removing the main reason for migration to Manchuria in the first place. What I've been calling the *deformal subsumption* of labor under necropolitical capital meant that Japanese imperialists were fully committed to neither systemic maintenance nor the reproduction of Chinese workers' lives.

Obviously the devaluation of Chinese lives was determined in part by the military impulse to kill all Chinese resisters after Japan's undeclared, full-scale invasion of China began in July 1937. This was compounded for some imperialists by the vast size of China's population at this time. With some 400 million people available to be manipulated by the superior power, what did it matter if twenty or thirty million died? As the Japanese gendarme told the Chinese forced laborer Liu Benzhang at a work camp in northern Manchukuo sometime in the early 1940s, "It's no big deal if all you people die [*nimen sile sile de hao*]; there are so many fucking Chinese anyway" (*RDQDZY*, vol. 14, 932). Although such a remark is certainly indicative of one aspect of necropolitics, we need to think beyond this straightforward population racism toward Chinese to find causes rather than merely symptoms.

Different from the axioms of Gotō Shinpei's colonial biopolitics, the five axioms of necropolitics in Manchukuo were colonial Taylorism, a generalized state of exception and extortion, an ethnoracial governmentality that denigrated Chinese, the deployment of sexuality as inducing death, not life, and, most important, an intensification of the reification of human life in neuropolitics. Again, these are only tendencies and not hegemonic everywhere, although I am arguing that the last phase of Japan's imperialism can't be fully understood without recourse to them. As I explained in the previous chapter, Kishi's version of labor management in Manchukuo required wages to be so low that they often could not reproduce labor power, making Chinese lives ideologically disposable and allowing war profiteers to make a killing off Chinese labor in Manchukuo. Inverting the paradigm I called in part I *business as an extension of war by other means*, the capitalist meltdown in 1929 led centrists and rightists in Japan to view imperialist war as the best way to secure the coal, oil, and steel necessary to guarantee industrial capitalist growth—and to wipe out Chinese and Euro-American competitors. For the many Japanese acting within this ideological formation, war was a way of directing investment away from finance and toward fixed and commodity capital, making war indistinguishable from capitalist business. Finally, part II of this book was devoted to analyzing the ways in which Japan's capitalism in its neuropolitical mode relentlessly dehumanized workers and stupefied consumers, aspiring to turn them into Pavlovian automatons to be manipulated and disposed of so as to serve the accumulation needs of a tiny capitalist directorate.

It is impossible to configure the widespread use of forced labor and other atrocities in Manchukuo from 1938 to the end of the Second World War without beginning with these necropolitical axioms, what I've been calling Kishi's "death principles." I want to insist that these axioms will arguably provide a more complete explanatory framework than the simplistic culturalist explanations of the emperor system and the militarist *bushidō* codes, which tend to trivialize this historical period. A more serious sin for materialist thinkers is that disregarding larger structural complexities prevents us from, in the words of Walter Benjamin, "grasp[ing] . . . the constellation which [our] own era has formed with a definitely earlier one" (1968, 263). To "blast a specific era out of the homogeneous course of history" is to take up Benjamin's challenge and highlight the extraordinary rendering of "enemy combatants," the water-boarding and other "enhanced" torture techniques against detainees (*RDQDZY*, vol. 14, 915), the routine disregard of international law in establishing zones of exception, the preemptive military invasion of sovereign countries for the purpose of pillaging resources, and, yes, the utilization of forced labor to build the huge Green Zone housing the U.S. bureaucracy in Baghdad, Iraq, as aspects of a recent North American constellation shared with Japan's imperialism in its necropolitical mode.

In chapter 8, I described an ideological milieu that increasingly naturalized forced labor in Manchukuo. In chapter 1, I tried to show how the constituent power of this labor in its "coolie" manifestation literally produced the infrastructure for the first phase of Japan's imperialism. David Tucker (2005) and the essays collected by Eda et al. (2002) have pointed to the continuities and changes in this nonforced labor market as it interacted with the new labor demands of the early Manchukuo state. However, in part III, I emphasized the overlooked sine qua non of necropolitical capitalism: forced, unremunerated labor.

In their war crimes testimony several Manchukuo corrections officers frankly admitted that many forced Chinese laborers had only two options: either escape or face probable death owing to the conditions of the work (*RDQDZY*, vol. 14, 924; Su 1995). Of the four distinct types of forced labor I enumerated in the previous chapter, it is clear that the cases of laborers worked to death occurred mainly in the first category, Manchukuoan *guonei* (delinquents), and the third category, non-Manchukuoan *guowai* (enemies). It may be difficult to believe that an imperial power threatened by constant labor shortages—but with vast pockets of laundered money available to conduct covert operations and allow elites to consume lavishly—would regularly work Chinese labor to death. However, when the revelations from Chinese forced laborers themselves are read together with the testimonies of Manchukuo corrections officers responsible for subjugating them, we can begin to grasp some of the ways this happened. The confessions of Chinese Manchukuoan collaborators like Wang Dehui describe how forced laborers weren't allowed to keep anything they had brought with them, including the clothes on their backs. All personal possessions were stolen from them and sold. With nothing left but exposed flesh, they resorted to cutting holes in the bottom of paper and hemp bags used for mortar (*yanghui zhidai*) and cement; this would be their only protection in the harsh winters (*RDQDZY*, vol. 14, 923). According to the corrections officer Qu Bingshan, forced laborers in Manchukuo often worked completely naked (*chisheng louti*) in the summertime, without shoes (879). When workers died in colder weather their paper bags or hemp sacks were stripped off their dead bodies and given to workers with no clothing at all (923). Workers were fed Chinese sorghum and grass for food, and thirteen- and fourteen-hour workdays were standard.

Beginning in 1942 pressures intensified to conscript more unremunerated labor from inside Manchukuo. The more humane of the Japanese *kempeitai*, however, realized that the Chinese who had been previously victimized by land and property seizures, punishing taxes, and the drug policy that flooded China with addictive substances would most likely be worked to death. In a report published in April 1942, the Chengde, Hebei *kempeitai* explained to the Guandong army high command that growing Chinese awareness of Japanese abuses made it difficult to press-gang North Chinese into Manchukuo, so they wouldn't be able to fill their quota of forced laborers. The only viable option was to round up workers from among the most oppressed strata of Manchukuoan Chinese: "The only available workers can be divided into three categories: landless renters; the homeless floating population; and opium addicts. . . . These people have clearly suffered oppressions, nevertheless they cannot but be forced to work [*bude bubei guyong*]. We should be conscious of the fact that this policy will result in an increased rate of death [*daoshi siwang*] among these workers" (*RDQDZY*, vol. 14, 885).

In ignoring the warnings of the increased death rate for forced laborers, Furumi Tadayuki, taking over Manchukuo labor management from his boss Kishi, went so far as to concoct a plan to reanimate what Marx called the "Lazarus layers" of society (Braverman 1974, 388). In the spring of 1944 Manchukuo officials surveyed unregistered opium addicts in the colony and quickly rounded up 1.2 million for a program pitched to "educate and cure" them (Sun 1993, 444–57). Under cover of an emergency opium eradication scheme, the Manchukuo police and Welfare Ministry officials ordered them, together with the "reserve of registered addicts" numbering 500,000, to report to the 180 vacant health centers originally set up as covers for the first fake opium detoxification program in 1937. Local officials were instructed to arrest any of the 1.7 million addicts who refused to report. The program was, in the words of the Manchukuo welfare minister, a thinly disguised "operation to exploit the labor power of opium addicts [*daqu yapian yinzhe laodongli de banfa*]" (*RDQDZY*, vol. 14, 820). Almost two million Chinese addicts were led through the entrance of the sham Manchukuo health centers promoting a healthy "biopolitics," only to be ushered immediately out the back exit (truth in advertising would mark this back exit as "necropolitics") into trucks carrying them off to work camps and graves. Two hundred thousand of the most incapacitated addicts not immediately Lazarus-ized by death threats and beatings were forcefully injected with drugs that Japanese doctors claimed were opium detoxification supplements. Manchukuo Welfare Minister Kaneda, who signed off on the program, confessed later that this was actually a strong amphetamine, designed to make them "feel younger and stronger [*nianli quangzhuang*]" so they could work like the infrahuman robots Furumi had dreamed of turning all Chinese into (820). It's a fitting necropolitical irony that this amphetamine was called by the same name that Japanese elites used publicly to refer to Manchukuo itself: *dongguanji*, or "Light of the East."

These Administrative Affairs tactics are directly linked to the condition of forced laborers from the first and third categories being routinely worked to death. Today one can see the monuments in Northeast China where huge numbers of these workers were buried. Called in Chinese "human dumps" (*wanrenkang*, "holes in the ground filled with ten thousand corpses"), these mass graves are memorials to Japan's necropolitics and lie adjacent to many of Manchukuo's notorious labor camps: the SMR's Fushun coal mines, Ayukawa's Shōwa Steel Works, and the large military installations near the Russian border. However, Japanese leaders operating in and around important military and industrial sites, not wanting to draw the locals' attention, would bury murdered Chinese in smaller holes so as not to leave visibly protruding human dumps.

The Japanese researcher Kubota Hajime has done the only detailed research on these atrocities. Kubota claims that it was "standard practice" for Chinese forced laborers to be massacred after completing work on military establishments (*yōki kensetsu*): "The Japanese military or military police would routinely have a celebration ceremony for the finished structure, and hand out food and alcohol. After the Chinese got drunk, the soldiers would murder them with their rifles" (2004, 76–77; see also Zhonguo Fushun zhanfan guanli suo 2005). The mysterious deaths of six thousand Chinese workers forced to build fortifications in Xinganling in northern Manchuria in 1944 were the culmination of this kind of necropolitical tragedy (*RDQDZY*, vol. 14, 862–64). So that the point I am trying to make here is not collapsed into the kind of liberal humanism that I think Agamben's work has a tendency to fall into, it is crucial to keep in mind that forced Chinese laborers from category one (delinquents), category three (enemy combatants), and category four (tricked forced laborers) perished while profiteers continued to suck surplus out of them; they died while being subsumed deformally to Japanese capitalist conglomerates like Nissan and Nakajima. Moreover, many of the Manchukuoan (*gounei*) Chinese who reluctantly performed their annual forced labor stints worked to death as well. Several of the testimonies we have of Chinese survivors report that 80 percent of those in their work groups died on the job, among them average Manchukuoan farmers fulfilling their annual unpaid work duty (976–83). Based on testimonies from survivors of forced labor from over twenty different sites and statistics compiled by the editors of the Jilin province historical archives, I estimate that, in addition to the millions drugged and starved to death in the colony, no fewer than 2.5 million Chinese forced laborers were worked to death in Manchukuo.

In attempting to answer the question of *why* Chinese workers were treated so brutally, we should revisit the last of the five necropolitical axioms. As I argued at length in part II, neuropolitics naturalized a world in which humans were indistinguishable from disposable commodity things, and the consumption of commodity things was essential and indispensable for the maintenance of the alienated existence of these same de-anthropomorphized subjects in metropolitan capitalism. In other words, already in neuropolitics commodity things are contradictorily both indispensable and disposable. When this situation of subaltern labor, characterized in Ken C. Kawashima's (2009) superb analysis as "indispensably dispensable," is connected to the partial awareness among imperial elites that otherwise disposable Chinese coolies *indis-*

pensably built the entirety of Japan's infrastructure in Northeast China and continued to be indispensable for total war mobilization and capitalist profit, we can understand more fully the simultaneity of disposability with indispensability in necropolitics. When we recall both that Kishi and Furumi, the Manchukuo elites responsible for labor policy, were "modern boys," frequenters of Asakusa, Tokyo, who consumed and disposed of feminized commodity things as their sovereign right as imperial capitalists, and that "the Chinese" had been profiled by Japanese imperialists as an excessive population programmed for the kind of self-annihilation that occurred during the Taiping and Boxer Rebellions, the indispensable-disposable circuit becomes clearer still. Moreover, as Mbembe has argued with respect to the perception of a similar abundance of black labor for white imperialists in South Africa, "because native life was seen as naturally doomed for self-destruction, it constituted wealth that could be lavishly spent" (2004, 381).

The disavowal of the indispensability of Chinese labor for Japan's imperial war and for the continued profiteering of necropolitical capitalists would have occurred routinely when the awareness of the unlimited abundance of China's reserve army of labor—available to Japanese for nearly free consumption and "lavish spending"—went hand-in-hand with the neuropolitical tendency to devalue Chinese labor as disposable consumables. Mbembe's notion of subaltern "superfluity"—meaning both numerically excessive and unnecessary—refers at once to what he calls the "dialectics of indispensability and expendability of both labor and life" and the "obfuscation of any exchange or use value that labor might have" (374–75). For Japanese imperialists, as the depreciation, denuding, and disposing of Chinese labor and life occurred simultaneously with a disavowed awareness of its indispensability for Japan's imperialism, this material and psychic contradiction contained the potential to elicit a kind of enraged delirium for Japanese on the ground, a delirium that fed back into the indispensable-disposable circuit as it redoubled the frequency and intensity of atrocities inflicted on the Chinese subaltern.

The disposing of human bodies like depersonalized garbage, as Mei Niang described the treatment of Chinese sex workers, provides evidence that both before the beginning of the Pacific War and after, Manchukuo's forced labor policies took the harshest toll on the most vulnerable segment of the colonized subaltern. While keeping in mind the indispensable-disposable circuit, when we identify the most intense instances of infrahumanization we are able to network the forced North Chinese workers in Manchukuo into a shared grid of intelligibility with the forced labor of the comfort women/sex slaves. For instance, the large comfort station at Andong, Manchukuo, near the Korean border was used from 1938 on to prepare (through physical and psychological humiliation) newly kidnapped Korean women for forced sex work, who were then dispatched to other sites throughout Japan's empire. In addition to this facility, there were approximately forty other stations in the colony.[2] The Manchukuo state is known to have built the second comfort station outside Fengtian for Guandong army use in April 1932. While we lack documentation, it was most likely the first comfort station to use non-Japanese women, a practice that became standard after the order to forcefully conscript non-Japanese women was sent out by the Army High Command in Tokyo on 3 March 1938, signed by Umezu Utsujirō.[3]

The transformation of coolie labor in biopolitics to Chinese forced labor in necropolitics is paralleled by the transformation of colonized forced sex workers. Feminist scholarship in Japanese refers to the shift from the biopolitical subjectivity of the Japanese sex worker and hysteric in Asia to the necropolitical subjectization of forced sex workers in the so-called comfort system as a shift "from *karayuki-san* to the comfort women." (Morisaki Kazue was the first to deploy this term [1976, 16–17].) In chapter 2, I detailed some of the horrors experienced by Japanese girls kidnapped by pimps like Muraoka Iheiji in western Japan and sold two, three, and four times before settling down in a Japanese-owned brothel in Fengtian, Shanghai, or Singapore. Most of these women were able to eventually close out their contracts and return to Japan or to find work inside Japanese concessions in continental Asia. This situation contrasts sharply with the women forced into sex work and submitted to deformal subsumption. Using methods pioneered by the biopolitical pimps, the Japanese *kempeitai* managed a system of sex trafficking without parallel in the twentieth century. We still don't have an accurate number of the women and girls subjected to this necropolitical operation, although estimates run from 150,000 to more than 400,000 (Su 1999).[4]

As in its biopolitical capitalism, Japan's imperial necropolitics displayed a rigid ethnoracial hierarchy that was strongly gendered. Although male Chinese were worked to death in Manchukuo's factories and labor camps, and poor Korean tenant farmers-turned-soldiers were sent off to die fighting for the Japanese emperor, there was no escape (through death or life) for female forced sex workers. As Nishino Rumiko and others have shown, the comfort women were systematically prevented from suicide; their condition was "absolute," rendered here as without means of escape (Nishino 2007; Jugun ianfu mondai uryoson nettowa-ku 1993). This applied even in the battlefield comfort stations close to front lines, where comfort women would often hear reports of men who had raped them the night before killed in battle the next day. In Burma and New Guinea in 1944, forced sex workers were prevented from committing suicide while the men around them were dying one after another from aerial attacks and sniper fire. There's little doubt that this experience would have been shared by comfort women sent to front-line stations in Manchukuo close to the Russian border in 1939. Yet despite their being watched closely by station owners and military police, some women were successful in taking their own life. Again, we come across the indispensable-disposable dialectical circuit.

It's standard knowledge among critical scholars that Japan's colonialism and imperialist wars were the impetuses for the system of forced sex work (Yoshimi Y. 2007). But the official rationale for the system—to prevent rapes of local women by Japanese solders and to control the spread of STDs to soldiers—must, in my view, be supplemented by acknowledging the extension of the logic of commodification in neuropolitical capitalism to Japanese civilian and military elites. Although I've already suggested some ways the neuropolitics of the mass culture erotic-grotesque (in the form of subscriptions to Umehara Hokumei's necrophilic offerings) invaded the psyches of Japanese military elites in Manchukuo and civilian elites like Kishi and Furumi, in mass culture sexology and in erotic-grotesque modernism alike men were naturalized as "modern primitives" who were instructed by the ideological codes of neuropolitics to treat women as disposable objects of male consumption. But, contradictorily, disposable women were the indispensable commodity bodies whose infrahuman state was the necessary condition for establishing this same heteromasculine primitivism. My reading of several of the modernist sexologists demonstrated how rape and other forms of erotic violence became naturalized in their discourse, producing what might be called, after Gilles Deleuze, an erotic-grotesque "image of thought." When this naturalization was combined with unchallenged authority in the colonial periphery—of Japanese elites over Chinese in Manchukuo; of Japanese and Korean soldiers over Korean, Taiwanese, and Chinese women and girls in the comfort stations; of Japanese soldiers over Chinese civilians remaining inside the Nanjing city walls in December 1937—the result was a monstrous necropolitical regime with few parallels in the twentieth century.

Manchukuo had "only" forty-two comfort stations. Except for the two periods of the failed offensive against the Soviet Union in 1939 and in July 1941, when between three thousand and eight thousand Korean females were forced to do unpaid sex work in Manchukuo (Kim P. 2000, 334), the problem of sexual slavery was in the background compared to places like Hainan Island and Okinawa. As Kim Puja has pointed out, there's plenty of testimony both from victims and colonizers about forced sex work in Manchukuo, but when one looks at the perpetrators' discourse it somehow seems less sharp than in other places. Maybe this was because there were so many male forced laborers in Manchukuo that the forced sex work of women and girls just wasn't as salient as it was elsewhere. Or maybe the reason forced sex work after March 1938 seemed insignificant was that Manchukuo was in a very real sense *one huge comfort station* constructed by the fateful articulation of the lower-class hustlers and traffickers with elite fascists like Amakasu Masahiko and Kishi Nobusuke—overdetermined by necropolitical capitalism. Concomitant with the explosion in commercial opium and heroin establishments in Northeast China's cities following Japan's military and colonial occupation was a dramatic increase in the number of brothels where women and girls were trafficked openly.

Despite Manchukuo's seeming disregard for women sex workers, the indispensable-disposable circuit was present here as well. Similar to the way disposable Chinese forced laborers generated indispensable surpluses for war profiteering conglomerates, profiteering occurred regularly at comfort stations and attracted unscrupulous capitalists. The fact that this expropriation regularly goes unrecognized by scholars proves the recent Marxist feminist point that the value created by sex work and feminized affective labor remains the most hidden (Tadiar 2009; Fortunati 1995). Advised not to compete with local commercial brothels, Japanese, Korean, and Chinese merchants who collaborated with Japan's military in consolidating the comfort system enjoyed steady revenues.

Even though these establishments were expensive to operate and prices were high—one short session with a forced sex worker normally cost between 1.5 and 2 yen (when the monthly salary of a Japanese soldier was between 6 and 10 yen)—many profited handsomely. Similar to the way Kishi designed the system of colonial Taylorism, profits were generated at comfort stations by paying forced sex workers as little as possible, sometimes less than nothing when they ran up debts for the exorbitant prices they were forced to pay for kimono, makeup, and drugs. Moreover, women who mistakenly thought they were saving a little money while undergoing the hellish ordeal of servicing twenty-five or thirty men each day also ended up with nothing when the Japanese military script (*gunpyō*), paid out occasionally as wages, became worthless after the Second World War. As far as the ethnoracial governmentality of necropolitics, Korean, Filipina, Taiwanese, and Chinese forced sex workers were controlled by Japanese or Koreans and their local surrogates. In turn, male Chinese forced laborers in Manchukuo were policed by Japanese and Koreans, with the occasional Chinese added as a translator or corrections officer.

Forced sex workers at comfort stations and the Chinese forced laborers at work camps were similarly determined by the deformal subsumption of necropolitical capitalism. Moreover, both were the recipients of the discursive violence of necropolitics: Japanese elites referred to comfort women as "toilets" (*benjo*), while Chinese forced laborers were designated as "robots" or "logs" (*maruta*). This allowed them to be similarly transformed into what Marx called infrahuman, "instrumentalized means of domination and exploitation" (1977, 799), and what Mbembe calls "commodity bodies" (2005). More than even they could have realized, when necropolitical common sense solicited Japanese elites to call comfort women "toilets," mutely receiving discharges with no effect at all on their composition, or "twenty-nine" (*nijūkyū*), objectifying them by averaging the number of soldiers each comfort woman was ordered to have sex with each day, they were robbing them of what made them sentient beings. Treating them as nonliving receptacles for semen, piss, shit, or the occasional lash with a sword or gun butt, Japanese militarists were reportedly surprised when these "toilets" tried to commit suicide as the only means to protest the necropolitical regime (personal communication, Nakahara Michiko, December 2007). Both as a way to restore the necropolitical hierarchy of death and life they had come to experience as common sense, Japanese leaders—in what was in effect a logical paradox, as nonliving things by definition can't take their own life—outlawed suicide; even these most disposable of commodity bodies were seen to be indispensable for the waging of total, imperialist war. From this point on they would become the fleshly object of the second part of necropolitics' command to, in my reading of Mbembe, "kill and leave living-dead." Neither killed nor allowed to die, the forced sex workers were banished into a necropolitical purgatory more existentially agonizing than violent death. They thus take center stage together with unremunerated, forced Chinese male labor as the central subjectivities of what I call, fusing Marx and Fanon, Japan's empire of the living dead.

In *Wretched of the Earth* Fanon decoded the ways colonial domination invasively snatched the bodies of the colonized, morphing them into "zombies" (later made popular by George Romero's 1968 horror film *Night of the Living Dead*). In *A Dying Colonialism* Fanon analyzed the ways colonialism, like capitalism for Marx, inverts the natural order of the world with respect to what is dead and alive and what is "normal and abnormal" (1965, 81). Necropolitics in Manchukuo *absolutized* these colonial capitalist tendencies. Passing first through the biopolitical production of living subjectivities whose labor was formally subsumed to late merchant capitalism, then moving through the commodification of all living things in neuropolitical capitalism, where human attention and desiring curiosity is submitted to real subsumption and labor is killed off and buried in machines, finally in necropolitical capitalism living labor is brought back from the death it suffered from neuropolitical capitalism and submitted as *living-dead* under deformal subsumption.

Fanon's call for normality in the face of the absolute (understood here as being completely detached or "absolved" from the norm) abnormality of colonialism brings us back to the standard signified of *hentai*, "abnormality." To return to the first erotic-grotesque novel, Umehara Hokumei's *The Killing Kapitalist Konglomerate* (1924), a phrase appears near the end as the writer's friend tries to find a way to describe modern capitalism: "the *hentai* of *hentai*." In biopolitical capitalism that allowed for degrees of reflexive negotiation, or what Tanabe Hajime called "mediated freedom," *hentai* can be translated as a modality of embodied transformation. However, once we arrive at the more complex regime of neuropolitical capitalism, *hentai* must be translated in Luxemburgian terms as "capitalist dispossession." "Dispossession" is the term all those social scientists I discussed in part II were groping for. Akagami Yoshitsuge came the closest to figuring *hentai* as "capitalist dispossession," but just as he published his major critique of erotic-grotesque modernism as the most advanced capitalist form of the expropriation of human attention and desire, the Manchurian Incident happened. If dispossession is the logical result of neuropolitical capitalism's commodification of all life, then "dispossession of dispossession" is what happens in the "Light of the East," Manchukuo. The effect of this was to populate the entirety of Japan's empire with living-dead, the third and final form of life I have tried to map in this book.

The Poverty of (Japanese) Philosophy

To conclude I'd like to return to Tanabe Hajime's imperialistic philosophical schema, which tried to enlist Korean, Taiwanese, and Chinese colonized to identify with the universality of Japan's empire. The dialectical immunology grounding his *Logic of Species* recommended that while all the subjects of Japan's imperialism maintain pathogens from their own ethnic species, their transference upward toward the universal genus occupied by Japan's empire would help guard against the restrictive confinement of their ethnic group. From the perspective of the imperial state, Tanabe's "absolute dialectics" promised to mediate and direct this transcendence of narrow species toward the universal genus for all individual subjects of the empire. However, as he specified in essays written in 1942 and 1943, after the outbreak of the Pacific War the absolute dialectical process involving the negating affirmations of the mother and ethnocultural group culminated in self-conscious "life" through the *death* of the male Japanese subject in imperial war. Tanabe rewrote his philosophical system to affirm Japan's total war: heroic male death halts the process of dialectical absolutism, while it is the only thing that guarantees imperial life, necropolitically.

While the act of self-consciousness that Tanabe styled after Martin Heidegger's *Gevorfenheit* launched individual subjects beyond their species toward the universal, this journey in the direction of the universal Other contained aspects of contingency and unknowability. Until, that is, Japan's total war. By the late 1930s the end result of the subject's dialectical journey was known in advance. In an essay titled "The Logic of Nation-State's Being" (1939) he wrote:

> In the act of self-negativity that offers the self up as a sacrifice for the nation-state, paradoxically, the self is affirmed. At this time, because the nation-state demands that the self be sacrificed for it, it harbors the source for the individual self's life, and therefore, this sacrifice doesn't have the sense of being for some vague Other at all. It is just the opposite of this; it is about restoring the self to its true self (to be found only in the state). (1963, vol. 7, 41)

No longer is the desiring, dynamic subject leaping into the unknown through the negation of its particular ethnoculture. The leap was only ever in the direction of the beck and call of Japan's imperial national command. By 1939 Tanabe had identified this command as calling for the sacrifice of the subject. A few years later he absolutized subjective freedom as that which is necessarily destined to die for Japan's empire.

Tanabe's essay "Life-in-Death" ("Shiyōji") was first presented as a talk to students at Kyoto University on 19 May 1943 and then was published in several places. The body of the essay discusses the problem of death in the history of philosophy and is primarily concerned with rejecting Heidegger's emphasis on the existential angst elicited by the personal and singular nature of death. Against Heidegger, Tanabe wants to "banish all anxiety and fear with respect to the problem of death" (1963, vol. 8, 252–53). Reassuring students who would soon be going off to die, he states, "Death is part of nature and should not be feared" (254). Opposing Heidegger again, he criticizes mere philosophizing about death: "We must face death directly and concretely and make the decision to die [kesshi]."

> [Such a decision is imperative given the] crisis situation facing Japan at this time. . . . Now we can't tolerate any separation between the self and the country. In times like this, when the self and the country become united, God is actualized. The three distinct entities of God, nation and self enter into a mutually constituting relation. When the self sacrifices its body for the nation it fuses immediately with it and actualizes divinity—this can only be the revelation of God [kami no keiji]. (260)

Astonishingly, Tanabe has forgotten his earlier formulations of antagonism, immunological contamination, and dialectics. In the period of total war the Japanese male subject is not immunized *with* different aspects of alterity, as in the earlier schema, but now becomes immune *from* Koreans, Chinese, North Americans, and all others in being ordered to die for the country of God: Japan. Advising Japanese men not to be anxious about this death, Tanabe explains that the cessation of life contradictorily generates a fuller life in necrological fusion with the imperial nation and God. Although he began turning his philosophy of dialectical absolutism from 1935 into a method to subjectivize all of Japan's imperial subjects, here only Japanese men are allowed sacrificial union with God. Tanabe's dialectical process has, to cite yet another etymological program of *absolute*, only "one solution," which is now to willingly commit suicide for Japan. This philosophical necropolitics could be said to "make sacrifices of" or kill Japanese men and "leave everyone else undead," as Mbembe, following Fanon, said of of necropolitics: "Its sovereignty subjects vast populations of the colonized . . . to the status of *living dead*" (2003, 40). With full life reserved solely for Japanese men killed in imperialist war, all other forms of life are relegated to the deontological condition of living-dead. Japanese subjects in the homeland ultimately become living-dead like the Chinese and Korean subaltern when, as Aimé Césaire uncovered the precedent for Nazism in Europe's colonial periphery, the modus operandi of colonial fascism in Manchukuo centripetally invades Japan's homeland (1955, 12).

All this is not to deny that the imperialists' necropolitical tactics in the war weren't also crimes against humanity. It is to argue that, saturated by the deformal subsumption of Manchukuo's necropolitics, capitalism itself must be seen as a crime against humanity. The criminal aggression that capital must always direct against workers in order for it to survive is unleashed with a delirious intensity in its necropolitical phase. The Smithian invisible hand guiding workers into a free market biopolitical capitalism becomes what several Chinese forced laborers in Manchukuo described as the "devil's claw [*mozhang*]" of necropolitics (*RDQDZY*, vol. 14, 980–81). Like the vampires of the erotic-grotesque media, this devil's claw extended day in and day out, not to ensnare "bare life" as identified in Agamben's humanistic philosophy, but what we might call, after Marx, Fanon, and the erotic-grotesque theorists introduced in this book, "bare labor"—disposable and nonsacrificial labor that served as the indispensable producer of surplus for insatiable capitalists. In his problematic modernizing mode, Marx prophesied that on some promised day in the future, capitalism would produce its own gravediggers. In its necropolitical mode in late Japanese imperialism, however, what capitalism did was generate living-dead zombies, many of whom ended up in mass graves, what were called by Chinese in Manchukuo "holes in the ground filled with ten thousand bodies."

NOTES

Introduction

1. In defending the peaceful, domesticated "cat" of Holland, the historian Peter de la Court has portrayed the military imperialist powers of France and England as "wild beasts" (cited in Arrighi 2007, 239).
2. I've drawn on Roberto Esposito's (2008) reading of immunization. Curiously, Esposito doesn't mention that Foucault explicitly linked immunization to security in biopolitics in *Security, Territory, Population* (2007).

1. Cool(ie) Japan

1. There are no reliable statistics on the percentage of emigrants from Shandong and Hebei remaining in Manchuria until 1923. In an important essay the SMR researcher Amano Motonosuke (1932, 33) divided immigrants into those returning in the same year they originally entered, and those staying beyond the first year. In 1923 only 30 percent of the 350,000 immigrants remained in Manchuria; however, in 1927 and 1928 over 60 percent of the more than one million immigrants in each of those years remained. Later years reflected the earlier pattern of 30 to 40 percent.
2. The only full-length study of the *batou* system, Nakamura Takatoshi's *Batou seidō no kenkyū*, published in 1944, seems concerned with depicting the innate corruption of all the Chinese actors in this drama except for the hapless coolies. The book is a thinly veiled justification for the Japanese occupation of China, in which Nakamura denigrates the batou system as "feudalistic."
3. Later SMR studies consistently contrasted the rational, forward-thinking behavior of Japanese industrial capitalists with the miserly, conservative attitudes of the Chinese merchants in Manchuria. See, for example, Hori 1942, 228–42.
4. The colonial Bank of Korea cited Chinese Maritime Customs figures in placing Dalian second after Shanghai in volume of trade in 1917 (Bank of Chōsen 1921, 78–109).
5. *Mantetsu chōsa geppo*, February 1941, 205–14. This is based on figures from the late 1930s, as no comparable figures exist prior to 1920.

6. The classic source on this is Franklin Ho's *Population Movement to the North Eastern Frontier in China* (1931). For the SMR's own studies, see Minami Man-shū Tetsudō Kabushiki Gaisha 1933: *Chūgokujin rōdōsha no chingin*.

2. Peripheral Pimps

1. All the documents in the Foreign Ministry Archive (Gaikō shiryōkan, here-after FMA) that were created prior to the Second World War are categorized by a general theme. The themes for the documents I focus on in this chap-ter are "Matters Relating to the Control of Japanese Conducting Improper Business" ("Honpojin fuseigyōsha torishimari kankei zakken") and "Collec-tions of Legal Problems Related to Japanese Conducting Improper Business" ("Honpojin fuseigyōsha torishimari kankei houki zasan"), hereafter "Collec-tions of Improper Business." There are seven large volumes of correspon-dence under the first theme, numbered 4.2.2.27, and two under the second, numbered 4.2.2.34.

2. The Paris Accords of 1909 banning human trafficking was signed by all the imperial powers, with the sole exception of Japan. After heated internal de-bate the Japanese government agreed to join the International Convention for the Suppression of the Traffic in Women and Children in 1925. Unfortu-nately, it refused to apply these laws to its colonies and mandates in Asia.

3. Nakahara Michiko pointed this out in personal correspondence in June 2003.

4. *Muraoka Iheiji jiden* was published in 1960 by a professor at St. Paul's Univer-sity in Tokyo named Kawai Yuzuru. In 1934 Kawai obtained his first teaching position at the Japanese Commercial College in Taipei, Taiwan. On a visit to the Philippines in 1936 he met Muraoka and became interested in his life story. Muraoka gave Kawai all his notebooks to edit and then in 1937 went to Japan's colonial capital in Taiwan for one month to work through some dis-crepancies in the notebooks. The notebooks then went through further edit-ing by Kawai before they were published in 1960.

There has been considerable debate among Japanese scholars about the veracity of Muraoka's account. The feminist scholar Yamazaki Tomoko claims in the preface to her important book *Sandakan Hachiban Shōkan* (Sandakan Brothel No. 8, 1999) that she finds very little truth in Muraoka's claims. Yamazaki argues that Muraoka's claims are dubious because none of the women she interviewed had heard of him. She also questions his reputa-tion as having been the preeminent Japanese pimp in Asia, arguing that the few scholarly pieces done on Japanese brothel keepers in Asia in the early twentieth century make no mention of him. However, Muraoka always used pseudonyms and expressly forbade his underlings from using his real name. It's very unlikely that any of the elderly Japanese sex workers that Yamazaki interviewed in the 1960s would have known his real name. Furthermore, some of the most respected scholars working on the history of Japanese–Southeast Asian relations find most, if not all, of Muraoka's claims legitimate. Mori Katsumi did ethnographic work in the areas around Nagasaki and Amakusa, where Muraoka claims his henchmen did most of their kidnapping, and finds that many thousands of women did disappear during this time; see his *Jinshin Baibai: Kaigai Dekasegi Onna* (1959). The historian of Southeast Asia and Waseda University professor Nakahara Michiko told me personally that she thought 75 percent of what Muraoka claims to be factual in his *Autobiography* is verifiable history.

5. The FMA record number for this is 3.8.5.5. Japanese women accompanied by white men came solely from the brothel district in Nagasaki called Maruyama-chō.

6. Kawai Yuzuru states in his detailed addendum to the *Autobiography* that Muraoka admitted to having sexual relations with all thirteen of "his women" in Shanghai at this time (Muraoka 1960, postscript 5).

7. Muraoka was officially listed with the Japanese consulate in Xiamen as the owner and operator of a barbershop, but it was widely known that most of these businesses in the treaty port cities were fronts for drug and human trafficking.

8. See Neferti Tadiar's brilliant reading of this passage in Marx in her *Things Fall Away* (2009), chapter 1.

9. Warren writes that in both Hong Kong and Singapore "sanctions had been given by the British government for the establishment of Japanese brothels, side by side with respectable Japanese businesses, and it proved extremely difficult under such circumstances for the Japanese Imperial government to carry out its intention of ending the traffic in girls for brothel prostitution in both colonies" (1993, 70). Japanese feminist scholars Fujime Yuki (1997) and Yamazaki Tomoko (1995) would strongly disagree with Warren's claim that Japanese officials were trying to terminate the trafficking of Japanese women.

10. The historical background to Japanese women submitting to regular venereal disease checkups began with the *Posadnik* Incident of July 1860 when the Russian warship the *Posadnik* docked in Nagasaki for food and repairs. After the local authorities gave the Russians permission to visit the brothels, the Russian doctor subsequently insisted that all Japanese sex workers submit to his medical examinations, as was de rigeur in Euro-America at the time. The standardization of these invasive examinations in the Japanese treaty ports by the mid-1860s was then transferred to Japanese brothels in continental Asia beginning in the mid-1870s. For more on this, see the fine essays by Susan Burns (1998) and Fujime Yuki (1995).

11. Katō Hisakatsu writes in his *Madorosu yanabanashi* that he heard of many

instances when, in demonstrating their absolute power over the kidnapped women, traffickers would sexually assault, strangle, and then throw overboard defiant women (1931, 62).

3. Empire in Hysterics

1. I have not been able to locate any issues of *Tairiku Fujinkai*; the advertisement for *Tairiku Fujinkai* is on p. v of *Korea Review*.

2. These are in the Gakushuin Special Collections Room. Thanks to Aoki Atsuko for bringing these to my attention.

3. There is very little natural correlation between modern militaries and licensed prostitution; in all modern military regimes men receive coercive, compulsory education in the technologies of aggressive heterosexuality, and nonhetero acts are often punished. The Japanese army consistently recommended frequent heterosexual intercourse for its soldiers. For a more complete discussion of this, see Driscoll 2005.

4. The *Manchuria Daily Newspaper* of 2 October 1919 reports an SMR census for that year of 26,135 men and 22,260 Japanese women living in Dalian, and suggests that Japanese women rather than men were the majority in the city of Harbin. The SMR statistics for northern Manchuria in 1915 report twice as many Japanese women as men. The *Manchuria Daily Newspaper* of 7 September 1920 gives the total Japanese population living in Manchuria in 1919 as 73,440 men and 69,149 women. The historian Kimura Kenji enumerates the official employed Japanese population of Korea in 1910 as 92,751 men and 79,792 women (1989, 12). The yearly figures I charted in Korea from the census published in the main Japanese newspaper in Korea, *Keijō Nippō*, show roughly the same figures until the early 1920s, with the number of women living in the Korean cities increasing slowly. There were large numbers of unregistered female sex workers in the Chinese and Korean cities, and several of the SMR censuses were based on people *in families* (while there was a standard 50 to 60 percent unmarried rate for Japanese women over eighteen in colonial cities until the 1920s), so occasionally these women were not counted in the Korean and Manchurian figures. Taking this into account led some contemporary commentators to the conclusion that the Japanese population in colonial urban areas during the first ten-year period of Korean colonization (1910–20) and Northeast Chinese settlements from the same period showed a slight female majority, doubtless the only time this has occurred in colonial history. The official Japanese census showed a slight male majority.

5. There were fairly regular features in *Keijō Nippō* in 1916–25 called "Japanese Women and Colonialism" (for example, 8 October 1921). In a feature of 21 September 1921 in the *Manchuria Daily Newspaper*, Japanese women were quoted as claiming the capacity to open the huge Manchurian frontier to Japanese development from north China to Mongolia all by themselves.

A two-part series in the same newspaper of 16–17 April 1922 on women and capitalist development states frankly in the first installment, "Women are better capitalists than men in the colonies."

6. See *Korea Review*, January 1916, for exposés about four Japanese women living in Seoul who had multiple lovers, including Koreans, Chinese, and Russians (seventy in one case!). The divorce rate in Dalian for women was three times higher than inside Japan in 1920 according to a *Manchuria Daily Newspaper* feature on 23 May 1921.

7. Recent Marxist-feminist work has identified reproductive and affective labor as fundamentally constitutive of all other types. See Neferti Tadiar's (2009) paradigm-shattering work and Leopoldina Fortunati (1995).

8. See Ishikaku Ryonosuke's work (1927), which features a completely biologistic reading of hysteria that emphasizes the "wandering womb" determinant, and the similar explanations in Nosō Yugi (1930). The sexologist and eugenicist Sawada Junjirō published some ten books between 1916 and 1930 on female biology that featured an essentialist reading of hysteria. If one must, see his *Hentai to hanzai* (1925).

9. This is only one among many inscriptions of the gendered specificity of the "assimilation" of Japanese with other Asians. Here, it's clear that it in no way means "Japanization," as the article mourns the fact that through the process of assimilation women have lost their sense of "Japaneseness."

10. I am drawing heavily on classic feminist psychoanalytic work throughout this chapter, in which hysteria is often read as refusing what is called "Symbolic identification." To my mind the best work on this is Catherine David-Ménard's *Hysteria from Freud to Lacan: Body and Language in Psychoanalysis*, trans. Catherine Porter (Ithaca, N.Y.: Cornell University Press, 1989). Another key text I draw on is Jane Gallop's *The Daughter's Seduction: Feminism and Psychoanalysis* (Ithaca, N.Y.: Cornell University Press, 1982).

11. The essential work on "poisoned women" and their ilk is Christen Marran's excellent *Geisha, Harlot, Strangler, Star* (Minneapolis: University of Minnesota Press, 2005).

12. The face of her Japanese boyfriend Takada is depicted as "really black" (*shin-kuroi*) in *Korea Review*, July 1914, 111.

13. Before Saitō Hikaru's (2002) twenty-page commentary to the reprint of *Modern Sexuality*, we had almost no information on Tanaka. Greg Pflugfelder's authoritative work on homoeroticism in Japan has some interesting things to say on Tanaka's take on the issue (1999).

4. Stubborn Farmers, Grotesqued Korea

1. As the two East India Company look-alikes, the SMR and the ODC were frequently compared, though the ODC always received lower grades. See "Mantetsu to Tōtaku," in *Chōsen oyobi Manshū*, December 1911, 10.

2. Cited in Moskowitz 1974, 96.

3. To counter the false official narrative of a pacified, supine Korea, some Japanese settlers in Korea began to publish pseudonymously their own accounts. One of the most popular of these was *Chōsen e iku no hito ni* (Ugaramon 1914). I learned of this from Helen Lee's terrific PhD thesis (2003).

4. The Korea Land Economic Research Center used the controversial 90 percent figure in *A Study of Land Tenure System in Korea* (Pak 1966). It also claims that Korean tenants had to pay the agreed-on rent "regardless of the success or failure," something the in-house history of the ODC denies. See *Tōyō Takushoku Kabushiki Gaisha* 1939, 40–41. Edwin Gregart's authoritative study of 1994 on landownership in colonial Korea works to displace many of the extreme claims made by the Korean Land Economic Research Center and others. However, he doesn't deal with the fact that Japanese corporations like the ODC tripled their Korean landholdings in less than a decade.

5. Among the several popular introductions to contemporary Korea written for a middle-brow Japanese reading public, Shimizu Kitsurō's *Chōsen jijō niwatori harawata* (1895) stands out as the central text, in Edward Said's phrase, "covering" Korea.

6. John M. Jennings refers to the extensive spread of Japanese drugs in colonial Korea as the "forgotten plague" (1995).

Intertext 1

1. See *Keijō Nippō*, 6 November 1920, and several commentaries in *Korea Digest* from June 1919 to May 1920. See also Park in Choi (1998).

2. See also Butler, "Phantasmatic Identification and the Assumption of Sex," *Bodies That Matter* (1993, 93–120).

3. Scholars are still trying to pin down the content and extent of Korean-Japanese intermarriages (*sōgo kekkon* in Japanese; *naeson kyorhon* in Korean). The official encouragement of intermarriage intensified after the anti-Japanese protests of 1 March 1919 when the son of the Korean King Gojong, Prince Yi Un, married the Japanese Princess Masako in a well-publicized ceremony on 28 April 1920. However, the encouragement did not become law until late January 1921 (*KN*, 2 Feb. 1921). Thereafter, the number of registered mixed-marriages went from 404 in 1925 to 1,038 in 1935 before exploding in 1937. The number of Japanese male to Korean female marriages inside Korea slightly outnumbered the Korean male to Japanese female type from 1925 to 1937, after which the Korean man hitched to a Japanese woman pattern dominates (Ch'oe 2000). My research shows that "unofficial" colonizer-colonized marriage and cohabitation during the 1910–21 period strongly favored the Korean man and Japanese woman pattern as well, which contrasts with the pattern in Euro-American colonialism. A

perusal of the two Japanese colonial monthlies, *Korea and Manchurian* and *Korea Review*, during the 1910s reveals that approximately 80 percent of the inter-ethnic couples shown are Japanese women with Korean men.

5. All That's Solid

1. Umehara and Sakai started *Kamashastra* in September 1927 while living in Shanghai. Umehara had been arrested several times for violating the censorship laws and thought that Shanghai would offer him some room to breathe. He continued the subscription service he started in Tokyo, sending his two thousand or so registered members monthly copies of *Kamashastra* in addition to other translations and works they produced in Shanghai. The so-called *kaiinsei*, or "members-only" distribution system, in Japan was, until 1934, a way for publishers to avoid the censorship laws by registering their business as a scholarly enterprise.

2. I have benefited from Harootunian's fine rendering of this passage (2000, 171).

6. Revolutionary Pornography

1. To the erotic-grotesque collector Jō Ichirō, Umehara was the "uncontested ringleader of erotic-grotesque modernism" (Jō, in Yonezawa 1994, 131).

2. Kanno Satomi argues that the signifier "bizarre" (*ryōki*) became a code for the erotic-grotesque in mass culture discourse from 1930 on, which is why I'm translating Akagami's book this way (2005, 130).

3. Uncannily similar to Adorno's and Horkheimer's essay "Enlightenment as Mass Deception" (1972).

4. Guy Debord wrote in *Society of the Spectacle*, "The alienation of the spectator to the profit of the contemplated object is expressed in the following way: the more he contemplates the less he lives; the more he accepts recognizing himself in the dominant images of need, the less he understands his own existence and his own desires" (1983, 30).

5. Yamaguchi Masao has written one of the only academic treatments of Umehara (1994, 341–78). There's a chapter on Umehara in Akita Masami's *Sei no Ryōki Modan* (1994), and there are several of Umehara's own references to his antiracist work in *Kamashastra* vol. 2, 1927, 2.

6. No fewer than four mass culture magazines published between 1928 and 1933 would include *Decameron* in their titles, including *Sekai Decameron Sokuron*, *Modan Decameron*, *Illustrated Decameron*, and, in Italian, *Decamarone*.

7. Because his focus tended to be on the sex lives of married men and women Tanaka Kōgai stopped printing his sexology journal *Modern Sexuality* in 1925, after only three years.

8. The media historian Saitō Takumi (2002, 57) claims that by 1934 *King* was the

"overwhelming" favorite among Japanese monthly magazines for Tokyoites fifteen to thirty-five years old. *King* began publishing in 1925 but had changed its style several times by the early 1940s, branching out into radio. It became an exuberant cheerleader for Japanese militarism in the early 1930s and frequently featured soldiers and tanks on its cover.

9. Personal correspondence with Jō Ichirō. In addition to Umehara's photojournalistic piece on the three classes of opium dens in Shanghai published in the January 1929 issue of *Grotesque* ("Ahen kō," 19–33), see Sakai's memoir published in 1933, *Kunen yobanashi*, in which he hints several times about smoking the drug as an aphrodisiac.

Intertext 2

1. Please see Alan Tansman's exciting new work on literary and cultural expressions of Japanese fascism (2009), in addition to the collection of interesting essays on fascism edited by him (2009).

2. Akechi Kogorō is to Rampo as Sherlock Holmes is to Conan Doyle and Hercule Poirot is to Agatha Christie.

3. Matsuyama Iwao's *Rampo to Tōkyō* (1984) is satisfied to read Rampo as a materialist guide to urban life in Tokyo. Pioneering work in English by Sari Kawana (2008) and Yoshi Igarashi (2005) takes Rampo's public disavowals of the critical force of his work at face value and not, as I do, as strategies to keep the police off his back.

4. One whole section of this collection of *bidan* is called "Dokudan senkō" (experts at self-authorization), where we find story after story of soldiers disobeying orders, acting arbitrarily, or going off on personal vendetta missions. See sections 1 and 4 of Kyōikusōkanbu (1933). I've benefited from Louise Young's excellent work on *bidan* (1996).

7. The Opiate of the (Chinese) People

1. My main reference materials for Manchukuo are, in Japanese, the Manshūkokushi hensan kankōkai's two-volume *Manshūkokushi* (1971) and Yamamuro Shinichi's *Kimera: Manchūkoku no shōzo* (1993), translated by Joshua Fogel in 2004; in English, Louise Young's *Japan's Total Empire* (1996); and in Chinese, Wang Chengli's *Zhongguo dongbei lunxian shisinianshi gangyao* (1991) and the resourceful fourteen-volume collection put out by the Jilinsheng shehui kexueyuan hebian, *Riben diguo zhuyi qinhua dangan ziliao xuanbian* (1991).

2. In "Japan's Atrocities of Conscripting and Abusing North China Draftees after the Outbreak of the Pacific War," Ju Zhifen (2002) claims that there were 5 million forced laborers sent from North China to Manchukuo from 1935 to 1941, and 4 million more from 1941. The numbers of forced laborers

reported by Manchukuo Welfare Minister Kaneda Sei largely corroborates Ju's numbers; he claimed that Manchukuo press-ganged 1.6 million forced laborers in 1944 and 1.8 million in 1945 (*RDQDZX*, 1991, vol. 14, 820). Furumi Tadayuki testified that between 1 million and 1.5 million were brought forcefully from North China to Manchukuo annually from 1941 (857–62). One of the only important Chinese bureaucrats in the Manchukuo regime, Gu Citing, claims that there were 3 million Chinese laborers forced annually to slave away in Manchukuo until 1941; after which the number levels off to 1.5 million. Gu claims the annual number from the period 1933–36 was 800,000, which would bring the total to just over 25 million Chinese forced laborers for the entire Manchukuo period, which seems impossible (876–77).

3. While the United States has used this "Japanese fanaticism" to justify the only use of nuclear weapons on a population to date, in studying the Japanese army's defense plans it becomes glaringly evident that Japan lacked the materiel to mount any real defense; thus combat training exercises were conducted using knives, sticks, and rocks.

4. The Japanese for this file set is *Shina rōnin kankei zakken.*

5. This can be found in a ten-volume collection entitled *Kyokutō kokusai gunji saiban sokkiroku,* 9524.

6. These are the IPS records kept by the International Military Tribunal of the Far East (1968), edited by Nitta Mitsuo and accessed at the National Diet Library in Tokyo.

7. There is little agreement about the number of opium users and addicts in Manchuria before the Incident. Out of a population of abut thirty million, estimates run as high as three million users, with about 10 percent of those being addicts, which is close to Kaneda's estimate of two hundred thousand Chinese addicts before the Incident (Merrill 1942, 108). Chinese critics were reporting to the League of Nations that they had evidence of ten million Manchukuoan Chinese being regular users by 1937, a number that seems high at first glance. However, in the internal estimates of addicts of Manchukuo's Opium Monopoly of 1935, not known until recently, the Japanese bureaucrats count 905,715 opium addicts (Kuboi 2007, 75). Using an 8–10 to 1 ratio of users to addicts, the internal Manchukuo numbers basically support what the Chinese officials were claiming. There's very little correlation between appearance and reality in what Japanese officials were claiming regarding drug use. Internally, opium addiction was thought to be around 1.6 million by July 1938, while the Manchukuo public figures enumerated 592,354 addicts (Merrill 1942, 109).

8. Frustrated Chinese in Manchukuo and in the second Manchukuo established in East Hebei in November 1935 occasionally resorted to targeted assassination against Japanese human and drug traffickers operating with impunity.

In the most famous instance of this in the capital of the second Manchukuo, Tongzhou, on 29 July 1937, Chinese resisters killed 223 Japanese, almost all of them drug dealers (Shinobu S. 1991).

9. In the fall of 1932 Hoshino directed Chinese officials to place opinion pieces in the major Chinese-language newspapers, such as Fengtian's *Shengjing shibao*, explaining that the rationale of the Opium Monopoly was first and foremost the Manchukuo regime's generous recognition that the "Chinese themselves covet opium," and, in addition to this demand side, many "poor farmer producers" rely on opium to keep their families alive (*RDQDZX*, 1991, vol. 14, 815). Hoshino outlawed all mention of drugs in the Japanese-language press.

10. Stephan Tanaka's (1993) insuperable work on Japan's historical relationship to China is the best single source on this issue.

11. Furumi may have argued that the salary differential for Chinese and Japanese in top administrative positions was already much better than in other Manchukuo agencies. A *kempeitai* based in northeast China during the 1930s, Hayashi Iku, revealed that the monthly salary for the Manchukuo police in the late 1930s was seventy-five yen for Japanese, twenty-five yen for Koreans, and ten yen for Manchukuoan Chinese (1993, 208).

12. For more on Amakasu, see my forthcoming book *Japan's Jihad*.

13. Writing back in the mid-1990s, Kathryn Meyer brilliantly intuited Amakasu's brokering of the marriage between the civilian elite and the hustlers. See Meyer and Parssinen 1998, 190.

14. The possibility of enriching oneself as a provincial Opium Monopoly officer was so well known among Japanese men that even with labor shortages in the first years of Manchukuo, there were over one thousand applicants for each of these positions (IPS Records, "Opium Monopoly in Manchukuo and Its Connection with the Kwantung Army," 196).

15. Jennings claims that the published revenues from 1939 were a mere third of the revenues Manchukuo reported internally to Japan's Foreign Ministry (1997, 138, n. 72). Yamada Gōichi (2002) cites 50 percent for the difference between the figures provided internationally in the *Manchukuo Yearbook* and the figures circulated internally in Japanese to banks and the Foreign Ministry.

8. Japanese Lessons

1. This is similar to the British system in its African colonies, producing what Mahmood Mamdani (1996) calls the "bifurcated state."

2. These talks were published in the Ministry of Commerce and Industry's journal *Sangyō Gōrika*, vol. 4 (January 1932) and vol. 9 (April 1932).

3. Kishi's Manchukuo buddies later testified that he went out to eat, drink, and fornicate *every night*, excessive even for the club kid standards of Japanese elites there (Iwami 1994, 57). When he first went to China he was provided

the standard new house and two live-in maids. From the diaries of other Manchukuo officials, we know that most of the Japanese elites had the maids prepare food regularly, as the elites went out only on weekends (Furukawa 2006). After the first year in his own house Kishi moved into a lavish suite in the Yamato hotel on the same floor as his friends Amakasu and Ayukawa.

4. Most policy for Manchukuo was drawn up in this way, with the Office of Administrative Affairs either drafting something directly or working in tandem with the other ministries. Policy would then be submitted to the State Council for rubber-stamping.

5. Furumi's testimony in China made it clear that the Office of Administrative Affairs continued to take the lead in formulating the policies of forced labor until 1944. See *RDQDZX*, 1991, vol. 14, 857–62.

6. See Marx's denunciations of alchemy in finance capital (1962, 515–20): money appears from money ($M{\rightarrow}M'$), as an "automatic fetish" disconnected from the real economy ($M{\rightarrow}C{\rightarrow}M'$).

7. The *Ayukawa Yoshisuke kankei bunsho* is a huge collection of documents given to the National Diet Library in Tokyo in 2000. The recent monograph by Haruo Iguchi, *Unfinished Business*, makes much of its use of this collection. But *caveat lector*: like most of the collections of correspondences in the Kensei Room, this collection has been cleansed by family members, and it's fair to say that we are given an idealized version of Ayukawa therein. Unfortunately this pruned and prettified version of Ayukawa is reproduced in *Unfinished Business* with little criticism or comment.

8. He makes these claims in an annual business journal's feature called *Tairiku ni yūhi suru*; see his "Greetings from Chairman Ayukawa," 1938, 115–19.

9. The published *Central Review* piece is only half the length of Ayukawa's submitted essay, which I'm drawing from here (*Ayukawa Yoshisuke kankei bunsho* 911.5).

10. Ayukawa is clearly referring to the important Manchukuo bureaucrat Okumura Kiwao's best-selling call for more fascism in Japanese politics in *The Reform of Japanese Politics* (1938).

Conclusion

1. I've benefited from the analysis of *Zhui* by Norman Smith in *The Social History of Alcohol and Drugs* 20 (2005), 66–104.

2. The Women's Active Museum on War and Peace in the Waseda Hoshien in Tokyo has the most complete archive of materials connected to forced sex work. I got the number of forty-two comfort stations in Manchukuo from their wall map of documented comfort stations in Asia. A rare early source in Japanese reports that there were thirty-eight comfort stations in Manchukuo (Mainichi Gurafu 1975).

3. A copy of this order is in Kum Pyondon (2007, 10–12).

4. The standard number at this point is 200,000. For background reading in English, see the Northeast Asian History Foundation's *The Truth of the Japanese Military "Comfort Women"* (2007), Tanaka Yuki (2002), and Yoshimi Yoshiaki (2000). For the best single work on the issue, see Sarah Chunghee Soh's *The Comfort Women* (2008).

BIBLIOGRAPHY

Archival Sites

Japanese Foreign Ministry Archives (*Gaikōshiryōkan*), Tokyo.

National Archives at College Park Maryland.

National Diet Library, Constitution and Politics (*Kensei*) Section, Tokyo.

National Diet Library, Rare Book Room, Tokyo.

University of North Carolina, Chapel Hill.

Works

Abe Hiroyuki. 2005. *Ishiwara Kanji*. Hōsei Bungaku Shuppankyoku.

Abel, Jonathan. 2005. "Pages Crossed: Tracing Literary Casualties in Transwar Japan and the United States." PhD diss., Princeton University.

Adachi Kinnosuke. 1925. *Manchuria: A Survey*. New York: R.M. McBride.

Adorno, Theodor W. and Horkheimer, Max. 1972. "Enlightenment as Mass Deception," in *The Dialectic of Enlightenment*. Trans. John Cumming. New York: Herder and Herder.

Agamben, Giorgio. 1995. *Homo Sacer: Sovereign Power and Bare Life*. Trans. Daniel Heller-Roazen. Palo Alto: Stanford University Press.

———. *State of Exception*. 2005. Trans. Kevin Attel. Chicago: University of Chicago Press.

Akagami Yoshitsuge. 1931. *Ryōki no shakaisō*. Shinchōsha.

Akita Masami. 1994. *Sei no ryōki modan*. Aōkyūsha.

Amano Motonosuke. 1932. "Manshū keizai no hattatsu." *Mantetsu Chōsa Geppō* 12, no. 7: 13–41.

Andō Hikotarō. 1965. *Mantetsu: Nihon teikokushugi to Chūgoku*. Iwanami Shoten.

Aoyagi Tsunatorō. 1923. *Chōsen tōchiron*. Keijō: Chōsen Kenkyūkai.

Arahara Bokusui. 1966. *Dai uyokushi*. Dai Nihon Kokumintō.

Arai Toshio and Fujiwara Akira, eds. 1999. *Shiryaku no shōgen*. Iwanami Shoten.

Aramata Hiroshi et al. 1993. *Minakata Kumagusu*. Kawade Shobō.

Arrighi, Giovanni. 2007. *Adam Smith in Beijing: Lineages of the Twenty-First Century*. London: Verso.

Asada Kyōji. 1968. *Nihon teikokushugi to kyūshokumichi jinushisei*. Ochanomizu Shobō.

Asada Kyōji and Kobayashi Hideo, eds. 1972. *Nihon teikokushugishita no Manshū*. Ochanomizu Shobō.

Asahi Shinbun Yamagata Shikyoku, ed. 1991. *Kikigaki, aru kenpei no kiroku*. Asahi Bunko.

Ayukawa Yoshisuke. 1938. "Greetings from Chairman Ayukawa" in *Tairiku ni yūhi suru*.

———. 1937. *"Nissan" no Manshū ichū*. Nihon Keizai Panfuretto.

Bank of Chōsen. 1921. *The Economic History of Manchuria*. Keijō: Chōsen Sōto-kufu.

Beller, Jonathan. 2006. *The Cinematic Mode of Production: Towards A Political Economy of the Society of the Spectacle*. Hanover, N.H.: University Press of New England.

Benjamin, Walter. 1968. *Illuminations: Essays and Reflections*. New York: Schocken.

———. 1973. *Charles Baudelaire: A Lyric Poet in the Era of High Capitalism*. London: New Left Books.

———. 2000. *One Way Street and Other Writings*. London: Verso.

———. 2008. *The Work of Art in the Age of its Technological Reproducibility*. Cambridge, Mass.: Harvard University Press.

Bōeicho bōei kenkyūjo senshishutsu. 1967. *Kokudo kessen junbi*. Asagumo Shinbunsha.

———. 1971. *Rikugun gunju dōin 1: Keikakuhen*. Asagumo Shinbunsha.

Bowlby, Rachel. 1985. *Just Looking: Consumer Culture in Dreiser, Gissing and Zola*. New York: Routledge.

Braverman, Harry. 1974. *Labor and Monopoly Capital*. New York: Monthly Review Press.

Brook, Timothy, and Bob Wakabayashi, eds. 2000. *Opium Regimes: China, Britain and Japan, 1839–1952*. Berkeley: University of California Press.

Brooks, Barbara. 2005. "Reading the Japanese Colonial Archive." *Gendering Modern Japanese History*, ed. Barbara Maloney and Kathleen Uno. Cambridge, Mass.: Harvard University Press.

Brown, Wendy. 1995. *States of Injury: Power and Freedom in Late Modernity*. Princeton: Princeton University Press.

Burns, Susan. 1998. "Bodies and Borders: Syphilis, Prostitution, and the Nation in Japan, 1860–1890." *U.S.-Japan Women's Journal, English Supplement* no. 15. Palo Alto, California: U.S.-Japan Women's Center.

Butler, Judith. 1993. *Bodies that Matter: On the Discursive Limits of "Sex."* New York: Routledge.

———. 2004. *Precarious Life: The Powers of Mourning and Violence*. London: Verso.

Césaire, Aimé. 1955. *Discours sur le colonialisme*. Paris: Présence Africaine.

Cheng, Anne Anlin. 2001. *The Melancholy of Race: Psychoanalysis, Assimilation, and Hidden Grief*. New York: Oxford University Press.

Chinese Emigration: Report of the Cuba Commission Sent by China to Ascertain the Condition of Chinese Coolies in Cuba 1874. Shanghai: Imperial Maritime Custom Press.

Ch'oe Sok-yong. 2000. "Singminji sigi 'naeson kyorhon' changrye munje." *Ilbonhak Nyonbo* 9, no. 9: 259–94.

Choi Chungmoo, ed. 1997. *The Comfort Women: Colonialism, War, and Sex. Position: East Asia Cultures Critique* 5, no. 1.

———. ed. 1998. *Dangerous Women: Gender and Korean Nationalism*. New York: Routledge.

Chōsen Chōsatsugun Shireibu, ed. 1913. *Chōsen bōto tōbatsushi*. Keijō.

Chōsen Sotokufu. 1935. *Chōsen no shuzoku*. 12th ed. Keijō: Chōsen Sotokufu Hensan.

Christy, Alan. 2010. *Ethnographies of the Self: Japanese Native Ethnology, 1910–1945*. Berkeley: University of California Press.

Chung Young-Iob. 2006. *Korea under Siege, 1876–1945*. New York: Oxford University Press.

Cumings, Bruce. 1981. *The Origins of the Korean War: Liberation and the Emergence of Separate Regimes, 1945–1947*. Princeton: Princeton University Press.

Daba Hiroshi. 2007. *Gotō Shinpei o meguru: kenryoku kōzō no kenkyū*. Nansosha.

Debord, Guy. 1983. *Society of the Spectacle*. Detroit: Black and Red Press.

de Grazia, Victoria and Ellen Furlough. 1996. *The Sex of Things: Gender and Consumption in Historical Perspective*. Berkeley: University of California Press.

Deleuze, Gilles and Felix Guattari. 1983. *Anti-Oedipus: Capitalism and Schizophrenia*. Trans. Robert Hurley, Mark Seem, and Helen Lane. Minneapolis: University of Minnesota Press.

———. 1987. *A Thousand Plateaus*. Trans. Brian Massumi. Minneapolis: University of Minnesota Press.

Doane, Mary Ann. 1991. *Femmes Fatales*. New York: Routledge.

Driscoll, Mark. 2000. "Erotic Empire, Grotesque Empire." PhD diss., Cornell University.

———. 2005. "Seeds and (Nest) Eggs of Empire." *Gender and Japanese History*, ed. Barbara Malony and Cathleen Uno. Cambridge, Mass.: Harvard University Press.

———. forthcoming. *Japan's Jihad: White Peril and Decolonization in the Greater East Asia War*.

Duara, Prasenjit. 2003. *Sovereignty and Authenticity: Manchukuo and the East Asian Modern*. Lanham: Rowman & Littlefield Publishers.

Duus, Peter. 1995. *The Abacus and the Sword: the Japanese Penetration of Korea, 1895–1910*. Berkeley: University of California Press.

Duus, Peter, Ramon Myers, and Mark Peattie. 1989. *The Japanese Informal Empire in China, 1895–1937*. Princeton: Princeton University Press.

Eda Kenji, Matsumura Takao, and Xie Xueshi, eds. 2002. *Mantetsu rōdōshi no kenkyū*. Nihon Keizai Hyōronsha.

Eguchi, Keiichi. 1988. *Ni-Chū ahen sensō*. Iwanami Shoten.

Esposito, Roberto. 2008. *Bios: Biopolitics and Philosophy*. Trans. Timothy Campbell. Minneapolis: University of Minnesota Press.

Fanon, Franz. 1965. *A Dying Colonialism*. Trans. Haakon Chevalier. New York: Grove Press.

———. 1967. *Black Skin, White Masks*. Trans. Charles Lam Markmann. New York: Grove Press.

———. 1968. *The Wretched of the Earth*. Trans. Constance Farrington. New York: Grove Press.

Figal, Gerald. 1999. *Civilization and Monsters: Spirits of Modernity in Meiji Japan*. Durham: Duke University Press.

Fletcher, William Miles. 1989. *The Japanese Business Community and National Trade Policy, 1920–1942*. Chapel Hill: University of North Carolina Press.

Fortunati, Leopoldina. 1995. *Arcane of Reproduction: Housework, Prostitution, Labor and Capital*. Trans. Hilary Creek. Brooklyn: Autonomedia.

Foucault, Michel. 1980. *The History of Sexuality, Vol. 1: An Introduction*. Trans. Robert Hurley. New York: Vintage Books.

———. 1994. "Les mailles du pouvoir." *Dits et Écrits, Vol. 4: 1980–1988*. Ed. Daniel Defert and Francois Ewald. Paris: Gallimard.

———. 1997. "The Punitive Society" in *The Essential Works of Michel Foucault, Vol 1: Ethics*. Ed. Paul Rabinow. New York: New Press.

———. 2003. *Society Must Be Defended*. Trans. David Macey. New York: Picador.

———. 2007. *Security, Territory, Population*. Trans. Graham Burchell. London: Palgrave.

———. 2008. *The Birth of Biopolitics*. Trans. Graham Burchell. London: Palgrave.

Frederick, Sarah. 2006. *Turning Pages: Reading and Writing Women's Magazines in Interwar Japan*. Honolulu: University of Hawai'i Press.

Freud, Sigmund. 1963. *Sexuality and the Psychology of Love*. New York: Macmillan.

Frühstück, Sabine. 2003. *Colonizing Sex: Sexology and Social Control in Modern Japan*. Berkeley: University of California Press.

Fujime Yuki. 1993. "Kindai Nihon no kōsho seidō to baishun undō." *Josei bunka to jendaa kenkyūkai genkō*. Heibonsha.

———. 1995. *Sei no rekishigaku*. Fuji Shuppan.

———. 1997. "The Licensed Prostitution System and Prostitution Abolition Movement in Modern Japan." Trans. Kerry Ross. *Positions: East Asia Cultures Critique* no. 5:135–70.

Fukuzawa Yukichi. 1960. "Datsua-ron." *Fukuzawa Yukichi zenshū*. Vol. 10. Iwanami Shoten.

Furukawa Takahisa. 2006. *Aru eri-to kanryō no Shōwa hishi.* Fuyo Shobō.

Furumi Tadayuki. 1978. *Wasurenu Manshūkoku.* Keizai Yukikisha.

Fuss, Diana. 1995. *Identification Papers.* New York: Routledge.

Gao Yuecai. 2000. *Riben "Manzhou yimin" yanjiu.* Beijing: Renmin Chubansha.

Gendaishi shiryō. 1986. *Ahen mondai.* Misuzu Shobō.

Gill, Insong. 1998. "Stature, Consumption and the Standard of Living in Colonial Korea." *The Biological Standard of Living in Comparative Perspective,* eds. John Komlos and Jorg Baten. Stuttgart: Franz Steiner Verlag.

Gionbō. 1999. *Ahen mitsubai jiken shimatsu.* Reprinted in *Nitancho Ōotozō: ahen kankei shiryō.* Fuji Shuppan.

Gonda Yosonosuke. 1974. *Zenshū.* Bunwa Shobō.

Gotō Masaji. 2002. *Minakata Kumagusu no shisō to undo.* Sekaishisōsha.

Gotō Shinpei. 1889. *Kokka eisei genri.*

———. 1911. *Gotō Shinpei ronshū.* Tokyodō.

———. 1921. *Nihon shokumin seisaku ippan.* Takushoku Shinpōsha.

———. 1944. *Shokumin seisaku ippan/Nihon bōchōron.* Nihon Hyōronsha.

———. 1978. *Kokka eisei genri.* (1889). Sōzō Shuppan.

———. 2004. *Gotō Shinpei to teikoku to jichi,* ed. Kojita Yasunao. Yumani Shobō.

Gottschang, Thomas. 1992. "Incomes in the Chinese Rural Economy, 1885–1935: Comments on the Debate." *Republican China* 18, no. 1: 41–62.

Gottschang, Thomas, and Diana Lary. 2000. *Swallows and Settlers: The Great Migration from North China to Manchuria.* Ann Arbor: University of Michigan Center for Chinese Studies.

Government-General of Chosen. 1935. *Thriving Chosen: A Survey of Twenty-Five Years' Administration.* Foreign Affairs.

Gramsci, Antonio. 1971. *Selections from the Prison Notebooks.* Trans. Quintin Hoare and Geoffrey Nowell. New York: International Publishers.

Gregart, Edwin. 1994. *Landownership under Colonial Rule: Korea's Japanese Experience, 1900–1935.* Honolulu: University of Hawai'i Press.

Gunn, Edward. 1980. *Unwelcome Muse: Chinese Literature in Shanghai and Peking, 1937–1945.* New York: Columbia University Press.

Habuto Eiji. 1919. *Fūzoku seiyokugaku.* Jitsugyō no Nihonsha.

———. *Ippan seiyokugaku.* 1920. Gakugei Shoin.

———. *Seiyoku to jinsei.* 1920. Jitsugyō no Nihonsha.

———. *Hentai seiyoku no kenkyū.* 1921. Gakugei Shoin.

———. *Seiyoku to kindaisichō.* 1921. Jitsugyō no Nihonsha.

Habuto Eiji and Sawada Junjirō. 1915. *Hentai seiyokuron.* Shunyōdō.

Hamashita Takeshi. 1988. "The Tribute Trade System of Modern Asia." *The Memoirs of the Toyo Bunko,* Vol. 46, 7–25.

———. 1989. *Chūgoku kindai keizaishi kenkyū.* Kyūko Shoin.

———. 2003. "Maritime Asia and Treaty Port Networks in the Era of Negotiation." *The Resurgence of East Asia: 500, 150 and 50 Year Perspectives*, Giovanni Arrighi and Mark Selden, ed. London: Routledge.

Hane Mikiso. 1982. *Peasants, Rebels, and Outcastes*: The Underside of Modern Japan. New York: Pantheon.

Hara Akira. 1976. "Manshū ni okeru keizai tōsei seisaku no tenkai." *Nihon keizai seisakushiron*, ed. Andō Yoshio. Tokyo: Daigaku Shuppankai.

Hara Yoshihisa. 1993. *Kishi Nobusuke shōgenroku*. Mainichi Shinbunsha.

———. 2007. *Kishi Nobusuke*. Iwanami Shinsho.

Haraway, Donna. 1991. *Simians, Cyborgs, and Women: The Reinvention of Nature*. New York: Chapman and Hall.

Harootunian, Harry. 2000. *Overcome by Modernity: History, Culture, and Community in Interwar Japan*. Princeton: Princeton University Press.

Haruna Mikio. 2000. *Himitsu no fairu*. Kyōdō Tsūshinsha.

Harvey, David. 2003. *The New Imperialism*. Oxford: Oxford University Press.

Hasegawa Tsuyoshi, ed. 2007. *The End of the Pacific War: Reappraisals*. Stanford, Calif.: Stanford University Press.

Hayase Yukiko. 1974. "The Career of Gotō Shinpei: Japan's Statesman of Research." PhD diss., Florida State University.

Hayashi Iku. 1993. *Shinpen: taiga nagareyuku*. Chikuma Shobō.

He Tianyi, ed. 1995. *Rijun qiang ci xia di Zhongguo lao gong ziliao ji yan jiu cong shu*. Beijing: Xinhua Chubanshe.

Hevia, James L. 2003. *English Lessons: The Pedagogy of Imperialism in Nineteenth-Century China*. Durham, N.C.: Duke University Press.

Hirakawa Hitoshi and Shimizu Hiroshi. 1999. *Japan and Singapore in the World Economy: Japan's Economic Advance into Singapore 1870–1965*. London: Routledge.

Hirano Kenichirō. 1983. "The Japanese in Manchuria, 1906–1931." PhD diss., Harvard University.

Ho, Franklin. 1931. *Population Movement to the North Eastern Frontier in China*. Shanghai: China Institute of Pacific Relations,

Hori, Tsuneo. 1942. *Manshūkoku keizai no kenkyū*. Nihon Hyōronsha.

Hotta Eri. 2007. *Pan-Asianism and Japan's War, 1931–1945*. London: Palgrave Macmillan.

Ichioka Yoji. 1977. "Ameyuki-san: Japanese Prostitutes in Nineteenth Century America." *Amerasia* 4, no. 1: 1–21.

Igarashi Yoshikuni. 2005. "Edogawa Rampo and the Excess of Vision: An Ocular Critique of Modernity in 1920s Japan." *Positions: East Asia Cultures Critique* 13, no. 2: 299–327.

Iguchi Haruo. 2003. *Unfinished Business: Ayukawa Yoshisuke and U.S.-Japan relations, 1937–1953*. Cambridge, Mass.: Harvard University Press.

Ikeda Hiroshi. 1997. *Kaigai shinshutsu bungaku*. Inpacuto Shuppan.

Ikegami Eiko. 1995. *The Taming of the Samurai*. Cambridge, Mass.: Harvard University Press.

Irick, Robert L. 1982. *Qing Policy toward the Coolie Trade, 1847–1878*. Taipei: Chinese Materials Center.

Iriye Akira. 1980. *The Chinese and the Japanese: Essays in Political and Cultural Interactions*. Princeton: Princeton University Press.

Irokawa Daikichi. 1985. *The Culture of the Meiji Period*. Trans. Marius Jansen. Princeton: Princeton University Press.

Ishikaku Ryonosuke. 1927. *Hentaiteki josei to hanzai*. Onko Shoten.

Iwami Takao. 1994. *Shōwa no yōkai: Kishi Nobusuke*. Asahi Sonrama.

Iwanami Koza, ed. 1992a. *Bōchō suru teikoku no jinryū*. Vol. 5 of *Kindai Nihon to shokuminchi*. Iwanami Shoten.

———. 1992b. *Bunka no naka no shokuminchi*. Vol. 7 of *Kindai Nihon to shokuminchi*. Iwanami Shoten.

———. 1992c. *Shokuminchika to sangyoka*. Vol. 3 of *Kindai Nihon to shokuminchi*. Iwanami Shoten.

Jansen, Marius. 1962. "On Studying the Modernization of Japan." *Studies on Modernization of Japan by Western Scholars*. Tokyo: International Christian University.

Jansen, Marius, ed. 1965. *Changing Japanese Attitudes toward Modernization*. Princeton: Princeton University Press.

Jennings, John M. 1995. "The Forgotten Plague: Opium and Narcotics in Korea under Japanese Rule, 1910–1945." *Modern Asian Studies* 29, vol. 4: 795–815.

———. 1997. *Opium Empire: Japanese Imperialism and Drug Trafficking in Asia, 1895–1945*. London: Praeger.

Jilinsheng shehui kexueyuan hebian. 1991. *Riben diguo zhuyi qinhua dangan ziliao xuanbian*. 14 vols. Beijing: Zhonghua Shuju Chuban.

Jō Ichirō. 1993. *Sei no Hakkinbon*. Kawade Bunko.

Jones, F. G. 1949. *Manchuria since 1931*. New York: Oxford University Press.

Jugun ianfu mondai uryoson nettowa-ku. 1993. *Shōgen: kyōsei renkōsareta Chōsenjin juguniafutachi*. Akaishi Shoten.

Ju Zhifen. 2002. "Japan's Atrocities of Conscripting and Abusing North China Draftees after the Outbreak of the Pacific War." Online at www.fas.harvard.edu.

———. 2005. "Northern Chinese Laborers and Manchukuo." *Asian Labor in the Wartime Japanese Empire: Unknown Histories*, ed. Paul Kratoska. London: M. E. Sharpe.

———. 2007. "Labor Conscription in North China: 1941–1945." *China at War: Regions of China, 1937–1945*, eds. Diana Lary and Ezra Vogel. Palo Alto, Calif.: Stanford University Press.

Ka Chih-ming. 1995. *Japanese Colonialism in Taiwan: Land Tenure, Development and Dependency, 1894–1945*. Boulder: Westview.

Kaneko Fumio. 1987. "Shihon yushutsu to shokuminchi." *Nihon teikokushugi*, ed. Ōishi Kaichirō. Tōkyō Daigaku Shuppankai.

———. 1995. "Shokuminchi tōshi to kōgyōka." *Shokuminchika to Sangyōka*, vol. 3 of *Kindai Nihon to Shokuminchi*. Iwanami Shoten.

Kang Chae-on. 1970. *Chōsen kindaishi kenkyū*. Nihon Hyōronsha.

Kang Chae-on and Iinuma Jiro, eds. 1982. *Shokuminchiki Chōsen no shakai to teikō*. Miraisha.

Kang Pyong-tae. 1977. *Chōsen shakai no kōzō to Nihon teikokushugi*. Ryūkei Shosha.

Kanno Satomi. 2005. *'Hentai' no jidai*. Kōdansha.

Kantō totokufu Minseibu. 1906. *Manshū sangyō chōsa*. 8 vols. Kokkōsha.

Kata, Kōji. 1985. *Shōwa jikenshi*. Iseisha.

Katō Hisakatsu. 1931. *Madorosu yabanashi*. Shokōdō Shobō.

———. 1924. *Sendō no nikka kara*. Shokōdō Shobō.

Katō Yōko. 2007. *Manshū jihen kara Nichū sensō e*. Iwanami Shinsho.

Kawakatsu Heita, ed. 1994. *Japanese Industrialization and the Asian Economy*. London: Routledge.

Kawana Sari. 2003. "Undercover Agents of Modernity: Sleuthing City, Colony, and Body in Japanese Detective Fiction." PhD diss., University of Pennsylvania.

———. 2008. *Murder Most Modern: Detective Fiction and Japanese Culture*. Minneapolis: University of Minnesota Press.

Kawashima, Ken. 2009. *The Proletarian Gamble: Korean Workers in Interwar Japan*. Durham: Duke University Press.

Kenchiku Gakkai Shinkyō Shibu, ed. 1940. *Manshū kenchiku gaisetsu*. Changchun: Manshū jijō annaisho.

Kenpeitai Shireibu. 1987. *Manshū jihen ni okeru kempeitai no kōdō ni kansuru shiryō*. Fuji Shuppan.

Khanna, Ranji. 2006. "Disposability." Lecture at the Franklin Humanities Center, Duke University, 11 October.

Kikakuin. 1939. *Kakyō*. Shōzanbo.

Kim Chōng-myōng. 1967. *Chōsen dokuritsu undo*. 6 vols. Hara Shobō.

———. 1979. *An chung-an to Nikkan kanseishi*. Hara Shobō.

Kim Hankyo, ed. 1983. *Studies on Korea: A Scholar's Guide*. Honolulu: University of Hawai'i Press.

Kim Hyun-kil. 1971. "Land Use Policy in Korea." PhD diss., University of Washington.

Kimijima Kazuhiko. 1973. "Tōyō Takushoku Kabushiki Kaisha no setsuritsu katei." *Rekishi Hyōron*, 282, November, 73–98.

Kim Ilmun. 1984. *Tenno to Chōsenjin to sōtokufu*. Tahata Shoten.

Kim Ilmyon. 1997. *Yūjo/Karayuki/Ianfu no keifu*. Onyamazai Shuppan.

Kim Puja. 2000. "Kantōgun ni yoru 'ianfu' dōin ni kansuru tegami." *Ianfu: senji seiboryoku no jitai*, vol. 3, ed. Violence Against Women in War Network. Ryokufu Shuppan.

Kimura Kenji. 1989. *Zaichō Nihonjin shakaishi*. Miraisha.

Kim Yong-sop. "The Landlord System and the Agricultural Economy during the Japanese Occupation Period." *Landlords, Peasants, and Intellectuals in Modern Korea*, ed. Pang Kie-chung and Michael D. Shin. Ithaca, N. Y.: Cornell East Asia Program.

Kinmonth, Earl H. 1981. *The Self-made Man in Meiji Japanese Thought*. Berkeley: University of California Press.

Kishi Nobusuke. 1932. "Sangyō gōrika undo ni arawaretaru keiken kōkan." in *Kōgyō keizai kenkyū*, July.

Kita Ikki. 1971. *Nihon kaizō hōan*. Masu Shobō.

Kitazaki Fukutarō. 1938. *Tōtaku sanjūnen no sokuseki*. Toho Tsūshinsha Shuppanbu.

Kobayashi Hideo. 1995a. *Chōkanryō*. Tokuma Shoten.

———. 1995b. "*Nihon kabushiki gaisha*" *o tsukutta otoko*. Shōgakukan.

———. 2004. *Teikoku Nihon to sōryokusen taisei*. Yoshikawa.

———. 2005a. *Manshū to Jiminto*. Shinchosha.

———. 2005b. *Mantetsu Chōsabu*. Heibonsha.

———. 2006. *Shōwa o tsukutta otoko*. Bijinesusha.

———. 2007a. "Jūgonen sensō." Lecture series at Tokyo Asahi Cultural Center, fall.

———. 2007b. "Kishi Nobusuke, dareka?" *Gendai Shisō* 35, no. 1.

Kōketsu Atsushi. 2005. "Senji kanryōron." *Sensō no seijigaku*, ed. Kurasawa Aiko and Narita Ryūichi. Iwanami Shoten.

Kong Jingwei. 1986. *Dongbei jingjishi*. Chengdu: Sichuan Renmin Chubanshe.

Kon Wajirō. 1929a. "Gendai no fūzoku." *Nihon fūzokushi* ed. Nakamura Kōya. Yūsankaku.

———. 1929b. *Shinpen DaiTōkyō annai*. Chūō Kōronsha.

———. 1973. "Kōgengaku to wa nanika." *Kon Wajirō shū*, ed. Kawazoe Noboru, Vol. 1. Domus Shuppan.

Kon Wajirō and Yoshida Kenichi. 1930. *Moderunoroji-*. Shunyōdō.

Kratoska, Paul, ed. 2005. *Asian Labor in the Wartime Japanese Empire: Unknown Histories*. Armonk, N.Y.: Sharpe.

Kuboi Norio. 2007. *Shien, dokuen "Daitoa" genei*. Tsuge Shobō.

Kubota Hajime. 2004. "Senjō no shinjitsu." *Tzūkiren*, no. 30 (fall).

Kum Pyondon. 2007. *Kokuhatsu: Jugun ianfu*. Dōjidaisha.

Kurahashi Masanao. 2005. *Nihon no ahen senryaku*. Kyōei Shobō.

———. 2008. *Ahen Teikoku, Nihon*. Kyōei Shobō.

Kurose Yūji. 2003. *Tōyō takushoku kaisha*. Nihon Keizai Hyōronsha.

Kyōikusōkanbu. 1933. *Manshū jihen chūyū bidan*. Kyōikusōkanbu Shuppan.

Lacan, Jacques. 1966. *Écrits*. Paris: Éditions du Seuil.

Laplanche, Jean, and J. B. Pontalis. 1986. "Fantasy and the Origins of Sexuality." *Formations of Fantasy*, ed. Victor Burgin and Cora Kaplan. London: Methuen.

Lary, Diana, and Stephen MacKinnon, eds. 2007. *China at War: Regions of China, 1937–1945*. Stanford: Stanford University Press.

Lee, Helen Jeesung. 2003. "Popular Media and the Racialization of Koreans under Occupation." PhD diss., University of Irvine.

Lee Chong-sik. 1965. *The Politics of Korean Nationalism*. Berkeley: University of California Press.

Lee Ki-baik. 1984. *A New History of Korea*. Seoul: Ilchokak Publishers.

Li Keyi. 1984. *Chuncao mushen: Changpiao xiaoshou "Beike" "Miansha" he ji*, ed. Gao Wen. Shenyang: Chunfeng wenyi chubanshe.

Lippet, Seiji M. 2002. *Topographies of Japanese Modernism*. New York: Columbia University Press.

Liu Mingshiu. 1983. *Taiwan tōchi to ahen mondai*. Yamakawa.

Lone, Stewart. 2000. *Army, Empire and Politics in Meiji Japan*. New York: St. Martin's Press.

Luxemburg, Rosa. 1968. *The Accumulation of Capital*. Trans. Agnes Schwarzschild. New York: Modern Readers Paperback.

Lu Yu. 1987. *Qingdai he minguo Shandong yimin dongbei shilue*. Shanghai: Shanghai Shehui Kexueyuan Chubanshe.

Mackie, Vera. 2000. "Modern Selves and Modern Spaces." *Being Modern in Japan: Culture and Society from the 1910s to the 1930s*, ed. Elise K. Tipton and John Clark. Honolulu: University of Hawai'i Press.

Mainichi Gurafu bessatsu. 1975. *Ichioku nin no Shōwashi*. Mainichi Shinbunsha.

Mainichi Shimbunsha, ed. 1978. *Nihon shokuminchishi: Chōsen*. Mainichi Shinbunsha.

Mamdani, Mahmood. 1996. *Citizen and Subject: Contemporary Africa and the Legacy of Late Colonialism*. Princeton: Princeton University Press.

Manchukuo Ministry of Information. 1940. *Japan-Manchukou Yearbook: 1940*. Manchukuo Yearbook Company.

ManMon sangyō kenkyūkai. 1920. *Manshū sangyōkai yori mitaru Shina no ku-ri-*. Dalian: Manshū Keizai Jihōsha.

Manshūkokushi hensan kankōkai. 1971. *Manshūkokushi*. 2 vols. Manmō Dōhō Engokai.

Manzhou yiminshi yanjiu hui. 1991. *Riben diguozhuyi zai Zhongguo dongbei de yimin*. Harbin: Heilongjiang Renmin Chubanhui.

Marx, Karl. 1962. *Capital, Volume 3*. Moscow: Foreign Languages Publishing House.

———. 1963. *The 18th Brumaire of Louis Bonaparte*. New York: International Publishers.

———. 1972. *Theories of Surplus Value*. New York: International Publishers.

———. 1973. *Grundrisse*. Trans. with a foreword by Martin Nicolaus. London: Penguin.

———. 1977. *Capital, Volume 1*. Trans. by Ben Fowkes. New York: Vintage.

———. 1988. *Economic and Philosophical Manuscripts of 1844*. Trans. Martin Milligan. New York: Prometheus.

Marx, Karl, and Frederick Engels. 1972. *On Colonialism: Articles from the New York Tribune and other Writings*. New York: International Publishers.

Matsui Ryūgo, ed. 1993. *Minakata Kumagusu o shiru jiten*. Kōdansha.

Matsumoto Takenori. 1998. *Shokuminchi kenryoku to Chōsen nōmin*. Shakai Hyōronsha.

Matsusaka Yoshihisa Tak. 2001. *The Making of Japanese Manchuria, 1904–1932*. Cambridge, Mass.: Harvard University East Asia Center.

Matsushita Yoshisaburō, ed. 1926. *Taiwan ahenshi*. Taipei: Taiwan Sōtokufu Senbaikyoku.

Matsuyama Iwao. 1984. *Rampo to Tōkyō*. Chikuma Bunko.

Mbembe, Achille. 2003. "Necropolitics." *Public Culture* 15, no. 1: 11–40.

———. 2004. "Aesthetics of Superfluity." *Public Culture* 16, no. 3: 373–405.

———. 2005. "Superfluity." Lecture at University of North Carolina, Chapel Hill, 2 March.

McCormack, Gavin, and Sugimoto Yoshio. 1988. Introduction to *The Japanese Trajectory: Modernization and Beyond*. New York: Cambridge University Press.

Mei Niang. 1940. *Di'er dai*. Xinjing: Wencong Han Xinghui.

Mei Niang. 1996. *Xie*, ed. Zhang Yumao. *Dongbei xiandai wenxue daxi*, vol. 5. Shenyang: Shenyang Chubanshe.

Merleau-Ponty, Maurice. 1964. *The Primacy of Perception*. Evanston: Northwestern University Press.

Merrill, Frederick. 1942. *Japan and the Opium Menace*. New York: Institute of Pacific Relations.

Meyer, Kathyrn. 2004. "Japan and the World Narcotics Trade." *Consuming Habits*, ed. Jordan Goddman et al. London: Routledge.

Meyer, Kathyrn, and Terry Parssinen. 1998. *Webs of Smoke: Smugglers, Warlords, Spies, and the History of the International Drug Trade*. Boulder: Rowman and Littlefield.

Mihalopoulos, Bill. 1993. "The Making of Prostitutes: The *Karayuki-san*." *Bulletin of Concerned Asian Scholars* 25:41–56.

Miki Kiyoshi. 1967. *Miki Kiyoshi zenshū*. Iwanami Shoten.

Mikuriya Tadashi, ed. 2004. *Gotō Shinpei: Jidai no senkakusha*. Fujihara Shoten.

Mimura, Janice Ann. 2002. "Technocratic Visions of Empire: The Reform Bureaucrats in Wartime Japan." PhD diss., University of California, Berkeley.

Minakata Kumagusu. 1951–52. *Minakata Kumagusu zenshū*. Kangensha.

———. 1985. *Minakata Kumagusu senshū bekkan*. Heibonsha.

————. 1992. *Minakata Kumagusu Korekusyon*. Kawade.

Minami Hiroshi. 1987. *Shōwa Bunka 1925–1945*. Keisō Shobō.

Minami Manshū Tetsudō Kabushiki Gaisha (Keizai Chōsabu), ed. 1919. *Minami Manshū Tetsudō Kabushiki Gaisha jūnenshi*. Dalian.

————. 1933. *Chūgokujin rōdōsha no chingin*. Dalian.

————. 1934. *Manshū no Ku-ri-*. Dalian.

————. 1937. *Gokanen keikaku ritsuan: Vol. 5, book 1: Rōdō bumon kankei shiryō*. Dalian; reprinted, Ryūkei Shosha, 1980.

Miyaoka Kenji. 1968. *Shōfu: Kaigai Ryūrōki*. Hyōronsha.

Mori Katsumi. 1959. *Jinshin baibai: kaigai dekasegi onna*. Shibundo.

Mori Ōgai. 1973. *Mori Ōgai zenshū*. Iwanami Shoten.

Morisaki Kazue. 1976. *Karayukisan*. Heibonsha.

Moriyama, Alan Takeo. 1985. *Imingaisha: Japanese Emigration Companies and Hawaii, 1894–1908*. Honolulu: University of Hawai'i Press.

Moriyama Shigenori. 1992. *Nikkan heigō*. Yoshigawa Kōbunkan.

Moscowitz, Karl. 1974. "The Creation of the Oriental Development Company: Japanese Illusions Meet Korean Reality." *Occasional Papers on Korea 2* (March).

Muraoka Iheiji. 1960. *Muraoka Iheiji jiden*. Nanposha.

Mushakōji Kinhide. 2006. "The Diaspora from Asia and Africa." Lecture presented at the Center for Asia-Pacific Partnership, Tokyo, 16 December.

Mutō Tomio. 1956. *Manshūkoku no dammen*. Kindaisha.

————. 1963. "Manshukoku ni kaketa yume." *Shisō no Kagaku* 21, December.

————. 1989. *Watashi to Manshūkoku*. Bungei Shunjū.

Myers, Ramon. 1982. *The Japanese Economic Development of Manchuria, 1932 to 1945*. New York: Garland.

Myers, Ramon H., and Mark R. Peattie, eds. 1984. *The Japanese Colonial Empire, 1895–1945*. Princeton: Princeton University Press.

Nagahara Yutaka. 1989. *Tennōsei kokka to nōmin: gōi keisei no soshikiron*. Nihon Keizai Hyōronsha.

Nagamine Shigetoshi. 1997. *Zasshi to dokusha no kindai*. Nihon Edita- Sukūru Shuppanbu.

Nakajima Kawatarō, ed. 1994. *Nihon suiri shōsetsushi*, vol. 2. Tokyo Sōgensha.

Nakamura Kokyo. 1921. *Saiminjutsu Kōgi*. Nihon Seishingakkai.

————. 1930. *Hentai Shinri to Hanzai*. Bukyōsha.

————. 1932. *Hisuteri- no ryōhō*. Shufu no Tomosha.

————. 1937. *Nijūjinkaku no onna*. Daitō Shuppansha.

Nakamura Takafusa. 1983. *Senji Nihon no kahoku keizai shihai*. Yamakawa Shuppansha.

Nakamura Takatoshi. 1944. *Batou seidō no kenkyū*. Nihon Hyōronsha.

Nakauchi Toshio. 1988. *Jugun bidan to kyōikusho*. Iwanami Shoten.

Nakayama Yuigorō. 1929. *Hentai Shoseigei*. Shumi no Hōritsu Fukyūkai.

Nakazawa Shin'ichi. 1993. *Mori no Barokku*. Sakariba Shobō.

Namikata Shōichi. 2000. *Kindai Nihon no keizai kanryō*. Nihon Keizai Hyōron-sha.

Natsume Sōseki. 2002. *Travels in Manchuria and Korea*. Trans. Inger Brodey and Sammy Tsunematsu. Kent: Global Oriental.

Negri, Antonio. 1991. *Marx Beyond Marx: Lessons on the Grundrisse*. New York: Autonomedia.

———. 2005. *The Politics of Subversion*. London: Polity Press.

Nelson, Diane. 1999. *A Finger in the Wound: Body Politics in Quincentennial Guatemala*. Berkeley: University of California Press.

Nihon Keieishi Kenkyūjo, ed. 1988. *Kōhon: Mitsui Bussan kabushiki gaisha hyakunenshi*. Nihon Keieishi Kenkyūjo.

Nishida Kitarō. 1970. *Fundamental Problems of Philosophy: The World of Action and the Dialectical World*. Trans. with an introduction by David A. Dilworth. Sophia University Press.

Nishino Rumiko. 1992. *Jugun ianfu: moto heishitachi no shōgen*. Akashi Shoten.

———. 2003. *Senjō no Ianfu*. Akashi Shoten.

———. 2007. "Higaisha no shōgen ni miru." Lecture at the Women's Active Museum on War and Peace, Tokyo, 5 October.

Nitta Mitsuo. 1968. *Kyokutō kokusai gunji saiban hōhan sokkiroku*, 10 vols. Omatsudō Shoten.

Noma Jirō. 1930. *Hentaiteki ero no kenkyū*. Kaichōsha.

Northeast Asia History Foundation. 2007. *The Truth of the Japanese Military "Comfort Women."* Seoul: Northeast Asia History Foundation.

Nosō Yugi. 1930. *Josei to Hanzai*. Bukyōsha.

Oda Susumu, ed. 2001. *"Hentai Shinri" to Nakamura Kokyo*. Fuji Shuppan.

Oguma Eiji. 1995. *Tanitsu minzoku shinwa no kigen*. Shinyosha.

Okabe Makio. 1987. "Kaisetsu." *Manshū Jihen ni okeru kenpeitai no kōdō ni kansuru shiryō*. Fuji Shuppan.

Ōta Naoki. 2005. *Manshū rishi: Amakasu Masahiko to Kishi Nobusukega seotta mono*. Kōdansha.

Ōya Sōichi. 1930. *Bungakuteki seijutsuron*. Chūō Kōronsha.

Pak Eun-sik. 1920. *Hanguo duli yundong zhixueshi*. Shanghai: Yuxinshe.

Pak Ki-hyuk. 1966. *A Study of Land Tenure System in Korea*. Seoul: Korea Land Economics Research Center.

Pang Kie-chung and Michael D. Shin, eds. 2005. *Landlords, Peasants and Intellectuals in Modern Korea*. Ithaca, N.Y.: Cornell East Asia Program.

Park Hyun Ok. 2005. *Two Dreams in One Bed: Empire, Social Life, and the Origins of the North Korean Revolution in Manchuria*. Durham, N.C.: Duke University Press.

Pauer, Erich, ed. 1999. *Japan's War Economy*. London: Routledge.

Pernikoff, Alexandre. 1943. *Bushido: The Anatomy of Terror*. New York: Liveright Publishing.

Pflugfelder, Gregory. 1999. *Cartographies of Desire: Male-Male Sexuality in Japanese Discourse, 1600–1950*. Berkeley: University of California Press.

Puar, Jasbir K. 2007. *Terrorist Assemblages: Homonationalism in Queer Times*. Durham, N.C.: Duke University Press.

Rampo Edogawa. 1956. *Japanese Tales of Mystery and Imagination*. Trans. James B. Harris. Rutland, Vt.: Charles E. Tuttle.

———. 1987a. *Kyūketsuki*. Shunyōdō.

———. 1987b. *Panorama tōkidan*. Shunyōdō.

———. 1987c. *Ryōki no hate*. Shunyōdō.

———. 1987d. "Yaneura no sanposha." Shunyōdō.

———. 1994. "Tantei shōsetsu to katarushisu." *Edogawa Rampo zuihitsusen*, ed. Kida Junichirō. Chikuma Shobō.

———. 1997. *Mōjū*. Shunyō Bunko.

Read, Jason. 2003. *The Micropolitics of Capital*. New York: State University of New York Press.

Saitō Hikaru. 1997. "Habuto Eiji no kingu obu kingusu." *Kyōto Seika Daigaku Kenkyū kiyō*, no. 12, 209–219.

———. 2002. "Gakujutsuteki to kairanteki no aida: *Hentai Seiyoku* to Nakamura Kokyo." *Kaisetsu* to the reprint of *Hentai Seiyoku*. Fuji Shuppan.

Saitō Minako. 2000. *Modan Ga-ruron*. Magajinhausu.

Saitō Takumi. 2002. *"King" no Jidai*. Iwanami Shoten.

Sakai Kiyoshi. 1929. *Rabu hiruta-*. Bungei Shijōsha.

———. 1930. *Ukiyo on Pare-do*. Sentōsha.

———. 1931. *Kōrei Majutsu*. Shunyōdō.

———. 1933. *Kunen yobanashi*. Shunyōdō.

Sakai Naoki. 1995. "Imperial Nationalism and the Law of Singularity." *Tamkang Review* 26, no. 1: 2.

Sakatani, Y. 1980. *Manchuria: A Survey of its Economic Development*. Prepared in 1932 for the Carnegie Endowment for International Peace. New York: Garland.

Sano Shinichi. 2008. *Amakasu Masahiko: ranshin no kōya*. Shinchosha.

———. 2005. *Ahenō: Manshū no yoru to kiri*. Shinchosha.

Sato, Barbara. 2003. *The New Japanese Woman: Modernity, Media, and Women in Interwar Japan*. Durham, N.C.: Duke University Press.

Sawada Junjirō. 1925. *Hentai to Hanzai*. Seiyokugakusha.

Schmitt, Carl. 2005. *Political Theology*. Trans. George Schwab. Chicago: University of Chicago Press.

Seagrave, Sterling, and Peggy Seagrave. 1999. *The Yamato Dynasty*. New York: Broadway Books.

Senga Motofumi. 2007. *Ahen Ō ichidai*. Kōjinsha.

Shibata Senga. 1999. *Senryōchi tsūka kinyū seisaku no kenkyū*. Nihon Keizai Hyōronsha.

Shimizu Kitsurō. 1895. *Chōsen jijō niwatori harawata.* Umehara Shuttyōden.

Shin Gi-Wook. 1991. "Social Change and Peasant Protest in Colonial Korea." PhD diss., University of Washington.

Shinobu Junbei. 1932. *Waga ManMon no tokushu keneki ron.* Nihon Hyōronsha.

Shinobu Seizaburō. 1991. "Tsūshū jiken." *Seiji keizai shigaku* 297.

Shiota Ushio. 2006. *Shōwa no kaibutsu.* WAC Bunko.

Silverberg, Miriam. 2007. *Erotic Grotesque Nonsense: The Mass Culture of Japanese Modern Times.* Berkeley: University of California Press.

Simmel, Georg. 1950. "The Metropolis and Mental Life." *The Sociology of Georg Simmel,* ed. Kurt Wolf. New York: Free Press.

Smith, Norman. 2007. *Resisting Manchukuo: Chinese Women Writers and the Japanese Occupation.* Vancouver: University of British Columbia Press.

Snow, Edgar. 1934. "Japan Builds a New Colony." *Saturday Evening Post,* 24 February.

Soeda Azenbō. 1982. *Soeda Azenbō chosakushū,* vol. 2. Tosui Shobō.

Soh, C. Sarah. 2008. *The Comfort Women: Sexual Violence and Postcolonial Memory in Korea and Japan.* Chicago: University of Chicago Press.

Sōma Jirō. 1929. *Hentai Shohōsen.* Kaichōsha.

Sommerville, Diane Miller. 2006. *Race and Rape in the Nineteenth-Century South.* Chapel Hill: University of North Carolina Press.

Song Youn-ok, and Melissa L. Wender. 1997. "Japanese Colonial Rule and State-Managed Prostitution: Korea's Licensed Prostitutes." *Positions: East Asia Cultures Critique* 5, no. 1: 171–217.

Sonoe Sachiko. 2000. "Facing Away from Japan: Japanese Prostitutes in Asia before World War II." *Researching the Fragments: Histories of Women in the Asian Context,* eds. Carolyn Brewer and Anne-Marie Medcalf. Quezon City: New Day Publishers.

Spivak, Gayatri. 1988. "Can the Subaltern Speak?" *In Other Worlds: Essays in Cultural Politics.* New York: Routledge.

Su Chongmin. 1995. *Laogong de xue yu lei.* Beijing: Zhongguo Dabaike Quanshu Chubanshe.

Sugihara Kaoru. 1996. "The European Miracle and the East Asian Miracle: Towards a New Global Economic History." *Sangyō to Keizai* 11, no. 12: 27–48.

———. 2003. "The East Asian Path of Economic Development: A Long-Term Perspective." *The Resurgence of East Asia: 500, 150 and 50 Year Perspectives,* Arrighi, Giovanni and Mark Selden, ed. London: Routledge.

Su Zhiliang. 1999. *Weianfu yanjiu.* Shanghai: Shanghai Chubanshe.

Sunaga Asahiko. 1993. *Chi no arabesuku.* Peyotoru Shuppan.

Sun Bang, ed. 1993. *WeiMan shiliao congshu,* vol. 7. Jilin: Jilin Renmin Chubanshe.

Suzuki Takashi. 1992. *Nihon teikokushugi to Manshū.* Hanawa Shobō.

Tadiar, Neferti X. M. 2009. *Things Fall Away: Philippine Historical Experience and the Makings of Globalization.* Durham, N.C.: Duke University Press.

Taiheiyō Sensō Kenkyūkai, ed. 1996. *Manshū Teikoku*. Kawade Shobō.

Takahashi Tomizo. 1928. *Tōyō Takushoku Kabushiki Kaisha nijūnenshi*. Tokyo Insatsu Kabashushiki Kaisha.

Takasaki Sōji. 2002. *Shokuminchi Chōsen no Nihonjin*. Iwanami Shoten.

Takazaki Tatsunosuke. 1953. *Manshukoku no shūen*. Jitsugyō no Nihonsha.

Takekoshi Yosaburō. 1907. *Japanese Rule in Formosa*. New York: Longmans Green.

Tanabe Hajime. 1963. *Tanabe Hajime zenshū*. Chikuma Shobō.

Tanaka Kōgai. 1922. *Ningen no seiteki ankokumen*. Osaka: Okugō Shoten.

———. 1923. *Josei to aiyoku*. Osaka: Okugō Shoten.

———. 1925. *Aiyoku ni kurū chijin*. Osaka: Okugō Shoten.

———. 1928. *Shumi no taishūkagaku*. Osaka: Osakayagō Shoten.

Tanaka, Stephan. 1993. *Japan's Orient: Rendering Pasts into History*. Berkeley: University of California Press.

Tanaka Yuki. 2002. *Japan's Comfort Women: Sexual Slavery and Prostitution During World War II and the US Occupation*. London: Routledge.

Tansman, Alan. 2009. *The Aesthetics of Japanese Fascism*. Berkeley: University of California Press.

Tansman, Alan, ed. 2009. *The Culture of Japanese Fascism*. Durham: Duke University Press.

Taylor, F. W. 1947. *The Principles of Scientific Management*. New York: W. W. Norton.

Terami-Wada, Motoe. 1986. "Karayuki-san of Manila: 1880–1920." *Philippine Studies*, 34:287–316.

Tosaka Jun. 1967. *Tosaka Jun zenshū*. 5 vols. Keisō Shobō.

Tōyō Takushoku Kabushiki Gaisha. 1939. *Tōyō Takushoku Kabushiki Gaisha sanjūnenshi*. Tōyō Takushoku Kabushiki Gaisha Shuppan.

Tsukase Susumu. 2004. *Manshū no Nihonjin*. Yoshikawa Kōbunkan.

Tsunoda Fusako. 2005. *Amakasu Taii*. Chikuma Bunko.

Tsunoda Jun. 1984. *Ishihara Kanji shiryō: kokubō ronsakuhen*. Hara Shobō.

Tsurumi, E. Patricia. 1967. "Taiwan under Kodama Gentarō and Gotō Shinpei." *Papers on Japan*, 4, ed. Albert Craig. Cambridge, Mass.: Harvard East Asia Center.

———. 1984. "Colonial Education in Korea and Taiwan." *The Japanese Colonial Empire, 1895–1945*, ed. Ramon Myers and Mark Peattie. Princeton: Princeton University Press.

Tsurumi Kazuko. 1978. *Minakata Kumagusu: chijyū ikō no hikakugaku*. Kodansha.

Tsurumi Shunsuke. 1982. *An Intellectual History of Wartime Japan, 1931–1945*. London: KPI Limited.

Tsurumi Yūsuke. 1937. *Gotō Shinpei*. 4 vols. Nihon Hyōronsha.

Tucker, David. 2005. "Labor Policy and the Construction Industry in Manchukuo." *Asian Labor in the Wartime Japanese Empire: Unknown Histories*, ed. Paul Kratoska. London: M. E. Sharpe.

Uchida Jun. 2005. "Brokers of Empire: Japanese Settler Colonialism in Korea, 1910–1937." PhD diss., Harvard University.

Uchida Ryoan. 2001. *Futabatei Shimei no Isshō. Meiji no Bungaku*, no. 11: 319–406. Chikuma Shobō.

Ugaramon. 1914. *Chōsen e iku no hito ni*. Ogura Shusetsu.

Umehara Hokumei. 1924. *Satsujin kaisha*. Akane Shobō.

———. 1928. *Barukan kuri-gu*. Translated from the 1926 text of Wilhelm Meiter. Bungei Shijōsha.

Umehara Hokumei, and Sugii Shinobu, trans. 1925. *Roshia daikakumei shi*. Chōkiya shoten.

Umehara Masaki. 1968. "Umehara Hokumei no ashiato." *Dokyumento Nihonjin 6*. Gakugei Shorin.

———. *Kindai kijinden*. 1978. Tairiku Shobō.

Vespa, Amleto. 1938. *Secret Agent of Japan: A Handbook to Japanese Imperialism*. London: Victor Gollancz.

Wang Chengli, ed. 1991. *Zhongguo dongbei lunxian shisinianshi gangyao*. Beijing: Zhongguo Dabaike Quanshu Chubanshe.

Warren, James Francis. 1993. *Ah Ku and Karayuki-san: Prostitution in Singapore, 1870–1940*. New York: Oxford University Press.

Weiner, Michael. 1994. *Race and Migration in Imperial Japan*. London: Routledge.

Weisenfeld, Gennifer. 2002. *Mavo: Japanese Artists and the Avant-Garde, 1905–1931*. Berkeley: University of California Press.

Williams, Eric. 1944. *Capitalism and Slavery*. Chapel Hill: University of North Carolina Press.

Women's Active Museum Documentary Evidence. 2005. "Nihongun seibōryoku higaisha no eizō kiroku #1." Lecture on 7 October.

Wright, Harrison, ed. 1976. *The "New Imperialism": Analysis of Late Nineteenth-Century Expansion*. Toronto: D. C. Heath.

Xie Xueshi. 1995. *Wei Manzhouguoshi xinbian*. Beijing: Renmin Chubanshe.

Yamabe Kentarō. 1966. *Nihon no Kankoku heigō*. Taihei Shuppansha.

Yamada Gōichi. 2002. *Manshūkoku no ahen senbai*. Kyūko Shoin.

Yamaguchi Masao. 1994. *Zasetsu no Shōwashi*. Iwanami Shoten.

Yamamoto Hideo. 1977. *Tachibana Shiraki*. Chūō Kōronsha.

Yamamoto Kiko. 1927. *Dalianshichū ni okeru kasō Chūgokujin no inshokubutsu shirabe*. Dalian: Minami Manshū Tetsudō Kabushiki Gaisha.

Yamamuro, Shinichi. 1993. *Kimera: Manshūkoku no shōzo*. Chūō Shinsho.

———. 2002. "Mensetsu" in *Kan: rekishi, kankyō, bunmei*. June.

———. 2006. *Manchuria under Japanese Dominion*. Trans. Joshua Fogel. Philadelphia: University of Pennsylvania Press.

Yamane Yukio. 1976. *Ronshū kindai Chūgoku to Nihon*. Yamakawa Shuppan.

Yamazaki Tomoko. 1972. *Sandankan hachiban shōkan*. Chikuma Shobō.

———. 1995. *Ajia josei kōryūshi*. Chikuma Shobō.

————. 1999. *Sandakan Brothel No. 8: An Episode in the History of Lower-Class Japanese Women*. Trans. Karen Colligan-Taylor. Armonk, N.Y.: M. E. Sharpe.

Yasutomi Ayumu. 1999. *Manshūkoku no kinyū*. Nihon keizai hyōronsha.

Yen Ching-Hwang. 1985. *Coolies and Mandarins*. Singapore: Singapore University Press.

Yonetani Masafumi. 2006. *Ajia/Nihon*. Iwanami Shoten.

Yonezawa Yoshihirō, ed. 1994. *Rampo no jidai*. Bessatsu Taiyō.

————. 1999. *Hakkinbon*. Bessatsu Taiyō.

————. 2001. *Hakkinbon II*. Bessatsu Taiyō.

Yoshimi Shunya. 1995. *Hakurankai no Seijigaku*. Chūō Shinsho.

Yoshimi Yoshiaki. 2000. *Comfort Women: Sexual Slavery in the Japanese Military during World War II*. Trans. Suzanne O'Brien. New York: Columbia University Press.

————. 2007. "Nihongun 'ianfu' mondai no kagai sekinin." Lecture presentation, Tokyo, 11 August.

Yoshimi Yoshiaki, and Hayashi Hirofumi, eds. 1995. *Kyōdō Kenkyū: Nippongun ianfu*. Ōtsuki Shoten.

Young, C. Walter. 1929. "Chinese Colonization and the Development of Manchuria." *Problems of the Pacific*. Chicago: University of Chicago Press.

Young, Louise. 1996. *Japan's Total Empire: Manchuria and the Culture of Japan's Wartime Imperialism*. Berkeley: University of California Press.

Zhang Yumao, ed. 1996. *Dongbei xiandai wenxue daxi*, vol. 5. Shenyang: Shenyang Chubanshe.

Zhonguo Fushun zhanfan guanli suo, ed. 2005. *Riben zhanfan de zaisheng zhi di*. Beijing: Zhonguo Tushuguan.

Zhuang Jianping. 2007. "Japan's Exploitative labor system in Quingdao: 1933–1945." *China at War: regions of China, 1937–1945*, eds. Diana Lary, and Ezra Vogel. Stanford, Calif.: Stanford University Press.

Žižek, Slavoj. 1989. *The Sublime Object of Ideology*. London: Verso.

————. 1991. *They Know Not What They Do*. London: Verso.

————. 1997. *The Plague of Fantasies*. London: Verso.

Note: Italicized page numbers refer to illustrations.

Mark Driscoll is an associate professor of Japanese and international studies at the University of North Carolina, Chapel Hill. He is the editor, with Gabriel Brahm Jr., of *Prosthetic Territories: Politics and Hypertechnologies* (1995) and translator of Kannani *and* Document of Flames*: Two Japanese Colonial Novels* by Katsuei Yuasa (Duke, 2005).

Library of Congress Cataloging-in-Publication Data
Driscoll, Mark.
Absolute erotic, absolute grotesque : the living, dead, and undead in
Japan's imperialism, 1895–1945 / Mark Driscoll.
p. cm.
Includes bibliographical references and index.
ISBN 978-0-8223-4740-8 (cloth : alk. paper)
ISBN 978-0-8223-4761-3 (pbk. : alk. paper)
1. Imperialism—Social aspects—Japan—History. 2. Japan—Foreign
relations—1912–1945. 3. Korea—History—Japanese occupation, 1910–1945.
4. China—History—1928–1937. 5. Manchuria (China)—History—1931–1945.
I. Title.
DS885.48.D75 2010
325'.35209041—dc22   2010000605